Leadership
Communication

Deborah J. Barrett
Jones Graduate School of Management
Rice University

Boston   Burr Ridge, IL   Dubuque, IA   Madison, WI   New York
San Francisco   St. Louis   Bangkok   Bogotá   Caracas   Kuala Lumpur
Lisbon   London   Madrid   Mexico City   Milan   Montreal   New Delhi
Santiago   Seoul   Singapore   Sydney   Taipei   Toronto

Irwin

LEADERSHIP COMMUNICATION

Published by McGraw-Hill/Irwin, a business unit of The McGraw-Hill Companies, Inc., 1221 Avenue of the Americas, New York, NY, 10020.

This book is printed on acid-free paper.

2 3 4 5 6 7 8 9 0 DOC/DOC 0 9 8 7 6 5

ISBN 0-07-291849-7

Editorial director: *John E. Biernat*
Publisher: *Linda Schreiber*
Sponsoring editor: *Doug Hughes*
Developmental editor: *Megan Gates*
Marketing manager: *Keari Bedford*
Producer, Media technology: *Damian Moshak*
Project manager: *Bruce Gin*
Lead production supervisor: *Michael R. McCormick*
Senior designer: *Adam Rooke*
Lead media project manager: *Cathy L. Tepper*
Developer, Media technology: *Brian Nacik*
Typeface: *10/12 Palatino*
Compositor: *GTS—New Delhi, India Campus*
Printer: *R. R. Donnelley*

Library of Congress Cataloging-in-Publication Data

Barrett, Deborah J. 1949-
    Leadership communication / Deborah J. Barrett.
        p. cm.—(Titles in business communication)
    Includes index.
    ISBN 0-07-291849-7 (alk. paper)
    1. Communication in management. 2. Communication in organizations. 3. Business communication. 4. Leadership. I. Title. II. Series.
HD30.3.B387 2006
658.4'5—dc22

                                                                2004058794

www.mhhe.com

Business Communication Titles

INTRODUCTION TO BUSINESS COMMUNICATION

Business Communication Design: Creativity, Strategies, Solutions with PowerWeb and BComm Skill Booster, 1/e
Pamela Angell, *Hudson Valley Community College*
Teeanna Rizkallah, *California State University–Long Beach*
ISBN: 0072859857
© 2004

Business Communication: Building Critical Skills, 2/e
Kitty O. Locker, *Ohio State University*
Steven Kyo Kaczmarek, *Columbus State Community College*
ISBN: 0072865717
© 2004

College English and Communication, Student Edition, 8/e
Sue C. Camp, *Gardener-Webb University*
Marilyn Satterwhite, *Danville Area Community College*
ISBN: 007825860X
© 2003

Business and Administrative Communication, 6/e
Kitty O. Locker, *Ohio State University*
ISBN: 0072551348
© 2003

Business Communication at Work, Student Text/Workbook 2003, 2/e
Marilyn Satterwhite, *Danville Area Community College*
Judith Olson-Sutton, *Madison Area Technical College*
ISBN: 0072829805
© 2003

The Gregg Reference Manual, 10/e
William A. Sabin
ISBN: 0072936533

Basic Business Communication: Skills for Empowering the Internet Generation, 9/e
Raymond Lesikar, *Emeritus, Louisiana State University*
Marie Flatley, *San Diego State University*
ISBN: 0072537531
© 2002

Professional Business Writing, 7/e
Elizabeth Kerbey, *San Jacinto College Central*
Marilyn Satterwhite, *Danville Area Community College*
ISBN: 0078211654
© 2002

BUSINESS ENGLISH

Business English at Work, 2/e
Susan Jaderstrom, *Santa Rosa Junior College*
Joanne Miller
ISBN: 0078290821
© 2003

The English Workshop: A Programmed Approach, Text/Workbook, 5/e
Keith Slocum, *Montclair State University*
ISBN: 0078262879
© 2003

English Made Easy, 5/e
Mary Margaret Hosler, *University of Wisconsin–Whitewater*
ISBN: 0072938021
© 2005

TECHNICAL/REPORT WRITING

Developing Proofreading and Editing Skills, 5/e
Sue C. Camp, *Gardner-Webb University*
ISBN: 007293798X
© 2005

Technical Communication, 2/e
Mary M. Lay, *University of Minnesota*
Billie J. Wahlstrom
Carolyn D. Rude, *Texas Tech University*
Cynthia L. Selfe, *Michigan Technological University*
Jack Selzer, *Penn State University*
ISBN: 0256220581
© 2000

Report Writing for Business, 10/e
Raymond Lesikar, *Emeritus, Louisiana State University*
John Pettit, Jr.
ISBN: 0256236917
© 1998

MANAGERIAL COMMUNICATIONS

Corporate Communication, 3/e
Paul Argenti, *Dartmouth College*
ISBN: 0072314028
© 2003

Managerial Communication: Strategies and Applications, 3/e
Geraldine E. Hynes, *Sam Houston State University*
ISBN: 007282915X
© 2005

Interpersonal Skills in Organizations with Management Skill Booster Passcard
Suzanne de Janasz, *James Madison University*
Karen O. Dowd, *James Madison University*
Beth Schneider, *James Madison University*
ISBN: 0072874260
© 2002

Management Communication: Principles and Practice, 1/e
Michael Hattersley
Linda McJannet, *Bentley College*
ISBN: 0072883561
© 2005

INTERNATIONAL BUSINESS COMMUNICATION

Intercultural Communication in the Global Workplace, 3/e
Linda Bearner, *California State University–Los Angeles*
Iris Varner, *Illinois State University*
ISBN: 0072829222
© 2005

Dedicated in loving memory of my father, Orland R. Burch
Dedicated to my mother, Wilhelmina E. Gray Burch, and
my children, Davy and Mary

—Deborah J. Barrett, Ph.D.

Brief Contents

Table of Contents

About the Author

Deborah J. Barrett is a senior lecturer of management and director of the M.B.A. Communication Program at the Jones Graduate School of Management at Rice University, where she teaches leadership communication, change management, change communication, management consulting, intrapreneurship, team dynamics, and negotiations.

Deborah has taught communication for over 25 years, specializing in business, technical, and team communication for the last 20 years. At Texas A&M University, she was a visiting assistant professor in technical writing; at Houston Baptist University, she was an associate professor in English and director of the writing specialization and English internship programs; and at Rice University, she was a lecturer of managerial communication before leaving teaching to work as a consultant full-time in 1991.

Deborah's leadership approach to business communication has developed over many years of teaching, but has been most influenced by her years as a consultant working independently and for McKinsey & Company and Hill & Knowlton. At McKinsey & Company, she was a communication consultant for over five years. She served as a leader in the change communication practice, developed and conducted Firm training, and led and worked with McKinsey teams on communication and general management consulting projects throughout the world. She was one of the few communication consultants Firmwide selected to attend McKinsey's Engagement Leadership Training, their advanced leadership training for senior associates. At Hill & Knowlton, Deborah was a senior managing director, brought in to build a change in employee communication practice.

In her consulting work, she has been able to put her academic experience and leadership communication concepts to the test. Her consulting work includes developing major change programs, designing and conducting vision/strategy development programs, writing strategic plans, creating communication strategy for mergers and acquisitions, and developing internal communication improvement programs. She has coached many senior-level executives, including CEOs of major corporations, in writing, speaking, and interpersonal skills and has conducted numerous executive workshops for managers at all levels.

Deborah has published articles in professional journals and presented papers at professional conferences around the world on communication ethics, change communication, employee communication, intercultural team communication, virtual teams, PowerPoint, effective M.B.A. communication, and leadership communication. She serves on the Editorial Boards of the *Business Communication Quarterly* and *Education Review of Business Communication* and is the chair of the Association for Business Communication's AACSB Liaison Committee.

Her B.A. in English and speech and her M.A. in English are from the University of Houston, and her Ph.D. in English is from Rice University.

Preface

Leadership Communication is a text to guide current and potential leaders in developing the communication capabilities needed to lead organizations effectively. The content is based on research in communication and leadership and on the author's years of experience teaching business communication and working as a consultant, independently as well as for one of the leading management-consulting firms and one of the leading public relations firms. As a consultant, the author has provided communication coaching for CEOs and other senior-level executives, developed and conducted executive training programs in communication and teams, led consulting projects in internal and external communication effectiveness, and developed change programs for major global companies representing many industries.

Leadership Communication's primary audience is senior-level managers, but all levels of managers will benefit from the content. Future business leaders need core communication skills in strategy, speaking, and writing. They also need to be able to communicate effectively with a diverse workforce, understand cultural differences, conduct productive meetings, manage global teams, create and communicate visions, lead change initiatives, and foster external relations. *Leadership Communication* includes all of these subjects and covers important fundamental communication skills needed by all leaders. It is designed to help managers become effective leaders by being better communicators.

Mastering leadership communication means you learn how to do the following:

1. Project a positive ethos in writing and speaking.
2. Analyze audiences and target your messages to them.
3. Develop an effective communication strategy for all situations.
4. Select and use the most effective medium or vehicles to reach your audiences.
5. Create well-organized, coherent documents.
6. Write clear, concise, correct business prose.
7. Deliver presentations with confidence.
8. Display emotional intelligence and cultural literacy.
9. Lead small groups, whether in teams or meetings, productively.
10. Develop a vision and internal messages that guide and motivate employees.
11. Design and deliver external messages to reach stakeholders with positive and effective results.

These are the primary objectives of this text. You will learn that leaders use all possible communication tools within reach and use them effectively. This text will help you know how to use those tools and show you how to improve your communication capabilities. As a result, you will learn to communicate more effectively and position yourself to be a leader in your organization and beyond it.

Acknowledgments

Before recognizing each individual to whom I am grateful, I want to thank three organizations for their direct and indirect contributions to the creation and publication of *Leadership Communication*:

- McGraw-Hill/Irwin—The editors for their guidance and support and the talented production staff for making the book a reality.
- McKinsey & Company—The Firm overall for the opportunity to work with some of the brightest business thinkers and with executives and managers who exemplify leadership communication, and the Firm Partners, who provided the opportunity for me to work with and lead client projects for some of the most successful companies around the world.
- The Jones School of Management at Rice University—The deans for their belief and support of communication, which allowed me to build a unique M.B.A. communication program and develop the concept of leadership communication in the classroom. The administrative staff who provided support; in particular, my administrative assistant, Josh DeMott, and my research assistant, Elise McCutchen.

I want to express my appreciation to the reviewers who were kind enough to review the manuscript and make valuable suggestions:

Bruce Bell, *Liberty University;* **Kim Sydow Campbell,** *University of Alabama;* **Mitch Carnell, Jr.,** *Webster University;* **Melinda Knight,** *Rochester University;* **Rachel Mather,** *Adelphi University;* **Craig Sasse,** *Rockhurst University;* **Carolyn Seefer,** *Diablo Valley Community College;* **Judith Swift,** *University of Sioux Falls;* **Deborah Valentine,** *Emory University;* **John Waltman,** *Eastern Michigan University; and* **Bonnie Yarbrough,** *UNC–Greensboro.*

Other colleagues contributed their time, energy, and expertise as I developed the book and I express my sincere gratitude to them:

- Chuck McCabe—Chuck's astute editorial expertise and his questioning of meaning improved the book's style and content. He constantly challenged me and contributed in so many ways to the final version of the text and to the instructor's manual.
- Beth O'Sullivan—Beth has contributed as a critical reader of the manuscript at various stages, as the creator of many of the exercises, as a major contributor to the content in the instructor's manual, and as the friend and colleague to whom I could always go for advice.
- Beth Peters, Gale Wiley, and Larry Hampton—Beth, Gale, and Larry who teach sections of the leadership communication course, willingly tried out portions of the text, the PowerPoint presentation lectures, and the exercises in their classes and collaborated with me on teaching much of the material.
- John Kim Kehoe—Kim's comments on an early version of the introduction helped me see the connections that needed to be strengthened in my discussion

of leadership; he also contributed to other chapters by making suggestions on ways to reinforce the leadership emphasis, in particular in the team chapter, where he suggested the table on the role of communication in leading a team.

- Linda Driskill and Melinda Knight—Two leaders in the practice of business communication, Linda and Melinda are role models and friends. I thank Linda for first starting me down the road of teaching business communication, for serving as my mentor over the years, and for being a source of professional support, challenge, and inspiration. And, I want to thank Melinda for her thoughtful comments as a reviewer of this text and for offering advice and encouragement in my other professional endeavors.

I owe thanks to all of my students over the years on whom I have tested many of my ideas. I recognize three students in particular because they directly contributed to the book: Sarah McGill, who provided criticism and comments from a student's perspective of the first draft of the book; Paul Trieu, who worked on obtaining copyright permissions; and Christina Jackson, who verified sources, confirmed documentation format, chased down the final few copyright requests, and played a major role in creating the Test Bank.

Finally, I want to thank Kramer, who sat beside me from the beginning to the end, adding support and providing stress release; and Butter, who tried to stay beside me, but who did not make it to the end.

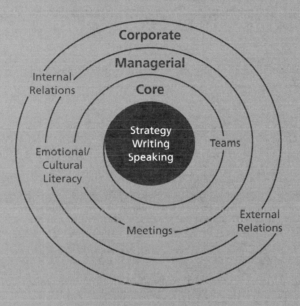

Introduction: What Is Leadership Communication?

> The difference between mere management and leadership is communication.
>
> Winston Churchill, quoted in James C. Humes, *The Sir Winston Method*

> Effective leadership is still largely a matter of communication.
>
> Alan Axelrod, *Elizabeth I, CEO: Strategic Lessons from the Leader Who Built an Empire*

Chapter Objectives

In this chapter, you will learn to do the following:

- Recognize the connection of leadership to communication.
- Apply the leadership communication framework.
- Appreciate the importance of projecting a positive ethos.
- Assess your own leadership communication capabilities and develop an improvement plan.

A leader must be able to communicate effectively. When asked to list the most important skills a business school graduate must possess, CEOs, senior managers, employment recruiters, and business school alumni, faculty, and deans all mention *good communication skills*. Managers spend most of their day engaged in communication; in fact, studies of how much time managers spend on various activities show that communication occupies 70 to 90 percent of their time every day.[1] The sheer amount of time you do spend or will spend communicating underscores how important strong communication skills will be to you in your career. Mastering leadership communication becomes a priority for managers who want their organizations or the broader business community to consider them leaders.

This introduction explains the concept of "leadership communication" and introduces the framework that governs the organization of the text. The discussion begins by defining leadership communication; then, it explains the importance of projecting a leadership image. It concludes by providing a self-assessment, to help you determine your own leadership communication strengths and weaknesses, and a worksheet, to help you establish your personal communication improvement goals.

CONNECTING LEADERSHIP AND COMMUNICATION

What exactly is leadership communication? Let's begin by defining "leaders."

Researchers seldom agree completely on how best to define leadership, but most would agree that leaders are individuals who guide, direct, motivate, or inspire others. They are the men and women who influence others in an organization or in a community. They command others' attention. They persuade others to follow them or pursue goals they define. They control situations. They improve the performance of groups and organizations. They get results. These individuals may not be presidents of countries or CEOs of companies, but they could be. They could also be employees who step forward to mentor less experienced or younger employees, managers who direct successful project teams, or vice presidents who lead divisions and motivate their staff to achieve company goals.

The fundamental premise on which this book rests is that *effective leadership depends on effective communication*. It is through effective communication that leaders guide, direct, motivate, and inspire. Good communication skills enable, foster, and create the understanding and trust necessary to encourage others to follow a leader. Without effective communication, a manager accomplishes little. Without effective communication, a manager is not an effective leader.

In fact, being able to communicate effectively is what allows a manager to move into a leadership position. An early Harvard Business School study on what it takes to achieve success and be promoted in an organization says that the individual who gets ahead in business is the person who "is able to communicate, to make sound decisions, and to get things done with and through people."[2] This text tackles the first of these capabilities directly, and by teaching you to communicate more effectively, it also helps you improve your ability to get things done with and through people. After all, communication is about people.

Now, to define communication: Communication is the transmission of meaning from one person to another or to many people, whether verbally or nonverbally. Communication from one person to another is often called the "rhetorical situation," which is commonly depicted as a simple triangle consisting of the context, the sender, the message, and the receiver (Exhibit I.1).

This exhibit shows very simple and ideal communication. There would be no miscommunication or misunderstandings. The sender would understand the

EXHIBIT I.1
The Traditional Diagram of the Rhetorical Situation

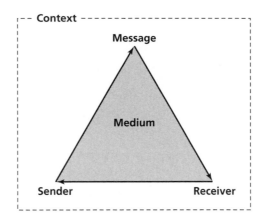

context and the audience (receiver), select the right medium, and send a clear message. The receiver would receive and understand that message exactly as the sender intended. In reality, communication more likely resembles some variation of the diagram in Exhibit I.2.

The complication in communication comes from the interruptions or interferences in that transmission, whether the sender causes them or the receiver. The context in which the information is sent, the noise that surrounds it, the selection of the medium, the words used in the message, the image of the speaker—all influence the meaning as it travels successfully, or as intended, from one person to another. Learning to anticipate the interruptions in the rhetorical situation, to appreciate the context, to understand the audience, to select the right medium, and to craft clear messages that allow the meaning to reach the specific receiver as intended is the foundation of effective business communication.

The goal of mastering all aspects of leadership communication is to move you as close as possible to the ideal of the rhetorical situation. Leadership communication necessitates anticipating all interruptions and interferences through audience analysis and then developing a communication strategy that controls the rhetorical

EXHIBIT I.2
Communication Reality or the Interruptions to Communication

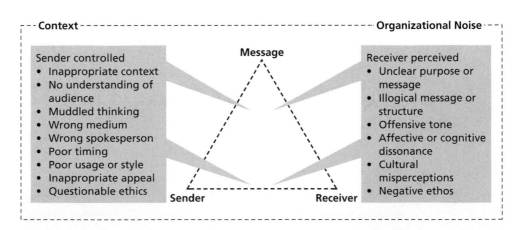

situation and facilitates the effective transmission of your message. So what is leadership communication?

Leadership communication is the controlled, purposeful transfer of meaning by which leaders influence a single person, a group, an organization, or a community. Leadership communication uses the full range of communication skills and resources to overcome interferences and to create and deliver messages that guide, direct, motivate, or inspire others to action.

APPLYING THE LEADERSHIP COMMUNICATION FRAMEWORK

Leadership communication consists of layered, expanding skills from core strategy development and effective writing and speaking to the use of these skills in more complex organizational situations. As your perspective and control expand, you will find that you need to improve your core skills to become effective in the larger, more complex organizational situations. *Leadership Communication* starts with the core communication skills represented in the center of the framework (Exhibit I.3). It moves out from these core communication skills to the managerial communication skills, and then expands further to the communication capabilities included at the broader corporate communication ring. Thus, this text moves from the inside of the spiral to the outside, expanding outward as you learn to apply the core skills to a wider array of audiences and increasingly complex organizational situations.

The model is not meant to suggest a hierarchy, which is why it is depicted as a spiral. All effective communications depend on the core skills at the center of the spiral. These are your more individual skills. To be a leader in any organization, you need to master the skills at the core. You also need to expand your skills to

EXHIBIT I.3
The Leadership Communication Framework

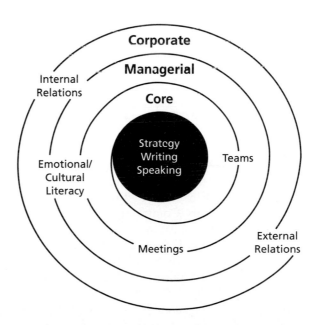

include those needed to lead and manage groups and, eventually, those on the outer circle, the corporate communication skills needed to interact successfully with all internal audiences and external stakeholders.

Core Communication Skills

Communication strategy is included in the section on core skills (Section One), but you will find you always need to take a strategic approach to be a master of leadership communication. Therefore, developing the communication strategy will be emphasized throughout all sections of the text as you move from inside to the outer rings of the spiral. Strategy is the foundation on which any effective communication depends. You need to be able to analyze an audience in every situation and develop a communication strategy that facilitates accomplishing your communication objectives.

You need to be able to structure and write effective simple and complex correspondence and documents, from e-mails and memos to proposals and reports. You need to be able to write and speak in the language expected of business leaders, language that is clear, correct, and concise. In addition, you need to be able to create and deliver oral presentations confidently and persuasively, using graphics that contribute to delivering your messages. These are the capabilities at the core of all business communication. Success in managerial and corporate communication depends on mastering these core capabilities.

Managerial Communication Skills

Managerial communication skills build on the core skills. They are the capabilities that more directly involve managing others, from one-on-one contact to interacting with groups and the broader organization. They are the skills needed to interact with individuals and to manage groups. Managerial communication skills begin with emotional intelligence and cultural literacy, the subject of Chapter 6, which covers the essential interpersonal and cross-cultural skills needed to interact effectively with others as individuals or groups. Although listening is a core skill in any rhetorical situation, it is included in the managerial section of the text (Section Two) instead of the core section because managing others effectively requires even greater attention to hearing what others say, not simply what we think we hear them say. The managerial section also includes leading meetings and managing teams, both essential capabilities for today's managers.

Corporate Communication Skills

Corporate communication (the topic of Section Three) involves expansion from the managerial skills to those abilities needed to lead an organization and address a broader community. Communication becomes even more complex when you need to think about how best to communicate to all internal and external stakeholders. Again, any good communication depends on having a strategy, but as the audiences become more diverse and larger, the communication strategy becomes more complicated. You will find as you move into higher levels of an organization that you become the leader of change programs and vision development. In addition, you become the company's face and voice for the public.

PROJECTING A POSITIVE LEADERSHIP ETHOS

Leadership communication depends on the ability to project a positive image, or more specifically, a positive ethos, inside an organization and outside. The word "image" is often associated with illusion or superficiality. It embodies what an audience thinks of you initially based on mostly superficial perceptions. Ethos refers to qualities of greater depth and substance. It ties more directly to your character, which your audience judges according to the culture in which you are communicating.

"Charisma" is another term often used to describe someone who has the ability to persuade others and move an audience. It resembles ethos in its effect on an audience, but it differs in that it suggests exuding a power over others based more in emotions than in reason. Examples of public figures who were charismatic leaders in their time include John F. Kennedy, Mahatma Gandhi, and Martin Luther King, Jr.

Both image and charisma can be used to describe leaders, but since ethos ties more directly to the character of the speaker or writer, it serves as a better word to use in capturing the positive qualities that we want our business leaders to possess. Projecting a positive ethos, then, better defines the goal you should seek in mastering leadership communication.

A positive ethos will take you a long way toward influencing your audiences with your intended message, whereas a negative ethos is one of the greatest barriers to effective communication. How you are perceived makes the difference in how well you are believed, how persuasive you are, and ultimately, how effectively you communicate. Successful leadership communication depends on projecting a positive ethos.

Defining Ethos

To understand ethos, it helps to look back at the original definitions found in the writing of the Greek philosopher Aristotle. Aristotle identified three types of persuasive appeals:

- Logos
- Pathos
- Ethos

Logos is an appeal based on the logic of an argument, while pathos is an appeal based on the use of emotions. Ethos is an appeal based on the perceived character of the sender of the message. Is the person trustworthy, confident, believable, knowledgeable, and a man or woman of integrity? If the audience does not trust or believe the speaker or writer, logic or emotion will have little persuasive force.

For Aristotle, ethos is the most important persuasive device and most critical ingredient in the rhetorical situation: the "character of the speaker may almost be called the most effective means of persuasion he possesses."[3] Therefore, "the orator must not only try to make the argument of his speech demonstrative and worthy of belief; he must also make his own character look right and put his hearers, who are to decide, into the right frame of mind."[4] An effective speaker can "inspire confidence in the orator's own character" and "induce" belief and acceptance in the audience.[5]

What is it that will help you to inspire confidence and induce others to listen to you? One of the primary requirements is *credibility*. In their extensive research on leadership, James M. Kouzes and Barry Z. Posner found that credibility is the number one reason people follow someone.[6] To be an effective leader, you must be credible to your followers. Credibility is essential to creating a positive ethos. Aristotle says, "Persuasion is achieved by the speaker's personal character when the speech is so spoken as to make us think him *credible*."[7]

For your audience to view you as credible, they must perceive you as knowledgeable, authoritative, confident, honest, and trustworthy. You can achieve the first two through hard work and position. For instance, if you are giving a presentation on the future of energy production in the United States, you must know the industry and the market as well as something about politics and regulatory policy. You can learn the facts and appear knowledgeable. In addition, if you are a CEO of a major energy company, your audience will probably perceive you as someone with the authority to talk about energy. You can exude confidence by being well prepared and feeling comfortable delivering presentations. You can even create an aura of honesty and trustworthiness by effective delivery techniques, such as steady eye contact, easy rapport with the audience, being well prepared to answer questions, and saying "I do not know" when you do not have the answer at hand. Thus, you can take specific actions to build greater credibility. By doing so, you can begin to establish a positive ethos.

Projecting a Positive Ethos

To build a positive ethos, you need to know how others perceive you; however, determining how all audiences perceive you is not easy. Research on the ability of managers to judge how they are perceived found that "most managers overestimate their own credibility—considerably."[8] Discerning how others perceive you takes honest self-reflection and often the assessment of others as well. Few people really see themselves as others see them. To see yourself completely honestly would be a powerful advantage. To quote the Scottish poet Robert Burns from his poem "To a Louse": "O wad some Power the giftie gie us/To see oursels as ithers see us!" In this famous poem, Burns tells the story of a woman dressed immaculately who exudes an air of great superiority. On closer inspection, however, her observers see that she has lice and realize she is not as immaculate as she appears on the surface. As the cartoon here illustrates, speakers may see themselves as geniuses, but the audience could just as easily see them as fools.

The idea that when two people meet, six people are really in the room—the persons as they see themselves, the persons as the others see them, and the persons as they may actually be—underscores the complexity of perception and self-perception.[9] Deciding which perception would be the most accurate would lead to a philosophical tangle, although determining which one is most important

would depend on the purpose of the encounter. If one of the individuals intends to influence the other, then the perception of the other takes on great importance and the need for that individual to know how he or she is perceived becomes critical.

What can you do to find out how you are perceived? You can develop greater emotional intelligence (see the self-assessment at the end of this chapter, which contains several questions related to emotional intelligence). In addition, you can obtain feedback from others; one popular performance tool is the 360-degree feedback, a multisource feedback process. It combines your self-evaluation with that of your superiors, peers, and direct reports to create a well-rounded evaluation of you. It provides an excellent method for uncovering discrepancies between how you see yourself and how others see you.

Self-exploration and some sought-after honest feedback from others will bring the greater self-awareness necessary to judge yourself more accurately and to recognize the signals others send back to you either in their words or, often more important, in their body language and their actions. This self-knowledge can help in building a positive ethos (for more information on self-assessments and ways to improve emotional intelligence, see Chapter 6).

In addition to critical self-reflection and the evaluation of others, you can improve your ability to suggest a positive ethos by building a positive reputation, improving your professional appearance, projecting greater confidence, and learning to communicate more effectively. Reputation could include title, organizational positions, past roles or accomplishments, and public opinion. You can achieve a positive appearance through appropriate and culturally expected dress and grooming. To suggest confidence to your audience, you can use eye contact, establish a rapport, and speak easily about a subject without notes when making a presentation. By using language effectively to capture the meaning and inspire trust, you can create believers in your message.

Connecting Ethos to Ethics

While you can control or develop some of the outward manifestations of a positive ethos, it is more difficult for an individual to change or for an audience to determine, for that matter, the true character of the communicator. Ideally, a positive ethos would exemplify a strong inner character (Exhibit I.4).

Unfortunately, history shows that the projected image may not be the reality of the person. Ethos and ethics are not always aligned; someone can project a positive ethos and appear honest and trustworthy, yet have little or no ethical foundation behind that projection. Someone skilled in deception can fool others; the absence of honesty and integrity is not always apparent to an audience.

When you think about your ethos, you have four possibilities:

1. You are ethical and project a positive ethos.
2. You are ethical but project a negative ethos.
3. You are unethical and project a negative ethos.
4. You are unethical but project a positive ethos.

Since effective leadership communication depends heavily on the ethos you project, you need to be sensitive to the ethical foundation below the surface. As James Kouzes and Barry Posner found in their research on leadership, "If people are going to follow someone willingly, whether it be into battle or into the board-room, they first want to assure themselves that the person is worthy of their trust. They want to know that the would-be leader is truthful and ethical."[10]

It is important for any leader to look critically at the motivation and meaning behind his or her words. Today in particular, businesses are looking for ethical leaders; therefore, your reflection on your ethos as part of the self-assessment suggested at the end of this chapter should include some analysis of the ethical foundation it reflects. For instance, does your ethos suggest the characteristics of an "ethical leader": "fairness, mutual well-being, and harmony"?[11] A positive ethos suggests a "good" character, and a suggestion of a good character makes you more persuasive. As Aristotle says, "We believe good men [and women] more fully and more readily than others."[12] A good character suggests an ethical foundation that makes your audience trust you and more receptive to believing what you say.

Projecting a positive ethos affects your success in communicating your messages and influencing your audience. Mastering the instruction provided in *Leadership*

EXHIBIT I.4
The Ingredients for Creating a Positive Ethos

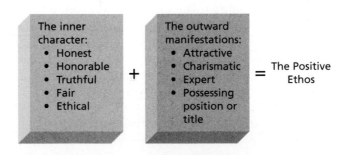

Communication will take you a long way toward projecting a positive ethos and achieving positive results. Some of the other aspects of ethos—such as your reputation, your skills, your knowledge, and your ethics—are, of course, up to you.

Connecting Ethos to Audience Motivation

The importance of understanding your audience cannot be overemphasized; therefore, several pages in Chapter 1 are devoted to analyzing audiences. An audience's receptivity to you, to your ethos, or to your message can assist or be a barrier to their receiving your message as you intend. Looking briefly at what makes an audience receptive to your message is helpful in expanding your understanding of ethos. What is it that makes others attend to your message? What is it that persuades them to listen and to act? In a recent article in *Harvard Business Review,* Robert Cialdini argues that "no leader can succeed without mastering the art of persuasion."[13] Just as creating a positive ethos aids in the art of persuasion, understanding what motivates others to listen and to act will help you as well.

People are obviously much more likely to listen to or care about what others say if the messages are meaningful to them or if they have an interest in them. Combine this interest with knowing how to encourage the audience to trust you and believe your message, and you will have an attentive audience. When the audience has a stake in your subject and is inclined to believe you, they are prepared to be persuaded.

The art (or, some might argue, science) of motivating people has been studied for years, from Freud and Jung to James to Maslow to Alderfer and others. One approach easily accessible to business leaders is that of John French and Bertram Raven. They diagnosed five sources of power to persuade others to attend to a message (Exhibit I.5).

The previous example of a CEO of a major energy company demonstrates creating an ethos based on the motivational power of expertise and legitimacy associated with title and position. When combined with the use of the "referent" appeal or the charisma of being a confident, effective presenter, the CEO establishes sources of persuasion. If we add to this scenario that the audience consists of energy analysts responsible for reporting on the industry's future, we have the appeal of "reward" and a very receptive setting for persuasion to occur with four of the five power influencers in place. The CEO's persuasive ability depends on an emotional appeal and a positive ethos, a combination that may work as well as or better than facts and figures in many cases: "Arguments, per se, are only one part

EXHIBIT I.5
French and Raven's Sources of Power

Source: French, J. R. P., and Raven, B. (1958). The bases of social power. In D. Cartwright (Ed.), *Studies in Social Power.* Ann Arbor: University of Michigan Press. Used with permission.

Power Type	Source of Persuasion
Coercive	The prospect of being punished
Reward	Prospective benefits or rewards
Legitimate	Recognized position or title
Referent	Personal attractiveness or charisma
Expert	Expertise of the speaker

of the equation. Other factors matter just as much, such as the persuader's credibility and his or her ability to create a proper, mutually beneficial frame for a position, connect on the right emotional level with an audience, and communicate through vivid language that makes arguments come alive."[14]

Knowledge of what motivates others can help you create a positive ethos, which will make you more persuasive. Words and how you use them reflect who you are. You can use the most effective words in any given situation, or put the right "spin" on a subject for a particular audience, but if you stray too far from what you believe, your audience will probably perceive you as untrustworthy. Being sensitive to the motivation of others is important to successful persuasion, but so is integrity and sincerity. Otherwise, you risk projecting a negative ethos.

Your ethos may be the most persuasive tool you possess. Although it may be difficult for a business leader to be perceived as honest and trustworthy, particularly in today's scandal-laden business world, the success of individuals and companies often depends on it. The extensive research into emotional intelligence has shown that company leaders set the tone, create the mood, and determine the actions of the organization. They and their companies are trusted because of their reputation, because they are good at what they do, because of their knowledge, because they appear confident, and because they are believed to be ethical. All of these conditions lead to a positive ethos.

This text is designed to help leaders become effective communicators in any situation. For some, that may mean changing their image to alter how others see them. It will certainly mean greater sensitivity to others since effective leadership communication depends on understanding your audience better in all communication events. This understanding will lead to greater self-awareness as well as increased awareness of others, resulting in improved emotional intelligence, which will help you project the positive ethos every leader needs.

ASSESSING LEADERSHIP COMMUNICATION SKILLS AND DEVELOPING AN IMPROVEMENT PLAN

Much of the success of any improvement approach depends on the necessary step of self-reflection. Before going any further in this text, you should step back, assess your leadership communication skills, and determine which areas need improvement and which simply need some polishing. The Checklist of Overall Leadership Communication Skills that follows is intended to get you started on your self-assessment. For even more insight, after you have completed your self-assessment, you may want to ask others to complete the checklist for you as well.

With this self-assessment behind you, you should be able to develop a plan for improving your leadership communication ability. The Worksheet to Help You Develop Your Personal Leadership Communication Plan will help you get started, and the instruction provided in this text should help you achieve your goals.

Checklist of Overall Leadership Communication Skills*

Read through the list of skills and for each one check off your present capability in the chart below.

1. Excel = You have mastered this skill and are excellent in it.
2. Competent = You are competent in this skill but could polish it some.
3. Need to Develop = This is a skill you need to develop further.

Area and Skill	Excel	Competent	Need to Develop
Part I—Assessment of the Core Skills			
Audience Analysis and Strategy			
1. Analyzing the context for communication			
2. Analyzing audiences			
3. Tailoring messages to different audiences			
4. Selecting the most effective medium (channel)			
5. Developing a complete communication strategy			
Written Communication Skills			
1. Deciding on communication purpose			
2. Clarifying your purpose			
3. Generating support for each purpose			
4. Organizing your written communication			
5. Using formatting effectively			
6. Using language correctly			
7. Writing clearly			
8. Writing concisely			
9. Writing confidently			
10. Using an appropriate tone			
11. Writing correspondence (e-mails, memos, letters)			
12. Writing formal reports			
13. Writing executive summaries			
14. Proofreading your own work			
Oral Communication Skills			
1. Delivering an impromptu presentation			
2. Delivering an extemporaneous presentation			
3. Organizing your presentation			
4. Creating PowerPoint slides			
5. Talking in small groups			

*The format and some of the content of this self-assessment were inspired by an assessment in the book *Client-Centered Consulting* by Peter Cockman, Bill Evans, and Peter Reynolds. The content has been significantly modified to correspond to the content and focus of *Leadership Communication*. Used with permission of McGraw-Hill.

Area and Skill	Excel	Competent	Need to Develop
Oral Communication Skills (continued)			
6. Talking in large groups			
7. Answering questions			
8. Asking questions			
9. Drawing others out			
10. Summarizing and clarifying others' ideas			
11. Keeping to the topic			
12. Summarizing a discussion			
13. Dealing publicly with more senior people			
Part II—Managerial Skills			
Ethos/Image			
1. Understanding how you are seen by others			
2. Knowing how your personal style differs from others			
3. Asking others to comment on your style			
4. Assessing your own strengths and weaknesses			
5. Setting goals for personal change			
6. Willing to work on improving personal effectiveness			
7. Influencing the behavior of others			
8. Inspiring trust in others			
9. Projecting confidence			
Skills at Dealing with Others			
1. Listening			
2. Being sensitive to others' feelings			
3. Asking people how they feel			
4. Acknowledging people's feelings			
5. Helping others express their feelings			
6. Dealing with anger			
7. Dealing with hostility and suspicion			
8. Being comfortable with conflict			
9. Withstanding silences			
10. Mentoring others			
11. Coaching others			
Observation and Feedback Skills			
1. Being aware of high and low participators			
2. Noting if people are excluded			

Area and Skill	Excel	Competent	Need to Develop
Observation and Feedback Skills (continued)			
3. Recognizing who talks to whom			
4. Being aware of who takes on leadership roles			
5. Giving feedback on behavior in the group			
6. Giving praise and appreciation			
7. Providing constructive feedback to individuals or groups			
8. Helping team members give each other feedback			
9. Soliciting feedback from others			
10. Receiving feedback without being defensive			
Team Communications and Dynamics Skills			
1. Sensing tension in the group			
2. Being sensitive to how people in the group are feeling			
3. Being aware of how open or closed the group is			
4. Identifying those issues that are avoided			
5. Identifying and clarifying goals and objectives			
6. Clearly defining the problem under discussion			
7. Examining all facets of the problem			
8. Exploring people aspects of the problem			
9. Surfacing vested interests and feelings about the problem			
10. Encouraging others to generate ideas			
11. Using creativity to develop new ideas			
12. Evaluating options			
13. Helping groups make decisions			
14. Helping groups explore their commitment to group decisions and/or agreements			
15. Encouraging groups to develop action plans			
16. Helping the team to confront difficult issues			
17. Drawing attention to unhelpful behavior			
18. Helping the team deal with conflict or other tension			
19. Supporting individuals against group pressure			
20. Helping team members acknowledge each other's strengths			
21. Facilitating team review and critique			
Skills at Dealing with Your Own Feelings			
1. Being aware of your own feelings			
2. Identifying your feelings			

Area and Skill	Excel	Competent	Need to Develop
Skills at Dealing with Your Own Feelings (continued)			
3. Asserting your own ideas and rights			
4. Stating your own needs			
5. Expressing feeling to others			
6. Expressing the following feelings			
• Warmth			
• Affection			
• Comfort			
• Discomfort			
• Anxiety			
• Frustration			
• Fear			
• Irritation			
• Annoyance			
• Gratitude			
• Satisfaction			
• Confidence			
• Uncertainty			
• Anger			
• Excitement			
• Determination			
Part III—Corporate Communication Skills			
1. Developing an internal communication strategy			
2. Developing a vision			
3. Communicating a vision			
4. Targeting messages to different levels in an organization			
5. Creating a change communication program			
6. Implementing a change communication program			
7. Developing an external communication strategy			
8. Managing corporate image			
9. Analyzing external stakeholders			
10. Developing targeted messages for all external stakeholders			
11. Communicating with the news media			
12. Dealing with a communication crisis situation			

Worksheet to Help You Develop Your Personal Leadership Communication Plan

Part 1—Assessing Your Own Leadership Communication Abilities

1. Using the information gained from completing the Checklist of Overall Leadership Communication Skills, assign a score for your improvement need in each skill area (use the scale provided next to the table).

Score	Skill Area
	Communication Strategy
	Written Communication Skills
	Oral Communication Skills
	Ethos/Image
	Skills at Dealing with Others
	Observation and Feedback Skills
	Team Communications and Dynamics Skills
	Skills at Dealing with Your Own Feelings
	Internal Corporate Communication
	External Corporate Communication

1 = substantial need to improve
2 = some need to improve
3 = little need to improve
4 = no need to improve at this time

2. What do you consider your major communication strengths?

3. What do you consider your major communication weaknesses?

4. What leadership communication roles do you currently play in your organization?

Part 2—Determining Your Leadership Communication Goals

Answer the following questions to help you develop your goals and plan.

1. What communication leadership roles would you like to play in the future (at your organization or in your career overall)?

2. What are your short-term and long-term leadership communication improvement goals?

3. What new skill do you want to work on first, second, third, etc.?

4. What barriers do you anticipate having to overcome to reach your improvement goals?

5. How long do you think it will take you to achieve your goals?

6. How will you know you are succeeding?

7. How will you obtain feedback?

Part 3—Developing a Plan to Achieve Your Goals

Use this grid to help you plan and track your improvement.

Improvement Goal	Action Steps to Achieve Goal	Deadline	Method to Measure Success

Notes

1. Mintzberg, H. (1973). *The Nature of Managerial Work*. New York: Harper & Row; Eccles, R. G., & Nohria, N. (1991). *Beyond the Hype: Rediscovering the Essence of Management*. Boston: Harvard Business School Press.

2. Bowman, G. W., Jones, L. W., Peterson, R. A., Gronouski, J. A., & Mahoney, R. M. (1964). What helps or harms promotability? *Harvard Business Review*, 42 (1), pp. 6–18.

3. Roberts, W. R., Trans. (1954). *The Rhetoric and Poetics of Aristotle*. New York: Random House, p. 25.

4. *The Rhetoric and Poetics of Aristotle*, p. 90.

5. *The Rhetoric and Poetics of Aristotle*, p. 91.

6. Kouzes, J. M., & Posner, B. Z. (1993). *Credibility: How Leaders Gain It and Lose It, Why People Demand It*. San Francisco: Jossey-Bass.

7. *The Rhetoric and Poetics of Aristotle*, p. 25.

8. Conger, J. A. (1998). The necessary art of persuasion. *Harvard Business Review,* 76 (3), p. 88.

9. Bamlund, D. C. (1962). Toward a meaning-centered philosophy of communication. *Journal of Communication*, 12, pp. 197–211.

10. *Credibility*, p. 14.

11. Solomon, R. (1998). Ethical leadership, emotions, and trust: Beyond "charisma." In J. B. Ciulla (Ed.), *Ethics: The Heart of Leadership*. Westport, CT: Quorum Books.

12. *The Rhetoric and Poetics of Aristotle*, p. 25.

13. Cialdini, R. (2001). Harnessing the science of persuasion. *Harvard Business Review,* 79 (9), pp. 72–80.

14. Conger, J. A. (1998), p. 87.

Core Leadership Communication

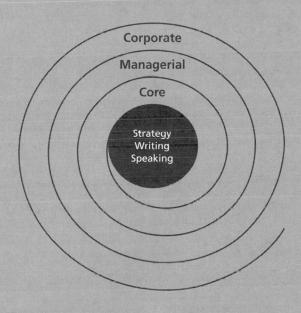

Corporate

Managerial

Core

Strategy
Writing
Speaking

Chapter **One**

Developing Leadership Communication Strategy

Indeed, the heart of strategy is at the business level where the dual facets of strategy (i.e., "where do you want to go?" and "how do you want to get there?") meld together.

Shona L. Brown and Kathleen M. Eisenhardt, *Competing on the Edge: Strategy as Structured Chaos*

Chapter Objectives

In this chapter, you will learn to do the following:

- Establish a clear communication purpose.
- Develop your communication strategy.
- Analyze your audiences.
- Organize written and oral communication effectively.

Leaders need to consider strategy in communication just as they do in other areas of their business. As traditionally defined in business, strategy consists of two pieces: (1) determining your goals and (2) developing a plan to achieve them. The same definition applies to communication strategy. You first determine exactly what your goal or purpose is in communicating with your audience, and then you decide how best to accomplish that purpose. In your role as a business leader, communicating with anyone inside or outside your organization without stopping to develop a strategy and analyze your audience could potentially harm both you and your organization. At a minimum, not developing a strategy could prevent your messages from reaching your audiences as you intend. If you look back at Exhibit I.2 in the introduction, you see that a sender can eliminate most of the interference or barriers to successful communication by taking time to develop a strategy and analyze the audience.

In this chapter, you will learn to apply communication strategy to achieve your communication goals. Effective communication strategy allows you to avoid the barriers and eliminate the interference that might prevent your messages from reaching your target audiences. Effective leadership communication depends on your mastering the lessons in this chapter. You will learn to establish a clear communication purpose, develop a strategic leadership communication plan, analyze audiences, and ensure that your message is well organized and logical so that it produces the results you intend.

ESTABLISHING A CLEAR PURPOSE

Leaders recognize that communication has consequences; you need to be sure the results you produce are those you intend. To achieve your intended results, you first need to establish a clear purpose. What do you want your audience to know as a result of your message? What do you want them to do? You will usually find that you have one of three general purposes:

- To inform—transferring facts, data, or information to someone.
- To persuade—convincing someone to do something.
- To instruct—instructing someone in a process.

Sometimes you may simply want to transfer information and are expecting no response or action as a result, but most often leadership communication is action-oriented. You want the receivers to respond, to follow up, or to do something in response to your communication. To ensure that their responses or actions conform to your expectations, you need to be very clear about your specific purpose. Breakdowns in communication frequently occur because the sender of the message has not taken the time to determine a clear purpose.

Clarifying Your Purpose

Just as leaders need to determine a strategic vision or a clearly stated direction for their companies, you need to establish a clear purpose or direction for your communication. If you are responding to a message sent to you, the sender's message may influence your purpose and determine your response. If you are initiating the communication, the purpose emerges from your own thoughts and ideas, and you may need to invent or generate the ideas to make it clear and support it.

In some cases, the purpose emerges easily. For example, if you need to tell your management team that you are planning to introduce a new product, your purpose would be to inform them of your decision and explain the product. If the product represents a radical departure from your company's current strategy or business line, your purpose becomes more complex since you may expect some resistance from the team. In this case, your purpose is to persuade them that the decision is a good one, which may require you to analyze the advantages and disadvantages and gather the support for your argument.

In addition, a further complication in this clarification step could occur if you need to establish in your own mind that the decision is valid. In that case, you might need to spend time generating ideas and even clarifying your purpose in your own mind so that you can state clearly and concisely your purpose as well as the reasons behind it to your audience.

In this phase of clarifying your purpose and analyzing your ideas, you should not be concerned with organizing or editing. People who struggle to get started are often trying to perform two functions at once: create and correct. The correcting side interferes with the creating side and can completely shut down the creativity. Instead, you want to turn off the internal censor and let the ideas flow. If you compose using a computer, you may find it helpful to turn off your monitor so that you are not tempted to stop and change the text or correct every error your word processing program highlights. You want to free up the creative side of your brain to think about your purpose, and your goal should be to capture your ideas quickly.

Although your purpose may be the first sentence you write, you will probably change the wording some to arrive at your exact meaning. Even if you are writing what appears to be a simple e-mail response to an e-mail sent to you, you should stop and think about your purpose and ensure that it is clear in your own mind, for if it is not, it will not be clear to your audience.

Generating Ideas

Once you determine your specific purpose, and sometimes while you are determining it, you can begin to come up with the supporting words and ideas and explore your thoughts about the subject. Clarifying your purpose is often an iterative process. You state the purpose, generate some ideas, and then restate the purpose once you see the direction your supporting ideas are taking. In addition, you may need to push your thinking to ensure that your ideas are complete, particularly if your communication is complex. In the previous example of introducing a new product, you would want to explore the pros and cons of introducing the new product before you attempt to persuade your management team that it is a good idea.

If you find you need to analyze an idea before presenting it to others, you will probably find one of the following four ways useful in helping you to push your thinking:

1. Brainstorming

Brainstorming in this context is conducting an internal discussion with yourself and jotting down the subject and any ideas related to it as they occur to you without concern for merit, order, or logic. You might look for the pros and cons, for instance, or attempt to isolate the main topics and list all examples that come to mind. You would want to use the same rules applied in any well-facilitated brainstorming group session for your individual brainstorming:

- Write down your purpose or overall idea.
- List all words or phrases that come to mind related to the purpose using free association.
- Remember, no idea is a bad idea, so suspend criticism or evaluation and turn off the internal censor.
- When you run out of ideas, look at your list to see if any of the ideas already recorded inspire other ideas.

Some people find that a time limit helps push their thinking; others find it hinders them by adding an element of stress. Do what works best for you.

2. Idea Mapping

Idea mapping, also called mind mapping, is similar to brainstorming in that you attempt to generate as many ideas as possible related to your main topic; it differs in that instead of a list of ideas, you create a visual representation of your ideas. You first write your main topic in the middle of the page, represented by the oval in Exhibit 1.1. Then, you write down all the ideas that come to mind in relationship to this idea, starting with the most general and working outward.

You may want to designate different shapes for different kinds of ideas, but you should not let the visual design slow you down. Again, you must avoid filtering, editing, or evaluating, and let your mind roam freely from topic to topic.

What you produce may appear rather random, although patterns will start to emerge that will help you refine your topic and hone in on what it is you really want to say. You can then draw similar shapes around related ideas or color-code them in some way. Later, you can come back and better organize your idea map, possibly regrouping some topics and removing others. The goal is to create an exhaustive page of ideas and thoughts that support your main idea. Then, you might

EXHIBIT 1.1   Generating Ideas through Idea Mapping

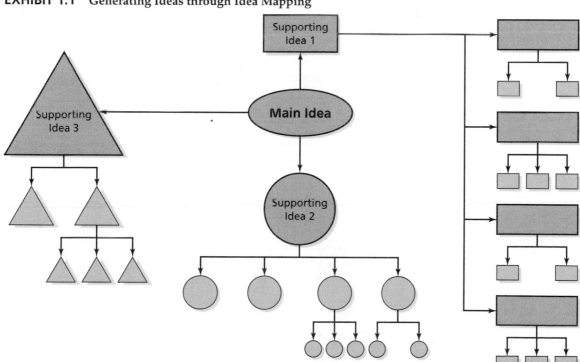

move to a new page to start collecting the facts and data for each of the supporting topics, represented by the smaller shapes in Exhibit 1.1.

Note that a real idea map will probably be messier than this example, but that is as it should be. The goal is to generate ideas and to attempt to be complete in doing so, not to create a neatly drawn diagram.

3. The Journalist's Questions: Who? What? Why? When? Where? How?

The following are the questions that journalists answer when generating ideas for a story. You may find them helpful in business communication as well, particularly for policy, process, or procedural topics.

For instance, if you need to write a memo describing a change in company policy, you would want to establish the following:

1. To whom does the policy apply?
2. What exactly is the policy? What has changed?
3. Why is the policy in place? Why have the changes been made?
4. When does the policy take effect?
5. Where would people needing more information obtain it?
6. How would they obtain it?

4. The Decision Tree

The decision tree is a way to break a topic into its parts so that you can see how the subtopics relate and whether you have the right support and enough support (Exhibit 1.2). It resembles idea mapping but is more structured and depends on an internal question-and-answer dialogue to be most effective. For example, if you were writing a memo to persuade your management team that the company should design and launch a new product, your argument might be as demonstrated in Exhibit 1.2.

EXHIBIT 1.2
An Example of a Decision Tree

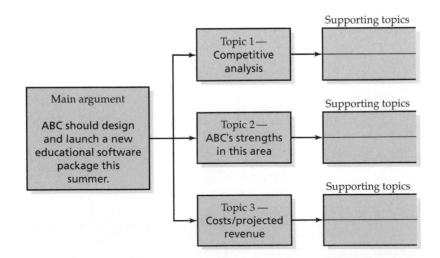

It may help you to use this approach if you think of it as a dialogue, beginning with the main topic, "ABC should design and launch a new educational software package this summer." This assertion leads to a series of "why" questions. The answers become the supporting topics. The why answers would be because (1) no one else is competing in this space, (2) we have the internal capabilities to design and launch the product efficiently and effectively, and (3) the costs would be low and the revenue potential high. Then, in developing the supporting topics, you would provide the data and facts for each of these. Once you have finished with the decision tree, you will probably have a very complete argument and be ready to develop the communication strategy to deliver it.

Working with these methods of generating ideas will help you gain an even clearer sense of your purpose for communicating with your audience. What you will find is that your thinking and your writing are intertwined. In his article in the *Harvard Business Review,* "Clear Writing Means Clear Thinking Means . . . ," Marvin H. Swift demonstrates the connection of clear thinking to clear writing and presents a very instructive example of how the relationship of writing and thinking might work when drafting a memo.[1] Here is the first draft of the memo:

First Draft of the Memo

To: All Employees
From: Samuel Edwards, General Manager
Subject: Abuse of Copiers

It has recently been brought to my attention that many of the people who are employed by this company have taken advantage of their positions by availing themselves of the copiers. More specifically, these machines are being used for other than company business. Obviously, such practice is contrary to company policy and must cease and desist immediately. I wish therefore to inform all concerned—those who have abused policy or will be abusing it—that their behavior cannot and will not be tolerated. Accordingly, anyone in the future who is unable to control himself will have his employment terminated. If there are any questions about company policy, please feel free to contact this office.

Source: Swift, M. H. (1973). Clear writing means clear thinking means . . . , *Harvard Business Review,* January–February, p. 59. Used with permission of Harvard Business School Publishing.

Notice that the tone in this first draft is accusatory and angry. The writer isolates himself from his audience and refers to the employees as "the people who are employed by this company." With his subject line, "Abuse of Copiers," and the statement that employees will be "terminated," he creates a negative tone making it doubtful that anyone would feel "free" to contact his office with questions.

If his purpose is to inform the employees of the problem, he has done that; however, if he thinks, as a leader should, about how best to motivate his employees, this memo would not accomplish his purpose. It would not create cooperation or support for him, the company, or the policy. Instead, it could alienate him from his employees and cause resentment.

As Swift discusses, when the writer wrote the first draft, his emotions were clouding his thinking. He is not thinking clearly and his writing shows it. After considerably more thought, particularly about how his audience will perceive his message and how he wants them to respond, he rewrites his memo several times to yield the final version.

The Final Draft of the Memo

To: All Employees
From: Samuel Edwards, General Manager
Subject: Use of Copiers

We are revamping our policy on the use of copiers for personal matters. In the past, we have not encouraged personnel to use them for such purposes because of the costs involved. But we also recognize, perhaps belatedly, that we can solve the problem if each of us pays for what he takes.

We are therefore putting these copiers on the pay-as-you-go basis. The details are simple enough . . .

Source: Swift, M. H. (1973). Clear writing means clear thinking means . . . , *Harvard Business Review*, January–February, p. 60. Used with permission of Harvard Business School Publishing.

In this final version, he is showing much more consideration for his audience and thinking about how best to motivate them. It does a much better job of accomplishing his purpose. His positive tone is more effective than the negative tone of the first draft. He now uses "we," which brings him and the employees together. The style is also more concise and the content clearer. He is no longer isolating himself from his employees and projecting a threatening, punitive image. He has assumed a positive ethos. This version will achieve the results he intended—to stop the misuse of the copiers—without alienating his employees.

This example also demonstrates one test you can use to see if your purpose is clear and exactly what you intend—the use of an effective subject line (or, in a longer document or presentation, a title). A subject line should capture the purpose of your memo or e-mail and set the tone. Notice the difference in the negative "Abuse of Copiers" and the more neutral "Use of Copiers." If you find yourself struggling to create a subject line that clearly reveals your intention in an e-mail or memo, or a title that specifically tells your audience the purpose of your report or presentation, then your purpose may not be clear in your own mind. If it is not clear to you, it will certainly not be clear to your audience.

This example illustrates the importance of clarifying your purpose before communicating it to others. It underscores that clear thinking about purpose as well as audience yields clearer, more effective communication. Your purpose establishes the direction you want to go and the results you intend to achieve with your messages, which sets the stage for you to develop a strategy to accomplish those results.

DETERMINING YOUR COMMUNICATION STRATEGY

Once you have clarified your purpose, you are ready to engage in the tactical side of communication strategy. Effective communication—whether a simple e-mail or memo, a complex report, a meeting, or a presentation—requires going beyond clarity of purpose to the plan for accomplishing your purpose, the second essential step in any good strategy. At this point, communication strategy shifts to determining how to achieve your communication objectives. Your strategic planning can be complex or simple, but you should build it around a methodical approach that calls on your analytical skills, just as you would call on those skills for any problem you need to solve.

The communication strategy framework (Exhibit 1.3) illustrates an approach to establishing a communication strategy that will ensure that you consider all the angles and anticipate any issues that might emerge to interfere with communicating the message you want to deliver. Your analysis begins with the context—what is going on in the organization, the market, the industry, the world—and places purpose at the apex. You then need to consider each of the components: messages,

EXHIBIT 1.3
Communication Strategy Framework

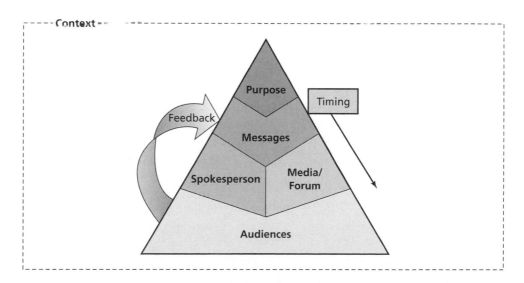

media/forum, timing, and, if appropriate, the spokesperson. At the base is your audience, the foundation on which all of these other strategy components rest. Audience analysis is critical to any communication strategy and is so important that the next section of this chapter discusses it at length. Connected to the audience is the need to devise a method for assessing the impact of your communication on your audience through a feedback loop.

The framework will help you develop the "how to" side of your communication strategy. You can use it for any communication need, but it is particularly useful in complex, critical situations, such as mergers and acquisitions, crises, and major change programs.

Exhibit 1.4 provides representative questions you should ask in analyzing each of the strategy components in the framework.

EXHIBIT 1.4
Key
Questions in
Developing a
Communica-
tion Strategy

Component	Key Questions to Ask Yourself
Context	What is going on that will affect how the messages are received (what is happening in the world, the industry, the market, the company, the department, etc.)? What are the cultural differences I should consider?
Purpose	What is my objective or what do I want to accomplish? Do I have different but related purposes for different audiences? How does my purpose relate to and support the company strategy?
Message	What is my overall message? How do I formulate my message to make it acceptable to my audience(s)? What do I expect others to do because of my message? What are my supporting messages? Do they differ for each audience?
Medium/Forum	What is the most effective means or channel for reaching each audience (e-mail, memo, letter, meeting, speech, etc.)? Do I need to consider costs, logistics, or other practical matters in selecting my communication medium or forum?
Spokesperson	Am I the best person to deliver the message? If not, who should deliver the message(s)? Who would be the most credible or otherwise effective presenter for different messages or audiences?
Timing	Does timing matter? If so, when should the message(s) be delivered and in what order?
Audiences	Who are my primary audiences? Secondary? Accidental? What are their interests in this situation? What are their stakes in the outcomes? How will they be affected by my messages?
Feedback	How will I determine if my audience is receiving my messages as I intend? How will I measure or assess the impact?

All communication occurs in a context of interrelated conditions that surround it. Leadership communication never exists in a vacuum. As you define your purpose and develop your strategy, you should recognize the context in which the communication occurs. Before you create any form of communication, from the simplest e-mail to the most complex report or presentation, you should ask yourself the following questions:

Questions to Determine the Context

1. What else is going on in the world, industry, or company that will affect how the audience will receive this communication?
2. Where does the communication fall in the overall flow of communication? First or last?
3. What has happened before and after?
4. What are the organizational implications?
5. What are the people implications?
6. What does the audience know or believe about the context compared to what the sender knows or believes?

Asking what is going on in the world, industry, or company is essential to ensuring your audiences will receive your message as you intend. For example, a few years ago an international energy company was implementing cost-cutting measures and announced the layoff of a large number of its employees. At the same time, the company was sponsoring a major golf tournament. Announcing the layoffs while continuing to spend money for the tournament made many employees and others in the community angry. The company had failed to consider the context for delivering their message. Leaders must be sensitive to what is going on around them and consider the context for the messages they send.

As discussed in the previous section, your purpose sets the stage for your communication strategy; and of course, in an organizational context, that purpose should link directly to the overall corporate strategy. You may have one overall purpose or many, depending on the complexity of the communication situation. You may also have several messages, with slightly different wording and tones for different target audiences. Your overall purpose and overarching message should be consistent from group to group; however, the emphasis, the submessages, and the expected reactions may differ from audience to audience. For example, investors may applaud a merger of your company with another, yet employees may be fearful and unhappy.

In addition, with more complex communications, such as those that affect the entire organization, you may need different spokespersons for different audiences and messages, and you will need to select the spokespersons carefully. In a merger or acquisition, for instance, you will have several spokespersons with slightly different messages for the different audiences. They could include the chief executive officer, chief financial officer, and chief public affairs officer, as well as the entire management team, area supervisors, and local representatives.

EXHIBIT 1.5   **Example of Communication Strategy Analysis (portion only)**

Target Audience	Medium	Purpose	Message	Spokes-person	Timing
Investment community	Meetings	Inspire confidence in company's stability and value	A strategic move designed to make both companies stronger	CEO	Day of announcement
Local media	Press conference	Generate positive public opinion and allay any fears of changes in their services	Good for the local economy and the people of the community	CEOs of both companies	Day of announcement
National media	Press release/ calls	Generate positive public opinion and assure potential investors	Good move for the industry, sound financial move, etc.	Public affairs official	Day of announcement
Employees (acquirer)	E-mail/ meetings	Keep good employees from leaving and reassure all that the company is stable	Good for all employees, creating stronger company, secure future for all	CEO, senior management team	Right after announcement
Employees (acquired)	Memo/ meetings	Keep good employees in place and make them as comfortable as possible	No layoffs, no major changes will occur (only if this is true)	CEO, senior management team	Right after announcement

Exhibit 1.5 illustrates how you might use the framework to develop a strategy for communicating a merger. It represents an excerpt from an actual strategy developed for a merger between two major high-profile companies. The complete communication strategy in this case consisted of several pages of an Excel spreadsheet containing over 25 different audiences and messages and with the timing broken down to minutes before and just after the merger announcement.

If you are preparing for a major communication event, or any communication that will reach multiple audiences and affect an entire organization, you should develop your communication strategy through an overall action plan similar to the one illustrated in Exhibit 1.6. The major phases of your strategy development and implementation are analysis, implementation, and assessment. The illustration suggests that the process is iterative since you will probably find that you need to make adjustments once you begin to implement the strategy.

In Phase 1, you use the strategy framework or a similar analytical tool to guide your analysis and frame your strategy. You then develop and communicate your plan. Finally, you monitor the impact and assess the success or failure of the communication strategy. The previous merger example, for instance, represents a portion of a much larger plan resulting from the analysis performed in Phase 1. Then, in Phase 2, the messages were transmitted to the identified audiences through the appropriate medium. In Phase 3, the organization conducted a survey to

EXHIBIT 1.6
Three-Phased
Communica-
tion Action
Plan

determine how well their messages had been received so that they could adjust the approaches if necessary. For more about how you might develop a complex communication strategy, see Chapter 9 on change communication and employee communication in Section Three of this text.

To summarize, effective communication depends on clarifying your purpose; developing a thorough, thoughtful communication strategy; and having an action plan for more complex communication.

ANALYZING YOUR AUDIENCES

Analyzing an audience is fundamental to any communication strategy since the characteristics of audiences will determine your approach and shape your targeted messages. As the communication strategy framework illustrates, audience is the foundation on which all of the other components in the framework rest. A leader addresses many different audiences, making it difficult to generalize about what approach to use in all circumstances; therefore, you will need to analyze your audience in every communication situation, and you should approach each audience as unique.

You may find Exhibit 1.7 helpful in determining your approach to audiences with different levels of expertise. The table on audience expertise helps you to appreciate the different levels of knowledge and experience of your audiences and to select how best to approach them to ensure that they are receptive to your messages. Recent research on how organizations learn has found that companies consist of communities of practice.[2] Communities of practice are groups that have common interests or a common knowledge base and interact frequently. The group could be a work group, a team, a function, a department, or even a company.

EXHIBIT 1.7
Audience
Expertise
Table

Source: Table created
based on information
from Houp, K. W.,
Pearsall, T. E., &
Tebeaux, E. (2000).
*Reporting Technical
Information*, 9th ed.
New York: Oxford
University Press.
Used by permission
of Oxford University
Press, Inc.

Audience	Medium	Purpose	Approach
Layperson/ nonexpert	Magazine article Newsletter Pamphlet	To entertain To inform	Make interesting and practical Give background Define terms Use narratives and analogy
Executive	Memo Letter Report	To inform To persuade	Focus on decision making Keep simple Be honest and direct Give conclusions and recommendations early
Expert	Journal article Report	To inform	State the how and why Present limited background information Use language of the discipline State inferences and conclusions Cite numerous references
Technical	Reports Procedure	To inform To instruct	State the how and why Provide limited background information Keep practical/avoid theory
Combined (diverse)	Memo Report	To inform To instruct To persuade	Avoid technical language and jargon Use sections, divisions, and headings Define terms/limit technical information to appendixes Keep prose clean, concise, and simple

Leaders need to communicate to audiences with a range of expertise from the layperson or nonexpert to the technical or highly specialized individual. As you assume higher leadership roles in the organization, you will find you communicate to a broader, more diverse, and less technical audience; thus, you will find you often use the approaches suggested for executives or the combined (diverse) audiences.

In addition, when you seek a decision from your audience, you might want to consider their decision-making style to ensure that you use a communication approach that will be persuasive with them. In a *Harvard Business Review* article, Gary A. Williams and Robert B. Miller provide one useful approach to analyzing decision-making styles and argue that "persuasion works best when it's tailored to five distinct decision-making styles." Their research indicates that "more than half of all sales presentations are mismatched to the decision-maker's style."[3] The table in Exhibit 1.8 explains the styles they identified.

In any situation, internal or external to your organization, knowing how your audience makes decisions will help you target your message. You should try to anticipate your audience's response, considering very carefully what they will do after reading what you have written or hearing what you have to say. Try to adopt the audience's point of view, the "you attitude." What is it that they need to hear to agree with your message? What will appeal to them? What will help them make the decision you want them to make?

You should also look closely at your audience in an organizational context: where are they, what do they know, and what do they need to know? When you

EXHIBIT 1.8 Decision-Making Styles

Style	Characteristics	Communication Approach
Charismatics	Talkative, captivating Easily intrigued by new ideas Make decisions based on information, not emotions	Begin with bottom line Focus on results Present straightforward arguments Use visual aids
Thinkers	Intelligent, logical, academic Impressed by arguments supported by data Tend to be risk averse Need time to come to their own conclusions	Openly communicate any concerns up front Have lots of data ready Provide all perspectives Be prepared to go through methods Be prepared for silence
Skeptics	Demanding, suspicious of every fact Aggressive, almost combative style Need to trust someone to believe their ideas Don't like being challenged or made to look uninformed in any way	Build credibility in yourself and your ideas by enlisting the help of someone they trust Emphasize the credibility of your sources Make arguments as concrete as possible, using specific examples
Followers	Cautious, responsible Risk averse Prefer innovative applications of proven solutions Make decisions based on track records, theirs or others'	Present proven methods, references, and testimonials Show how the idea is safe yet innovative Use case studies Present options Provide details
Controllers	Logical, unemotional, sensible, detail- oriented, analytical Abhor uncertainty and ambiguity Focus on the facts and analytics of an argument	Carefully structure your argument Provide details from experts Don't push too hard Provide the facts and leave them to decide

Source: Adapted and reprinted by permission of *Harvard Business Review.* From "Change the way you persuade," by G. A. Williams & R. B. Miller, 80 (5), pp. 65–74. Copyright © 2002 by Harvard Business School Publishing Corporation; all rights reserved.

communicate in business, you are communicating within an organizational context. Whether the communication is simple or complex, you will need to think carefully about organizational relationships and how they affect motivation. The questions in Exhibit 1.9 are designed to help you not only determine who your audience is but also understand better what motivates them in a particular organizational context.

You will probably be too busy to answer all of these questions every time you send a memo or e-mail, and in many cases, your familiarity with the audience will minimize the need for analysis. But with any important correspondence or report, you must stop and consider your audience. These questions will help you focus on what you should consider. If you do not have the time to work through all of them for all of your communications, you should at a minimum be able to articulate very clearly your purpose in writing to them and your expectations of them as a result of this communication. This clarity of purpose combined with a good sense of your audience supports any successful communication strategy.

EXHIBIT 1.9
Questions to Clarify Audience and Organizational Context

1. Does the document or presentation respond to a previous document or particular request? If so, what? Where is this document or presentation in the overall flow of communication?
2. What is the organizational context for this communication?
3. Who are the primary audiences (the persons who will act) and who are the secondary audiences? Who might be an unintended or accidental audience?
4. If they are the decision makers, what motivates them and how do you best persuade them?
5. If they are not the decision makers, what is their relationship to the decision maker?
6. How much do they know about the subject? What do they need to know?
7. What do I expect them to do in response to this communication?
8. How do I expect them to feel?
9. What do they have to gain or lose by accepting my ideas/recommendations?
10. How will the document or presentation affect the organization?
11. Overall, what do I expect to happen as a result of this communication?

ORGANIZING WRITTEN AND ORAL COMMUNICATION EFFECTIVELY

Once you have clarified your purpose, conducted your audience analysis, and created a strategy, you are ready to select the best structure for organizing your communication. You must include the organization of your communication in your early thinking about how best to present your ideas to your audience.

Organization depends on purpose, audience, and strategy. For instance, if your purpose is to persuade a hostile audience, you might want to begin indirectly, saving your main message or recommendation for the end. If you are addressing a decision maker who needs to see the details before making a decision, you may want to present the facts up front. If you are in a culture where relationships are valued more than results, you might want to begin by talking about general, non-business topics before introducing the main subject of your communication. If, however, your audience consists of typical busy U.S. executives, you will need to get to the main subject quickly, right up front, or you risk losing their attention and trying their patience.

In thinking about your presentation or document, you should adopt the perspective of the audience, and select and organize your information for that particular audience. If you used the decision tree or idea mapping to develop your ideas, you have already begun to organize them and done some selecting and discarding of information. You should now be concerned with the logical ordering of your writing or speech. You can pose the following questions to determine the best approach to organizing your communication:

- What is the most effective way to begin the document or presentation with *this* audience?
- How should I organize the content to ensure that the audience can follow the argument easily and understand the main ideas?
- What is the most effective way to conclude?

Your readers are busy, just as you are, and will be much more likely to respond positively to a memo, e-mail, or any communication if it gets right to the main ✓ message, stays on topic, establishes relevance to them, and is organized to be immediately accessible to them and to the way they think and make decisions. How you start your document or presentation will depend on your audience analysis. The general rule for business communication, however, is that your purpose for ✓ writing or speaking usually will come first. Background information is included only if you need it to establish a context for your communication or your relationship to the problem addressed. Likewise, you should place your recommendations ✓ at the beginning unless you have a specific reason for delaying them. If you delay the conclusions or recommendations until the end, many readers will go looking for them anyway, and the listener will become impatient waiting for them. Your audience wants to know immediately why you are writing or speaking to them. Therefore, with most business audiences, you need to deliver your main message immediately.

How you organize your communication once you move into the body of your discussion will depend on your analysis of your audience; however, the logic of the entire document or presentation, as well as that of each section of it, should be obvious to anyone. Your argument should be so logical that anyone can follow your reasoning and understand why one point follows another.

Selecting Organizational Devices

You will probably use one or more of the following methods to organize individual sections and even the entire document or presentation:

1. **Deduction** (general to particular)—conclusions or recommendation, then the supporting facts, arguing from general principles to specific situations.
2. **Induction** (particular to general)—supporting information, facts that build to the conclusions or recommendation.
3. **Chronological**—first, second, and so forth, used to describe a process or procedure or relate events in the order they occurred as a narrative.
4. **Cause/effect**—Because of X and Y, Z happened; a powerful and common form of analysis.
5. **Comparison/contrast**—similarities, then differences.
6. **Problem/solution**—explanation of the situation or problem, followed by ways to solve it.
7. **Spatial**—organization based on relationship of steps, pieces, or items to each other.

Frequently the structure of your communication is either deductive or inductive. If deductive, you begin with an overarching argument or general principle, and you then provide levels of facts grouped logically by topic to support your major assertion. If inductive, you present your facts or groupings of facts first and build your argument from point to point, ending with a "therefore" and your conclusion.

Using the Pyramid Principle

In *The Pyramid Principle*, Barbara Minto illustrates how to structure an effective discussion in a business context by applying classical deductive and inductive logic.[4] You begin with your main argument and, then, establish a dialogue that supports each part of the argument with specifics that answer the questions "why," "what," or "how." This dialogue is similar to the approach you use to create a decision tree to generate ideas. You start with your conclusion or recommendation at the top and then work through the levels of support, testing each level to make sure it answers "why," "what," or "how" for the level above it (Exhibit 1.10).

Using the pyramid principle helps you structure a complete and logical argument. As you create the pyramid, you can easily see gaps in your evidence, establish the balance of your argument, and determine if each level logically supports the next. You can see if you have too much support for any one topic and not enough for another. A pyramid also makes it easy for you to see that each level of your argument clearly and logically supports the level above it and that you have not duplicated support under any of the topic boxes. In addition, drawing a pyramid helps if you are working with a team to create a document or presentation. With all topics and supporting details visually displayed, you can easily divide the topics into tasks, avoid duplication of effort, and determine quickly where the team needs to do more analysis.

Creating a Storyboard

Another technique for working out the structure of your communication is a storyboard. A storyboard is particularly useful if you are working in a team to prepare a presentation. It allows everyone to see the logical flow and encourages you

EXHIBIT 1.10 **Example of a Pyramid**

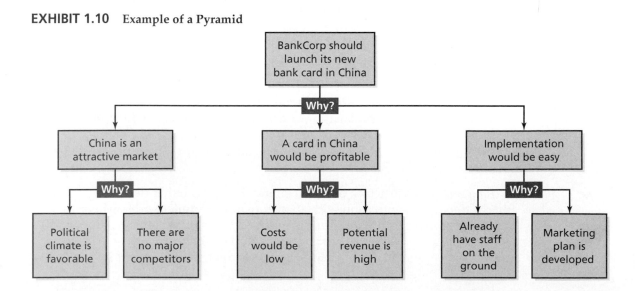

EXHIBIT 1.11
Example of a Storyboard for a Presentation

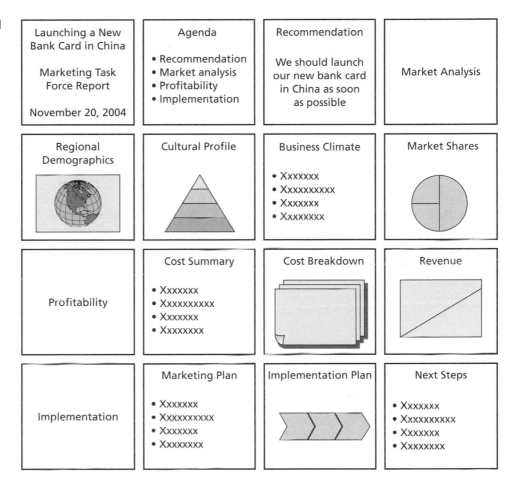

to think about the individual slides you need to support each section. It also helps you to divide these pieces up for completion by the individual team members (Exhibit 1.11).

Ensuring a tight, logical organization for any communication requires a plan or map of the argument, whether a pyramid, an outline, a decision tree, or a storyboard. You want to establish a logical structure and think carefully about the organizational devices that work best with your audience.

This chapter has focused on clarifying your messages and developing a communication strategy, both essential skills for anyone wanting to master leadership communication. In addition, you have learned to generate and organize your ideas to ensure that they reach your audience with your intended message. Applying the principles and guidelines in this chapter to all types of communication discussed in the remaining chapters of the book will help you ensure that your communication accomplishes your purpose and results in the action you desire, the hallmarks of effective leadership communication.

Exercise 1.1: Using the Pyramid Principle to Organize an Argument

Use the pyramid principle to structure an argument based on the facts provided here. First, establish an assertion at the first level in answer to the following question: Should AmeriHotels build a new, upscale hotel in Metroburg, near a new major downtown convention center and sports arena? Second, identify at least three primary supporting ideas. Third, group the facts under the supporting ideas.

1. No other hotels exist within walking distance of Metroburg's new convention center or the sports arena.
2. Experts predict a downturn in hotel bookings for at least the near term (one to three years) and possibly for a longer term.
3. No restaurants exist outside of the convention center or sports arena, and the restaurants that do exist within the convention center offer "fast food" fare only.
4. Members of several ethnic groups and other local residents, many of whom had residences displaced by the convention center and sports arena developments, may oppose building permits.
5. The new convention center is in a high-crime area.
6. There are three other four-star, upscale hotels in the vicinity (within short driving distance) of the new convention center.
7. The city of Metroburg has obtained funds for park and landscaping efforts in the area.
8. Studies indicate that businesses thrive in the areas surrounding large urban convention centers and sports complexes/arenas, particularly in the accommodations/dining sectors.
9. Some statistics indicate a high correlation between sports arenas in large urban areas and increased numbers of outside visitors who stay overnight.
10. The city of Metroburg has committed to increased police presence/patrol in the area.
11. AmeriHotels has a spotty record concerning minority hiring and relationships.
12. Last year, AmeriHotels adopted a new vision statement promising that the company would make diversity and community-based hiring a top priority.
13. AmeriHotels has experience building in inner-city locations.
14. There is land near the new convention center and sports arena available for purchase and development.
15. Property values in the Metroburg downtown area have skyrocketed in the last year.

Source: This pyramid exercise was adapted from an exercise originally designed by June Ferrill, Rice University.

Exercise 1.2: Communicating Bad News

The Case: Superior Foods Corporation Faces a Challenge

On his way to the head office, Jason Starnes passed by the production line where hundreds of gloved, uniformed workers were packing sausages and processed meats for shipment to grocery stores around the world.

Jason's company, Superior Foods Corporation, based in Wichita, Kansas, employed 30,000 people in eight countries and had beef and pork processing plants in Arkansas, California, Milwaukee, and Nebraska City. Since a landmark U.S.–Japan trade agreement signed in 1988, markets had opened up for major exports of American beef, now representing 10 percent of U.S. production. Products called "variety meats"—including intestines, hearts, brains, and tongues—were very much in demand for export to international markets.

Jason was in Nebraska City to talk with the plant manager, Ben Schroeder, about the mad cow disease outbreak in the United States and its impact on their plant. On December 23, 2003, the U.S. Department of Agriculture had announced that bovine spongiform encephalopathy, or mad cow disease, had been discovered in a Holstein cow in Washington State. The global reaction was swift: seven countries imposed either total or partial bans on importation of U.S. beef. Superior had moved quickly to intercept a container load of frozen Asian-bound beef from its shipping port in Los Angeles, and all other shipments were on hold.

After walking into Jason's office, Ben sat down across from him and said: "Ben, your plant has been a top producer of variety meats for Superior, and we have appreciated all your hard work out here. Unfortunately, it looks like we need to limit production for a while—at least three months, or until the bans get relaxed. I know Senator Nelson is working hard to get the bans lifted. In the meantime, we need to shut down production and lay off about 25 percent of your workers. I know it is going to be difficult, and I'm hoping we can work out a way to communicate this to your employees."

The Assignment

After reading the Superior Foods case, complete the following actions.

1. Clarify your purpose(s) for communicating with the employees at the Nebraska plant. Consider what the employees will want to know and how they will need to feel about Superior Foods.
2. Use one of the idea-generation approaches introduced in this chapter to determine your primary messages.
3. Draft a memo or e-mail to the employees, paying very careful attention to the organization of the messages.

Source: Case developed by Beth O'Sullivan and assignment by Deborah J. Barrett, Rice University, 2004. Used with Permission.

Exercise 1.3: Developing Communication Strategy

The Case: Spree Cruise Lines

At 9:00 a.m. on Monday, Tara Hoopes, manager of corporate communications for Spree Cruise Lines, arrived at her office at Spree's corporate headquarters to find several messages already taped to her chair.

Please call the investor relations office at ext. 3620—need to discuss the upcoming shareholder meeting.	Please call the City Attorney in New Orleans—she's claiming that several small, historic buildings incurred foundation and mortar damage yesterday. Thinks it might have been caused by vibrations from the *Sensation* leaving.

The 750-foot *Sensation* had set sail from New Orleans on Sunday afternoon, bound for a five-night cruise to Cozumel and Cancun. Tara checked the statistics on the vessel and its itinerary:

- Built in 1974, cruising speed 20 knots, gross tonnage 50,000, slated for dry-dock repairs in several months.
- Carrying 1200 passengers on board, mostly Americans, about 35 percent under age 35, 40 percent between the ages of 35 and 55, and the remainder senior citizens.
- Staffed by Captain Hernan Galati, Chief Engineer Scotty Ferguson, and veteran Cruise Director Ned Carnahan. Additional staff on board: 650 crew members representing 20 different countries.
- Cruising to Cozumel with a Sunday departure, followed by a day at sea on Monday and arrival in Cozumel on Tuesday morning. On Tuesday night the vessel was scheduled to depart for Cancun, docking there all day Wednesday before returning to New Orleans on Friday.

Tara reached for the phone just as it rang. Ned Carnahan and Captain Galati were on the line. Before she could tell them about the full situation in New Orleans, they presented her with some problems of their own.

Sunday Night Aboard the *Sensation*

Ron and Marilyn Nelson stood on the stern deck enjoying the view. It had been an exciting day, watching the huge ship dwarf the buildings on shore as they departed New Orleans. They had already explored the ship, delighted to find an Internet café, a sushi bar, two pools, and the rock-climbing wall. They had listened carefully to the announcements over the ship's public address system and had skimmed the *Spree Fun,* the ship's newsletter, which listed a wide array of excursions to book before their arrival on shore. As they had waited in line to book their excursions, Marilyn noticed the weather maps hanging on the wall in the main deck lobby.

"Looks like a tropical storm over in the Bay of Campeche," she noted.

"Don't worry," Ron said. "This is a huge vessel, and its engines are strong enough to out-run any storm!" Ron was an ocean engineer by trade, and he was an authority on anything that floated on or happened under water. He added, "We're on vacation—let's enjoy it!"

They booked a catamaran sail/snorkel trip and a horseback-riding excursion to visit the Mayan ruins at Tulum, leaving plenty of time for shopping in Cozumel and Cancun.

Now, standing on the stern of the vessel, there was no evidence of a storm. Ron and Marilyn watched the two wakes made by the twin engines—frothy white foam that trailed from the ship into a moonlit sea. They came down the back staircase into a quiet, unused bar and lounge area. The glassware on the metal shelving was clinking together loudly, making an eerie echo across the room. Other parts of the ship were noisy with the voices of excited passengers, but as they passed into the quiet cigar lounge, they could clearly hear a loud, rhythmic bumping sound. Ron remarked, "There is something wrong here; it sounds like the dual engine props aren't synchronized."

Later that night, Marilyn could not sleep. It seemed that the vibration was getting worse and the plastic grids over the lighting system in the cabin were rattling loudly. As she put in some foam earplugs, she thought to herself that she never realized a cruise ship would be so loud.

In the Captain's Quarters

At 6:00 a.m. Monday morning, Scotty Ferguson, chief engineer, knocked at Captain Galati's door. He said, "Sir, the propulsion unit running the left engine prop won't hold up—we've got to shut it down. Running it could result in permanent damage, but we might have to restart if we need the full 20-knot engine speed to outrun the storm later in the cruise."

"Scotty, are you sure?" asked the Captain. "It will take us three days to reach Cozumel if we travel on half power. And we'll have to skip Cancun and turn right around to get back to dock by Friday. The guests have already booked their on-shore excursions. Let's get Ned up here."

Ned, the cruise director, grumbled to himself as his stateroom phone rang. He thought to himself, just one last cruise on this old ship; corporate promised I could move to a European route if I just finished this one last cruise. He spoke briefly with the captain and told him he would be right up.

On his way to the captain's quarters, he thought about what Captain Galati had told him and his mind worked quickly—I think we'd better call Tara at corporate, tell the passengers, refund or reschedule all the on-shore excursions, monitor the Internet café to see how many people have already contacted travel agents to disembark in Cozumel—and what about that storm?

Even though passenger tickets clearly stated that itinerary changes could occur and that Spree would reimburse only $30 per person, it was Ned's job to keep the passengers happy—not to mention what this could mean for *Sensation*'s future marketing plans. He was already calculating the financial impact to the cruise line and he couldn't help wondering if the minor engine troubles on the last cruise hadn't been properly repaired.

Tara's Phone Call

"Hello Tara, we've got a delicate situation here," Ned said.

Captain Galati interrupted, "We have to shut down one engine immediately; I know the passengers will be upset, but the integrity of the ship is my first concern."

"Of course, Captain," Tara said. "Tell me what's going on."

They reported the damage to the engine's propulsion system and their decision to shut down one engine and reduce their cruising speed to 10 knots. The arrival into Cozumel would be delayed; rather than arriving at 9:30 a.m. on Tuesday, they would most likely arrive at 4:00 p.m. To ensure a timely return to New Orleans by Friday, they would have to depart Cozumel at 2:00 a.m. Wednesday, skipping the Cancun destination altogether and cruising straight through.

Tara thought for a moment and said, "Ned, Captain Galati, is there a possibility that the engines could have set up a vibration significant enough to damage some buildings as you left port?" She told them about the call from the City Attorney.

"There's a lot at stake for Spree here. I think we'd better talk about how best to approach the situation."

The Assignment

1. Identify all of the key audiences for the communication surrounding this incident. What do you know about each of them? Are there other audiences linked to this audience, either as secondary or "future" audiences?

2. Answer the following questions about the audiences identified in question number 1.

   a. What is the message you want to send to each key audience?

   b. What information does the audience *already know* and what information do they *need or want to have* about the situation?

   c. How does this audience feel at this point and how would you like them to feel at the conclusion of the situation or after receiving your communication?

   d. How will you motivate or persuade them to accept your messages?

3. Develop a communication strategy considering the following questions:

   a. What are your key objectives for this communication? (Consider personal as well as departmental and corporate objectives.)

   b. Who is the best spokesperson to deliver this message and why? What other people could serve as spokespersons?

   c. What is the best channel or medium to use to communicate with this audience? Also consider the option of using several channels for these communications.

   d. When is the best time to communicate the information?

   e. Are there cultural or other context considerations you should keep in mind?

   f. How will you know if your communication has been successful?

Source: Spree case and assignment developed by Beth O'Sullivan, Rice University, January 2004. Used with Permission.

Notes

1. Swift, M. H. (1973). Clear writing means clear thinking means . . . , *Harvard Business Review,* January–February, p. 60.

2. Wenger, E. (1998). *Communities of Practice: Learning, Meaning, and Identity.* Cambridge: Cambridge University Press. Also, see Wenger, E., McDermott, R., & Snyder, W. M. (2002). *Cultivating Communities of Practice.* Boston: Harvard Business School Press.

3. "Change the way you persuade," G. A. Williams & R. B. Miller, *Harvard Business Review,* 80 (5), pp. 65–74. Copyright © 2002 by Harvard Business School Publishing Corporation; all rights reserved.

4. Minto, B. (1996). *The Pyramid Principle: Logic in Writing and Thinking.* London: Minto International.

Chapter **Two**

Creating Leadership Documents

Developing excellent communication skills is absolutely essential to effective leadership. The leader must be able to share knowledge and ideas to transmit a sense of urgency and enthusiasm to others. If a leader can't get a message across clearly and motivate others to act on it, then having a message doesn't even matter.

Gilbert Amelio, *president and CEO, National Semiconductor Corporation*

Chapter Objectives

In this chapter, you will learn to do the following:

- Select the most effective communication medium.
- Create individual or team documents.
- Organize document content coherently.
- Conform to content and format expectations in correspondence.
- Include expected contents in reports.
- Format business documents effectively.

In business, documents usually fall into one of two broad types: (1) correspondence (e-mails, memos, and letters) and (2) reports (including proposals, progress reviews, performance reports, and chart packs). Leadership documents are correspondence and reports by which managers and executives assert their influence in a wide range of organizational settings. Leaders write correspondence several times daily. They also write different kinds of reports, from complicated studies and white papers with recommendations and pages of analysis to shorter progress reviews. Business audiences carry with them certain expectations when they receive and read the various genres or types of business documents. In addition, they judge the leadership qualities of the writer. The audiences ask: Is the message clear? Is the argument logical and complete? Is the tone appropriate? Has the writer been careless in the content or prose? Problems in any of these areas can prevent your message from reaching your audience as you intended.

The inability to create a clear and coherent document has hindered countless business careers. Even something as apparently innocuous as an internal e-mail can hurt you and your organization. For example, an e-mail discussed in this chapter damaged a midwestern CEO's reputation and resulted in a substantial dip in his company's stock price. Once you are in a leadership position, your documents become powerful and can change the entire direction of your company. By knowing the importance of every document you create, you begin to appreciate the importance of making sure you approach the writing of all documents with utmost care, from the simplest e-mails to the most complicated reports.

This chapter focuses on helping you create leadership documents that accomplish your communication purposes. Chapter 1 emphasized that leadership communication depends on your establishing a clear purpose, developing a communication strategy, analyzing an audience, and ensuring you use the most effective organizational structure. This chapter will begin by applying these principles to creating documents. In addition, this chapter discusses how to make your documents coherent to your audience. You achieve coherence by using a logical structure and effective organization and by making sure your documents conform in content and format to typical business expectations.

SELECTING THE MOST EFFECTIVE COMMUNICATION MEDIUM

As with any effective leadership communication, you need to clarify your purpose, analyze your audience, and develop a communication strategy before you put pen to paper or fingers to the keyboard to create a document. You have a few options to consider when selecting the best document medium. When writing, people generally reply in kind: for example, if someone sends you an e-mail, you send an e-mail back. When you are initiating the chain of communication, the usual communication practices of the organization will probably guide your choice of medium. If the organization uses e-mail for everything, then you will as well. If you have complete freedom to select the medium and are not limited by the previous chain of communication or the practices in the organization, you should select the medium best suited for the context and your message. Exhibit 2.1 lists some of the pros and cons for each written medium to help you decide which is best in your situation.

CREATING INDIVIDUAL AND TEAM DOCUMENTS

Once you have developed your strategy and selected the most appropriate medium, you can then create and perfect your written communication. Whether you are creating your document alone or in collaboration with a team or other

EXHIBIT 2.1 Pros and Cons of Each Written Medium

Medium	Advantages	Disadvantages
Text Message	Fast, easy, immediate	Too abbreviated for more complex communication
E-Mail	Fast, immediate Easily distributed to one or many Creates a permanent electronic trail	Easily distributed to the world, accidentally or on purpose Discoverable in litigation Formatting sometimes lost in transmission
Memo	Usually considered informal and for internal use Creates a permanent paper trail Allows writer to control layout	Slower than e-mail Thought of as more informal than a letter Creates a permanent paper trail
Letter	More formal, primarily reserved for external use Creates a permanent paper trail Stands out from the crowd Allows writer to control layout	Slower than e-mail Creates a permanent paper trail
Discussion Outline	Informal Tends to encourage discussion	May be seen as too casual and even careless unless positioned effectively
Chart Pack or Deck	Can be informal or formal depending on the setting Easy to create effective data charts	Usually requires discussion in person or (at a minimum) text explanation to accompany it
Reports	Usually viewed as formal Allow fuller discussions and analysis of subjects Come in numerous shapes and sizes	Are seldom read in their entirety May require additional time and effort to compile and to format

group, having some plan will help you be more productive and streamline the document creation process considerably.

Creating Individual Documents

Exhibit 2.2 provides a phased approach you might follow if working alone, from the initial steps of establishing your purpose and strategy to the final step of producing a completed document. Approaches to creating documents differ from person to person. Some people work best from an outline, while others feel more comfortable using the idea mapping or brainstorming techniques discussed in Chapter 1. You should find the approach that works best for you, but realize that you will be more productive if you follow some sort of step-by-step plan. For example, one of the greatest barriers to idea generation is editing as you write. The brain cannot be creator and critic at the same time.

Ideally, you should go through each step in order, making sure that you leave all editing until the final phase. Your purpose and strategy affect content, organization, format, and style. They will, of course, govern how you approach the process and how you complete it. Your purpose will usually be clear by the time

EXHIBIT 2.2
Individual
Document
Creation
Process

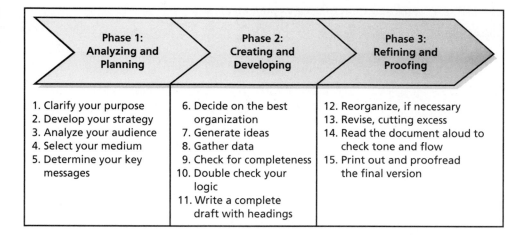

Phase 1: Analyzing and Planning	Phase 2: Creating and Developing	Phase 3: Refining and Proofing
1. Clarify your purpose 2. Develop your strategy 3. Analyze your audience 4. Select your medium 5. Determine your key messages	6. Decide on the best organization 7. Generate ideas 8. Gather data 9. Check for completeness 10. Double check your logic 11. Write a complete draft with headings	12. Reorganize, if necessary 13. Revise, cutting excess 14. Read the document aloud to check tone and flow 15. Print out and proofread the final version

you reach Phase 2, although sometimes you may find that you start writing the draft before you know exactly where you are heading. Sometimes you simply need to get words on the page or screen to help the ideas flow, and as they do, you gain greater clarity in your message. For example, when sending e-mails, you may sometimes write a few sentences that you end up deleting once you realize what it is that you really want to say. If you find you are hitting a writing block, you may want to go back to brainstorming or mind mapping to free up your ideas.

Creating Team Documents

Leaders must often manage the process of document creation within a team setting. Doing so requires more preplanning and a clearly defined approach. Without a plan, team document creation can involve extra work and result in a lower quality document. Teams often struggle with dividing up the labor and run into difficulties managing the versions of the documents.

Teams use one of two ways to divide the tasks: (1) one person on the team does all of the writing with the others providing the content to the scribe, or (2) the team divides the writing among the team members according to the sections for which they have provided most of the content.

The Single-Scribe Approach

The single-scribe approach ensures consistency in style and format. However, one person ends up with tremendous control over the document's content and style, as well as a heavy work burden at the end of the project. With this approach, the fate of the team's project essentially rests in the hands of one member's ability to communicate the team's ideas effectively. In addition, despite the amount of work involved, scribes may feel that other members of the team minimize their contribution to the team effort. Thus, to ensure that the single-scribe method works well, the members must share in the ownership of the document by reading and contributing to the drafts. They must also make sure the scribe's contribution is recognized, and that he or she is included in all team meetings.

When using the single-scribe approach, the team needs to build the compilation step into the work plan and be very specific about what each team member is expected to give to the scribe. Teams frequently multitask, with different team members working on different tasks; therefore, the team may want to assign one person to oversee the document production deadlines, ensuring that the schedule is on target.

Despite the best intentions and scheduling, often the final compilation of the document occurs at the last minute. If team members submit material that is at radically different stages of completion, then the scribe has a huge challenge that could end up harming the quality of the final product. For instance, if one team member brings an outline, another brings a list of bullets, another goes off task and writes on someone else's material, and then another does what is expected and writes out the entire section in detail, the scribe is forced to manage the uneven contribution and fill in the blanks without being in full command of the content. In addition, the compilation time expands fourfold. Agreeing specifically to what each team member will give to the scribe will help with efficiency and quality.

The Multiple-Writer Approach

The multiple-writer or collaborative approach divides the writing among team members. This has advantages and disadvantages as well. One of the major advantages can be efficiency. When various team members write individual sections of a document, the work will usually go much faster than the single-scribe approach. The team members know the content well and can ensure that it is complete and correct. Also, they avoid the delays caused when a team member has to rewrite his or her section because the scribe, who is often not close to the content, has misrepresented the meaning in some way. Collaborative writing makes the team labor more efficient and also makes it seem more equitable. In the end, the entire team feels greater ownership of the finished product.

However, the approach has some problems. One danger is that the team may be confused about the precise scope of individual assignments, resulting in duplication of effort or neglected tasks. The team may have trouble dividing the sections equitably, and the resulting sections may be uneven and inconsistent. Also, the style and tone will probably differ from section to section. If the differences are extreme, the document can easily come across as fragmented and even incoherent.

To ensure that the writing is performed completely and evenly, you can divide the document into its different sections and assign responsibilities for them using the pyramid or storyboard. A good pyramid shows the major topics with no overlap. A storyboard can serve a similar function for a team working on a presentation.

To avoid formatting issues or time-consuming mechanical changes in the compiling phase, the team must specify all details of format ahead of time. For example, the team should decide on margins, spacing, body and heading fonts, and the positioning of headings and subheadings. It is desirable for the team to outline the document, using the pyramid or a similar structural approach to guide them. If they use the pyramid, the major organizational topics at the first level of their pyramid become the major section headings, or in a longer document, the chapter titles. Using the pyramid from Chapter 1 as an example, the team's outline would be as follows:

Launching a New Bank Card in China

I. Market Potential
    A. Political Climate
    B. Competitive Analysis
II. Profitability
    A. Cost Analysis
    B. Potential Revenue
III. Implementation Plan
    A. Staffing Requirements
    B. Marketing Plan Actions

From the outline, the team could assign sections and also establish the formatting. If all members are comfortable with Word templates, the team could create one for the document, and then each writer would simply need to type in his or her content.

Finally, to ensure that the document is consistent and coherent, the team must take time at the beginning to agree on style and format, but also allow time at the end to have one person do the final editing after the entire team reviews the document. Although this person does the final editing, the entire team shares the responsibility for the quality of the end product; therefore, every member of the team should read the final document, with one person giving it the final proofing and quality check before it is delivered.

Controlling Versions

Whether working alone or with a group, you need a method for controlling the versions of your documents. Version control is essential when creating a team document, since multiple team members will touch the document at various times during the writing process.

To keep the versions straight, the team should decide together when drafts are due, who is to receive them, and in what order they are to circulate through the team. In addition, you should establish a tracking method for the versions. One approach is to insert the date and time in the footer and use it as the file name while the document is in drafting stages. You will want to adopt a similar approach for your documents when working alone. Once you have finished all editing, you should make sure to delete this footer from the final version. In addition to the time and date, team members should get in the habit of inserting their initials in the footer and also when saving the document. For example, a team might use the footer "9:00 a.m. 17 09 05 AS" and the file name "Brand Study 17 09 05 AS1."

Agreeing on a method for tracking your versions and establishing a writing and version control plan will save you time and help you ensure a higher quality document. Such procedures will also help teams avoid some of the conflict that can occur when individuals collaborate in the writing of a document.

ORGANIZING THE CONTENT COHERENTLY

The initial stages of creating a document may be rather messy, particularly the idea generation stage. When you are generating ideas, you are engaged analytically, which means you are breaking things apart and probably even free-associating as one idea leads to another. Once you have exhausted the sources of ideas, you move into the stage of organizing them to present them to others. A business audience expects order and logic in a document; they expect it to make sense to them, to be coherent.

To "cohere" means to hold together, which is what you want your documents to do. You want the pieces—paragraphs and sections— to conform to a systematic arrangement or plan that is logical and apparent to readers. In Chapter 1, you learned different approaches to organizing a document or a presentation and the dependence of organization on communication strategy and audience analysis. This section focuses specifically on creating coherence when writing typical business documents by organizing your content and including the content expected by your audience.

Organization and Content

Chapter 1 discussed how organization depends on purpose, audience, and strategy, and explained some of the options for organizing your communication. You need to anticipate your audience's response and stay focused on your purpose. You will want to select the organizing device that best matches your purpose and content, such as deductive, inductive, or chronological. In some cases, the type of document will dictate the organizational structure. For instance, if you are describing a process or procedure, you will usually use a chronological structure, taking your reader through each step in turn. In a proposal, however, you might use any number of logical structures—including deductive, problem solution, comparison and contrast, and cause and effect—to organize the document or sections in the document. These different structures will be applicable despite the similarity of informational content from one proposal to another.

The logic of the entire document, as well as that of each section, should be obvious to your readers. You want the logic to be so clear and the organization so tight that no one wonders, "Where did that come from?" Although they are useful references, too frequent use of the following expressions in a report may signal that the organization may need to be stronger: "As mentioned or discussed earlier," "Returning to point A again," or "In the previous section."

You usually will want to organize your document deductively, stating your main message, conclusion, or principle recommendation directly at the very beginning of the document and proceeding through secondary arguments and supporting information. You might select inductive organization if you have a hostile or resistant audience and decide it is best to take an indirect approach by explaining and presenting your evidence before stating your main message or recommendation.

Again, you will find traditional outlines, storyboards, decision trees, and the pyramid principle to be effective techniques for organizing your document. You should anticipate your readers' questions and attempt to organize the document so that you answer the questions as they would occur to the audience.

Opening with Power

In your opening, most of the time you should begin strongly by quickly stating your main message, but let your analysis of your audience guide you. You may want to begin indirectly for the following reasons:

- To establish the context for the communication if it is part of a chain of communication.
- To include a more gentle opening with some appropriate pleasantries if your audience's culture would expect it.
- To provide some information to soften the bad news you must deliver.
- To explain the reasoning or logic if you have complicated information to deliver.

Again, use your analysis of your audience to determine how best to begin, but try to state your main point as early as possible in your document so that the reader knows your reason for writing.

In the first paragraph of most business correspondence—letters, memos, and e-mails—you need to establish the context briefly before the purpose. For example, if you are responding to an e-mail or memo sent to you, you might begin as follows:

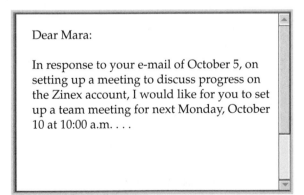

Starting by stating your purpose ("I would like for you to set up a team meeting for next Monday, October 10, at 10:00 a.m.") without the context ("In response to your e-mail of October 5, on setting up a meeting to discuss the progress on the Zinex account") would make the exact meeting topic you have in mind ambiguous for Mara. While the company may be small enough and the number of clients few enough to make ambiguity unlikely, it is always best to make the exact context clear in the openings to your correspondence.

If the correspondence is longer, you might want to prepare the reader for what is to come by listing the topics covered as well. Then, you address the topics in the order introduced, using headings to set off each major section. To expand on the previous example, for instance, you might begin as follows:

> Dear Mara:
>
> In response to your e-mail of October 5, on setting up a meeting to discuss progress on the Zinex account, I would like for you to set up a team meeting for next Monday, October 10 at 10:00 a.m. In the meeting I have three primary objectives, which I have discussed below: (1) progress, (2) issues, and (3) next steps.

You would then include a discussion of each of these topics, using the topics as your headings.

The next example demonstrates a very indirect opening to a letter. In fact, it is so indirect you cannot even be sure what the writer's purpose is in writing to Ms. Watson.

> Dear Ms. Watson:
>
> This past weekend I watched the Florida Golf Classic on television and was impressed by the show of support for the tournament. Obviously, the senior golf tour has progressed to a serious competitive level, and I applaud your efforts in having a part in the evolution. I am an avid fan of all sports, especially golf, and am happy to see greats such as Arnold Palmer and Jack Nicklaus continuing to play competitively. I know that your organization has only 10 people who work directly on the tournament, yet you have made the Classic the second largest on the tour, in terms of prize money. This status is quite an accomplishment, and I would certainly enjoy contributing to the effort to make the Classic the most recognized tournament on the senior tour.

This amiable, rambling opening paragraph leaves you wondering about the purpose and asking "so what?" By the end of the paragraph, you may have determined that the writer wants to apply for a position, but you cannot be sure. The writer could be asking about donating money or volunteering in some way.

In the second paragraph, this job applicant finally makes the purpose clear:

> Joanne Brownstone, who held an internship in public relations in your organization last year, spoke enthusiastically of her work with the tournament. She suggested that I contact you about an internship since my current studies in business administration and my involvement in the sports field would contribute to your efforts in planning future tournaments and events.

This paragraph would have made a much better opening to the letter. The applicant establishes a context for writing (the source of the information about the possible internship opportunity) and then states the purpose of the letter (to apply for an internship).

In leadership communication, it is particularly important to make sure you deliver your main message very early. You want to start your letters, memos, and e-mails fast and get to the point quickly, providing only enough background information to establish the context. Getting to the point quickly demonstrates greater respect for the busy reader on the receiving end. The reader must know within the first couple of sentences why he or she is receiving this document. You can check whether you are getting to the point directly by applying the "so what?" test. Broadcasters have used this test and it works well to remind you to think about the value of the information you are providing to the reader. You do not want your readers to say "so what?" to anything that you write.

Developing with Reason

You should aim for the same directness and brevity in the discussion or development section of your documents as you do in your introduction. Your logical structuring should be MECE, which is defined in a handy site called www. acronymfinder.com as Mutually Exclusive, Collectively Exhaustive. MECE means your supporting topics do not overlap, and you have provided adequate justification for each one. MECE also suggests a balance for your sections. If, for instance, you find that for one topic you need several pages and for another only a short paragraph, then you need to reassess your topics and consider grouping that short one with another or breaking the longer section down into several distinct topics. Once you know you have the right topics and can develop each topic adequately, you should feel comfortable that your discussion section will appear reasonable to your audience.

EXHIBIT 2.3
Example of a
Poorly
Organized
and Formatted
Policy
Statement

Training Division Policy #4503.11

This policy applies to all employees except Production Division employees below the rank of supervisor and clerical employees below the rank of Junior Administrative Assistant. In order to encourage personnel to develop greater professional competence in their respective fields and to prepare for professional advancement, personnel registering in credit courses at the college or graduate level in state-accredited institutions of higher education will be reimbursed for the direct costs of tuition, registration fees, and required course textbooks and other materials upon successful completion of such instruction. Certification that the college course will contribute to the employee's professional growth will be provided by the employee's direct supervisor and countersigned by the supervisor's direct superior unless the supervisor be at the rank of vice president or higher. Successful completion is defined as completion with the grade of C or higher (or equivalent). Costs of travel and costs of nonrequired materials such as paper and clerical help will not be reimbursed. Submission to the Training Division of receipts for all expenses, approval of the direct supervisor that the course fulfills the requirements of this policy, and documentation of successful completion are required before reimbursement through the Training Division budget. Supervisors are encouraged to allow released time for personnel to enroll in credit college courses for professional development when departmental or divisional schedules permit. Released time is encouraged only when scheduled meetings of credit college courses occur during regular working hours. If possible and necessary, personnel may be required to make up working time outside normal working hours. If the credit college course can be taken outside the individual's normal working hours, no released time should be given. To receive reimbursement, personnel should submit Training Division Form 4503B to the Training Division in accordance with the instructions on that form.

In solving many of the business problems that you tackle, you will collect more information than you can or should present to your audience. You need to be carefully selective in the information you include in your discussion. You want to include only what is necessary to support your message. You must avoid the inclination to include all of the analysis simply because you or your team has done it. Select only the data that are necessary to make your point, and place other relevant information in an appendix or attachment.

If you are unsure of the importance of certain information, you should probably leave it out or consign it to an appendix. Most of your audiences are more interested in your interpretation of the data than in seeing the data itself, so you should be particularly careful to be selective. Again, ask yourself, can anyone say "so what" to this?

Finally, once you know the content is logically organized and reasonable in its balance, you want to consider how to make it accessible to your audience. You can make the document easy to read by formatting and careful use of headings. You will want to use meaningful (message-driven) headings and avoid long paragraphs. You want your readers to be able to easily scan your document and locate what they want to read.

Most businesspeople read documents selectively, which means they go to the section that is of interest to them or that is relevant to their department or function. Studies have shown that very few businesspeople read a longer document from cover to cover. Researchers found that most decision makers read the executive summary, but only 60 percent read the introduction and conclusions, and only 15 percent read the discussion or main body.[1]

You should avoid lengthy paragraphs and long sections of discussion between headings. Find the places in a long paragraph where you can break it up into shorter paragraphs, and use headings and lists. Also, make sure to provide clear transitions from idea to idea within paragraphs and between them (see Appendix A, "Transition Words"). It is fine to have one-sentence paragraphs. In fact, it is better to have shorter paragraphs, particularly in e-mails, since the added white space makes them easier to scan.

The policy statement in Exhibit 2.3 illustrates a poorly organized, lengthy paragraph. Notice how difficult it is to follow the logic and how tedious it is to read this paragraph. In fact, you would probably avoid reading it if it came across your desk.

Before turning to a reorganized and reformatted version, look closely at this policy statement and think about how you would reorganize and reformat it. As with most policy statements or procedures, this statement could be restructured using the journalist's questions of who, what, when, where, and how.

Reorganizing and reformatting the policy statement makes it much easier to read (Exhibit 2.4). Readers can now scan the reorganized and reformatted policy quickly and find what they need to know. This example illustrates the importance of organizing your documents into a logical structure, as well as the value of headings in making that logic clear and aiding your audience in reading your prose quickly. Apply your analytical skills to organizing and developing your documents and their sections, and use your reasoning ability to select the most important content and establish the most effective structure.

Closing with Grace

Once you have taken your audience through your discussion, you should end as quickly and directly as you began. You should, however, provide a sense of polite, unrushed closure. Traditional academic writing requires closings that restate or summarize what has already been said. A letter, memo, or e-mail is too short to require such repetition of ideas. A conclusion in a letter, memo, or e-mail should call for action, mention contact information or follow-up arrangements, anticipate any problems, and offer a courtesy closing (see Exhibits 2.5 and 2.6).

EXHIBIT 2.4
Example of an Effectively Organized and Formatted Policy Statement

ABMC's Policy on Reimbursement of Educational Expenses
Training Division Policy 14503.11

The purpose of ABMC's Policy on Reimbursement of Educational Expenses is to encourage its employees to develop their professional skills and prepare for advancement through the completion of college-level courses. The following outlines who is eligible, what is covered, and how to file.

Who Is Eligible

All product division employees above the level of supervisor and clerical employees above the level of junior administrative assistant are eligible for the reimbursement.

What Is Covered

The following are the expenses covered under this policy:
• Direct costs of tuition
• Registration fees
• Required texts and other required materials

Travel costs and costs of general school supplies, such as paper and pens, are not reimbursable.

How to File

To file for reimbursement, take the following steps:

1. Obtain certification that the course will contribute to your professional growth from your direct supervisor, countersigned by his/her superior (if your supervisor is a Vice President, the counter signature is not necessary)
2. Register for the course at a state-accredited institution of higher learning
3. Complete the course successfully (a minimum grade of "C+" or equivalent)
4. Submit the following to Sam Gates, Training Division Office, Building C, Room 209:
   • Training Division Form 4503B
   • Proof of successful completion of course(s)
   • Certification from supervisor
   • Receipts for all expenses

Note that classes should be taken outside of working hours. If the class is offered only during working hours, release time may be allowed as divisional schedules permit; however, you may be required to make up missed time.

If you have any questions or need help, call Sam Gates (Ext. 9933).

EXHIBIT 2.5
Sample of
Preferred
Formatting for
a Business
Letter

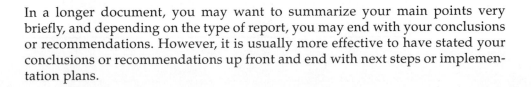

Global Communication Services
6108 Martin Lane
Houston, Texas 77000

August 4, 2005

Ms. Kerith Karetti, CEO
Hamill Brothers, Inc.
2708 W. 43rd Street
New York, New York 10036

Dear Ms. Karetti:

We have enclosed our final draft of the marketing analysis you requested.
We have enjoyed working with your team to identify the potential to
expand your product into Asia. In the report, we have provided not only the
analysis of the market but also some ideas on how you might move ahead.

Our analysis indicates a tremendous opportunity for your company, and we
suggest you move forward in developing a complete marketing plan as
soon as possible. We believe you and your team are positioned to move
quickly using this analysis as your launching point.

If we can be of any further help as you move into this project, please let me
know. We always enjoy working with your group and look forward to
continuing our relationship in the future.

Sincerely,

Janette Zuniga

Janette Zuniga
Senior Managing Director

Enclosure: Final Marketing Analysis to Determine Expansion Opportunities
in Asia

In a longer document, you may want to summarize your main points very
briefly, and depending on the type of report, you may end with your conclusions
or recommendations. However, it is usually more effective to have stated your
conclusions or recommendations up front and end with next steps or implementation plans.

EXHIBIT 2.6
**Sample of an
Effective
Business
Memo**

Date: August 11, 2004
To: All marketing team members
From: Alan Zhang, Scribe this week
Subject: Meeting notes with next steps from August 8 meeting

As our team decided, we want to keep notes of our meetings and send them to each other weekly. As the scribe this week, that task fell to me. Therefore, I am sending you a summary of the meeting organized into the two main topics that we discussed: (1) making team meetings more effective and (2) organizing our team tasks. Please review this memo and let me know before 8:00 a.m., Wednesday, August 13, if I need to add anything and resend these before our next meeting.

Making Team Meetings More Effective

We decided that we can definitely make our meetings more effective. Some of the methods we discussed were as follows:

- Schedule more face-to-face interactions, but keep a "get it done and make it productive" attitude
- Agree to meeting times and maintain communication lines regarding availability
- Designate a leader for every team meeting
- Distribute an agenda with 24 hours notice
- Follow up all team meetings with minutes that express decisions and agreed upon next steps

Organizing Tasks More Effectively

We also discussed ways to organize our tasks more effectively. We came up with two actions:

- Create a team action plan with tasks and responsibilities allotted to specific members
- Divide up tasks according to project phases

We ran out of time, so we will be continuing this discussion at our next meeting.

Establishing the Next Steps

Our next step is a phone conference Wednesday at 11:00 a.m., to discuss the progress on the marketing project and to finalize our approach to organizing our work more effectively.

I look forward to our next meeting and again, if I left anything out of this summary, please let me know by Wednesday morning so that I can send out a revised version before our conference call. You can reach me at x6785 or through e-mail at zhangA@swiftly.com.

CONFORMING TO CONTENT AND FORMATTING EXPECTATIONS IN CORRESPONDENCE

You will determine the actual content of your letters, memos, and e-mails based on your purpose, strategy, and audience, but these types of business communication do carry with them some expectations of what you should include. In addition, you want to use a format that follows standard business writing conventions, which are designed to make your documents accessible as well as attractive. Good formatting reveals and supports the organization, as you can see from the rewritten version of the policy statement in Exhibit 2.4. Format is important in helping your audience see the structure and logic of your document and in making it easy for them to skim or read.

This section illustrates the formatting of typical types of correspondence (e-mails, memos, and letters) and provides information about and examples of the standard content you will want to include. In particular, it provides guidelines for e-mail since it has become such a common medium for business communication and is often used ineffectively.

If your company does not have a style guide for the format of letters and memos, you should follow the conventions included in most business writing handbooks and in college dictionaries. The examples provided here follow these conventions.

Letters

Most businesspeople today prefer the block format for letters illustrated in the letter of transmittal (Exhibit 2.5) with a simple "Sincerely" to close the letter.

Memos

Memos should include all of the preliminary elements of date, to, from, and subject (avoid "re" unless it is used by your organization). Two warnings about memos: (1) make sure your subject line captures the "so what," the purpose for writing very specifically, and (2) repeat that purpose in the first sentence of the memo (see Exhibit 2.6).

E-Mails

E-mail has rapidly become the most frequently used medium for business communication today. It is also the most common use of the Internet. Sixty-eight percent of respondents to a recent Harris poll said that they often to very often send and receive e-mail, and daily e-mail usage is projected to hit 60 billion messages by 2006.[2] Although we still send and receive printed letters and memos, they are becoming rarer and are often transmitted as e-mail attachments rather than as hard copy.

E-mails follow a format similar to that of a memo, but they do have some special guidelines you should follow to ensure that they are effective. The subject line takes on tremendous importance since it will usually determine if your audience will open your e-mail. You should take special care in the subject line of e-mails to tell recipients why they should read your message. Look at the following and decide which you would open if they came from your peers.

Subject: For your information
Subject: Forward: Forward: Forward: Funny!!!!!!!!!
Subject: Reminder
Subject: Agenda for Tomorrow's Meeting
Subject: How are you?

The context of the e-mail will influence your inclination to open it. When your boss sends the e-mail, instead of a peer, you will probably open it no matter what the subject line says. Most of us do not have time for e-mails that require no action on our part, as is suggested by "for your information"; and few of us have the patience or interest to open forwarded messages since they are often mass-mailed and include jokes or lame examples of someone else's sense of humor.

You also need to be particularly careful with the tone and content of your e-mails. A harsh tone will be perceived even more harshly in an e-mail than in a hard-copy memo because people expect e-mails to be informal. You should be extra cautious about what you say in an e-mail because receivers can easily forward them to the world. Even if e-mails are not sent to unintended audiences, they still become a permanent, easily accessed record. The e-mail in Exhibit 2.7 provides a wonderful example of the damage a harsh message in electronic format can do. The CEO of a midwestern computer company actually sent it to his management group. The capitalization, the formatting, and all the content are exactly as written by the CEO. The only changes are in the company name, changed to MWCC to stand for Mid-Western Computer Company, and in the CEO's name.

McCutcheon sent this e-mail to his 400-member management team on March 13, and by March 21, it made its way across the Internet. Shortly afterward, it appeared in its entirety in *The New York Times*, and MWCC's stock dropped by 22 percent.

If you compare this e-mail to the first version of the copier memo discussed in Chapter 1, you see some similarities. Both were written when angry feelings clouded rational thinking. Fortunately, the writer of the copier memo realized before he sent it that he needed to reconsider his approach. The CEO of MWCC did not, and with the speed of the Internet, his message went global, and his company suffered because of it. This example serves as a warning for everyone using e-mail: think carefully about all of your possible audiences before hitting "send."

Given the importance of e-mail in the workplace, it is surprising people still take it so lightly. For example, a recent *Business Wire* article states, "E-mail, the electronic equivalent of DNA evidence, is playing an increasingly common role in workplace lawsuits and regulatory investigations. A primary source of evidence in high-profile discrimination, sexual harassment, and antitrust claims, e-mail is regularly used to bolster cases, embarrass organizations, and damage reputations. A new survey of 1,100 U.S. companies reveals that 14% of respondents have been ordered by a court or regulatory body to produce employee e-mail, up from 9% just two years ago."[3] The evidence of the detrimental effects that follow when

EXHIBIT 2.7
The Mid-Western CEO's E-Mail to His Managers

From: McCutcheon, Bill (name changed)
Sent: Tuesday. March 13, 2001 11:48 a.m.
To: DL ALL MANAGERS;
Subject MANAGEMENT DIRECTIVE: Week #10_01: Fix it or changes will be made
Importance: High

To the HQ_based managers:

I have gone over the top. I have been making this point for over one year.

We are getting less than 40 hours of work from a large number of our HQ_based EMPLOYEES. The parking lot is sparsely used at 8 a.m.; likewise at 5 p.m. As managers—you either do not know what your EMPLOYEES are doing; or YOU do not CARE. You have created expectations on the work effort which allowed this to happen inside MWCC, creating a very unhealthy environment. In either case, you have a problem and you will fix it or I will replace you.

NEVER in my career have I allowed a team which worked for me to think they had a 40 hour job. I have allowed YOU to create a culture which is permitting this. NO LONGER.

At the end of next week, I am plan to implement the following:
1. Closing of Associate Center to EMPLOYEES from 7:30 a.m. to 6:30 p.m.
2. Implementing a hiring freeze for all HQ based positions. It will require Cabinet approval to hire someone into a HQ based team. I chair our Cabinet.
3. Implementing a time clock system, requiring EMPLOYEES to 'punch in' and 'punch out' to work. Any unapproved absences will be charged to the EMPLOYEES vacation.
4. We passed a Stock Purchase Program, allowing for the EMPLOYEE to purchase MWCC stock at a 15% discount, at Friday's BOD meeting. Hell will freeze over before this CEO implements ANOTHER EMPLOYEE benefit in this *Culture*.
5. Implement a 5% reduction of staff in HQ.
6. I am tabling the promotions until I am convinced that the ones being promoted are the solution, not the problem. If you are the problem, pack your bags.

I think this parental type action SUCKS. However, what you are doing, as managers, with this company makes me SICK. It makes sick to have to write this directive.

(continued)

an internal e-mail finds its way to the Internet, let alone the growing use of it in litigation, should encourage people to approach it more cautiously as a medium for communication.

Many observers agree that e-mail has led to poorer business communication.[4] In addition to carelessness in content, hurried e-mail writers are also careless about how they compose their e-mails. Perhaps because it is so easy to use or is perceived

EXHIBIT 2.7
(continued)

[MWCC e-mail continues]

I know I am painting with a broad brush and the majority of the HQ based associates are hard working, committed to MWCC success and committed to transforming health care. I know the parking lot is not a great measurement for 'effort', I know that 'results' is what counts, not 'effort'. But I am through with the debate.

We have a big vision. It will require a big effort. Too many in HQ are not making the effort.

I want to hear from you. If you think I am wrong with any of this, please state your case. If you have some ideas on how to fix this problem, let me hear those. I am very curious how you think we got here. If you know team members who are the problem, let me know. Please include (copy) Sarah in all of your replies.

I STRONGLY suggest that you call some 7 a.m., 6 p.m. and Saturday a.m. team meetings with the EMPLOYEES who work directly for you. Discuss this serious issue with your team. I suggest that you call your first meeting tonight. Something is going to change.

I am giving you two weeks to fix this. My measurement will be the parking lot: it should be substantially full at 7:30 a.m. and 6:30 p.m. The pizza man should show up at 7:30 p.m. to feed the starving teams working late. The lot should be half full on Saturday mornings. We have a lot of work to do. If you do not have enough to keep your teams busy, let me know immediately.

Folks this is a management problem, not an EMPLOYEE problem.

Congratulations., you are management. You have the responsibility for our EMPLOYEES. I will hold you accountable. You have allowed this to get to this state. You have two weeks. Tick, tock.

Bill. . . . .
Chairman & Chief Executive Officer

as informal, e-mail encourages carelessness. E-mails often contain typos, spelling mistakes, usage errors, inappropriate capitalization (particularly the annoying use of all caps and all lowercase), and overall poor formatting—all mistakes people are not as likely to make in a printed memo or letter.

E-mail can be an extremely effective medium, but an e-mail deserves as much care as a letter, perhaps even more since it can much more easily be sent to the world. At a minimum, you should aim to avoid the following e-mail blunders, identified as the ten most common mistakes of business e-mail correspondence:

Ten Most Common Mistakes of Business E-Mail Correspondence[5]

1. Unclear subject line.
2. Poor greeting (or none at all).
3. Unfamiliar abbreviations.
4. Unnecessary copies (CCs).
5. Sloppy grammar, spelling, and punctuation.
6. All caps in the message.
7. No closing or sign-off.
8. Rambling, unformatted message.
9. Unfriendly tone.
10. No clear request for action.

Source: Leland/Customer Service for Dummies; copyright © 2000. This material is used with permission of Wiley Publishing Inc., a subsidiary of John Wiley & Sons, Inc.

The bottom line on e-mails is to treat them with care. Take the time to write them well, paying attention to organization and format as well as style and tone. Tone is especially important since it is very easy for your audience to misinterpret your intention in an e-mail. Read your e-mail aloud, and even read it to someone else, if the subject is sensitive and you want to ensure that you will not offend the audience or come across as negative, harsh, or insensitive. In fact, if the content is sensitive, you might want to reconsider e-mail as your medium.

Take the time to proofread each e-mail, printing out important ones, since it is very difficult to see mistakes on a computer screen. Finally, do not be misled into thinking that your audience will overlook carelessness just because they view e-mail as informal. Although most readers are a little more forgiving with e-mail, many are not. Carelessness of any sort can hurt a career; an insensitive or careless e-mail could result in your ending up in *The Wall Street Journal*.

INCLUDING EXPECTED CONTENT IN REPORTS

Business audiences also have expectations for longer documents and reports. The type of report, the company style, as well as the industry standards will often dictate content and organization. As a leader in an organization, you may write reports that inform, instruct, or persuade. Often, you may team up with or supervise others in writing these reports. They may be long or short, formal or informal. They may even tell a story; for instance, you might first provide an overview of the current situation, then discuss the details that have complicated the situation, and finally suggest a resolution or recommendation to improve the situation. Although many reports serve multiple purposes, such as informing and persuading, Exhibit 2.8 lists typical types of leadership communication reports organized by their primary purpose.

One type of document that you may also be creating that is not listed in Exhibit 2.8 is a case report. You will find case analysis and report contents discussed in Appendix B.

EXHIBIT 2.8   Purposes and Types of Leadership Communication Reports

Purpose	Report Type	Focus of Content
Inform	Progress	→ Outlines the status of the tasks in a project, including work completed, work remaining, and anticipated delays (see typical contents below) → Sometime includes analysis for discussion or preliminary conclusions for testing with audiences
	Financial	→ Includes financial performance for reporting purposes, such as to the SEC for public companies (for example, 10-Ks and 10-Qs)
	Sales/ marketing	→ Provides the sales achievements and figures for a standard period of time (a week, month, or quarter) → Often includes sales prospects and projections and could focus on market trends, positioning, and product development
	Operational	→ Varies across industries and companies, but may include overall operational/project performance or compliance to regulations, such as health, safety, and environmental
	Meetings (minutes)	→ Provides a summary of the major topics discussed → Usually includes date, attendees, old business, new business, and action items
	Research/ investigative	→ Reports on the results of research and often provides recommendations on actions → Includes investigative research, analysts reports, benchmarking
Instruct	Procedure	→ Explains the steps to be completed to accomplish some goal → Usually presents the actions in chronological order
	Policy	→ Summarizes the organizational regulations or guidelines that govern employee behavior
	Performance appraisals	→ Documents the quality of an employee's work with the intention of creating needed legal records and providing feedback to improve performance
	Request for Proposal (RFP)	→ Provides guidelines on the information to include in a proposal
Persuade	Annual	→ Reports on the financial performance of an organization with the intent of influencing external and internal constituencies, primarily investors and analysts → Frequently includes a company's mission, vision, accomplishments, and plans
	Feasibility	→ Argues that an approach or idea will work; recommends action → Usually focuses on economic, technical, and cultural aspects
	Proposals	→ Seeks acceptance for a product, service, or potential solution by defining the needs and benefits (see typical contents below) → Often responds to an RFP and is seen as a sales document that is legally binding
	Business plans	→ Discusses all of the important components of a business or business idea, including value proposition, feasibility, and profitability → Follows standard content expectations, such as those provided by the Small Business Administration

A Formal Full-Length Report

When the different types of reports in Exhibit 2.8 are formal, they include the contents outlined and discussed below. Most full-length formal reports conform to the content and sequencing pattern in Exhibit 2.9.

A formal full-length report should have a table of contents. The table of contents reveals the organization of your report. It allows your readers to see the overall content and select the sections relevant to their needs and interests. The two examples here illustrate a poorly created table of contents and then a more effective one (Exhibit 2.10). The first example does not suggest any form of organization or grouping of ideas; it appears to be a random list of topics. The second example, although containing too little information, at least suggests some logic in organization.

EXHIBIT 2.9
Formal Report Content

Content	Purpose
1. A Letter or Memo of Transmittal or Preface	Sets the stage for the report and is usually addressed to the decision maker. It should identify the purpose of the attached report, may provide highlights of the content, and always ends with a statement of what the writer expects the receiver to do next in response to the report. It will also contain contact information for the sender. Exhibit 2.5 is an example of a letter of transmittal.
2. Cover	Contains a title that captures the "so what" of the report. Usually, contains the sender's name and the receiver's, as well as the date.
3. Title Page	Contains the same information as the cover, but may also contain a short abstract or descriptive summary of the report contents.
4. Table of Contents	Lists all important sections of the report (see examples below). It will usually list the main headings and second-level subheadings from the discussion section.
5. Executive Summary	Summarizes the main idea(s) from the body of the document, including conclusions and recommendations. Generally, approximately 10 percent of the discussion section length; however, it must be long enough to capture the central content of the report, so it may need to be longer than 10 percent. See discussion below.
6. Introduction	Provides context for the report, including any information the reader needs to understand the background and impetus for the report.
7. Discussion	Differs from report to report (see discussion of proposals and progress reviews below). It contains the developed content or argument organized logically.
8. Next Steps, If Appropriate	Outlines actions you expect the reader to take in response to the report as well as any follow-up actions you may be taking as well.
9. Appendix	Contains any data or other support for your report that is too lengthy or detailed for the discussion section. It may also contain qualifications, any graphs or diagrams not needed in the body of the document, and examples of survey instruments. Note: Any item included in an appendix must be mentioned by number in the report and then included in the order referenced.

EXHIBIT 2.10
Examples of
Table of
Contents

Example of a Poorly Organized and Poorly Formatted Table of Contents

Contents

Example of a More Effectively Organized Table of Contents

Table of Contents

If your report contains numerous graphs or data charts, you may need a list of figures with their page numbers following the table of contents (see Chapter 5 for guidelines on creating and using graphs).

Including Exhibits in Reports

Many types of business documents include exhibits, from memos to letters to reports. An exhibit (table, graph, diagram, and the like) should never be inserted into your documents without some discussion of its contents and relevance or without being assigned a number and given a title, whether it is inserted directly into the text or placed in an appendix.

Exhibit Placement

It is best to insert the exhibit as close as possible to the text that discusses it, which means that most of the time you should embed it in your document so that it follows closely after any discussion of it rather than in an appendix. At times, however, the exhibit may supplement your message but not be immediately necessary to the understanding of it, in which case you may place it in an appendix at the end of the document.

Exhibit Labels

You will need to assign a number and provide a title for each exhibit inserted in your document or attached in the appendix. Exhibits are always numbered consecutively. You must reference the exhibit by its number in your text discussion just prior to its appearance. If you decide to place exhibits in an appendix, they will need numbers and titles as well, and they should be in the order of their reference in the body of your document.

Handling Research Information in Reports

Business documents usually include information that you have obtained from primary research (that you conduct directly through surveys, interviews, or direct observation) or secondary research (which is research using published materials in books and on the Web). You need to ensure you handle both carefully, fully documenting your methods for primary research and your sources for secondary research, and placing correct citations within your documents.

If you have used information that you gained by reading what others have said or written, you must include notes and a bibliography, which would come just before the appendix. The notes can be parenthetical, placed at the bottom of the page or slide, or listed at the end of your document just before your bibliography. You should follow some standard guide for documenting sources, such as *The Chicago Manual of Style*, the *Publication Manual of the American Psychological Association* (APA Style Guide), or the *MLA Style Manual*.

Since Web research is still relatively new, you may not be sure what to document or how to reference it. Basically, anything that you read on the Web and use in your report must be documented. You need to include the complete URL so that the reader can go to the exact source. Using the home page address alone is not sufficient anytime the site provides links to other pages within the Web site.

For example, the following would be an incorrect Web reference of a direct quotation:

> Since 1980, Bain's clients have outperformed the S&P 500 index by a 3 to 1 margin. This success is not serendipitous, but a natural result of the approach that Bain takes to consulting, which always considers maximization of shareholder value (http://www.bain.com).

The correct method for handling this same reference would be as follows:

> "Since 1980, Bain's clients have outperformed the S&P 500 index by a 3 to 1 margin. This success is not serendipitous, but a natural result of the approach that Bain takes to consulting, which always considers maximization of shareholder value" (http://205.134.84.25/bainweb/about/expertise/expertise_capability.asp? capability_id+56).

Since the reference is rather cumbersome, you could use an abbreviated version in the body of your document and then place this complete reference in your bibliography.

As a reminder of what needs to be credited within the body of your documents, the rules are as follows: *All words or ideas of others and all copyrighted, published, or Web information* that you use in your documents if taken word for word and placed in quotation marks, or if paraphrased (written in your own words), must have the complete references placed immediately after the idea, the quotation, or the paraphrased statement.

Proposals and Progress Reports

Since proposals and progress reports are two of the most common leadership communication reports with expected content that is specific to each, the following sections outline the typical contents with discussion of each major section.

A Proposal

A proposal may be written as a formal report with a letter of transmittal, executive summary, and so forth, or it may be presented as a formal letter. Whichever format is appropriate for your communication situation, you will want to include the sections discussed in Exhibit 2.11.

A Progress Report

Progress reports are common in business. They may be presented formally as reports or more informally as memos or e-mails. They allow you to highlight progress on a project or task and also, if appropriate, to showcase your work. They will usually include the following sections:

1. Introduction.
2. Project description.
3. Work completed.
4. Work in progress.
5. Work remaining.
6. Overall appraisal of progress.

You may find that a table works best if the project consists of fairly simple tasks. It could be set up to include the following columns:

Task	Work Completed	Work in Progress	Work Remaining	Comments

EXHIBIT 2.11
Proposal Contents

Section	Contents
1. Introduction	Sets the stage with a statement of the problem and background or establishes the context for the proposal by discussing appropriate company and industry background (more detailed background or industry research may belong in other parts of the document or in an appendix). The introduction should also include a general overview of the purpose of the proposal.
2. Needs and benefits	Provides a detailed discussion of the organization's current problem or issue and your assessment of its needs and then discusses how the proposed solution will meet the needs and be of value to the receiver.
3. Scope	Specifies the boundaries of your proposed work by answering the following questions: (1) What areas are included in the study and which are not? (2) What is the main focus of your work? (3) What specifically are you proposing to deliver?
4. Method and working relationship	Establishes your research methods or analytical approach with your plan for working with clients if appropriate. For example, do you plan to use a team and include members of the department or company on that team? The round-table document included in Chapter 4 includes an example of a team structure approach (Exhibit 4.3).
5. Task and time breakdown	Shows proposal phases and timing, specific tasks, deadlines, and responsibilities. Often a very detailed Gantt chart, Critical Path Method (CPM), or similar work plan is included in the appendix. Often includes a discussion of contingencies (other approaches or what you will do to keep on track if some "what ifs" occur).
6. Costs	States the fees or costs for completing the work. Often proposals will provide different approaches and price them on a scale from the highest to lowest cost.
7. Qualifications	Summarize your key background and experiences, profiling capabilities. A more detailed description of qualifications, such as descriptions of similar projects or evidence of special certifications, may be included in the appendix if necessary.
8. Acceptance clause	Requests a signature from the receiver to indicate acceptance of the proposal and agreement to pay if appropriate. An acceptance clause may appear at the end of a formal proposal or in the letter of transmittal.

Executive Summaries

Since the executive summary is so critical to a business report, and since it is the section of the report that your readers will most likely read, you should know how to write one that captures the appropriate content of your report. An executive summary must accurately, yet concisely, summarize the major messages of the original document so that your reader understands the substance of your report without reading further. You should see the executive summary as an independent document even though it includes only information discussed in the report. This independence means that although it may contain a graph or other figure in support of the content, it should not reference graphs or figures in the body of the document.

As mentioned in Exhibit 2.9, an executive summary is typically no more than 10 percent of the length of the report. Although it may need to be longer to cover the content of the report adequately, you still will only have a small amount of space to capture the content. It should include your major conclusions and recommendations and enough support to persuade your audience to accept both. The tone should be direct and the style concise without being too abbreviated. See Exhibit 2.12 for an example of an executive summary.

FORMATTING BUSINESS DOCUMENTS EFFECTIVELY

Formatting is important in creating a professional appearance for all of your documents, correspondence, and reports. It makes them accessible to your audiences and easier for them to read. You should organize and format all of your documents so that readers can easily skim them, find your key messages, and select what they want to read. You also should use headings and lists frequently to break up the text, separate main ideas, and avoid long blocks of text without frequent line breaks and meaningful headings.

If you do not have a style guide to follow in your organization, then your documents should conform to the following business writing standards:

Layout

A letter or memo should follow standard conventions illustrated in the sample letter and memo in Exhibits 2.5 and 2.6. Allow adequate margins, which usually means at least one inch on all sides. If you have letterhead, you will want to align the margins with it. Never crowd the page, but avoid placing only a sentence or two and a closing on the second page in a letter. Instead, go back and cut some words. Also, avoid "widow" words, a single word at the end of a paragraph appearing on a line by itself. A report format should be appropriate for the method of delivery to your audience. For instance, if it is to be bound, you will need to leave a larger left-hand margin. With all business correspondence and reports, allow plenty of white space for easy reading and for a more attractive appearance.

Spacing and Alignment

Business documents should be single-spaced with a double-space (the equivalent of a one-line gap) between the paragraphs. You should not indent the first line of a

EXHIBIT 2.12 Example of an Effective Executive Summary

Executive Summary:
Determining the Relationship between CEO Compensation and Company Performance

In response to a request by Chris Moellar, President of Executive Recruiters (ER), Performance Consultants, Inc. (PCI) was hired to determine what measures Fortune 500 companies use to establish the compensation of their chief executives. In particular, Ms. Moellar wanted to know if the CEO's compensation correlates directly to the financial performance of the CEO's company.

Analytical Methods

To determine what drives the compensation of top executives, the PCI team selected CEOs from a representative sample of Fortune 500 companies. For these CEOs, we performed statistical analysis to determine whether CEO compensation is positively correlated to performance. The average compensation of the 100 CEOs in our study was $3.1 million, ranging from a low of $0.5 million to a high of $10 million. In assessing company performance, we used five-year Return on Investment (ROI) as our primary measure, the companies in our 100-company survey group reported a five-year average ROI ranging from ($.5) Billion to $5 Billion.

Performance Impacts Compensation

We found a definite relationship between the five-year ROI of a company and the total compensation that the CEO receives. Based on our analysis, the CEO compensation increases with every 10 percent increase in a company's ROI level (Exhibit 1). In addition, besides performance, we found only one other factor that significantly influences CEO compensation: Age. The older the CEO, the more salary he or she received.

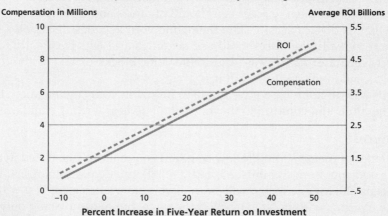

Exhibit 1 CEO Compensation Correlates Directly to Average Five-Year ROI

Recommendation

Based on PCI's findings, CEO compensation is directly related to company performance, but other factors, such as CEO age, also have an impact on compensation. Given our results, ER should continue to monitor company performance and use the 10 percent increments as the basis for your recommendations to your clients on compensation levels and on adjustments.

paragraph. Text should be fully aligned on the left but not on the right. Full alignment (or justification) causes gaps when the document is printed, making your text more difficult to read; therefore, you do not want to use it for letters, memos, e-mails, or reports. Many of the Microsoft Word templates for business correspondence include full justification, so you will need to override this format as the default. The only time you should use full justification is in a brochure or other similar promotional material, which will be professionally typeset and printed.

The table here illustrates how you should not align text and how you should:

How Text Should Not Be Aligned: Fully Justified Right Edge	How Text Should Be Aligned: Ragged Right Edge
Text should be fully aligned on the left but not on the right. Full justification causes gaps when printed, making your text more difficult to read. Therefore, you should not use it for letters, memos, e-mails, or reports.	Text should be fully aligned on the left but not on the right. Full justification causes gaps when printed, making your text more difficult to read. Therefore, you should not use it for letters, memos, e-mails, or reports.

Regarding the spacing at the end of a sentence and the beginning of another, you can allow one or two spaces after the end mark, although skipping two spaces in correspondence and in most documents makes them easier to read. Microsoft Word lets you set as your default whichever spacing you prefer, which makes it easy to be consistent and to follow your preferences or the standards of your organization for all documents.

Font Type and Size

For legibility in text documents, you should use one of the traditional serif (the tails on letters) fonts illustrated here:

Times New Roman

Palatino

Garamond

Bookman Old Style

Century Schoolbook

Times New Roman has become the preferred font and is used most frequently in business documents, but any of the ones here will work in most cases.

The serifs help the eye move across the page, thus making pages of text easier to read; however, for charts in oral presentations and for brochures or other documents where the span of text is short, a sans serif font (such as Arial or Helvetica) is usually best. For online documents (e-mail in particular), most people seem to prefer sans serif fonts although experts are still debating which is better to use. Since screen resolution is poorer than hard-copy printouts of documents, the sans serif fonts are usually sharper and thus probably the better choice. On Web sites, you will often see mixtures of fonts with lengthy text inserts in a serif font and the titles and links in sans serif fonts.

The bottom line on fonts is to be consistent and, in general, use serif fonts for text documents and sans serif for presentations and online correspondence.

A font size of 11 to 12 points is best for correspondence and reports. A smaller size is difficult to read and causes legibility problems when faxed since faxes decrease the size of the type.

Using Headings

Headings are essential in all but the shortest of formal documents, and you should make frequent and logical use of them. You should also conform to the standard expectations that govern the handling of headings, all of which reinforce the major rules of logic, consistency, and accessibility. Your goal with headings is to make it easier for the audience to access the information in the document; therefore, you need to make all headings meaningful by capturing the "so what," the specific message of the text that follows. Headings should add to your document and not distract from it in any way.

Traditional heading hierarchy follows the formatting illustrated here:

Chapter or Other Major Heading
(bold, centered, may be a larger font)

First Subheading (flush left on a line by itself)

Text that follows the first subheading starts with a capital letter and appears one line below the heading.

Second Subheading (flush left with period after it). Text that follows the second subheading starts with a capital letter and appears on the same line.

   Third Subheading (indented five spaces with a period after it or flush left if numbered as demonstrated below). Text that follows the third subheading starts with a capital letter and appears immediately after it. If you choose to number this heading, it would appear as follows:

1. **Third Subheading.** The text would start two spaces after the period.

Note that all major words in headings usually begin with an initial capital letter in business documents although some disciplines and some companies choose to capitalize only the first letter of the first word. If you do not have a style guide in your company that specifies this detail, you should probably capitalize each major word; however, either way is acceptable as long as you are consistent throughout the document. Also, note that your headings should be grammatically parallel, the same part of speech: all nouns or all the same verb form, for example, all infinitives (to + the verb constructions) or all participles (-ing forms of the verb) or all command form verbs (keep, make, use, etc.).

In business documents, you will rarely see all capital letters or large cap/small cap used in headings today since it makes the text more difficult to read and takes up more space on the page. In addition, underlining is used very sparingly today; instead, most people use **bold** when they want to draw attention to a word or statement. Underlining cuts off the lower portion of letters, reducing the graphic appeal of the document. All caps and underlining are both remnants from the days of typewriters when people had fewer options to distinguish their text and headings, so in addition to making your text more difficult to read, they make it look dated.

If you look at the examples below, you will see the problems created by using all caps and underlining:

ALL CAPS SHOULD BE AVOIDED IN HEADINGS AND TEXT

AND SO SHOULD LARGE CAPS/SMALL CAPS

Stay Away from Underlining Completely since

Using It Cuts Off the Bottom of Letters

Although computers make it easy to format your text—allowing you to vary font size, style, and color—it is usually better to maintain the same style of font throughout a business document. For example, you usually would not mix Arial font, or a similar sans serif font, with Times Roman, or a similar serif font, in correspondence or reports, although you might mix them in a brochure or Web site.

Instead of mixing font styles, you should use bold and increase the size of the font as illustrated here:

Avoid Mixing Font Styles	Use Bold or Larger Font Instead
Advantages (Arial)	Advantages (Times Roman 14)
Cost Advantages (Times Roman)	Cost Advantages (Times Roman 12)

Finally, the heading does not take the place of the text, just as a subject line does not take the place of your opening statement of purpose in an e-mail or memo. You should start your discussion as if the heading were not there.

How Not to Use Headings	How to Use Headings
<u>Nontransplant program:</u> This program will use only dialysis treatment. <u>Maximum transplant program:</u> This option is the most cost-efficient and practical in my opinion.	**Nontransplant program.** The nontransplant program will use only dialysis treatment. **Maximum transplant program.** The maximum transplant program is the most cost-efficient and practical.

To summarize, when you use headings, you should follow the principles listed here.

Principles for Creating and Formatting Headings

1. Keep headings short, meaningful, and consistent in style.
2. Make sure that all headings are parallel—the same part of speech.
3. Use the same font used in the rest of the section, but make it bold, larger, or centered.
4. Be consistent in handling capitalization (either initial cap each major word or only the first word and avoid capitalizing every letter).
5. Avoid underlining headings.

Remember, you should format your report for accessibility and appearance. Use headings to label the sections so that your readers can find them with ease and your document looks good. Your company may have a style sheet or templates that dictate your format. If not, you should follow the guidelines discussed here and make sure your headings are logical, consistent, and accomplish the overall purpose of making the document accessible to the reader.

Formatting Lists

Lists are formatted using bullets or numbers. One rule of thumb on the use of bullets is that if you have more than five items in your list, you should use numbers instead since it makes it easier for the reader to keep track. How you punctuate the items depends on the logic of what you have written or on aesthetics; there are no hard-and-fast rules. You would usually aim for some form of consistency, but even that is not always necessary in a longer document. Some lists treat items as separate units, while others treat items as grammatical units.

Two Examples of Separate Item Lists

A proposal contains the following sections:
1. Introduction
2. Needs and Benefits
3. Costs

Or

A proposal contains the following sections:
- Introduction
- Needs and Benefits
- Costs

A Sample List with Items Treated as Grammatical Units

A proposal contains
1. An introduction,
2. A section on needs and benefits, and
3. A section on costs.

Note that there is no colon after the word "contains," before the list. You should avoid using a colon between the introduction to your list and the list unless the introduction is a complete sentence and includes the object of the verb as in the following two examples.

As with headings, you should keep the items grammatically parallel, introducing each item with the same part of speech.

Incorrect Handling of Listed Items	Correct Handling of Listed Items
When writing a formal report, you perform the following: 1. Draft the report. 2. Establishing the format. 3. Design of the graphics. 4. Publication of the report.	When writing a formal report, you perform the following: 1. Draft the report. 2. Establish the format. 3. Design the graphics. 4. Publish the report.

If you use bullets instead of numbers, as we frequently do in leadership communication, the same guidelines apply. The previous list might appear as follows:

When writing a formal report, you perform the following:

- Draft the report.
- Establish the format.
- Design the graphics.
- Publish the report.

Placing periods at the end of each item is a matter of taste and appearance; just be consistent. If you use periods at the end of one item, use them in all others.

Documents are integral to leadership communication. You will spend a good amount of your day writing and reading e-mails, memos, letters, and various types of reports. This chapter has provided guidelines to help you become more proficient and more effective in creating documents of every sort.

Exercise 2.1: E-Mail Subject Line Exercise

Read the four scenarios below and write a brief and complete e-mail subject line for each.

1. You are working on the budget for next year and members of your department met last week to discuss all the changes. You need each member to provide you with their budget figures so that you can roll up the various subaccounts. The budget is due tomorrow, and you really need their input by 4:00 p.m. so that you will have time to complete your part of the work.

2. To streamline processing of expense reports, your accounting office has adopted new software that will enable employees to scan receipts. The new software also streamlines the categorization of expenses and totals each category automatically. Employees should have their reimbursements more quickly and you will save hours in staff time. The new software is a bit tricky, though, and you need employees to come to one of three training sessions so that they will know how to use it. All sessions will be held over lunchtime, with the first on Tuesday, one on Thursday, and one next Monday.

3. Your company recently adopted and rolled out a new benefits plan. After the rollout, you received word that there is one new addition that was not included in your materials: a child care advisory service that helps employees locate quality, affordable child care for their family. You want to let the employees know about this new feature.

4. You are the head of the Information Technology Division and your company will be implementing a new enterprise resource planning system companywide over the coming weekend. Bringing the system online will entail a significant effort by your team together with the consultants, and you will need to shut down the system at 5:00 p.m. Friday to get started. Since many people in your company work until 6:00 or 6:30, even on Fridays, and sometimes come in on the weekend, you need to inform everyone of the necessity to shut down the system at 5:00 on Friday. You believe this will enable your team to finish by mid-day on Saturday, with time to test and troubleshoot the system before Monday.

Source: Developed by Beth O'Sullivan, Rice University, March 2004. Used with permission.

Exercise 2.2: Writing Memos

The Case—Refinery Managers Face Budget Challenges

You work for a major international petroleum company, and you find yourself in a difficult position. As the budget coordinator for a large business unit made up of several key refineries, you have noticed that costs are rising so quickly that the refinery sites may soon become uncompetitive.

To begin getting costs under control, your team analyzes the budget and finds that a major component of refinery costs consists of an "overhead" allocation of costs from site services managers, as opposed to direct refinery costs. The site services managers provide an array of critical services to each refinery, such as central maintenance, storehouse services, security, HSE (health, safety, and environmental) services, human resources, and training/development services. The costs of these services across the full business unit's refineries are combined in a centralized cost center; that cost is subsequently allocated among the various refineries that use these services.

Your team knows that you must find a way to cut these allocated costs, so you decide to hold a meeting to talk with the site services managers about the budget and how it can be reduced so each refinery can maintain a competitive advantage as a site. Of course it is also important that refinery operations are safe and secure, so all of the services provided play an important role in the successful operation of the refineries. However, you need to find out from the site services managers what items can be cut or reduced while minimizing the impact on people and assets at the business unit level; and if certain items in the site services budget are true necessities, you need to have more information about what makes them critical to the business.

You have no direct control over the site services managers, although a component of their annual bonus comes from how well the various refineries perform, so you should think carefully about how you will ask them for information.

The Assignment

Draft a memo to the site services managers scheduling a meeting to discuss the budget. Since you have no direct supervisory control, it will do little good to demand cuts; in fact, a demand to cut budget might result in the loss of a service that matters most to you! Therefore, consider your strategy and your persuasive approach carefully as you prepare the e-mail. You may also consider whether to use a direct or indirect approach to the memo. Remember to craft a clear and complete subject line for the memo, provide all the information they need to attend the meeting, and close with the next steps or how to contact you for further information.

Source: Developed by Beth O'Sullivan, Rice University, March 2004. Used with permission.

Exercise 2.3: Creating an Executive Summary

The Case—Merging Benefits at Huge Computer Company

Two major high-tech companies, Huge Co. (HC) and Computer Co. (CC), have recently merged to form Huge Computer Company (HCC) and are now starting to combine the operations of both. A key issue of the integration has been how to treat the benefit and retirement plans from the two companies and, in particular, how to blend the plans for the software engineers, who are key to the continued success of the new company. Read the case below and write an executive summary of your key findings for the partner of the Human Resources Consulting firm.

Two Companies—Two Cultures

HC has been an industry leader for the past 20 years in both hardware and software. HC is a large company, with an employee base of about 22,000 in four different countries. Its corporate culture is relatively formal: HC does things "by the book." About 3500 software engineers work for HC, and all operate out of the Silicon Valley offices. The average tenure among the software engineers is ten years. HC redesigned the software engineers' benefits package two years ago, based on their research in industry best practices. HC spends about $20,000 per employee on annual benefits but has done no surveys to determine employee satisfaction with the new benefit plan.

CC is a young software company headquartered in Austin, Texas. CC is known for its leading-edge developments and has risen to the top over the last seven years. In fact, *CORP. Magazine* recently recognized CC as one of the "Top 100 Companies to Work For in the U.S." Its corporate culture still has a casual collegiate feel and its business practices are highly flexible, stressing the need for creativity and innovation. CC has about 8000 employees, including 2000 software engineers. Gaining access to those engineers was one of the key reasons for the merger. CC spends about $26,000 per employee on annual benefits. CC has had essentially the same benefits package for six out of its seven years of existence.

A Consulting Team Gathers Information on Benefits

Although the two companies have technically been combined into one company, they are still operating independently and are just starting to combine their separate workforces. The COO of the new entity has hired your consulting firm to assess the current plans of both companies. It is her goal to develop a blended system that represents the best features of both benefit plans and a plan that will be well received by software engineers in both groups.

To learn more about the retirement and benefits plans at both companies, your team decides to interview HR managers and departmental managers at both companies. For both HC and CC, you want to gather information on the following topics:

- Strengths and weaknesses of current benefits programs and areas for possible improvements.
- An assessment of how well the current plan meets the needs of software engineers.
- Each company's perceptions of the plans of the other company.
- Key areas software engineers will be concerned about regarding the adoption of a common benefits plan.

Your team holds several interviews, from which you gain managers' perceptions and information on both of the existing plans. Notes from two interviews are included here.

Notes from the Interview of the Computer Co. Benefits Manager

Date:	February 17, 2005
Interview Objective:	Obtain the CC manager's perspective on the merger of benefit plans between HC and CC and on the perceived strengths and weaknesses of both
Interviewee:	Mariel Salinas, Benefits Manager at CC
Interviewers:	Two of your team members

Background: The benefits manager, Mariel Salinas, has six years of experience in human resources and joined CC three years ago. Her previous employer was a cutting-edge advertising agency, and she feels that the way CC treats its employees is very consistent with what she experienced at her former job. Both industries depend on their "human capital" to achieve success; rewarding creativity and independence is critical to the company's performance.

When Mariel came to CC, she initiated a benchmarking study to review the hiring and benefits practices of the top 50 technology companies to familiarize herself with the industry. She also discovered that CC is way above average on granting stock options and way below average on employer contributions to 401K plans. In addition, the results showed that CC has earned a reputation as one of the top 100 best working environments in the country because of flexible hours and benefits options.

Quotes from the interview:

About Benefits at CC

"Our company is comprised primarily of younger workers. They focus more on perks like vacation packages, on-site concierge, and the company fitness center. They aren't really worried about retirement packages, dental insurance, or life insurance."

"To meet our employees' diverse needs, we use a 'cafeteria plan' approach. That means we supply an à la carte system of point-based options. Employees can distribute their points to the categories of benefits that appeal to them. As a result, every employee has a different benefits package, but the dollar values are consistent."

"I think one of the weaknesses of our benefits and retirement program is the lack of long-term focus on retirement. The interests of our employees would be better served if they were a little more focused on their future."

Notes from the Interview of the Computer Co. Benefits Manager (continued)

"Several employees have complained that our vision plan doesn't include Lasik eye correction surgery, but you know, I think that's over the top. I'm not sure that we should focus too much of our attention on that sort of thing, or we'll soon be paying for all kinds of cosmetic surgery!"

About Benefits at HC

"HC was included in a benchmarking study that we did, but that was three years ago. And they have revamped their benefits program since then."

"When we did the study, the problems HC had were tremendous. In fact, I think they may have revamped the system when they got the benchmarking data. The worst part of their program was how it didn't even begin to compete with the other benefits packages. In fact, if their employee base wasn't so old and set in their ways, they would surely have moved on to a different company by now . . ."

"No, I guess I'm not too familiar with their current system. I've heard rumors, but I don't really know how it works. I guess the strength of their program is that it must work for their people. Retention at HC is very good. But their employee base has such a different demographic from our software engineers."

On Merging the Benefits

"I am very concerned that the people in charge might decide to use HC's benefits system since they have so many more employees than we currently have on our system. And I'm guessing that their program is less expensive. The problem is that our system is so much better. It's nationally recognized as being progressive and friendly to our employees. But since HC recently redid their program, we'll probably get stuck with their way of doing things."

"I think the employees are most concerned that the merger is going to rob them of the innovation and flexibility they've come to expect around here. In addition, I'm afraid that changing the benefits system will send a negative signal to our folks that the HC system and employees are more valuable in this merger relationship. I anticipate a huge attrition problem."

Notes from the Interview of the Huge Co. VP of Human Resources
---

Date:	February 17, 2005
Interview Objective:	Obtain the HC perspective on the merger of benefit plans between HC and CC and on the perceived strengths and weaknesses of both
Interviewee:	Adam Nagami, VP of Human Resources for HC
Interviewers:	Two of your team members

Background: Adam Nagami has been in the Human Resources business for 20 years, having started his career as a junior HR analyst at HC. He has "grown up" with the company and prides himself on keeping current with trends in HR. As the current VP of Human Resources, he directed the redesign of the HC benefit and retirement plan two years ago and feels that it is now an excellent plan. Although he did not survey the employees to assess their level of satisfaction with the plan, he based his changes and recommendations on industry "best practices" and what he felt was most appropriate for HC's employee base.

Notes from the Interview of the Huge Co. VP of Human Resources (continued)

Quotes from the interview:

About Benefits at HC

"Our employee base consists of mostly people in their late 30s and 40s. Many of them have families and are focused on having good health benefits. They also care about long-term savings and we have active participation in our 401K program."

"As you know, we revamped our benefits and retirement programs two years ago, and so far, I haven't heard any negative feedback from our employees, so I haven't spent the time or money to conduct any surveys, but let me tell you about a few key features."

"We use a standard cafeteria plan that allows a choice between two types of medical plans and choices on coverage for life insurance and dental. We've also recently added a flexible spending account option to our plan—this allows for pretax dollars to be set aside to reimburse employees for items not covered by our regular plan—for example, they can use it to reimburse themselves for out-of-pocket medical expenses or expenses the plan wouldn't ordinarily pay for, such as eyeglasses or Lasik surgery. They can also use it for dependent care—for their children or older relatives—so it offers lots of flexibility."

On Merging the Benefits

"I don't know much about the CC plan although I know it is highly ranked. I think that CC's software engineers are a much younger group and that they don't care that much about life insurance or reimbursement for care of elderly parents, but I think the key here is to show them the flexibility we can offer and help educate them about planning for their future. As they start families, they might appreciate some of our benefits. The combined company will now have almost 30,000 employees, so we can expect to negotiate some real economies of scale with our providers. I think if we can convince the CC engineers that our way is best, the transition will go quite smoothly."

The Assignment

As the head of the consulting team, you need to brief the senior partner on your findings so that he can then meet with the COO at Huge Computer Company. You need to synthesize the information from the interviews, consolidate your key findings, and *develop a one-page executive summary* comparing the key features of the plans and making any observations or recommendations you have about merging the plans. Remember that the senior partner may or may not read your full report, so any key findings and your recommendations need to be easy to access and understand.

Source: Case and exercise developed by Deborah J. Barrett, Beth O'Sullivan, and Beth Peters, Rice University. Used with permission.

Notes

1. Dodge, R. W. What to report, as quoted in Kenneth W. Houp and Thomas E. Pearsall, *Reporting Technical Information.* New York: Macmillan, 1984, p. 85.
2. Harris Poll Survey conducted in December 2003. www.harrisinteractive.com/harris_poll/index.asp. Worldwide Email Usage Forecast, 2002–2006: Know What's Coming Your Way (IDC #27975).
3. *Business Editors New York Business Wire*, May 28, 2003.

4. Leonard, D., & Gilsdorf, J. (2001). Big stuff, little stuff: A decennial measurement of executives' and academics' reactions to questionable usage elements. *Journal of Business Communication* 38 (4), 439–475.

5. For more guidance on e-mail, you may want to go to www.albion.com/netiquette/corerules.html. Virginia Shea's *Netiquette,* which she defines as "network etiquette, the do's and don'ts of online communication," was one of the first sources to provide rules of Internet communication; her site still remains one of best of the many that are now available.

Chapter **Three**

Using Language to Achieve a Leadership Purpose

Just as an artist works from a palette of colors to paint a picture, the leader who manages meaning works from a vocabulary of words and symbols to help construct a frame in the mind of the listener.

Gail T. Fairhurst and Robert A. Sarr, *The Art of Framing: Managing the Language of Leadership*

Without the right words, used in the right way, it is unlikely that the right actions will ever occur. . . . Without words, we have no way of expressing strategic concepts, structural forms, or designs for performance measurement systems. In the end, there is no separating action and rhetoric.

Robert G. Eccles and Nitin Nohria, *Beyond the Hype: Discovering the Essence of Management*

Chapter Objectives

In this chapter, you will learn to do the following:

- Achieve a positive ethos through tone and style.
- Communicate in a style that is clear and concise.
- Use business language correctly.
- Employ efficient editing techniques.

Leaders lead and inspire others to action through their effective use of language. In *The Art of Framing: Managing the Language of Leadership*, Gail Fairhurst and Robert Sarr argue that "leadership is a language game, one that many do not know they are playing. Even though most leaders spend nearly 70 percent of their time communicating, they pay relatively little attention to how they use language as a tool of influence."[1] The introduction to this text discussed how leaders use language as a tool of influence every day. Their ability to influence their audience positively, overcoming barriers to effective communication, is the essence of leadership communication.

The goal of this chapter is to help you create a positive ethos through the effective use of language—the use of the right words in the right way to achieve the outcome you intend. You reveal your ethos through the language you use. If you are unsure and lack confidence in your writing or speaking abilities, your choice of words, your style, and your tone will reveal it. If, on the other hand, you are confident in your ability to use the language of leaders, that confidence will resonate in your words and enhance your influence with all your targeted audiences.

In one of the best and most concise books on style, *The Elements of Style,* E. B. White says, "Every writer, by the way he uses the language, reveals something of his spirit, his habits, his capacities, his bias. This is inevitable as well as enjoyable. . . . No writer long remains incognito."[2] And no speaker does either. You reveal who you are through your use of language. Look, for instance, at the following speech given a few years ago by the then CEO of Pennzoil, Hugh Liedtke, during a legal battle between his company and Texaco over a company they were both seeking to buy:

> There is perhaps a greater question involved [than the legal details]. It turns on the crucial point of integrity in our industry.
>
> It's one thing to play hardball. It's quite another thing to play foul ball. Conduct such as Texaco's is not made legal simply by protestations that the acts involved were, in fact, legal. All too often such assertions go unchallenged, and so slip into some sort of legal limbo, and become accepted as the norm by default. In this way, actions previously considered amoral somehow become clothed in respectability.
>
> Pennzoil's litigation challenges this mindless slip into acceptability. We seek to test the acceptable standards of behavior in our industry.
>
> A contract is a contract. We used to say that in the oil industry, business was done on a handshake. Should it now require handcuffs?
>
> . . . We believe that integrity is more than just a word. It is a standard of conduct in a world perhaps gone slipshod. Our industry was built on that standard, and Pennzoil will continue to make every effort to see to it that this standard is upheld.[3]

From this short portion of his speech, without knowing anything about Mr. Liedtke, you have formed opinions about his ethos. His language suggests an ethos of confidence, honesty, dedication to his company and his industry, and a rather folksy and down-to-earth quality with his baseball metaphor and comment about business being done on a handshake. Since this was a prepared presentation to his stockholders, Mr. Liedtke may have had some help from a speechwriter, as CEOs quite often do for important speeches, although he was well known for his communication abilities and for writing his speeches himself. Speechwriter or not, the words would have to be natural to him, or he would not have sounded sincere. Overall, Mr. Liedtke creates a positive ethos and influences his audience to trust him and to follow him. He presents himself as a leader—through the use of clear, confident, resonant language.

As a leader, you want your audience to perceive a positive ethos in your tone, to see you as confident, and to trust and believe you. This chapter begins by discussing how you can achieve a positive ethos through your writing and speaking style, which your audience perceives as your tone. It provides ways to make your style more concise and, by doing so, ensure that you sound more forceful and confident. It then reviews briefly the correct use of language expected in leadership communication and concludes by showing you techniques to help you edit your own work.

ACHIEVING A POSITIVE ETHOS THROUGH TONE AND STYLE

To project a confident tone when you speak and when you write, you need to possess confidence not only in your knowledge on the subject but also in your ability to capture the content in the right words used in the right way. You want to sound confident and speak with authority. You want to be clear and crisp in your language yet not sound too harsh or brusque as the sample letters illustrate in Exhibits 3.1 and 3.2. The words you select and how you decide to combine them in sentences create your style; your audience perceives that style as your tone, and through that tone, they make assumptions about your ethos. The tone, or what your readers perceive as your attitude toward them or toward the subject, influences the success of your message to such a great extent that you must always be aware of its impact.

EXHIBIT 3.1
Dismissal Letter with a Harsh, Uncaring Tone

Braniff Airlines
121 No. 20th Blvd.
New York, New York 10021

April 10, 19–

Dear John:

Effective with the close of business on Wednesday, May 10, 19–, your job will be abolished and no further work will be authorized on that position.

Your support and assistance of Braniff Airlines in its sales efforts have been most appreciated.

Sincerely,

James T. Cole
Director of Reservation Sales

TL/hh

cc: Personnel file
     Employee
     Original mailed to above address.

EXHIBIT 3.2
Rejection
Letter with an
Alienating
Tone

One Hundred First Congress
U.S. House of Representatives
Committee on the Budget
Washington, D.C. 20515

March 8, 2005

Blakeman Brown
6500 South Main
Houston, TX 77030

Dear Blakeman:

Thank you for applying to the Budget Committee Republican staff for an internship.
I am sorry that we will not be able to accept you to our program this summer.

We had several dozen applicants. However, we have room for only two interns this
summer. Our selections process, therefore, was fairly arbitrary in light of these odds.

Again, thanks for applying.

Sincerely,

Martha Phillips

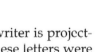

As you read these letters, ask yourself what kind of ethos the writer is projecting in them. What are the connotations of the language? (Note: These letters were
written as you see them here. Only the names have been changed; everything else
is as it appeared in the originals.)

The first letter (Exhibit 3.1) shows no concern for the audience. It begins with the
harsh statement that John's job has been "abolished" and then ends with an attempt
to soften the brutal effect by thanking John for his "efforts." The thank-you seems
insincere and even out of place in this otherwise cold, bad-news letter. One element
of style that contributes to the distancing, uncaring tone is the use of passive voice
sentence constructions: "will be abolished," "will be authorized," and "has been
most appreciated." These distance Mr. Cole from his audience and from the actions.
Imagine the difference if he had written the following sentences instead:

As of May 10, 19–, I will abolish your job and authorize no more work on your position.

And

I appreciate your support and assistance of Braniff Airlines in its sales efforts.

The first would be too direct, and besides, it is unlikely Mr. Cole has made this
decision. It is a decision people above Mr. Cole have made, so selecting a direct,

active style in the opening sentence would not make this letter more effective. The following letter delivers the same message with a better ethos:

Dear John:

As you know, Braniff has encountered extremely difficult financial times over the last few months. We have done everything we can to keep the airline functioning as in the past so that we can serve our public and keep all of our employees employed. Now, however, we have come to a point where we must make some difficult decisions. The most difficult decision is having to let some of our people go. Regrettably, your department is one that we must cut. Therefore, as of May 10, 19–, we will no longer authorize work in your department.

Your severance package will include the following. . . .

We all regret that the layoffs are necessary. We value your department and your individual contributions to Braniff Airlines. We appreciate your sales efforts over the years and wish you the best for the future.

Sincerely,

James T. Cole

The message has not changed—John is still out of a job—but at least Mr. Cole has shown some concern and seems sincere in his regrets and in his appreciation. Since it is a bad-news letter, the indirect style is more appropriate. In addition, the words selected in the second version create a more positive ethos for Mr. Cole.

The letter in Exhibit 3.2 is also a rejection letter with a problem in tone. How would you feel if you received it?

The opening to this letter is probably acceptable. It is direct and expresses some regret. The second paragraph, however, alienates the reader and makes the sender seem foolish. To admit that a decision is "arbitrary" makes it sound as if it had no basis in logic, as if they drew the name out of a hat. The wording may, in fact, distort the writer's intentions and may be inaccurate.

Both of these letters, as well as the Liedtke speech, illustrate how important the words are that you choose to convey your messages.

In a classic *Harvard Business Review* essay on style, "What Do You Mean You Don't Like My Style?" John Fielden illustrates and analyzes the different styles that a business writer might use in response to a letter from a business acquaintance. The sender (Frank Scalpel) has asked the receiver to serve on a committee. This could be perceived as a conflict of interest since it could place the receiver in the position of evaluating his own company's proposals to automate the hospital's information flow. However, it is not clear if Frank is aware of the potential conflict or if he is simply being careless and not thinking that the receiver's company might be submitting a proposal that the committee would then be reviewing.

Fielden includes four possible responses to the letter, all reprinted here. As you read each one, think about the tone and the perceived ethos of the sender, and ask: Which style most resembles your own style?

Response 1

Mr. Frank J. Scalpel
Chairman, Executive Committee
Community General Hospital
Anytown, U.S.A

Dear Frank,

As you realize, this litigious age often makes it necessary for large companies to take stringent measures not only to avoid conflicts of interest on the part of their employees but also to preclude even the very suggestion of conflict. And, since my company intends to submit a proposal with reference to automating the hospital's information flow, it would not appear seemly for me to be part of an evaluation team assessing competitors' proposals. Even if I were to excuse myself from consideration of the SYZ proposal, I would still be vulnerable to charges that I gave short shrift to competitors' offerings. If there is any other way that I can serve the committee that will not raise this conflict-of-interest specter, you know that I would find it pleasurable to be of service, as always.

Sincerely,

Response 2

Dear Frank,

Your comments relative to your respect for my professional opinion are most appreciated. Moreover, your invitation to serve on the hospital's data processing evaluation team is received with gratitude, albeit with some concern.

The evaluation team must be composed of persons free of alliance with any of the vendors submitting proposals. For that reason, it is felt that my services on the team could be construed as a conflict of interest.

Perhaps help can be given in some other way. Again, please be assured that your invitation has been appreciated.

Sincerely,

Response 3

Dear Frank,

Thank you for suggesting my name as a possible member of your data processing evaluation team. I wish I could serve, but I cannot.

XYZ intends, naturally, to submit a proposal to automate the hospital's information flow. You can see the position of conflict I would be in if I were on the evaluation team.

Just let me know of any other way I can be of help. You know I would be more than willing. Thanks again for the invitation.

Cordially,

Response 4

Dear Frank,

Thanks for the kind words and the invitation. Sure wish I could say yes.
Can't though.

XYZ intends to submit a surefire proposal on automating the hospital's information systems. Shouldn't be judge and advocate at the same time!

Any other way I can help, Frank—just ask. Thanks again.

Cordially,

What is the tone of each of these? What is the projected ethos of the writer? Which writer appears more confident and at ease with himself? In addition to asking yourself which one is closest to your natural style, you should also ask which one of these you might use even if not your usual style, and which would you never use. Answering these questions will help you get a sense of your own style and the tone that is typical of your writing.

Every person has an individual style. It is your voice; it is the "you" that your reader perceives and your "natural" style and tone. However, if the situation justified it, you might adopt any one of these styles, although Response 1 and Response 4 are probably a little far from a style you would consider using. Most people would probably see the first response as too formal and stilted, the second too passive, and the fourth too casual.

Most businesspeople select Response 3 as closest to their own and as preferable for the situation. Although it is a good letter, it contains some problems with tone in the second paragraph in the context of the case. Since Frank's motivations are unknown and you do not want to offend him, you would not want to say "naturally" or "you can see." These words imply that Frank knows he is asking you to do something questionable. This implication, in turn, casts doubt on Frank's ethos and will result in a loss of face that will damage your relationship with Frank.

That you would select Response 3, the one most others would select, tells you that you are already comfortable with an expected style in business writing. You probably use the same style consistently, and your audiences probably perceive your tone as fairly consistent; you most likely vary it only slightly when the situation calls for a different tone or when your feelings are influencing your thinking and writing, as in the copier abuse memo in Chapter 1. You may not even be aware of the tone you project, although you need to be. After looking at the examples provided in this chapter, you should have a better idea of your natural style and realize how your ear detects tone in writing and speaking without your even being aware of doing it. You should apply the same scrutiny to hearing your own tone that you applied to analyzing the tone in the previous examples. You should read what you have written out loud and practice a presentation aloud or, even better, record what you plan to deliver and play it back to yourself. If you are still not sure how you sound, you should ask others to read what you have written and listen critically to you.

You need to know how others perceive the language that you use, your tone. The more you can anticipate the audience's response and hear how you sound to others, the better able you will be to control your tone and use it to influence your audience. Being aware of your style and tone moves you one step closer to developing a leadership style. You never want to move too far away from your natural style, since to do so will make you sound insincere. You can, however, learn from specific techniques used by leaders that will make your language more powerful and help in creating a positive ethos, an ethos that signals to your audience that you know what you are talking about and can be trusted (Exhibit 3.3).

To test your style, try stepping back and looking critically at something you have written. Put yourself in the shoes of your audience. Ask yourself, "How do I come across?" "Is there confidence in my tone?" "Do I project a positive ethos?"

The next section will provide some guidance on making your style more forceful by making it more concise.

EXHIBIT 3.3
Guidelines for Creating a Positive Ethos

1. Do not try to imitate someone else's style. Although you can adjust your tone slightly to different situations, you do not want to move too far away from your natural voice. If you do, you risk sounding artificial and perhaps superficial.

2. Read what you have written aloud to see how you sound, and if something is particularly sensitive, read it to someone else.

3. Never send something out when you are angry or upset. Always wait until you have control of your emotions and can select your language carefully.

4. Be careful in your use of complex language or "thesaurusitis," finding a word in a thesaurus and using it because it is a "big" word when a simple one would be better (for example, saying "utilize" instead of "use").

5. Use strong verbs and avoid passive voice unless you have a specific reason to use it (see discussion below).

6. Select a positive over a negative construction when possible. For example, say "We will begin implementing the changes you recommended on January 22" instead of "We will not be able to implement your recommended changes before January 22."

7. Avoid using too many modifiers or empty words, such as "sort of," "kind of," "possibly," and too many "ly" words in particular.

8. Be careful in the use of qualifiers, such as "in my opinion," "I think," "I believe," "probably," and "I feel." They can make you sound too unsure of yourself and hesitant.

9. Eliminate fillers, such as "you know," "uh," and "um" from your speech.

10. Be careful with the use of jargon (see discussion below). Use it only when it is the best way to say what you want to say and when you know for sure the audience will understand it.

COMMUNICATING CONCISELY

One way to make your writing clear is to make it concise. Clear writing is direct, to the point, and free of jargon, pomposity, and wordy constructions. Again, look at Mr. Liedtke's speech. He says, simply: "A contract is a contract" and "We believe that integrity is more than just a word." He could have said: "Contracts are legal documents that are meant to be obeyed" or "It is believed by most people that integrity means being trustworthy and honest." If he had, his presentation would not have been as powerful, and his ethos would not have been as positive. His sentences are very concise and contain only the words he needs to deliver his meaning. Additional words might only dilute that meaning.

Unfortunately, early education may have influenced some of our writing habits negatively. Teachers probably gave you writing assignments that specified a certain length. As a result, you may have counted words and added fillers to meet the required length, when what we should have been doing was saying the most with the fewest words. Instead of looking for what the French call "le mot juste" (just the right word), we chose bigger, more impressive words and wrote sentences full of deadwood—words that could and should be removed because they are meaningless—because we had to fill up the page to meet the length requirement.

To achieve conciseness in your writing, you may need to break old habits of wordiness that you do not even realize you have. Writing concisely requires practice and a critical eye for your own style. To help you make your writing more concise, this section offers a series of guidelines. *These guidelines are not rules on style,* because "rules" suggest "right" or "wrong." The guidelines only demonstrate what is *usually* preferred when communicating as a leader. As you master your own leadership style, you will find that you may break away from the guidelines when you feel you have good reasons to do so. For example, you may want to be vague at times, or you may want to be wordy. You may want to write in passive voice or begin a sentence with "there is." The meaning you intend should guide your choice to write or speak as it seems best to you. You will simply want to ensure that carelessness or haste is not the reason for your wordiness. As Pascal wrote years ago, when he apologized to a friend for writing such a long letter: It takes much longer to write something short than to write something lengthy.

Following the ten guidelines below will help you achieve greater conciseness and a style that is more direct and forceful.

1. Avoid the Overuse of the Passive Voice—The Actor Should Usually Come First in the Sentence

Passive Voice	Active Voice
The report was written by the committee. (seven words)	**The committee wrote the report. (five words)**
Object *action* *actor*	*Actor* *action* *object*

Choose the active voice unless you have a specific reason for using the passive, such as the following:

- You want to protect the actor in the sentence.
- You are not sure who is responsible for the action.
- The actor is unimportant.
- The company style or some other mandate dictates otherwise.

The lesson here is to use the passive voice because you intend to use it, not out of haste or carelessness. Beware of using grammar/style checkers to determine if you are using passive voice. While they can be useful in flagging passive construction, they cannot distinguish between past tense sentence constructions and passive voice; therefore, they will often label a sentence passive when it is not.

2. Avoid Expletives, Such as "There Is" or "It Is"—Watch for the "It Is . . . That" Construction in Particular

Construction with Expletives	Nonexpletive Construction
There is one manager at BDC who is not very efficient.	**One manager at BDC is not very efficient.**
There are two fundamental issues in the area of effectiveness that the team must analyze first . . .	**The team should analyze two fundamental issues in the area of effectiveness first: functional capability and decision-making processes.**

Use your meaning and emphasis to guide your use. For instance, in the second example, the emphasis shifts from the issues to the team, when you may want to highlight the issues.

3. Avoid the Use of Prepositional Idioms

Idioms to Avoid	Concise Replacements
due to the fact that	➢ **because**
during the time that	➢ **while**
for the purpose of	➢ **to**
for the reason that	➢ **because or since**
if the conditions are such that	➢ **if**
in order to	➢ **to**
in the event that	➢ **if**
in the area of	➢ **in**
in the case of	➢ **in**
in the interest of	➢ **for**
in the nature of	➢ **in**
in the region of	➢ **around**
next to	➢ **by**
on the top of	➢ **on or above**
over and above	➢ **beyond**
with regard to	➢ **regarding**
with the purpose of	➢ **to**

While usually these idioms are unnecessary, you may want to use them to ensure clarity, particularly if your writing will be translated into other languages, or you may decide the rhythm of your prose necessitates their use. Again, use them intentionally, not out of carelessness.

4. Avoid the Overuse of Relative Pronouns—"Who," "Which," and "That"

Unnecessary Relative Pronouns	Sentences without Relative Pronouns
Mr. Bigelow is a man **who** never misses a meeting.	**Mr. Bigelow never misses a meeting.**
The documentation **which** was written by Joan Browning is helpful.	**Joan Browning's documentation is helpful.**

5. Avoid the Repetition of Words and Ideas

Look at the following introduction and conclusion from a one-page letter:

We on the board of the United Way were disheartened by the statement you made yesterday. We feel that there is a grave **misunderstanding.** If this **misunderstanding** is not cleared up, it will harm both the needy and the unity we are all trying to foster in the community. I wish to have a personal meeting with you to clear up this **misunderstanding** immediately.

If this boycott is carried out, the needy will suffer. Organizations such as the Red Cross, the Boy Scouts, and Catholic Counseling, all badly in need of contributions, will suffer. If we can iron out this **misunderstanding,** all these worthy charities will benefit. Solving this **misunderstanding** is in all of our best interests. This **misunderstanding** will also harm the unity that we are trying to bring to El Paso. All of the races and religions of the community must live in harmony. We must not let this **misunderstanding** polarize the community.

Obviously, a misunderstanding exists, but the needless repetition weakens the effect of the letter. The writer needs to think a little deeper to give the argument substance. Needlessly repeating words and ideas suggests shallow thinking and careless writing.

The following repetition, based on the policy statement discussed in Chapter 2, illustrates a common type of repetition found in lists:

In order for an employee to qualify for reimbursement, the **employee must** satisfy all of the following requirements:

(1) **employee must** be of production foreman level or higher or the rank of secretary or higher

(2) **employee must** enroll in a state-accredited institution in courses of the college or graduate level

(3) **employee must** complete the course with at least a "C."

If you find you are repeating the same words at the beginning of each item in a list, you need to move the repeated words into the introductory sentence. Usually you can set up the list so that you start each item with an active verb, which will make your writing more direct and forceful (see example here):

For employees to qualify for reimbursement, they must

- **Be of production foreman level . . .**
- **Enroll in a state accredited institution . . .**
- **Complete the course with at least a "C".**

Excess words or verbiage can be very irritating to your audience, so you should try to make every word you write and speak significant. You should repeat words or ideas only to emphasize an important message or to create a particular rhetorical effect. For instance, you usually want to state your primary message and the main supporting topics in both the introduction and conclusion of a presentation, and if some discussion intervenes in a document, you may find that you need to restate your main message later.

6. Do Not Overuse Descriptive Words, Particularly Adverbs (-*ly* Words)

Ineffective Use of Words Ending in -*ly*	Example with -*ly* Words Removed
I **personally** felt that the CEO's **wonderfully** articulated presentation **decisively** swayed the stockholder in his favor.	**The CEO's presentation convinced the stockholders.**

The first version sounds insincere and exaggerated in addition to being too wordy.

7. Avoid Weasel Words, Ambiguous Noncommittal Words
Such as the following:

almost	elements	manner
as much as	feel	situation
aspect	field	special
basis	help	things
can be	like	up to
different	look	virtually

8. Be Aware of Jargon (Language Used in Particular Disciplines) and Other Kinds of Gobbledygook
Legal documents are full of jargon, creating the perception that lawyers are always talking only to other lawyers, or as cynics might say, legal language perpetuates the need for more lawyers:

The aforementioned documents for the application of the captioned corporations for a Certificate of Authority to Transact Business in Texas are enclosed.

The legal profession is not alone in the tendency to use jargon; all professions use the language of their disciplines. Writers and speakers create problems anytime they continue to use the specialized language of their disciplines when communicating with others outside their discipline. For example, engineers, IT professionals, accountants, or investment bankers should feel comfortable using the language of their group with their group. The higher up you move in an organization, however, the more diverse and less specialized your audience becomes. As an organizational leader, you are addressing all employees and even external stakeholders. Jargon can make portions of your audience feel excluded or lead to their misunderstanding your message.

Jargon is so widespread in business that you probably find it handy shorthand and use it daily without realizing it, but you need to learn to avoid it. In fact, a number of Web sites have emerged dedicated to fighting the overuse of business jargon. They provide lists of jargon, translations of jargon terms, and even ways to avoid jargon.

One site provides the following passage as a way to test your recognition of business jargon. They ask their readers to answer the following questions:

- How many examples of jargon can you find in the excerpt below?
- What do you think this company does?

Unicorp: Dedicated to Excellence

One of Unicorp's corporate objectives is to develop strategic relationships with key customers and be recognized for our ability to deliver services of superior value. This competitive advantage will be achieved through continued focus on our core competencies, management attention to the development of operations and process management excellence in all parts of our business, the identification and application of best processes, and continued attention to direct and indirect cost management. The focus on core competencies will promote the concentration of knowledge in select areas consistent with the tenets of Unicorp's strategic plan, Unicorp 2000. Management's attention to operations and process management excellence in all business areas will be achieved through the continued expansion of our management and technical staff, as well as through consistent application of corporate quality programs such as benchmarking and continuous improvement, leading to the establishment of Unicorp's superior business processes in each core competency. Finally, continued attention to direct and indirect cost management will enable Unicorp to offer customers a superior, value-added package of high-quality service at a competitive price.

Source: http://www.westegg.com/jargon/

To combat the overuse of business jargon, the firm Deloitte Consulting promotes a free software program called "Bullfighter," which will help get rid of such jargon as the following used as an introduction to its product:

- "A value-added, leverageable global knowledge repository."
- "Repurposeable, leading edge thoughtware that delivers results-driven value."
- "A future-proof asset that seamlessly empowers your mission-critical enterprise communications."

Source: http://www.dc.com/insights/bullfighter/

Deloitte Consulting claims Bullfighter will be an "online conscience," running in Microsoft Word and PowerPoint and working similarly to spelling and grammar checkers.

Although we all use jargon, you need to be sensitive to its use and abuse. Jargon is a particular problem in international settings where it can cause miscommunication. If you recognize that jargon has its place and use it only with audiences who share your cultural and business context, you will be safe. Be careful, however, that you do not let jargon or gobbledygook become your only way of conversing because your communication will seldom be clear or concise if you do.

9. Avoid Nominalizations (a Jargon Word Used by Linguists That Means Turning Verbs into Nouns by Adding *-tion*)

Nominalization Example	Active Verb Example
The product management team will perform an **investigation** of the marketing strategy.	**The product management team will investigate the marketing strategy.**

Your communication will be much more powerful if you avoid nominalizations and use active verbs whenever possible. Review your sentences to determine if you have, in fact, selected the most appropriate word to serve as the verb.

10. Finally, Avoid Redundancies

The redundancies in Exhibit 3.4 are more common in speech than in writing, but you should be careful to avoid them in both. This guideline warrants a few words of caution, however:

- You do not want to become so obsessed with cutting redundancies that you hinder your natural voice or flow. The result can be choppy, disjointed prose.
- Occasionally, the rhythm of your prose or the need to translate your communication into another language may necessitate your using redundancy.

The list in Exhibit 3.4 should make you sensitive to common redundancies so that you can avoid them or at least be more aware of how often you hear them and use them.

As George Orwell in "Politics and the English Language" says, "If it is possible to cut a word out, always cut it out." You want to keep all your communication as short and simple as possible and eliminate everything that is not relevant and necessary. In addition, you should use the simple word over the complex in most cases. For example, look at how complex, exaggerated language can destroy the beauty and effectiveness of a familiar Christmas poem:

Twas the nocturnal segment of the diurnal period preceding the annual Yuletide celebration, and throughout our place of residence, kinetic activity was not in evidence among the possessors of this potential, including that species of domestic rodent known as *Mus Musculus.* Hosiery was meticulously suspended from the forward edge of the wood burning caloric apparatus, pursuant to our anticipatory pleasure regarding an imminent visitation from an eccentric philanthropist among whose folkloric appellations is the honorific title of St. Nicholas.

Source: By GIMS, otherwise author unknown.

EXHIBIT 3.4
Popular
Redundancies

actual **experience**	difficult **task**	**my** personal **opinion**
advance **planning**	direct **confrontation**	old **antique**
advance **warning**	**during** the course of	one and the **same**
all meet together	**each** and every	pair of **twins**
alongside of	**either** and/or both	past **history**
and **moreover**	end **result**	**period** of time
as **for example**	established **fact**	personal **friend**
at 12 **midnight**	**few** in number	**plan** ahead
at 12 **noon**	final **end**	**postponed** until later
at about	foreign **imports**	**raise** up
at some time to come	grand **total**	**reason** is because
basic **fundamentals**	**I** myself personally	**reason** why
but **however**	**introduced** for the first time	**refer** back
but **nevertheless**	ir**regardless** (not even a word)	**remand** back
chief **protagonist**	**is** now **pending**	**repeat** back
climb up	**lift** up	**return** back
close **proximity**	major **breakthrough**	**revert** back
combine together	mass **media**	rough **rule of thumb**
commute back and forth	**may** possibly	**sufficient** enough
complete **monopoly**	**merge** together	sworn **affidavits**
consensus of opinion	most **equal**	true **facts**
continue on	most **unique**	usual **custom**
definite **decision**	mutual **agreement**	when and **if**
different **kinds**	mutual **cooperation**	**whether** or not

This passage exemplifies "thesaurusitis." It demonstrates the danger of selecting the complicated over the simple. In leadership communication, you want to apply Henry David Thoreau's dictum on life: "Simplify, simplify, simplify." Simplifying your language will allow you to connect more easily with your audience and help them perceive the positive ethos you want to project.

To conclude this section on conciseness with some repetition of a key message, wordiness can indicate careless communication. Beyond carelessness, your audience may also interpret wordiness or use of complicated language as deception or purposeful obfuscation. The resulting lack of clarity can even suggest your thinking is careless, superficial, and imprecise or that you are too busy or do not care enough about your audience to take the time to make your communication clear and concise. It takes time to find "le mot juste," but the more positive ethos you create should be worth the time you spend.

USING BUSINESS LANGUAGE CORRECTLY

A concise and confident style and an appropriate tone contribute to a positive ethos. In addition, studies have found that the correct use of language affects ethos as well: Beason (2001) writes that "Errors [grammatical] create misunderstandings of the text's *meaning,* and they harm the *image* of the writing (and possibly the organization to which the writer belongs . . .). Errors affect a person's credibility as a writer or employee."[4] Business audiences are surprisingly adept at detecting errors in writing or speaking, and their judgments can be harsh and unforgiving. Errors in grammar, spelling, and mechanics may cause an audience to characterize the speaker or writer as hasty, careless, indifferent, uninformed, a faulty thinker, ignorant, stupid, a poor oral communicator, poorly educated, or not a detail person—to the detriment of the ethos of the individual and the organization.[5] As one investment banker wrote in the previously referenced study:

> The banking industry is more or less thought of as being a perfect industry. . . . And we try to do everything right, and I guess it bothers me if we present something on a piece of paper that is not . . . as near perfect as it can be. If I'm going to write you a letter, then my image went out in the letter, or my company's image. My bank's image needs to be nearly perfect, and a grammatical error, I think, would be offensive to some of my customers.[6]

The letter in Exhibit 3.5 sent by a vice president to a placement center director and the deans of a major university reinforces the importance of being very careful in your use of language.

Correct use of language in business communication is indeed important. For a leader, it is crucial. Your credibility as a leader, your ability to represent yourself and your company, and your ethos all depend on using language carefully. Careless errors are potentially damaging to a company: As Leonard and Gilsdorf (2001) found in their research, "Usage errors in business messages can cause misreading[s] that carry a high price. (Not all business messages with potential legal or financial consequences get reviewed by editors and legal counsel.) Error-prone writers might, for example, inadvertently obligate themselves or their firms financially, compromise themselves or their firms ethically, or erode their own and their firms' credibility."[7]

The Language Rules That Matter

The rules that govern the English language are numerous; however, some are more important than others and, according to survey findings, matter more than others in contemporary business communication. What follows is a brief overview of the rules that matter to business professionals today and a guide to *traditional business grammar* (as opposed to journalism or other contemporary usage). If you see yourself as very strong in standard business grammar, you could skip the short review provided here. If you are unsure, you might want to pause before reading the next section to complete the "Usage Self-Assessment" (Appendix C). If you suspect you need more review or have forgotten some of the terminology used in discussing grammar, you should read Appendix D ("Business of Grammar").

This section emphasizes rule violations or errors that can cause misreading or suggest that the writer is careless or not well informed: in other words, the rules that affect ethos. The principle that governs this review of rules is that it is better to be safe and follow traditional business grammar than to adopt what you see or hear in other contemporary settings, particularly in the media. Therefore, you may find some of the rules more conservative than those you have learned in the past or observed in some business settings or in the media. The goal is to prepare you as a leader to make educated choices. You will be prepared to choose to ignore a rule rather than violate it from lack of knowledge.

EXHIBIT 3.5
Letter to
Placement
Center
Director and
Deans

Dear Jerry, Martin, and Susan:

I am pleased to tell you that shortly I will be extending offers for positions to two of your graduating students. A colleague and I interviewed 20 students on campus and brought four in for follow-up office interviews. Without exception the students were bright, articulate, and well prepared analytically. The comments back from my colleagues following the office interviews were glowing about the students' abilities and personalities.

That is the good news.

The bad news is that some of the students have serious problems on paper, specifically in writing their cover letters and resumes. One candidate is getting his MBA at "The University of XXX." One worked at "Merill Lynch." One doesn't know the difference between "perspective" and "prospective." The examples are endless. Everyone makes mistakes, and that's part of being human. However, I would think that students' resumes and cover letters would be a place where they would do more than spell-check—they would carefully read line by line; they would ask their friends or Placement Center advisors to review the documents, etc.

I eliminated some strong candidates from consideration because of errors, but others slipped through my review. I will not let that last part happen again. In the future, I will eliminate from my review any candidate with these kinds of errors, without regard to their experience. I'm sure that is the approach that most recruiters take anyway, which brings me to my core point:

As an alumna who spends a great amount of her personal time working to advance the university's recognition, I am gravely embarrassed to think that these kinds of errors are circulating throughout the business community. I do not buy the story that these students should be responsible for themselves. They should be responsible for much more than that—representing the school and their alumni as well as themselves. I am more disappointed than you know that this is not the case. I am not sure how best to communicate my concerns to the students, but I am confident that among the three of you, the correct approach will be taken.

Best regards,

Lauren

Lauren LeBlanc
Vice President of Investments

Surveys of executives and of members of the Association for Business Communication have identified the types of errors that business professionals find most bothersome.[8] Exhibit 3.6 lists the top 20 types of errors executives found most distracting. The second column contains the sentence used in the survey to illustrate the error.

EXHIBIT 3.6 **Most Distracting Grammatical Errors to Executives**

Type of Error	Example Sentence with Error
1. Sentence Fragment	Although the Department of Transportation has implemented rules making it legal for employers to test an employee for drugs if he or she works in the airline, trucking, gas pipeline, or maritime industries. And Small companies suffer in a tight labor market. One of their problems being that they can't compete for qualified personnel.
2. Unpunctuated Parenthetical Expression [Interrupter]	When the time came for the representatives to sign the contract **however** the bid was withdrawn. And The chairman fired five department heads **among them Jerald Destefano.**
3. Run-On Sentence	He focused all his energies on his personal goals he never wavered from his chosen path.
4. Faulty Parallel Structure	Most people he encounters are impressed by **his calm manner, meticulous attire, and being ambitious.**
5. Dangling Modifier	**Looking very tired and worn,** a decision was finally reached by the committee.
6. Apostrophe in Plural Noun	Signs at the lot instruct motorists to park between the **line's** and not back into any parking space.
7. Comma Splice	Only 1,000 new full-time jobs will be **created, management** will fill the remaining 9,000 positions by urging part-timers to apply for existing full-time positions.
8. Use of Reflexive Pronoun When Objective Case Is Needed	After lunch, the chairman introduced Jameson and **myself** to the assembly.
9. Use of *Less* for a Count Noun	After the recession, Textron rehired **less** technicians than Puritan Mills did.
10. Use of Nominative Case Pronoun in Compound Indirect Object	The vice president directed my associate and **I** to submit reports to the executive committee.
11. Use of *Between* for More Than Two	The three buyers talked **between** themselves and decided to use the same vendor.
12. Adverbial Clause as Complement to Linking Verb	The reason I fired him after two years with our company **is because** he was incompetent.
13. Its/It's Confusion	Specific Dynamics claims that **it's** agreement with our company has been violated. As McAuliff pointed out, **its** a good thing that the auditors talked to the department before making the findings public.
14. Use of Adverb "Badly" with State-of-Being Verb "Feel"	The accounts supervisor felt **badly** yesterday.

(continued)

EXHIBIT 3.6 (continued)

Type of Error	Example Sentence with Error
15. Misspelling of "Principle"	I voted against the provision as a matter of **principal.**
16. Lack of Apostrophe in Possessive Noun	Our **firms** performance has been excellent.
17. Starting a Sentence with "But"	A recent IRS effort attempted to scan tax returns. **But** because the scanner could not decipher the taxpayers' handwriting, the process ended up costing more than the manual method.
18. "Which" Used to Refer to Entire Preceding Clause	Customers find it hard to locate the store, **which** affects business.
19. Use of Plural Pronoun to Refer to Singular Noun	Auto retailers on the Internet let **the buyer** configure a vehicle to **their** taste and see the firm price of the car **they** want.
20. Use of Plural Verb with Either/Or Subject Structure	**Either** the vice president **or** the marketing director **are** going to the reception as a company representative.

Source: Leonard, D., & Gilsdorf, J. (2001). Big stuff, little stuff: A decennial measurement of executives' and academics' reactions to questionable usage elements. *Journal of Business Communication* 38 (4), p. 440. Reprinted by permission of Sage Publications.

These are the errors that are most bothersome to business professionals because they suggest that the writer is being hasty and careless. The errors in the top ten are also the types of errors that can cause the reader to misinterpret or fail to understand your meaning.

The following sections discuss some of the rules behind the mistakes found in Exhibit 3.6, starting with a review of the correct use of punctuation in business writing.

The Power of Punctuation

Why does punctuation matter? It allows us to follow the complete thoughts embodied in sentences and distinguish between them. Punctuation makes reading easier and can lead to misreading if used incorrectly. Look at the challenge of sorting out the writer's meaning in the following passage, for example:

> That that is is that that is not is not that that is not is not that that is that that is is not that that is not is not that it it is[9]

Believe it or not, with the proper punctuation, this passage makes perfect sense. Of course, this example exaggerates the issue, but it makes the point that punctuation has power, some marks more than others. (If you need additional help beyond this brief review of punctuation, see Appendix D.)

The strongest marks of punctuation are the end marks (? ! .), and the weakest are *commas (,)* and *dashes (–)*. Confusion usually comes over what to do with the marks in between—the *colon (:)* and the *semicolon (;)*. The colon is used to introduce lists or to signal that what follows explains or elaborates what has come before. The semicolon is used to separate closely related independent clauses not joined by a coordinating conjunction (and, or, but, for, so, yet, nor); to separate independent clauses joined by conjunctive adverbs (accordingly, also, besides, consequently, further, however, moreover, nevertheless, then, therefore, thus, etc.); or to separate a series of phrases or clauses containing numerous commas.

The following chart illustrates what marks can and cannot do between independent clauses.

Independent Clause	Strongest	Independent Clause	
Mary balanced the books	**? ! .**	John paid the bills	**ok**
Mary balanced the books	**;**	John paid the bills	**ok**
Mary balanced the books	**:**	John paid the bills	**ok**
Mary balanced the books	**–**	John paid the bills	**no**
Mary balanced the books	**,**	John paid the bills	**no**
	Weakest		

You should avoid using a dash (–) unless you are sure how to use it. A dash signals that the information within the dashes is parenthetical but deserving of more emphasis than using parentheses or commas would suggest. You should avoid using a dash to separate two independent clauses. The comma is also too weak to separate two independent clauses, but it could be used if you provided help with a coordinating conjunction: Mary balanced the books, *and* John paid the bills.

Additional Punctuation Rules

The following provides an overview of additional punctuation rules.

Quotation Marks

In the United States, quotation marks should always be placed outside periods and commas, inside semicolons and colons, and inside or outside (depending on the context) question marks and exclamation marks. In other countries (for example, in Europe, Canada, and Australia), the comma and period are placed outside the quotation marks, so you will need to follow the custom of the country in which the document is written or the country that serves as the headquarters of the company.

."	,"	**Always correct.**
";	":	**Always correct.**
"?"	"!"	**Depends on the sentence.**

Even if the construction seems illogical to you, as in the following example, the rule in the United States remains the same.

> Shing-Hwa expects to make good grades in all of her classes; even in Economics 598, she expects to make an **"A."**

Commas after Introductory Phrases

Always place a comma after an introductory clause beginning with a subordinating conjunction (after, although, as, because, before, during, even though, if, since, than, though, unless, when, where, whereas, etc.). Also, it is always safer and easier to place commas after introductory phrases instead of trying to decide if the phrase is short or not.

> From a humble beginning, Marion Manufacturing Company has grown to be an enormous multinational corporation.

A comma should always follow an introductory absolute phrase as illustrated here:

> The surveys completed, we were ready to start analyzing the results.

Commas with Items in a Series

Contemporary usage (journalism in particular) has led to the demise of the comma before the "and" with items in a series. For example, people write, "The flag is red, white and blue." Leaving out the comma, however, can create ambiguity and cause misreading; therefore, it is safer to follow traditional usage and place a comma before the *and*. For instance, look at the change in meaning in the following example:

> The steering committee recommended that they start their analysis by looking at the following departments: personnel, benefits and insurance, production, human resources and social services.

Or,

> The steering committee recommended that they start their analysis by looking at the following departments: personnel, benefits and insurance, production, human resources, and social services.

In the first example, it is not clear if "human resources and social services" is one department or two; thus, the comma is needed to avoid confusion. Your decision to use a comma or not should be based on your being absolutely sure that omitting the comma does not change the meaning or leave the possibility of misreading. Going through this reasoning, however, requires more time and energy than just placing the comma before the "*and*" anytime you have items listed, which is the most appropriate choice for business writing.

When writing for other than business audiences, however, you need to be flexible and sensitive to their conventions; for instance, since journalists do not use the comma, when writing journalistic copy or for the news media, as in press releases, you may want to omit the comma, but again you should test the meaning.

Commas with Nonrestrictive Clauses

Use commas with nonrestrictive clauses (meaning that they can be removed from the sentence without changing the meaning). Clauses beginning with *that* are restrictive, but clauses beginning with *who* or *which* may be either restrictive or nonrestrictive. You must ask yourself: "If I remove the clause, will the sentence still make sense?" For example, look at what happens when you remove the clause from the following sentence:

> The data **that accompanies the report** came from his database.

Without the bolded clause, it is not clear what data the writer means. Therefore, the clause is necessary (restrictive) and does not require commas around it.

Contrast the following—

> The analysis, which includes his formulas, accompanies the report.

The clause provides additional information, but the information that the analysis "includes his formulas" is not necessary to understand the meaning of the sentence.

Apostrophes

Apostrophes are added with an "s" to nouns to show ownership; "'s" is added to singular and plural nouns not ending in "s"; plural nouns ending in "s" take the apostrophe alone in most cases, although the pronunciation usually determines when to add the "s" as well. Apostrophes are also used to create contractions (can't, don't, etc.). Apostrophes are not used to create possessive forms of personal pronouns (hers, not her's; its, not it's).

You will also still see the apostrophe used before an "s" after numbers, acronyms, or abbreviations. For example, "MBA's" instead of "MBAs" or "1990's" instead of "1990s." Although most modern guides to usage say to omit the apostrophe here, technically, either is correct as long as leaving the apostrophe out does not cause a misunderstanding. For instance, "As" looks like "as" when you might mean "A's" as in, "I expect to make 'A's.'" Whichever option you choose, be consistent.

Parentheses

Parentheses are used in pairs to set off interrupting information in a sentence when dashes would give the information too much emphasis and commas might lead to misreading. Note: The period is placed inside the parenthesis if the entire sentence is parenthetical and outside if not; see the discussion of apostrophes for an example.

Ellipses

The ellipsis is defined as "three spaced periods." Please note the word "spaced." This means that you literally hit the space bar key before, between, and after each period; thus, it should look like . . . when you use the ellipsis in a sentence, which is not the way Microsoft Word wants to treat it. If you use the ellipsis at the end of the sentence, then you should use four periods, thus. . . . Note: No space before the periods, in this case. Also, the ellipsis is usually not needed at the beginning of a direct quotation if you work the quotation into your prose. The ellipsis indicates that the writer has omitted some words from a direct quotation. It should not be used as you see writers sometimes use it (particularly in e-mail) to suggest they have more to say but are not taking the time right now to say it. In other words, they are using the ellipsis to mean "in addition" or etcetera. This usage is careless and even irritating to the reader, so you should avoid it.

Sexist Language

Leaders in contemporary business culture avoid sexist language. Sexist language shows a bias or preference toward one gender over another, often by implying exclusion of the nonpreferred gender. Using "man" or "he" all the time is not appropriate in most environments, particularly in the workplace. The issue creates problems for writers because the English language does not provide easy alternatives for the singular masculine and feminine pronouns; therefore, you will often need to rewrite sentences to make your subjects plural so that you are not locked into using "he" or "him."

> For instance, instead of saying
> > **Everybody** must pay **his** income tax.
> You can say,
> > **Taxpayers** must pay **their** income taxes.
> Or,
> > **All Americans** must pay **their** income taxes.

Of course, it is not always so easy to avoid sexist constructions, but you should take care that you do not offend anybody. In some situations, however, it is difficult to find a totally inoffensive construction that avoids doing violence to the language.

Since the 1960s, attempts to find substitutions for *he, him,* and *his* have led to two rather awkward replacements:

1. **He or she, him or her, he/she, him/her,** or **his/her.**
2. **S/he** (no equivalent has been created for him/her or his/her).

The first replacement (*he or she*) is grammatically correct and is sometimes the best alternative; however, it becomes rather awkward when overused and interrupts the flow of the language. The second replacement has received negative response since it looks so strange and is impossible to pronounce, so it should be avoided.

Again, trying to make the antecedent plural, as in the previous taxpayer example, is usually your best choice. Remember, although some people are now intentionally using a plural pronoun to refer to a singular antecedent to avoid the problem, you should *never do so.* You are better off being perceived as slightly sexist than being perceived as illiterate. To write "*Everybody* should pay *their* income taxes" is still considered *substandard* and probably always will be since it violates a basic grammatical rule about agreement of pronouns and the nouns to which they refer.

The Use of Ms.

Ms. is a convenient and well-accepted way to address a woman of unknown marital status; however, if you know the marital status, you may use Mrs. or Miss if you are sure that your audience prefers to be addressed that way. Follow your audience's lead, if possible. If the individual has written to you and signed her letter Mrs. Brown, then address her as Mrs. Brown when you write to her.

A Note on Letter Salutations

When you are not sure of a woman's marital status, use "Ms." in the salutation of letters. If you are unsure of the sex, then use the first and last name:

> Dear Leslie Smith:

If you do not know the name, address the person by position:

> Dear Customer:
> Dear Managers:

Never begin a letter with "Gentlemen:" or "Dear Sir:"

You may also remove the salutation and just use a subject line, although you should use this as a last resort:

> Expert Computer Systems
> 2920 Main Street
> Houston, Texas 77002
> Subject: Defective Computer Parts

Or use an attention line:

> Expert Computer Systems
> 2920 Main Street
> Houston, Texas 77002
> Attention: Computer Parts Department

The Use of Words Ending in "man"

The suffix "-man" has been replaced by "-person" in words such as "chairman," although in many cases complete substitutions have been offered. Thus, *chairman* has become *chair; mailman, letter carrier; policeman, police officer;* and so forth. You only need to consider these changes in general references; if you know the subject is male, you can use the masculine form of the word.

EMPLOYING EFFICIENT AND EFFECTIVE EDITING TECHNIQUES

Editing is an important skill that requires discipline and practice. It is particularly difficult to edit your own work. Many business writers are not sure what it is that they need to watch for besides the obvious typos and spelling. The advanced editing technique shown here works well for leadership communication. Try it or develop your own method based on what you know are your particular strengths and weaknesses. The key is to develop a method of some sort; otherwise, your editing will lack focus and may become haphazard.

The following acronym will help you remember this editing method: "*Do Save Money.*"

> D = *Document* (overall coherence, organization, formatting, tone)
> S = *Sentences* (structure, clarity, conciseness)
> M = *Mechanics* (typos, spelling, usage, diction)

Document
---

1. Read the complete document aloud for flow (logical progression and adequate transition) and tone.
2. Map the structure, noting major and minor ideas.
3. Add headings if necessary and make sure all are consistent and capture the "so what."
4. Break up long paragraphs into smaller paragraphs or make lists if appropriate.
5. Circle all pointer or transition words at the beginning of paragraphs. Do you have too few or too many? Are there places where you need more variety?
6. Check to see that attachments and exhibits are identified in the text of the document.
7. Now, look at the document; does it look neat, logical, accessible, and consistently formatted?

Sentences
---

1. After you have made any necessary organizational changes, go back through and underline conjunctions.
2. Try combining short simple sentences into compound or complex sentences and breaking long sentences into shorter ones.
3. Cut out prepositional idioms and other wordy expressions.
4. Check for lack of parallel structure and misplaced or dangling modifiers (note each use of an introductory participial phrase such as "having finished" to be sure that the first noun in the next clause can perform the action described).
5. Highlight each "this" and "it" to make sure your reference is clear.
6. Mark "to be" constructions to see if you can substitute a strong active verb. If you find passive voice constructions, make sure that they are necessary.

Mechanics
---

1. Check for comma splices, run-ons, and fragments. Underlining the conjunctions should help you find sentence errors.
2. Note use of punctuation marks, such as dashes, colons, commas, question marks.
3. Next, proofread the entire document, looking for typos, spelling, and diction.
4. Finally, proofread the document backwards to catch typos and spelling errors. Actually start at the end of the page and sentence and work your way to the beginning. When we proof our own work, we tend to read what we think we have written instead of what is actually on the page. By reading backwards, your eye is forced to look at each word.

The following provides a few final reminders on proofreading:

1. Do not proofread as you write. Proofread after you think you are finished.
2. Try to put some time between when you write something and when you proof it.
3. Know what errors you tend to make or overlook, and watch for them in particular.
4. Watch for common trouble spots, such as transposed letters, confused words, pronoun/antecedent disagreement, dangling modifiers, and misused apostrophes.

Even though the *D-S-M* approach to editing your work takes some time, try it, following the steps in order. Soon, you will find that it becomes second nature and won't take more time than any method of editing that you have used before.

MAKING COMPUTER TOOLS WORK FOR YOU

Word processing programs have made creating documents much easier, but they have also caused some problems that deserve mention:

1. Jumping into the writing of a document without adequate planning.
2. Seeing only the screen version, causing us to lose sight of the document as a whole.
3. Relying too much on spell checkers when they can catch only some of the mistakes.
4. Depending on grammar checkers when they are extremely limited in what they can correct.
5. Proofreading from the screen, thus missing many typos and other errors.
6. Moving words and phrases around easily, causing us to leave in extra words and omit necessary ones.

If you are aware of the possible problems and follow the guidelines below, you can make the computer work for you and use it to make your writing more efficient and effective.

1. When you use the computer to perform your idea generation, recognize that what you enter at this brainstorming stage seldom qualifies as a final version ready for your audience because it will probably lack coherence or clear organization. You should not let the desire to get it just right or to organize the ideas at this stage slow down the composition. Use the computer instead to overcome writer's block and get ideas down quickly; then, go back through and organize them.
2. Take advantage of features such as word search to look for common redundancies, wordy expressions, unclear references with "this" and "that," or words you may tend to misuse, such as "affect."
3. Experiment with different formatting to see what makes your document more accessible and readable. For letters and basic documents, Microsoft Word has templates that you can use. However, the spacing and text font selected are not always the most effective. Thus, you may want to do your own formatting, perhaps postponing it until after you have entered all of your text.
4. Recognize the limitations of spell checkers, but always run them to catch careless errors; just do not expect the spell checker to find all mistakes. It will not catch "there" and "their," for instance.
5. Also, be wary of style/grammar checkers. The English language is too complex and irregular for a style/grammar checker to recognize what is right or wrong in many cases. For instance, style checkers often label past tense sentences as passive voice. Thus, unless you know grammar rules and style best practices well enough to determine when the style/grammar checker is incorrect, it can be more dangerous to use one than not. In fact, in addition to missing many major errors, these checkers tend to add errors. You should only rely on a grammar checker to highlight possible mistakes, and you must know what to follow and what to ignore; otherwise, you will add more mistakes than you will correct.
6. Do the final proofreading from a hard copy, not on the computer screen.

When possible, you might want to have someone else look over your work to provide the "fresh eye" that leaders sometimes need, so allow time not only for them to read the document but for you to correct it if necessary. Remember that audiences will connect you to what they see written, and while most audiences may overlook an occasional slipup, errors in the use of language can harm you and your company.

In conclusion, this chapter has provided instruction in creating a positive ethos through the use of leadership language. You need to develop a confident style and reflect an appropriate tone in all that you write and say. You need to be concise and ensure that your language is clear, crisp, and meaningful. You need to avoid careless grammatical and usage errors. As a leader, you manage meaning for those who follow you by the words you select and how you put those words together to create sentences. The more control you have over the use of language, the greater your influence and your ability to lead.

Exercise 3.1: Passive Voice

Try your hand at recognizing and changing the passive voice constructions in the following sentences. First, underline each passive voice construction; then, rewrite the sentence making it active. Be prepared to discuss why the passive might be the better choice in some of the sentences.

1. An order for 5000 T-shirts was placed by the MBA Student Association.
2. Requests for class transfers will be accommodated if the request is made in person, the receipt of payment for the class is shown, and a $1 processing fee is paid.
3. Data were selectively collected to allow computation of the unique ratios utilized by "corporate raiders" in assessing a buyout candidate.
4. "The coming of the British has been observed!" (Paul Revere)
5. Detailed information on filling out the form is presented forthwith.
6. It has been decided that your proposal does not follow the RFP guidelines as outlined and, therefore, it must be rejected.
7. To implement the policy, a memorandum will be issued to all management personnel in my division.

Exercise 3.2: Conciseness

Eliminate the unnecessary words in the following sentences:

1. We are in receipt of your expense report, but due to the fact that it contains errors, we need to discuss it with you as soon as possible.
2. Per your e-mail, we are sending you the report in regard to our analysis of the Patrick Co. reengineering project.
3. Please be advised that as of January 10, 2006, we will no longer authorize work on the Javia account.
4. To ensure that the optional conclusions will be drawn, it is absolutely essential for you to ensure the analysts are given any and all data that are necessary for effective completion of the analysis assigned to them to complete.

Exercise 3.3: Positive Messages

Rewrite the following sentences to make the message positive:

1. Please don't waste ink and paper. Don't print PowerPoint in anything but Pure Black and White format.
2. I cannot meet with you before Monday to discuss the report, so you should not wait for my approval to create the final version.
3. We are not hiring any new employees until the next quarter earnings are available. Please do not contact us until then.
4. I don't think it will be too much trouble to change the policy as long as no one disagrees with the changes.
5. Our market presence was weak internationally, so we have launched a new marketing campaign in Bolivia, Italy, and India.
6. Our refineries do not release dangerous particles into the air.

Exercise 3.4: Parallelism

Rewrite the following sentences to make them parallel:

1. Highland Services offers friendly, fast responses to all customers, our technicians are professional, and lowest cost is our goal.
2. To persuade your audience, you must:
   - Consider the audience's motivation.
   - Include your bottom line message early.
   - The strongest arguments should come first.
   - Key points summarized at the conclusion.
3. The team gave the following reasons for not completing the business plan on time:
   - Not enough time.
   - Computer problems.
   - They lacked the necessary data.

Exercise 3.5: Clarity and Conciseness

See how much you can cut and how much clearer you can make the following excerpt from a report on how managers can motivate their employees. Your goal should be to capture the meaning in as few words as possible. You will probably do best if you step back and read the whole numbered passage as a unit rather than getting caught up in the words and sentences.

1. Intrinsic, indigenous motivation comes from job enrichment rather than job enlargement. Increasing the volume or amount of work done does not motivate. A manager can motivate through increasing the quality of the work experience, if the conditions are such that for more recognition and more opportunities for advancement are provided.
2. Enriching jobs takes more effort from managers than enlarging jobs. There are some cases in which a manager may feel that she cannot think of any ways to enrich the job. One strategy for a manager to follow is that of training a person as if they were training their own replacement. This enriches the job of the subordinate due to the fact that it frees the manager for more personal advancement, in the eyes of the firm's directors.

3. When managing technical workers, the manager must make sure the enrichment is in a direction that is right for both the person and the firm. Anyone can get bored doing the same thing repeatedly over and over again. Allowing a worker to learn new skills and improve abilities is one way to motivate without promoting them in the firm. It is an established fact that some technical types are happy performing the difficult technical tasks. A manager must not force a happy, hardworking chip designer into being a poor, dissatisfied manager. Similarly, motivation strategies should be planned with the best interests of the firm in mind. In the long run, new activities undertaken must be of more value to the firm than the old activities they replace.

4. Management is sometimes defined as providing the tools for the workers to use to do their jobs. This is especially true with technical workers, who often have a high competency motivation. The workers know how to do their jobs, and want to do them if properly motivated. Management of a well-motivated group is not so much management of activities as it is leadership, as described in "Let's Get Rid of Management" from the *The Wall Street Journal*.

Exercise 3.6: Usage and Mechanics

The following paragraph contains usage and mechanical errors. Correct the errors in the space provided within the passage. Sentences may contain more than one error or none.

(1) Group leaders must prepare the program agendum and should distribute it at least several days before the meeting. (2) They should also ensure that the group have a satisfactory place to meet. (3) A designated conference room or a suitable substitute. (4) If the meeting is a formal conference and has a number of people which are not acquainted leaders should place name cards on the table in front of each persons chair. (5) Having started the meeting, name cards make discussion easier. (6) Once the meeting has started, discussion leaders must keep it moving. (7) Each of the members have to assume the same responsibility. (8) A group sometimes drifts off course into trivial and unrelated matters, therefore, leaders must guide them back to the central problem. (9) Though leaders must have kept the group process moving, they must often be careful about revealing their own position. (10) This has been of great importance to my colleagues and I. (11) We recognize that a high status person for example a company president, can cut off discussion by revealing their own view to clearly.

Exercise 3.7: Use of Language Overall

After you have read the following letter from Mr. Thompson, answer the questions below Note: Again, this is a letter that was actually sent.

Questions

1. How do you like the way the letter looks—letterhead, formatting, and the like?
2. Does the appearance of the letter influence your response to the letter? How?
3. What mistakes in usage do you notice?
4. Are there any expressions that Mr. Thompson uses that bother you in particular? What are they, and why do you they bother you?
5. How do you feel about Mr. Thompson? Do you like him or not? Do you trust him? Why or why not?
6. What would you change about the way the letter is written?

Executive Consultants, Inc.
*"Where True consultants Meet
Worthy Client's Needs"*

August 29, 2002

Mr. Robert Browning, General Partner
Robertson and Co.
2020 Westheimer, Suite 250
Houston, Texas 77025

Dear Robert:

We're in receipt of your good letter of July 20, 1090, and it's good to hear from you again... Good to learn that you're doing well. As for myself, still trying desperately to 'Catch-up' after having returned this past Monday, from a very enjoyable vacation. All this past week has been devoted to 'Wading thru papers', which I am sure you fully understand...

The purpose of our letter to you today is to get your response as to the 'Common-denominators' 'which are prevalent in the acquisitions you've made thus far, in relationship to the types of situations you are desirous of pursuing at this time...

I am seeking to 'Get a handle' on the main points of your acquisition thrust in order that we may approach your needs more intelligently, and therefore ultimately aid/be beneficial and/or instrumental with such needs...

Look to hear from you with this written documentation in order that we PRESS ON in your behalf...

I'm out of here for the entire week of 20th for NCN in Chicago, and look to hear from you as soon as possible...

Robert, that's the news from the Thompson Tower.

With the Best of Regards, I remain

Very truly yours,
Charles J. Thompson, Jr., President

CJT/ms

*P.O. Box 44296, Houston, Texas 77005
Phone 713-562-7471 Fax 713-733-1234*

Notes

1. Fairhurst, G., & Sarr, R. (1996). *The Art of Framing: Managing the Language of Leadership*. San Francisco: Jossey-Bass.

2. Strunk, W., Jr., & White, E. B. (1959). *The Elements of Style*. New York: Macmillan, p. 53.

3. Petzinger, T., Jr. (1987). *Oil & Honor: The Texaco-Pennzoil Wars*. New York: Berkley Books, pp. 271–272.

4. Beason, L. (2001). Ethos and error: How business people react to errors. *College Composition and Communication* 53:1 (September), pp. 33–64.

5. Beason (2001).

6. Beason (2001), pp. 56–57.

7. Leonard, D., & Gilsdorf, J. (2001). Big stuff, little stuff: A decennial measurement of executives' and academics' reactions to questionable usage elements. *Journal of Business Communication* 38 (4), p. 440.

8. Hairston, M. (1981). Not all errors are created equal: Nonacademic readers in the professions respond to lapses in usage. *College English* 43, pp. 794–806. Results based on a survey of 101 professional people, asking them what usage and mechanical errors bothered them the most. Leonard, D., & Gilsdorf, J. (1990). Language in change: Academics' and executives' perceptions of usage errors. *The Journal of Business Communication* 27, pp. 137–158. Results based on a survey of 133 executive vice presidents and 200 Association for Business Communication members. In 2000, Leonard and Gilsdorf repeated their survey, but they changed the format slightly. Instead of the categories of lapses used above, they used a scale ranging from "most distracting" to "least distracting." The survey respondents totaled 64 executives and 130 academics. They found that the usage errors that "distracted" both the executives and the academics were very similar to those that they had found in their 1990 survey. They also found very little difference between the two groups.

9. Ravenel, W. B., III. (1959). *English Reference Book*. Alexandria, VA: Newell-Cole Company, p. 143. With added punctuation, the passage reads as follows:

    That, that is, is. That, that is not, is not. That, that is not, is not that, that is. That, that is, is not that, that is not. Is not that it? It is.

For similar punctuation challenges, see Barrett, D. J. (1986). From "Thinking Man" to "Man Thinking": Exercises requiring problem-solving skills. *Activities to Promote Critical Thinking*. Urbana, IL: National Council of Teachers of English.

Chapter **Four**

Developing and Delivering Leadership Presentations

A speech or talk should be the oral projection of your personality, experience, and ideas.

James C. Humes, *The Sir Winston Method: The Five Secrets of Speaking the Language of Leadership*

A speech is like a symphony. It can have three movements, but it must have one dominant melody.

Sir Winston Churchill

Chapter Objectives

In this chapter, you will learn to do the following:

- Plan your presentation, including developing a communication strategy.
- Prepare a presentation to achieve the greatest impact.
- Present effectively and with greater confidence.

The leader's skills are most visible to others when speaking, whether informally, with a few people around a conference room table, or formally, standing before a large group delivering a prepared presentation. Much of the 70 to 90 percent of ✓ their time that managers spend communicating is spent in conversations or in presenting, either talking to others one-on-one or speaking in groups or to groups. According to Eccles and Nohria in their book *Beyond the Hype: Rediscovering the Essence of Management* (1992), "Through their speeches and presentations, managers establish definitions and meaning for their own actions and give others a sense of what the organization is about, where it is at, and what it is up to."[1] As managers move higher in the organization, their pronouncements become even more public and they spend greater amounts of time engaged in public speaking, whether internally to their employees or externally to the community. Leaders must master

EXHIBIT 4.1
The Three "P's" Approach to Presentation Development and Delivery

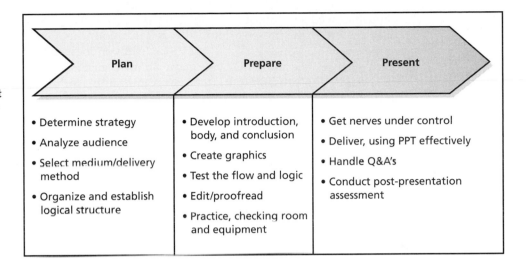

Plan	Prepare	Present
• Determine strategy	• Develop introduction, body, and conclusion	• Get nerves under control
• Analyze audience	• Create graphics	• Deliver, using PPT effectively
• Select medium/delivery method	• Test the flow and logic	• Handle Q&A's
• Organize and establish logical structure	• Edit/proofread	• Conduct post-presentation assessment
	• Practice, checking room and equipment	

public speaking, becoming comfortable and confident in all kinds of presentation situations so that they project a positive ethos for themselves and their companies.

This chapter applies the tools and techniques of previous chapters—determining the strategy, structuring communication coherently, and using language effectively—to the art of public speaking. The chapter will take you through each of the action steps in the Three "P" process: planning, preparing, and presenting (Exhibit 4.1). The process provides an approach to developing presentations that will help you move through each step strategically so that you can deliver any type of presentation with confidence.

PLANNING YOUR PRESENTATION

In the planning phase of developing your presentation, you need to (1) determine your strategy, (2) analyze your audience, (3) select the medium and delivery method, and (4) organize and establish your logical structure.

Determining Your Strategy

Just as you clarify your purpose to write effectively, you must define the purpose of your presentation clearly and specifically and develop a communication strategy using the communication strategy framework: context, messages, spokesperson, media/forum, timing, and audience (Exhibit 1.3). In presenting, as in writing, you first need to consider the context for your presentation. What is most important about what is going on in your company or industry or even the world that will be first in the minds of your audience? There might be an event or something happening to which you might want to refer to help frame your presentation, or you might need to establish some background for your presentation to provide the context that the audience needs to understand your purpose. The more you can relate your presentation to what is on the mind of the audience, the more easily you will be able to garner their attention.

You also need to establish a clearly defined purpose. What is most important for you to achieve in the presentation? What is it that you want your audience to do in response to what you say? These questions lead you logically into the analysis of your audience. The more that you know about your audience, the more at ease you should be in presenting to them. At a minimum, for any presentation, you should be able to answer the following questions:

1. What is my primary purpose in delivering this presentation to this audience?
2. Who is my primary audience? Will there be secondary audiences affected by what I say?
3. What is motivating the audience to attend and how do I motivate them to listen to me?
4. What do I expect the audience to do as a result of hearing my presentation?
5. How do I expect them to feel?

You will also want to consider the timing of the presentation and determine if feedback is possible and, if so, how best to obtain it. You should be able to tell from the audience's reaction to your presentation how they have received your message, but obtaining more structured feedback may be important as well. Of course, the purpose of your presentation will shape the feedback. If, for example, you are presenting the quarterly performance to the board, they will probably tell you what they think while you are presenting, and you will be able to discern their response by the questions they will ask you during and after the presentation. If you are presenting to analysts, they too will tell you how they feel about what you have said by their questions, and then you will see if you have succeeded in delivering your message by what they write. If, on the other hand, you are delivering a presentation to a large group at a professional meeting, the only feedback you receive might be the expressions on the faces of the listeners.

Selecting the Medium and the Delivery Method

In developing a strategy for a presentation, you will be able to choose from several options for the medium and the delivery method. Recognizing the advantages and disadvantages of each method will help you select the right one for each situation (Exhibit 4.2). All of the presentation delivery methods compared here are assumed to be extemporaneous, a prepared presentation spoken without notes or text. It is very rare in business situations to deliver a memorized presentation or to read a prepared speech, although occasionally you will see presenters using teleprompters at large trade shows and conventions.

The three common types of presentations found in business today—the round-table, the stand-up presentation, and the impromptu—are discussed here.

Round-Table Presentations

The round-table presentation method has become increasingly popular for business settings. Using this delivery method, you sit at the table with your audience and deliver a prepared document instead of standing up in front of your audience to deliver the presentation. The typical round-table is an interactive exchange between the presenter and the audience. Round-table presentations encourage discussion and tend to

EXHIBIT 4.2   Pros and Cons of Each Delivery Method for Oral Communication

Delivery Method	Advantages	Disadvantages
Stand-Up without Visuals	Allows flexibility in delivery of content Makes you appear confident Makes it easier to connect with audience and establish rapport	Requires careful preparation and comfort with content Means keeping close track of timing, particularly if questions are allowed
Round-Table	Allows for interactive discussion With printed presentation pack, appeals to auditory and visual audiences Makes it easier to establish real contact with audience	Makes it more difficult to control flow of discussion Seems more informal than stand-up presentation Presents some delivery challenges
Stand-Up with Computer Projection	Allows some flexibility of delivery Provides visuals to support your messages Appeals to both auditory and visual audience preferences	Calls for comfort with the technology and creates dependence on it Requires backup plan Makes it harder to keep audience focused on you
Stand-Up with Overheads	Allows some flexibility of delivery Provides visuals to support your messages Appeals to both auditory and visual audience preferences	Seems old-fashioned Limits what you can do with graphics Poses some potential technical problems
Stand-Up with Flip Charts/White Boards	Offers complete flexibility Encourages discussion Eliminates technical problems Allows easy recording of audience contributions	Takes presenter away from audience when writing on boards Makes presenter appear less prepared May be difficult to read
Videoconferencing	Allows interaction across time and space With chart pack, can appeal to auditory and visual audiences	Delays in voice transmission cause some distraction Limits what you can do with visual aids Makes it difficult to establish rapport Poses potential technical problems
Phone Conferencing (Conference Call)	Allows interaction across time and space	Limits what you can do with visual aids Makes it difficult to build rapport Causes loss of body language cues

be less formal than stand-up presentations, although they require as much or even more preparation on the part of the presenter. You need to feel so comfortable with the content that the audience's questions, interruptions, or desire to jump to the end of the document do not throw you off course. Also, you must be very familiar with the content on each page so that you do not need to look down at it too much.

You should select the round-table approach any time you want to achieve one of the following:

1. Encourage an informal, interactive discussion.
2. Receive input from audience members.

3. Build consensus or gain agreement on conclusions or recommendations.
4. Check the accuracy of facts or identify sources of missing facts.
5. Surface and resolve major issues.
6. Present a lot of information in a short amount of time.

Delivering a Round-Table Presentation

Most of the principles that apply to stand-up presentations also apply to round-table discussions, but round-table presentations differ in the handling of the materials and in delivery:

1. You hand out the presentation pack to the group before you start, which means you will need to control the situation by guiding the audience through the pack and by keeping them focused on the page you want to discuss.
2. Since the audience has a printed copy of the presentation in front of them, you can usually place more information on a page than you would with an overhead or computer projected presentation, although you should still be careful not to overcrowd your page.

Your delivery should follow the same guidelines for any good presentation; however, you need to be even more aware of the importance of establishing and maintaining eye contact. It is very easy when sitting at a table with a document in front of you to look down instead of up, so you need to make sure you are so well prepared that you do not need to look down at the page after turning to it. You should be looking up and at your audience most of the time.

When you deliver a round-table presentation, the following guidelines will help you control the pace and flow of the discussion:

1. Direct your audience to the specific page.
2. State the major message of the exhibit.
3. Explain any legends or symbols.
4. Guide the audience through any diagrams or graphs.
5. Allow the audience time to scan the page.
6. Be flexible and responsive to the discussion.
7. Provide transition before turning to the next page.
8. Be sensitive to body language.

Whenever you deliver a round-table presentation, be very careful to give your audience enough time to skim the page and be alert to their body language. If they need time to think about what you have given them, do not feel that you must keep talking: silence is okay. Finally, remember that you want to encourage discussion, so welcome questions as you present.

Formatting a Round-Table Presentation Handout

The round-table presentation pages resemble the slides in a stand-up presentation except for the following:

1. The pages are numbered; otherwise, you will not easily be able to tell people which page you are discussing.

2. The page may contain more information than a slide for a stand-up presentation.

3. A smaller font is appropriate.

You may elect to use a chart pack with only the graphs included, but it is usually better to create an entire presentation, with cover page, agenda, and appropriate text, as well as the graphs since people often pick up the packs without having the opportunity to hear the presentation. The round-table presentation pack should be complete enough that anyone picking it up will understand your main messages. Exhibit 4.3 demonstrates selected pages from a typical round-table presentation pack.

EXHIBIT 4.3 Typical Round-Table Presentation Pack

**Establishing a Marketing Plan
for Brown & Peterson**

Round-Table Discussion Proposal
Presented by
L&B Consulting Firm

September 29, 2005

Today's Discussion

❐ Our understanding of the current situation

❐ Study objectives and proposed approach

❐ Suggested team structure and our capabilities

❐ Outstanding questions and next steps

2

**Our Understanding of Your
Current Situation**

❐ Offices in Houston; Dallas; Los Angeles; London; Paris

❐ Three primary practices: litigation, business, and government

❐ Specializing in areas such as energy, taxation, labor and employment, corporate, real estate, and finance

❐ Brown & Peterson (B&P), along with its peers, is caught in the transition in the legal profession from no marketing or self-promotion to need to establish marketing campaign and public profile

3

**The Largest Law
Firms by Revenue**

$ Millions

Source: *Lawyer Reports*, July 7, 2005.

4

(continued)

EXHIBIT 4.3 **Typical Round-Table Presentation Pack** (continued)

Success factors

- ❑ Total revenue
- ❑ Number of attorneys
- ❑ Courtroom wins
- ❑ Recognition for speaking and writing
- ❑ Membership on law school faculties
- ❑ Bar pass rates and percentile rankings
- ❑ Ability to attract and retain top recruits

How do you leverage your critical success factors to build corporate reputation?

5

Project Objectives

- ❑ Obtain a better understanding of B&P's competitive market
- ❑ Establish profile of B&P's current image, reputation, and market perception
- ❑ Determine the firm's value proposition, other key messages, and target audiences
- ❑ Develop a marketing communication plan and materials to reach target audiences
- ❑ Define ongoing communication needs

Establish and maintain a highly respected, recognizable public image for B&P

6

Summary of Proposed Approach

Areas of focus	Competitive analysis	Brand identity/image research	Niche capability building	Ongoing communication
Action items	• Identify competitors • Establish benchmarking criteria • Perform basic competitive research • Develop survey • Conduct surveys • Assess promotional materials	• Profile current image/ market perception • Identify gaps • Determine value proposition and messages • Identify audiences	• Define pra-ctice area capabilities • Create materials to illustrate niche capabilities • Identify niche audiences	• Determine communication marketing needs • Link plan with other initiatives • Define individual communication responsibilities • Establish ongoing communications program
		• Develop communication plan • Create marketing materials • Establish media campaign • Identify other public relations opportunities		
Timing:	October–November	December–February		February–March

10

Potential Team Structure and Responsibilities

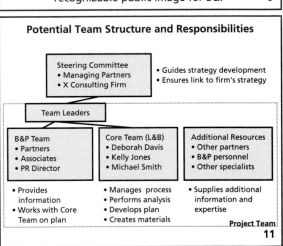

Steering Committee
- Managing Partners
- X Consulting Firm

• Guides strategy development
• Ensures link to firm's strategy

Team Leaders

B&P Team
- Partners
- Associates
- PR Director

Core Team (L&B)
- Deborah Davis
- Kelly Jones
- Michael Smith

Additional Resources
- Other partners
- B&P personnel
- Other specialists

• Provides information
• Works with Core Team on plan

• Manages process
• Performs analysis
• Develops plan
• Creates materials

• Supplies additional information and expertise

Project Team

11

Questions

- ❑ Will we have access to previous relevant research, such as the X Consulting Firm findings?
- ❑ How accessible will partners and associates be for interviews and fact finding research?
- ❑ Will B&P be able to free up resources to participate in team problem solving?
- ❑ How much in the way of promotional materials has already been completed?
- ❑ What will a successful strategic corporate image campaign look like in your eyes?

14

Immediate Next Steps

- ❑ Determine B&P's success factors
- ❑ Establish scope of competitive analysis and benchmarking
- ❑ Identify target audiences
- ❑ Develop interview guides and targets
- ❑ Collect all previous research and complete gathering of promotional materials
- ❑ Assemble the B&P team
- ❑ Formally launch the engagement

15

Stand-Up Extemporaneous Presentations

One of the most popular delivery methods for business presentations is still the stand-up extemporaneous presentation. It is the most difficult but also the most effective form of presentation if structured and delivered correctly. Extemporaneous presentations offer three major advantages over any other method. They allow you to

1. Maintain eye contact and rapport with your audience.
2. Make adjustments based on the audience's response.
3. Appear confident and knowledgeable.

You should strive to deliver your extemporaneous presentation without relying on external promptings, such as reading from your computer screen or from notes. You should resist the temptation to memorize the presentation or to write everything down because if you do, you will sound unnatural and will be unable to adjust easily should you need to vary the presentation. On the other hand, you will probably want to resist the other extreme of not having any notes because no matter how experienced you are, you may need to refer to them for supporting information or numbers.

In most presentation settings today, you will be able to have your laptop computer screen in front of you with the audience seeing a projected presentation on a large screen behind you. This arrangement allows you to face your audience but glance at the large screen to ensure the correct slide is being projected. You do not want to rely on your laptop screen, however, since doing so will decrease your eye contact with your audience and make you appear less confident. If a laptop or similar smaller computer screen is not available for you to see but you have a podium or table nearby, you will probably want to print out your presentation in handout version of six slides per page. That way you can glance down to see where you are, yet not have to turn the page each time you change slides.

Impromptu Presentations

Many of the presentations you will deliver will be impromptu, which means you are called on to deliver them without much, if any, warning. For example, you may find yourself in the elevator with a superior who asks how the project you are leading is coming along. This is the classic "elevator speech," in which you only have the time the elevator takes to go between floors to answer the question. You can prepare for these kinds of encounters by making frequent mental or written notes of the project status. Essentially, you prepare yourself for the elevator speech by anticipating that it will occur and periodically formulating the key message— the "so what?"—to convey the status of the project or analysis you are doing.

Of course, at times, you are called on to speak impromptu without benefit of any preplanning or strategizing. In those cases, the following techniques will help you perform more effectively:

1. Do not rush into speaking. Take a deep breath and gather your thoughts. A few seconds of silence will not bother anyone.
2. If appropriate, start by giving your name or by saying something informal to break the ice, such as a positive comment about the surroundings or the meal.

3. If appropriate, refer to something that a previous speaker said, but again be positive.
4. Think very simply of the primary message you want to deliver and isolate only a couple of supporting topics.
5. State your message and your supporting topics before you dive into details, and then come back at the end and repeat the main points.

You should practice impromptu speaking frequently even if it means creating a bunch of topics, putting them in a hat, and drawing one out daily in your own office or at home (see the impromptu exercise at the end of this chapter for a few topics to get you started).

Establishing a Logical and Effective Presentation Structure

The organization or structure of a presentation proceeds from the needs and interests of the audience, your purpose, and the demands of the subject matter. When you start to outline or map out your presentation, you will refer first to the analysis of your audience to determine the most effective structure. Do you want to start with your recommendation and then present the data to support it (direct approach), or do you want to present the facts and lead to the conclusion (indirect approach)? In most cases, it works best to state the conclusions or recommendations first and then provide the supporting data; however, if your audience will be resistant to your conclusions or recommendations, then you may want to build your argument and present the evidence first. Think carefully about which pattern will work best with this audience. Then, consider the nature of your subject matter and your overall purpose to develop a logical structure for the body of your presentation that will appeal most effectively to your audience.

Also, if you are presenting on a controversial topic and some audience members are opposed to your view or approach, you should prepare your refutation and place it either in the body of the presentation or even at the beginning. To ignore the opposition completely may cause some to question your objectivity and the validity of your analysis. Although it is usually better to work the refutation into the body, if you know your audience may be so focused on it that they will not listen to you, you may want to address it in your opening. You will want to be careful not to spend too much time on the refutation though, since doing so could weaken your own argument.

As you map out your preliminary plans for the organization of the presentation, remember that in a speech the audience cannot go back and look at the preceding message as they might in a document. You thus need to make sure that each point is logically related to the ideas that precede it and the information that follows, and that you use adequate, even obvious, transitions from point to point. Also, use repetition more than you would in writing, particularly in the body and conclusion since an audience's memory is short and attention span fleeting.

When creating and organizing a presentation as a team, you should establish the format first, and since most presentations routinely use PowerPoint templates, you should select one that meets your needs. In fact, the team may want to create a ghost pack (a pack that establishes the format and contains the slides they think they are going to use, even if only an idea exists at this point). With a ghost pack, the team can easily assign each section or chart to a specific team member. The storyboard in Chapter 1 serves as an example of a ghost pack (Exhibit 1.11). The ghost pack establishes the format and layout as well as the preliminary outline for the presentation.

PREPARING A PRESENTATION TO ACHIEVE THE GREATEST IMPACT

After you have analyzed your audience, developed your communication strategy, and determined the overall structure, you are ready to start preparing the actual presentation. The preparation consists of developing the introduction, body, and conclusion; creating the graphics; testing the flow and logic; editing and proofreading; and practicing.

Developing the Introduction, Body, and Conclusion

Modern expectations for good presentations have not changed that much from the expectations of the past. What the ancient Greeks taught about the introduction, the body, and the conclusion is as applicable today as then, in fact, maybe even more applicable considering our short attention span and poor listening habits.

Therefore, for almost every presentation, you should follow the traditional rule:

Tell them what you are going to tell them.
Tell them.
Then, tell them what you have told them.

If the presentation is very short, you may be able to avoid repeating your topics at the beginning and the end. For a longer presentation, it is helpful to your audience to hear your messages repeated. Most audiences will pay more attention to the introduction and the conclusion than the middle or body. In a longer presentation, it is important to remind them of your main arguments. You can be sure you will gain the full attention of every listener when you utter the magic words, "And in conclusion."

The Introduction

The introduction to your presentation starts as soon as you stand up and start walking to the podium or front of the room. You will want to take command of yourself and the situation the moment you stand up, and you need to be aware that your posture and the way you carry yourself will affect the audience's perception of you before you even start to speak.

After you have established your presence in front of the room, you will want to arouse interest and create a positive atmosphere for the presentation. You have numerous options for how to start your presentation. You can start with a fact, a quotation, an example, an anecdote, a question, or a reference to the occasion or something else in the context of the presentation. You can start with humor if it is appropriate to the occasion and if you are absolutely sure it will not offend anyone. It is usually better though to tell a humorous anecdote rather than a joke.

What you do not want to do is joke about your subject or apologize for being unprepared; it destroys your credibility and diminishes everything that you say afterward. You should be prepared, or you should not be there. Remember that you are addressing fellow human beings with similar interests and problems who have come to hear you because they expect you to say something meaningful. You want to start quickly, get to the point, and establish a positive relationship with your audience.

You should introduce your overall message and each of your supporting topics. You might say something like, "I am going to cover (1), (2), and (3)." Then, you can discuss each of these supporting points in order and say in the conclusion, "I have covered (1), (2), and (3)." If you used the pyramid principle or wrote out a storyboard, you should have a tight, logical story that flows easily from slide to slide. You can test the presentation logic by creating a one-sentence summary that includes your overall message and supporting topics. If you can create a meaningful, logical sentence, then you probably have a logical story to tell. This story will serve as the guide to the creation of your agenda slide for the presentation.

If you are using visual aids, such as overheads or computer-generated slides, you can use the slides to help cue the audience to the structure and main messages of your presentation. In addition to telling them what you will discuss, you will want to show the audience an agenda or today's discussion slide or, if appropriate for your topic, the framework or model around which your presentation is organized.

The agenda page may be a few bullet points of the main sections of the presentation (note that this agenda should not consist of a list of all of your slides). The agenda page could be a list of topics or it could capture your story, which you will present using a narrative structure. Your first bullet would summarize the current situation, the next one or two would discuss the complication, and the last would suggest a resolution. Even if you do not actually write this story on your agenda page, the audience should at least be able to determine what the story is by looking at your bullet points.

An agenda or setup page should be concise but meaningful. Your agenda pages should not contain a list of your slide topics; such a laundry list suggests a poorly organized presentation. Also, you should avoid using the following as bullet points on your agenda: Introduction, Conclusion, and Questions. These take up space without communicating anything to your audience. Every bullet should capture a "so what?" Exhibit 4.4 shows the dos and don'ts of agenda pages.

EXHIBIT 4.4
Examples of Agenda Pages for a Presentation

How Not to Do an Agenda	How to Do an Agenda
Today's Agenda	**Today's Agenda**
• Introduction • Understanding of current situation • Competitive analysis • Niche capabilities • How you measure your success • Project objectives • Overview of approach • Proposed approach • Team Structure • Next steps • Conclusion • Q&A	• Understanding of current situation • Project objectives and approach • Team structure and our capabilities • Next steps

The Body

The body of the presentation, which usually accounts for 80 percent, should be concise and specifically focused. The effective presenter will follow a storyboard or similar outline or plan, judiciously selecting the main points and being careful not to overwhelm the audience with too much detail. Keep in mind that your audience only wants to know what is relevant to them and, in some cases, what you can do for them. Beware of anything in the presentation to which the audience can say, "so what?" Elaborate each main point with specific examples or explanations accompanied by graphics if appropriate. You should, however, be selective in your use of graphics. Know when they are appropriate and effective and when they are not (see Chapter 5).

Throughout your presentation, provide transitions to lead from one topic to the next and one graphic to the next. Make sure that your presentation is so well organized and logical that when you move from topic *a* to *b*, no one could question why you are doing so. It is usually best to organize a presentation directly, giving the general point (usually your recommendation) first and then the facts to support or illustrate it. However, as discussed previously, the organization depends on your audience analysis and your communication strategy.

The Conclusion

In the conclusion, summarize what you have said by going back over the main points and reinforcing them. If you are using visual aids, you should show the audience a summary slide that highlights your main messages. You may want to bring the agenda slide back at this point. You may also want to make your recommendation if you did not make it in the opening or repeat it if you did. Do not just stop talking or say, "Well, that's all." Also, do not just trail off. Remember, this is your last chance, make the most of it and go out strong. The tone should be just right, and you should work on the conclusion as much or even more than on the introduction and body.

Creating the Graphics

You should plan to use graphics in your presentations. Many people are better able to take in and process information presented visually than orally. Adding graphics to your presentations will help you reach everyone. Further, several categories of information—including quantitative, structural, spatial, and highly complex—can be conveyed more efficiently and effectively in visual rather than auditory form.

You do, however, want to be selective in the use of graphics. Unfortunately, graphics are sometimes overused or misused. The result is a presentation in which the graphics offer more distraction than support, making the presentation appear to be all show and no substance. Since the next chapter discusses when to use graphics, which graphs to use, and how best to design graphics using PowerPoint, the only point to be made here is that you want to use graphics when possible, but you also want to use them with care.

Testing the Flow and Logic

You should take time after planning and preparation and before practicing to ensure your presentation flows smoothly and that it is logical. Test the flow by telling the story of your presentation aloud to yourself and to someone else. Can you tell the story in a couple of minutes? What are your main messages? Do they flow logically from one to the other? You may find after you perform this test that you need to go back and do some reorganizing, but it is worth the time. A presentation has to be clearly logical to your audience or they will not stay with you.

Editing and Proofreading

A presentation should be clear, concise, coherent, correct, and confident. One of the major differences between written and most oral business communication is that more time must be spent in preparing an oral presentation because once it starts, you cannot go back and correct as you can with written copy. If you are using visual aids, you will want to edit them and proofread them very carefully. In the editing process, first look at each slide title and make sure it is meaningful: does it capture the "so what?" of the chart below it? Also, look at how much you might be able to cut from bullets and not lose the meaning. Make them as concise as possible. Finally, proofread each slide carefully. Mistakes are magnified on a slide. You should print out your slides and go over each one, reading from the bottom to the top. Then, project each slide and look at it once more.

Practicing to Facilitate Effective Delivery

Practicing a presentation is often the key to delivering it successfully in front of your audience. You should find a practice method that works for you and make sure that you allow time for it.

Giving the Presentation Out Loud

Just going over your presentation in your head is not sufficient. You must go through your presentation at least twice out loud. Try to re-create the speaking situation as closely as possible, in the scheduled location and with the same equipment. Try to practice at least once in front of a mirror and be sure to speak aloud. Practicing in front of a mirror allows you to see how others see you and gives you a chance to see how well you are establishing eye contact. Better yet, video yourself, or deliver the presentation to friends and listen to their feedback. It is particularly important to set time aside for a group practice if you are delivering a team presentation. Practice is the only way to establish smooth transitions from speaker to speaker and to ensure all sections are complete and coherent.

Checking the Room and Setup

If you are delivering a presentation using overheads or computer projection, it is particularly important to check the room ahead of time if at all possible. You want to be familiar with the equipment and the layout before you present. In some circumstances, it may be possible to adjust the layout or setup to accommodate your specific needs. You should load your presentation onto the computer hard drive and make sure it projects as intended. This test is particularly important because computer projectors often alter the colors of your slides, and you need to see them exactly as they will appear when you present them. Also, you will need to check the size of your font for the particular room. Make sure the person sitting in the very last row can read your bullet points and see your graphics without straining.

Timing

For most business occasions, you will be speaking under a time constraint. You want to obey the time limits. If you are allowed to go overtime, you may finish your talk but irritate your audience. If you are stopped before you finish, just think about what you have lost—the chance to reiterate your main ideas and to end strongly. Also, prepare for the inevitable. Organize your presentation so that you can adjust it if it needs to be shortened. One approach is to build in two or three examples to support each main point and then cut them back to one or two if you see you are short on time. Another approach is to cover the most important points first, but that can lead to an anticlimactic presentation in which you lose your audience toward the end. Audiences tend to be more attentive when they perceive that the speaker is almost finished. Much of what is in the middle is often lost. It is generally best to introduce your main ideas at the front but try to save some of the meat for the end. Practice your presentation with a timer and adhere to the time limit exactly. However, be prepared to make adjustments. When it comes to time limits, be prepared, be flexible, and anticipate the unexpected.

PRESENTING EFFECTIVELY AND WITH GREATER CONFIDENCE

When it comes time to present, you should concentrate on your delivery style, focusing particularly on eye contact, stance, speech, and overall effect. You want to appear comfortable, confident, enthusiastic, and professional. Since much of the success of your presentation will be determined by how your audience perceives you right at the beginning, you should be prepared to establish your expertise and your value to the audience immediately and maintain that positive ethos throughout.

Getting Nerves under Control

Public speaking is often cited as one of humankind's greatest fears, and everyone has advice about how to overcome nervousness when presenting, from practicing some yoga deep-breathing exercises to pretending everyone in the room is naked. Some techniques are more reliable than others. Before the presentation, visualize your success. Sports trainers use this technique to help their athletes, and it works. They teach the athletes to see the moves they are making and imagine themselves serving that ace, making that goal, or hitting that home run. You have to find what works best for you. The most important way to overcome nerves is to be well prepared. If you know your subject, have your story down pat, and are prepared for whatever the situation may throw at you, you will not be as nervous.

Nervousness is not all bad. It releases adrenaline, which catalyzes the energy that usually enhances performance, so a little nervousness is good. Too much, however, could hurt your credibility.

If you suffer from too much nervousness, it may help if you put the presentation into perspective and remember that the audience is human and, most of the time, forgiving. You are the only one who will notice most mistakes (a typical audience hears only a small portion of what a presenter says, and remembers even less). Your attitude will shape the audience's attitude. If you are at ease, they will be at ease.

Try taking a few deep breaths, thinking of something pleasant, and being yourself. It helps if you are able to laugh at yourself. A smile, if the situation is appropriate, will go a long way toward helping you relax and connect with your audience. It relaxes your face muscles and makes you appear more at ease with the audience. If your nervousness makes you forget what you are planning to say while speaking, try "shirttailing," which is repeating what you just said. The audience will think you are doing it for emphasis, and it will trigger the next idea in your head.

Focus on the audience and not on yourself. Find that friendly face (and there will be one) and establish eye contact with him or her. Although you should make sure you look at the rest of the audience as well, keep coming back to the friend. If possible, get into the room ahead of time and start to establish a rapport by chatting with the audience. If you can "get out of yourself" and worry more about the audience, you will not be nervous, and your overall performance will be much more effective. Remember, it is the ability to connect with the audience that makes a great presenter.

Finally, if you find that you cannot get your nerves under control, you may want to try some of the newer virtual reality exposure therapy (VRE), a conditioning technique using software that is being applied to overcome phobias, such as fear of flying, fear of heights, and fear of public speaking. Although VRE is fairly new and only a few tests have been conducted to see how well it will work for public speakers, the early results suggest some success.[2]

Eye Contact

When leaders present, they seem to connect with everyone in the audience. If you are in their audience, you feel as if they are talking to you personally. They do this by looking at different people in the audience for a few seconds and actually establishing eye contact with them. Depending on the cultural expectations, your looking directly in the eyes of as many of your audience members as possible will suggest confidence as well as an interest in them. You do need, however, to be sensitive to cultural differences since some cultures may consider looking someone directly in the eye offensive, in which case your eye contact may need to be glancing and indirect. You want to avoid a rapid movement approach in which you glance quickly from person to person, since it makes you appear unfocused and nervous. Also, you do not want to stay locked on one person too long since it will make that individual uncomfortable. Be aware that every speaker tends to favor one side of the room; therefore, you may need to concentrate on ensuring that you do not neglect half of the people you are addressing.

Good speakers really look at the people in their audiences, not over their heads or out the window. Presentation trainers sometimes advise presenters to look at people's foreheads instead of in their eyes; however, people can tell where you are looking, and by not looking people in the eyes, you are not establishing a connection with them.

Finally, do not look down at your notes or read from them; only glance at them as necessary (although, again, if you are well prepared, you will not need many reminders). Be careful that you only glance at your computer screen briefly as well, and never turn your back to your audience to look at the slide screen.

Stance and Gestures

Your stance and your posture reflect your attitude toward your subject and your audience and reveal your confidence. Someone who has his or her head down with shoulders slumping appears unsure or distracted. To project confidence and establish a positive ethos, you want to stand straight and tall and look out at your audience. Usually, you will want to assume an open stance with your feet shoulder-width apart and your weight evenly distributed. Your goal should be to maintain a comfortable, relaxed stance, appropriate to the situation.

Use your hands as you would in a conversation, although if you tend to move them too much, you may need to be more restrained when presenting. Usually people look and feel most natural if they bend their arms, keeping elbows at their sides. You should avoid pointing or gesturing at your projected slides. Instead, use the features in PowerPoint to highlight the areas of the slide on which you want the audience to focus. If you find yourself in a situation that requires you to point to the screen, you should be careful not to turn your back. Instead, move back even with the screen, face the audience, and gesture to your side. Also, since few people are steady enough to hold laser pointers completely immobile and positioned exactly over what it is they want to highlight, you will be more effective presenting if you do not use one.

If possible and appropriate, it is best to come out from behind a podium. The podium creates a barrier between you and your audience, and establishing a rapport with them will be easier if you remove the barrier. You do not need to stand in one place unless the space in the room is limited or your movement might make your audience uncomfortable. In a large room in particular, you may need to walk toward the audience and maybe even from one side of the room to another to connect with the entire audience. Just be careful that your walking is purposeful and not random pacing.

If you tend to rock excessively and are having trouble breaking the habit, you might try standing in a box or a garbage can, as strange as it may sound, so that you become aware of where your feet are and that you are moving. Tennis coaches sometimes use this technique to teach beginners where to place their feet.

Here are some common problems with stance that you want to avoid:

Common Problems with Stance and Gestures to Avoid

1. Slouching or assuming a similar informal stance more appropriate to the company picnic than the boardroom.
2. Leaning to one side or the other.
3. Pacing up and down or around the room too much.
4. Clasping your hands in front or behind you.
5. Standing with your hands on your hips.
6. Gripping the podium until your knuckles turn white.
7. Gesturing too much or when not appropriate or natural.
8. Fidgeting with keys, pens, a pointer, tie, and the like.
9. Rocking or shifting your feet.
10. Leaning on the podium or sitting on the table.

Few presenters realize exactly what they are doing or how they are moving when they present, so the best way to see what you *actually* do in front of an audience and not what you *think* you do is to have someone video your presentations. You will be amazed at what you do. You may find that you are better than you think. If not, you will certainly be able to see what you are doing wrong or badly so that you can begin the improvement process. If you watch the video without the sound, you will focus more on your movements, and if you play the video in fast-forward, your repeated gestures will be exaggerated, which may help you see them more objectively.

Although you want to develop your own leadership presentation style, you may find it helpful to watch some good presenters. How do they stand? How do they move? What gestures do they use? Try some of their techniques that seem to work particularly well.

Voice and Speech Patterns

Most of your individual speech patterns are established by the time you are five; however, you can make changes if you need to and if you are aware of what you are doing and what you need to change. Common problems occur in articulation, pronunciation, inflection, rhythm, volume, and the use of fillers, such as "uh" or "um." The key to changing your speech patterns is knowing what you do now, and a recording is the best way to find out. If you are working with a video, to hear your speech patterns, you should not watch the video, only listen to it. You may not be aware of how many fillers you use, for example, so listening only and not watching will help you notice. You may even want to count the fillers as they do in Toastmasters.

If you watch leaders present, you will see that they speak clearly so that the audience can understand them. They speak loud enough for the people in the back of the room to hear them. They pause between sentences and use few, if any, fillers. They sound confident, which comes from making statements and avoiding "up-speak," an inflection which occurs if you emphasize the last word of a sentence as you do when asking a question.

Try to observe the following guidelines for the vocal qualities of your delivery:

1. Speak to the last row in your audience, but raise the volume naturally. If you find you must strain to be heard, then you need to use a microphone.
2. Articulate clearly, making sure you pronounce all important syllables, particularly the last.
3. Do not talk too fast. Build in pauses between main ideas and be careful not to run ideas together.
4. Vary your rhythm and pitch appropriately so that you do not sound monotone. Your voice should reflect the enthusiasm you feel for the topic and the energy that generates. Relaxing your face muscles and smiling will often help.
5. Know the words you tend to stumble over and either avoid them or practice them until you can say them perfectly ten times in a row.

As a leader, your ability to present will be an important part of your job. To ensure you are effective, you probably will want to video one of your presentations and observe closely how you look and sound. Seeing and hearing yourself on a video recording is the best way to become aware of bad habits or mistakes in delivery.

Delivering Effectively with Visual Aids

The good techniques for delivery using PowerPoint, overheads, or other visual aids vary little from delivering a presentation without aids. You want the audience to focus on you, so your goal should be to make the handling of your visual aids as unobtrusive as possible. In particular, you need to be aware of your eye contact, stance, voice, transitions, and timing. In addition, you need to test the projection or display equipment and any other technology (for example, remote mice, speakers, microphones) ahead of time.

Eye Contact

The need to maintain continuous eye contact becomes a problem for presenters who are accustomed to looking at the projection or laptop screen. You should look at your audience, not back at the projection screen or down at your laptop. You should seldom look back, although you may want to glance at the screen occasionally to ensure the right slide is up if you do not have a monitor in front of you. Your goal should be to maintain your eye contact with your audience at all times. If you turn your back, you lose this contact and also your voice will be less audible since you will be projecting at the screen instead of out toward the audience. In most presentations, your delivery should proceed as if there were no projected images behind you or in front of you.

Stance

You should assume a firm stance and position yourself so that you are facing forward and have easy access to whatever device you are using to change your slides. Be sure you do not block the screen from the view of the audience in any part of the room. There is no one best place to stand since it will depend on the layout of the room. In the interests of good rapport, you should position yourself as close to your audience as possible and not next to the screen, which is usually located too far from the audience.

Voice

You should be careful to maintain your volume. Presenters have a tendency to let their voices fade when they move to change slides. You should finish your thought on the current slide and complete your introduction to your next slide; then, stop talking for a second and change to the slide you have just introduced. Volume goes along with eye contact. If you maintain strong eye contact, you will also maintain the right volume of sound; it is when you look away from the audience that you are most likely to drop your volume.

Transition

You want to make the transition from slide to slide as seamless as possible. One technique is to introduce each slide before you show it. Most presenters wait for the slide to appear and then start talking about it almost as if they do not know what is coming up until they see it. For a much more effective transition, introduce the topic, which should be the "so what?" or main message, of the next slide before it appears. Displaying your slide only after you have introduced it will help make you appear more confident and your presentation flow more smoothly.

Timing

Practice with your slides to ensure you do not have too many for your allotted time. The rule of thumb is to allow at least two to three minutes per slide. Give your audience time to absorb complex graphic information and be prepared to walk your audience through it if necessary. Also, do not use the automatic timing in PowerPoint; it is next to impossible to make it match exactly your timing as you present. Having the slides advance ahead of you or even behind you will be distracting to you and to your audience.

Technology

If possible, check the technology and the room in advance. You want to make sure you know how to use it and that everything is working. You also want to see how your presentation projects. Are the colors as you intend? Are the font sizes large enough for the audience to see all text from the back of the room? You may find that the projector distorts your colors and you need to adjust them. You will want to see where the screen, the projector, and the computer are positioned so that you will know where to stand to establish eye contact and the best rapport with your audience. Also, you will probably want to load your presentation onto the computer you are using instead of running it from a CD.

Even if all the technology checks out, you will want to come prepared in case technical problems occur and bring handouts or overheads or both as a backup. Never rely on computer projection to work flawlessly. It may falter in some way or fail entirely. You need to be prepared to handle any situation.

Handling Q&A

It is not unusual for presenters to spend more time preparing for the question and answer session than for the presentation itself. Effective handling of Q&A requires thorough preparation, careful listening, and the humility to say, "I do not know, but I will find out for you." You control the presentation content, but you never know what questioners might ask you. At that now famous analyst conference call shortly before Enron collapsed, Jeff Skilling, then Enron's CEO, delivered his prepared remarks effectively; but when faced with hostile questions, he lost his poise and called one persistent questioner an obscene, derogatory name.

Leaders manage Q&A sessions by being prepared, even overprepared, particularly for the difficult questions. They anticipate all questions and prepare answers just in case. They also practice staying in control of the topics and of themselves. When you are presenting with a team, all participants should work out a plan, stipulating who will answer which types of questions. If the presentation is formal, team members should position themselves at the end of the presentation to indicate which members are ready to answer the questions. During the Q&A session, the following tips will help you better manage your audience:

Tips for Handling the Q&A Session

---

1. Determine and announce the timing of questions before starting your presentation.
2. Listen very carefully to the question.
3. Repeat the question or paraphrase it for the sake of ensuring you understand it and so that your audience can hear it. This also provides you some time to formulate an answer.
4. Keep your answer short and simple: answer the specific question, then stop. Avoid talking too long or going off on a tangent.
5. Do not try to bluff your way through an answer. It is better to say very politely, "I am not sure I have an answer for that question at the moment, but I will find out for you."
6. Move away from any questioner who tries to isolate you in a two-way conversation so that you break eye contact with him or her and reestablish it with the rest of the room.
7. Handle difficult questions or multilayer questions by answering them as completely as time allows and in the order they are asked by the questioner, but be prepared to say, "I will be glad to discuss this question in more detail after the presentation."

After you have answered the last question, you will want to make sure to summarize the discussion and repeat your main message. You want to control the way the presentation ends rather than letting the audience leave with the answer to the last question in their minds; you want them leaving with your main message in their minds.

OVERALL EFFECT

Ultimately, your ethos will determine the overall effect of your presentation. A leader must project a strong, positive ethos in all presentation situations. Your credibility, knowledge, and integrity must be without question or you will lose your audience no matter how logical your presentation may be. You want to appear poised and confident.

The best way to project a positive ethos is to believe in what you are saying and to be fully prepared. As obvious as it may sound, nothing will take the place of preparation. To deliver an effective presentation, you must be prepared. Some guidelines suggest spending one hour in preparation for each minute that you will be presenting. While that may be too much in some cases and would certainly need to be modified depending on the type of presentation and your knowledge of the subject, it suggests emphatically how important it is not to neglect or underestimate preparation time. The success of your presentation and, in the long run, your career may depend on it.

In summary, to appear confident and project a positive ethos when presenting, you need to do the following:

1. Focus your energy on your audience.
2. Create and maintain rapport.
3. Adopt a secure stance.

4. Establish and maintain eye contact.

5. Project and vary your voice.

6. Demonstrate your messages with gestures.

7. Adjust pace of delivery based on the audience response.

The self-evaluation form that follows is designed to allow you to assess your presentation strengths and weaknesses by watching yourself on a video and, then, using the form to assess your presentation and establish an improvement plan.

Exercise 4.1: Oral Presentation Self-Evaluation

Video one of your presentations, and then use the following form to assess it. You should watch the video three times: (1) watch with the sound turned off to focus on body movements and delivery; (2) listen without watching so that you can hear what you really say; and finally, (3) watch and listen. In addition, if you have a problem with fillers, you might want to listen one additional time to count the "uhs."

	Needs Work	Average	Good	Excellent	
Delivery					**Strengths:**
Leadership image _____					
• Confidence					
• Stance & movement					
• Approach & departure from podium					
Gestures _____					**Areas to improve:**
Eye contact _____					
Fillers (uhs, etc.) _____					
Energy level _____					
Voice, articulation, language, grammar _____					**Strengths:**
• Tone					
• Volume					
• Pauses					
• Rate/pace					**Areas to improve:**
• Fillers					
• Articulation					
• Language usage					
Content and organization					**Strengths:**
Introduction _____ (context, purpose, & topics)					
Organization _____ (coherence & logic)					
Knowledge & _____ control of content					**Areas to improve:**
Conclusion _____ (summary of main points)					

	Needs Work	Average	Good	Excellent	
Graphics					**Strengths:**
Quality of graphics (conforms to graphic basics—simple, easy to understand)					
Ability to present charts & graphics effectively (introduce before showing, walking audience through them if needed)					**Areas to improve:**
Effectiveness of chart titles (capture meaning of the chart)					

Overall presentation and improvement plans:

1. What was the best part of your presentation? Why?

2. What are key areas to improve?

3. How do you propose working on improvement areas?

4. How will you measure your progress in these areas?

Exercise 4.2: Practicing Impromptu Presentations

Select a couple of the topics from the following list and practice delivering a three-minute presentation on them. Allow yourself only two to four minutes of preparation time for some of them, but also practice reading them and then starting to talk.

1. Discuss three key reasons for the failures of so many dot.com companies.
2. Discuss what it takes to be a successful entrepreneur.
3. Discuss why so many start-up businesses fail.
4. Review the three key features to consider in purchasing a new laptop computer.
5. Review tips for planning a successful meeting.
6. Discuss something you wish you had learned in school but didn't.
7. Explain some time management tools that you find helpful.
8. Describe the essential elements for having a productive team.
9. Of the current market leaders in any industry, which do you think will continue to dominate their industry, and why?
10. What does it take to be a good leader?
11. Review the pros and cons of day trading.
12. Discuss factors to consider in setting up a balanced investment portfolio.
13. Discuss ways of doing business in another country and how it is different from doing business in the United States.
14. Select a city and argue the merits of living in it.

Exercise 4.3: Developing a Round-Table Presentation

Huge Co Revisited

Review the circumstances surrounding the Huge Co merger with Computer Co presented in the exercise section of Chapter 2. Assume the role of the head of the consulting team that has interviewed the human resources managers at both Huge Co and Computer Co. You have been asked to develop a round-table presentation to deliver to the senior partner and two new consultants who will be joining the project team. Consider the need for background information as well as the synthesized information from the interviews, and create the ghost pack for the round-table presentation.

Notes

1. Eccles, R. G., & Nohria, N. (1992). *Beyond the Hype: Rediscovering the Essence of Management*. Boston: Harvard Business School Press, pp. 47–48.
2. Anderson, H. V. (2003). A virtual end to stage fright. *Harvard Management Communication Letter* (January).

Chapter **Five**

Using Graphics and PowerPoint for a Leadership Edge

Charts are an important form of language. They're important because, when well conceived and designed, they help us communicate more quickly and more clearly than we would if we left the data in a tabular form.

Gene Zelazny (2001), *Say It with Charts*

Presentations largely stand or fall depending on the quality, relevance, and integrity of the content. The way to make big improvements in a presentation is to get better content.

Edward Tufte (2003), *The Cognitive Style of PowerPoint*

Chapter Objectives

In this chapter, you will learn to do the following:

- Recognize when to use graphics.
- Select and design effective data charts.
- Create meaningful and effective text layouts.
- Employ fundamental graphic content and design principles.
- Make the most of PowerPoint as a design and presentation tool.

Leaders need to know how and when to use graphics. Graphics improve presentations and documents, particularly if the material is primarily quantitative, structural, pictorial, or so complicated that it can be illustrated more efficiently and more effectively with a visual aid than with words alone. Graphics will contribute to the success of your oral and written communications. Most people are more visually oriented today than in the past, and they expect and respond to graphics in presentations and printed documents. Even though it is a cliché, the expression "a picture is worth a thousand words" conveys a powerful truth. People respond to visuals. In fact, research has proven that presentations with visual aids are 43 percent more persuasive.[1]

Leaders use visuals that are integral to the communication of their intended meanings and not ones simply added for show. When selected appropriately and designed carefully, graphics embody and carry the meanings that create your message. With the introduction of PowerPoint, the default presentation graphics program for business presenters, and the improving graphic capabilities of MS Word, adding graphics to communications has become increasingly easier. However, the ease of use has also led to gratuitous and poorly designed graphics and presentations with more flash than content.

Managers often create their own presentations, which has in some cases unleashed an unsophisticated graphic artist and led to presentations with too little content packaged in poorly designed slides. Edward Tufte says that PowerPoint's "cognitive style routinely disrupts, dominates, and trivializes content."[2] However, PowerPoint presentations can and do contain solid content and can and do communicate content effectively—but only if the content is solid to begin with and if the slides conspire fully in communicating the speaker's message.

Used appropriately, graphics and PowerPoint provide a leadership edge. Knowing how to deliver messages effectively with words and pictures is a powerful combination, and developing even a basic understanding of the principles of graphic design can provide an advantage.

This chapter will focus on when and how to use graphics effectively, provide some basic guidelines for designing effective graphics, and deliver some guidance on designing and presenting graphics using PowerPoint.

Glossary of Terms Used in This Chapter

- **Visual Aid**—object, picture, drawing, diagram, graph, table, and the like, included in a presentation to help the audience understand the message.
- **Graphics**—visual designs, drawings, diagrams, tables, or graphs, intended to support, explain, illustrate, or clarify a presenter's message. Note: When Zelazny says "charts" in the opening quotations, he means graphics as defined here.
- **Graph**—representation of numerical information in a line, bar, pie, or similar conventionally scaled depiction of data.
- **Slide**—used in PowerPoint to define the separate pages in a presentation even though technically they are not intended to be shown with a slide projector, but using computer projection.
- **Chart**—page in a presentation, could be text or graphics, often used interchangeably for "slide."
- **Pack or Deck**—a hard-copy collection of slides/charts intended for support and as handouts in stand-up or round-table presentations.

RECOGNIZING WHEN TO USE GRAPHICS

Graphics should never be gratuitous; they should always be purposeful. They should add to the content of the presentation or the document. For presentations, in particular, graphics should supplement the content and never detract from it. They are not meant to replace the speaker.

Specifically, graphics should serve the following purposes:

1. Reinforce the message.
2. Provide a road map to the structure of a presentation.
3. Illustrate relationships and concepts visually.
4. Support assertions.
5. Emphasize important ideas.
6. Maintain and enhance interest.

Reinforce the Message

Reinforcing the message means that the chart captures and emphasizes the main ideas expressed by the speaker. Recognizing that many people are visually oriented, you can ensure your audience will remember more of what you say if you reinforce your words with visuals. Although you do not want to overuse text charts, even a simple one can help reinforce your message. You should ensure, however, that what is on the screen is consistent with what you are saying. A common problem in presenting with word charts is that the speaker says something very different from the words projected on the screen. This discrepancy causes the audience to be confused: do they listen to the speaker or read the screen?

Remember, the words on the screen should echo what you say. You may paraphrase or expand on the words, but you should not say anything that diverges too far from what is projected. Also, you should never simply read from the screen. After all, this is your presentation; you should know the subject matter well enough to speak about it without reading.

You may also want to use graphic charts to reinforce your message. For instance, if your message is that sales are down, you can reinforce that message with a line graph showing how much and over what length of time. If your message is that the company needs to be involved in community outreach, you might show pictures of some community efforts currently under way, such as inner-city cleanup or Habitat for Humanity.

The bottom line is to think of ways to use charts, whether verbal or graphic, to help your audience remember your message.

Provide a Road Map to the Structure of a Presentation

Using a text chart to establish the agenda or discussion topics is one very common method of establishing a road map for the structure of a business presentation. One common mistake, however, is to list all or most of the slide titles on the agenda chart (see Exhibit 4.4 in the previous chapter). This laundry list of topics does not suggest the "structure" of the presentation. In fact, it can suggest a lack of

EXHIBIT 5.1 **Using a Framework as a Road Map for a Presentation**

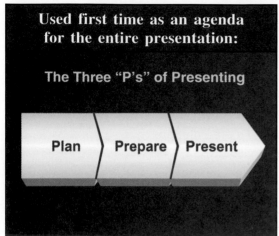

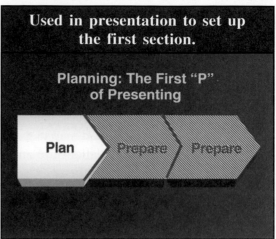

structure, an aimless stringing together of ideas. Instead, use the agenda slide to reflect the logic of your presentation. Think back to the pyramid principle or other structuring device you used and group your slides into like ideas so that the agenda tells the story in miniature. In other words, think of the agenda as an executive summary with only the headings included. Then, you will create an effective agenda slide that your audience will more likely remember.

If your topic is complex, you might want to use a structural graphic as a road map for your presentation. For instance, if you think back to the discussion in Chapter 4, you remember a graphic used to set up the steps in developing and designing a presentation. You could use this same graphic to introduce each section in the presentation, thus keeping the entire framework in the audience's mind at the same time as you introduce the specific pieces in the presentation (Exhibit 5.1). When you use a framework or even a text slide to set up the entire presentation and then each of the major sections, the slide serves as a tracker, a slide designed to help your audience keep track of where you are in the presentation.

If you decide to use a framework, you need to be careful that it is not so complex that your audience gets lost in it or that your presentation is so short that repeating the same graphic becomes tedious. Some presenters take a tracker too far, placing a small version of it on every slide in the presentation. You should avoid using a tracker in this way since it diminishes your work space and must be so reduced that to your audience, it will only be a distraction that adds little, if any, meaning (see Exhibit 5.2).

The one exception to using this type of tracker might be if you are presenting a process flow in which the audience must be reminded of the whole to appreciate the parts.

Illustrate Relationships or Concepts Visually

Graphics usually work better than words to help an audience understand relationships or concepts. For example, the triangle used in Chapter 1 to introduce strategy is a concept graphic. It shows how all of the components of a communication

EXHIBIT 5.2   Misusing a Framework as a Tracker on Each Slide

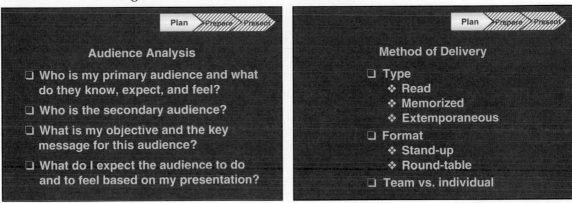

strategy connect to the others, build on them, and influence them with audience analysis as the foundation for every other component above it.

Exhibit 5.3 is a concept chart designed to show the relationship between the components of an individual communication improvement plan. The framework shows the individual development at the center with the team experiences and

EXHIBIT 5.3   Graphic Showing Relationships

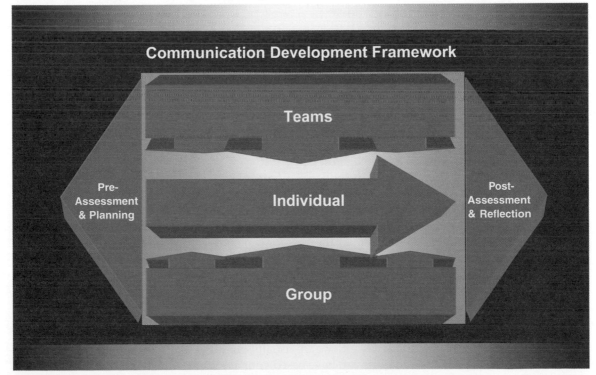

EXHIBIT 5.4 Concept Graphic

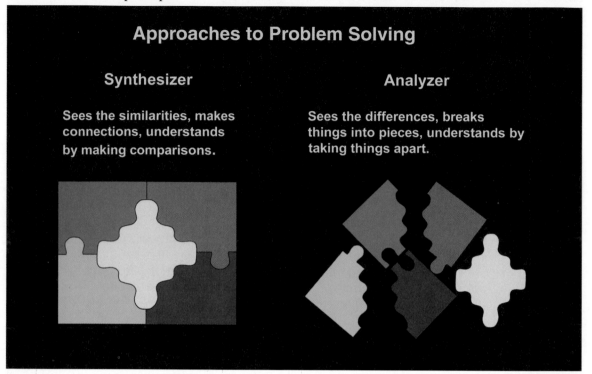

group instruction influencing the development from the top and the bottom. Framing the development on each end are the beginning self-assessments with an improvement plan and then the post-assessments with reflection to measure the improvement results. The presenter could use color and shading for each arrow and PowerPoint's building capabilities to introduce the components one at a time so that he or she could make their meaning and their relationship to the other components clear to the audience.

Concept graphics are useful in clarifying ideas and also in creating a mental picture for the audience. For instance, in Exhibit 5.4, a standard Microsoft clip art of a puzzle shows different approaches to problem solving. On one side, you have the "synthesizer" or the person who puts things together and sees similarities, and on the other, you have the "analyzer" or the person who takes things apart and sees differences.

Exhibit 5.5 illustrates a few of the most commonly used business concept charts. If you would like to see more examples of concept graphics, Gene Zelazny in his book *Say It with Charts* dedicates an entire chapter to examples of visual concepts and another chapter to visual metaphors.

Support an Assertion

Graphics to support assertions are usually quantitative charts; however, you might use qualitative charts if you have based your assertions on interviews or open-ended surveys and want to show your audience quotations from your subjects. Exhibit 5.6

EXHIBIT 5.5   Common Concept Charts

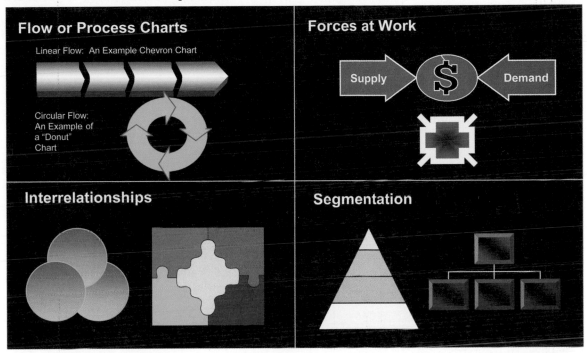

EXHIBIT 5.6   Example Quantitative Chart to Support an Assertion

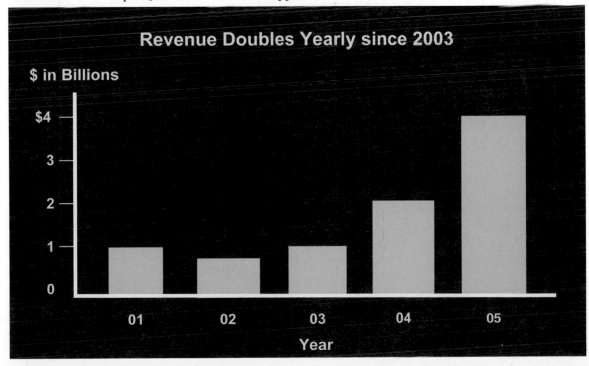

EXHIBIT 5.7
Example
Qualitative
Chart to
Support an
Assertion

Communication Important in Performance Reviews at ABC	
Interview Findings	**Representative Quotations**
Employees beginning to realize communication is important in reviews.	• "My communication ability was highlighted as one of my main strengths in my performance review." • "My communication weaknesses kept me from receiving a good review."
Employees think communication is important to management.	• "Communication effectiveness seems to be a high priority to management in reviews now." • "This is such a bottom-line company, I was surprised management put so much value on what I see as a soft skill—communication."
Employees evaluated as "high" in communication effectiveness are rewarded.	• "Employees who are rated high on communication in reviews receive the promotions." • "No matter what kind of deal maker you are, only the good communicators rise to the top here."

demonstrates a typical quantitative chart supporting the assertion that ABC's revenue has doubled each year since 2003. While this assertion is fairly simple and you could probably get away with making it orally, adding a graphic that shows the numbers will bring greater credibility and can have a greater impact on your audience.

Exhibit 5.7 shows a qualitative chart created to support the assertion that communication is a priority in performance reviews. It demonstrates how you might use quotations from interviews to support your findings and overall conclusion.

Emphasize Important Ideas

All presenters hope that orally emphasizing the important points, and maybe even repeating them, will fix them in the audience's memory. Studies show, however, that audiences remember more of what they see than what they hear, although they do not retain much of that either. To put it simply, as taught in one ancient Chinese proverb,

> I hear and I forget;
> I see and I remember;
> I do and I understand.

The common English expression indicating understanding suggests the importance of the visual as well: "I see." Thus, if you want to emphasize important ideas, do so in words and in visual aids, whether you use word charts or graphics.

Maintain and Enhance Interest

Using graphics to maintain and enhance interest requires a word of warning. Essentially, adding interest means introducing some variety in your slides and looking for ways to make your presentation graphically interesting; it does not mean throw in wild colors, crazy cartoons, or superfluous animation just for the sake of doing so. As always, the most important rule for the use of graphics applies here: graphics should add to the presentation and the presenter and not detract in any way. You should think about ways to make your presentation more visually appealing, but approach the task with caution. For instance, a presenter using Exhibit 5.8 would probably get your attention but would run the risk of your being so distracted by the graphics that you might not hear the intended message. Imagine the darts flying into the target with a swooshing sound, and you might decide this chart goes too far to make a point.

If the presenter used this slide with others on presentations to reinforce a lesson in what not to do, it could be effective by its contrast to the previous charts as a bad example. People do seem to remember bad examples better than they do good ones. Also, it could accomplish the purpose of breaking up the purely instructional slides with something a little lighter. Such a poorly designed chart does, however, need the appropriate context to convey this message, which again brings us back to the cardinal rule of using graphics. *Graphics should enhance the delivery of your message, not detract from it in any way.*

EXHIBIT 5.8   Example of a Graphic That Risks Going Too Far to Add Interest

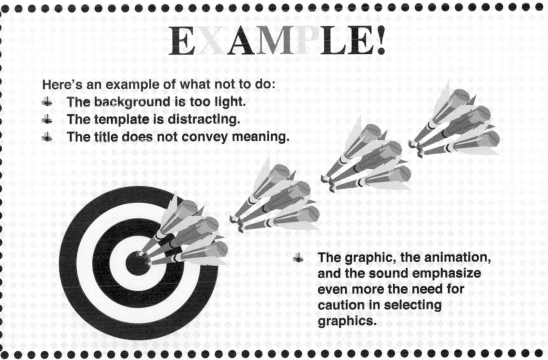

EXAMPLE!

Here's an example of what not to do:
- The background is too light.
- The template is distracting.
- The title does not convey meaning.

- The graphic, the animation, and the sound emphasize even more the need for caution in selecting graphics.

SELECTING AND DESIGNING EFFECTIVE DATA CHARTS

For data charts to add to your presentation or document, you first need to clarify your message and then you can determine the type and content of the graph that will add to, support, or explain that message best. Although you may have someone to help design your graphics, particularly if you have reached a high level in an organization, you will find it useful as you manage others and oversee the creation of your presentations to possess some knowledge of the best types of graphs, as well as the best designs, to ensure the clarity and accuracy of the different kinds of data you will be conveying to your audiences.

Edward Tufte, a Yale University statistician and author of several books on graphic design, provides the following best practice guidelines for creating data charts:

Excellence in statistical graphics consists of complex ideas communicated with clarity, precision, and efficiency. Graphical displays should
- Show the data.
- Induce the viewer to think about the substance rather than methodology, graphic design, the technology of graphic production, or something else.
- Avoid distorting what the data have to say.
- Present many numbers in a small space.
- Make large data sets coherent.
- Encourage the eye to compare different pieces of data.
- Reveal the data at several levels of detail, from a broad overview to the fine structure.
- Serve a reasonably clear purpose: description, exploration, tabulation, or decoration.
- Be closely integrated with the statistical and verbal descriptions of a data set.

Source: Tufte, E. R. (1983). *The Visual Display of Quantitative Information*. Cheshire, CT: Graphics Press, p. 13. Used with permission.[3]

Tufte emphasizes that graphs should be carefully selected and designed to ensure that the meaning of the numbers dominates, not the method of analysis. The goal of the graph should be to aid the audience in understanding the data and your central message. Selecting the best type of graph for the type of information that you want to convey and then following a few basic design principles for graphs will help you communicate your message more effectively. Exhibit 5.9 demonstrates the most commonly used data graphs in business, explains when you should select one or the other, and includes pointers on how to make them easier for your audience to grasp the content in a presentation.

Knowing when to use graphics and the best graph to select will help you ensure the graphics add to your presentation and document, but you also should consider the integrity of any graphics that you use, particularly your data charts.

Ethically Representing Data

Tufte emphasizes the importance of the integrity of graphic representation of data: "Graphical excellence begins with telling the truth about the data."[4] Ethical leaders would not intentionally distort the data through manipulating the

EXHIBIT 5.9   Selecting the Most Effective Graphic Format for Data Charts

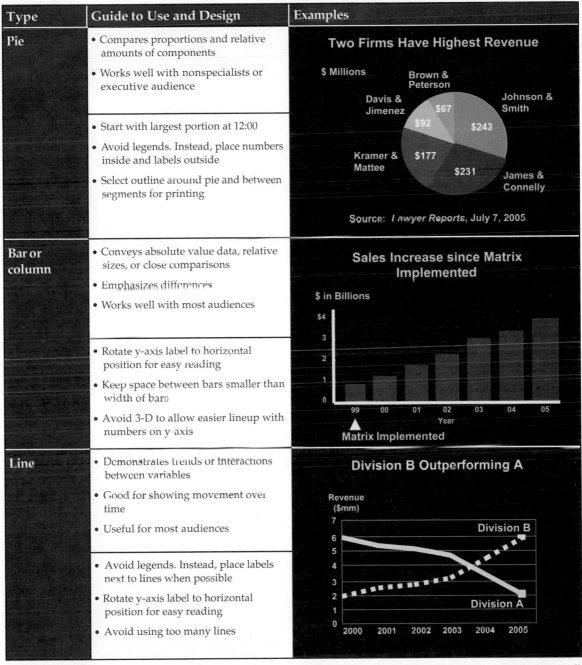

Type	Guide to Use and Design	Examples
Pie	• Compares proportions and relative amounts of components • Works well with nonspecialists or executive audience • Start with largest portion at 12:00 • Avoid legends. Instead, place numbers inside and labels outside • Select outline around pie and between segments for printing	**Two Firms Have Highest Revenue** $ Millions — Brown & Peterson — Davis & Jimenez $67 — Johnson & Smith — $92 — $243 — Kramer & Mattee $177 — $231 — James & Connelly Source: *Lawyer Reports*, July 7, 2005.
Bar or column	• Conveys absolute value data, relative sizes, or close comparisons • Emphasizes differences • Works well with most audiences • Rotate y-axis label to horizontal position for easy reading • Keep space between bars smaller than width of bars • Avoid 3-D to allow easier lineup with numbers on y-axis	**Sales Increase since Matrix Implemented** $ in Billions $4 / 3 / 2 / 1 / 0 99 00 01 02 03 04 05 Year ▲ Matrix Implemented
Line	• Demonstrates trends or interactions between variables • Good for showing movement over time • Useful for most audiences • Avoid legends. Instead, place labels next to lines when possible • Rotate y-axis label to horizontal position for easy reading • Avoid using too many lines	**Division B Outperforming A** Revenue ($mm) 7 / 6 / 5 / 4 / 3 / 2 / 1 / 0 Division B Division A 2000 2001 2002 2003 2004 2005

(continued)

EXHIBIT 5.9 **Selecting the Most Effective Graphic Format for Data Charts** (continued)

Type	Guide to Use and Design	Examples
Stacked bar	• Conveys differences • Captures a lot of data in a small space • More suited to technical or other analytical audience • When using colors in bars, ensure contrast shows when printed in black and white • Align numbers across as much as possible and align labels with numbers	**Desserts Increasing at Ice Cream's Expense** % of Total 8 — 19 — 20 — 21 — 21 — Other Desserts 23 — 23 — 22 — 22 — 23 — Ice Milk 69 — 58 — 58 — 57 — 56 — Ice Cream 2001 2002 2003 2004 2005
Histogram	• Shows frequency distributions, indicating how many in each class being measured • Not immediately intuitive for most people • Best used with statistically oriented audience • Rotate labels for ease of reading • Avoid double y-axis if possible	**Corvettes Sold in 2005** Frequency / % of Total Sales 90 — 28 67 — 21 45 — 14 22 — 7 3 5 7 9 11 Car Sales
Scatter plot	• Shows correlations, how well a variable follows the expected pattern • May need to be explained more than most charts making the title even more important in delivering the "so what?" • Rotate y-axis label for ease of reading • Make sure title explains meaning of content	**Work Experience Does Not Affect GMAT Scores** GMAT Scores 700 680 660 640 620 600 2 4 6 8 10 12 14 16 Years of Experience

numbers or purposely designing graphs that mislead the audience. In addition, they should be careful that they do not confuse their audience or accidentally mislead them by using poorly designed graphs or incorrectly selected graphs or by taking or presenting information out of context.[5] As you consider the type of graph to use, you should test the integrity of your graphics by asking the following questions:

1. Does the data set completely support the message I wish to convey?
2. Have I provided or will I be able to provide enough context for the data to be interpreted accurately?
3. Are the numbers accurate and depicted honestly and accurately?
4. Does the design distort or hide the data in any way?
5. Are all axes and data accurately and adequately labeled?

You want to make sure that your graphics add to the substance of your presentation and that they do not distort, distract, or confuse the audience in any way. You should aim for meaningful and clear content, honest and accurate depiction, and simplicity. If you then select the most effective graph to demonstrate or support your message, the graphics should help you communicate more powerfully.

CREATING MEANINGFUL AND EFFECTIVE TEXT LAYOUTS

Text slides are the staple for most presentations and, in fact, are often overused. They may seem fairly simple and straightforward from a design point of view; however, Exhibit 5.10 contains a few guidelines and examples (first bad and then good) that will help you make your text slides more effective. In addition to the guidelines and examples, Exhibit 5.10 also contains a few technical tips on using PowerPoint.

The goal with any text chart is to make it as readable as possible and to make sure that it contains meaningful content. Achieving both of these objectives is not always easy because to ensure legibility you must minimize the words, which means every word must count.

EMPLOYING FUNDAMENTAL GRAPHIC CONTENT AND DESIGN PRINCIPLES

This section focuses specifically on the content and design principles that you should follow whenever creating data or text charts for leadership presentations. For charts to add to the presentation, they should convey your messages clearly and effectively to your audience. In addition, they should be legible and designed so that they contribute to communicating your messages.

EXHIBIT 5.10 Guidelines for Creating Effective Text Slides

The Guidelines and PPT Hints	The Bad Examples
1. **Do not put too many words on the slide** as done on the slide at the right. You should not have too many bullets or too many words at each bullet. 2. **Do not have only one bullet or sub-bullet as a category**. If you do, you should rephrase your points or elevate your bullets. Thus, the single bullet below "Expansion Division" needs to be broken into two.	**Key Current Quarter Priorities** **Global Division:** • Maintain consistent price pressure against competition • Execute toward lower alternative targets • Implement new global/local philosophy **Technical Division:** • Use SWAT team and various Area projects such as ACE in So America and Thrust in Europe to impact customer acceptance of the Newline 2000 and families and increase channel sales out on Newline 2000, 2500, and 3300 • Analysts removed Newline products from problem watch in July; communications deliverables sent to Global Marketing groups worldwide **Expansion Division:** • Deplete Technical inventory by end of Q1 to pave the way for AMstart (launch AMstart with European mono availability in Q3; European and So American color models in Q4)
3. **Use hanging indents for text lists of more than one line.** **Technical Tip:** To create the "hanging" indent, it is easiest to make your ruler visible in \<View\> and then adjust the bullets. Each bullet level will adjust when you adjust one of them. 4. **Avoid having too many "widow words" (see right).** **Technical Tip:** To get rid of "widow" words, cut words, decrease font, or increase margins, but be careful to stay as close to a consistent font and margin as possible.	**Key Current Quarter Priorities** **Global Division:** •Implement new global/local philosophy that the structure **Widows** •Work with Area divisions to increase/monitor attach rates **Technical Division:** ♦Use SWAT team and various Area projects such as ACE in So America and Thrust in Europe to impact customer acceptance of the Newline 2000 ♦Analysts removed Newline products from problem watch in July; communications deliverables sent to Global Marketing groups worldwide **No hanging indent**
The Guidelines and PPT Hints	**The Good Examples**

5. **Keep the text simple but present meaningful content.** Note the use of hanging indents and the spacing between the lines and between the bullets and the text.
 	
 6. **Make sure all bulleted items are parallel in structure.**
	Key Current Quarter Priorities
	 ❏ **Global Division**
	    ❖ **Maintain consistent price pressure**
	    ❖ **Execute toward lower alternative targets**
	    ❖ **Implement new global/local philosophy**
	    ❖ **Increase/monitor attach rates**
	 ❏ **Technical Division**
	    ❖ **Improve customer acceptance of Newline**
	    ❖ **Achieve target market share**
	    ❖ **Increase channel sales on Newline families**

(continued)

EXHIBIT 5.10 (continued)

The Guidelines and PPT Hints	The Good Examples (continued)
7. Use some variation in how you lay out the text (slide after slide of lists of bullets can get rather boring). See example. **Technical Tip:** It is usually easier to create each column of text as one text box. In this example, "Division" is in the same box as "Global" and "Technical." You can control the spacing between the items to ensure alignment across columns, by using <Line spacing> in <Format>.	**Current Priorities by Division** **Division Priority Actions** Global ❖ Implement global/local philosophy ❖ Work with Area divisions to increase attach rates Technical ❖ Use SWAT team to impact customer acceptance of Newline families ❖ Increase channel sales on Newline families to achieve market share
8. Maximize the impact of your title slide. In other words, communicate the main message and the who, what, and when. See good example to the right. **Technical Tip:** Use the title master for the first slide so that you can format it differently from the rest of the presentation. Also, you will usually need to change the font size on PowerPoint title master. Use shadow fonts with care; check readability since the shadows often make the letters look fuzzy. Selecting bold fonts is usually best.	
9. Work the text and graphics together to convey the message as at the right. **Technical Tip:** When using text with AutoShapes, it is better to create a separate text box than to link the shape and the text, which is the default in PowerPoint. That way you can move the text where you want it easily and align it within an object and from object to object.	**Steps to Creating Charts** **Determine the message** **Choose the comparison** **Draw the chart** Adapted from Gene Zelazny, *Say It with Charts.*

Conveying Messages Clearly and Effectively

The following guidelines apply to all data and text charts:

1. Keep charts simple *but* meaningful. Often instruction in creating and using graphics will include the adage "Less is more, " originally used by Ludwig Mies van der Rohe (1886–1969), an architect and designer who started the minimalist school. Effective leaders keep their graphs simple enough for their audience to understand easily, yet they also know that the graphs still need to communicate something. While you should strive for simplicity in whatever graphs you create or slides you design, you must avoid reducing the content on the slide so much that the meaning evaporates.

The content of slides, whether graphics or text, should never be mere decoration or embellishment. Empty pictures and hollow words add nothing and should never be part of the presentation. Always ask yourself: Is the graphic useful? Is it necessary? You have probably sat through presentations with slides that were not much more than decorative pictures, objects, or cartoons that added little to the message. If the visual aid does not add to the presentation, cut it, no matter how attached you may be to the graphic or even how much time you spent creating it.

In Edward Tufte's *Cognitive Style of PowerPoint* (2003) he argues that PowerPoint is so flawed that it is impossible to communicate anything meaningful using it; however, it is not the medium that is flawed—it is the users of it. Many of the standard presentation templates force you to use few words and fairly simply graphics, but that does not mean that you cannot create a presentation that contains solid, thoughtful, and meaningful content. You simply have to make sure your message is clear in your own mind and then make every word and every graphic work for you to convey your message. Remember you are delivering the main messages; the graphics are there to support you.

2. Include only one main message per chart or slide. If you have too many messages, you risk losing your audience. Back away from the slide and ask yourself the following questions:

- What is it that I am trying to communicate?
- If the audience leaves with only one message from this slide, is it what I intend?
- Do the words say this?
- Do the graphics support this?

3. Make sure your chart title captures the "so what?" The title on the chart should clearly announce your main message or provide adequate information for interpreting the graph. You have probably heard someone say, "The numbers speak for themselves." In fact, the significance of numbers is seldom transparent, and numbers can be made to convey a range of potential meanings. So simply putting a graph up displaying some numbers does not ensure your audience will see them the way you do. It is your responsibility to make sure the numbers as configured and displayed carry the meaning you intend and that they cannot be interpreted otherwise. You can help ensure your audience interprets the numbers as you do by putting a title on the slide that tells the audience the meaning of the numbers or other data you are showing them.

Selecting the Most Effective Colors

The right colors and fonts can make a difference in how effective your Power-Point presentation is. Selection should focus on colors and fonts that show up best when a presentation is projected. Often company logos determine colors and fonts; however, these are not always the best choices to make for entire presentations. To make effective decisions on colors, it will help you to know something about color psychology and graphic design. What follows provides some of both.

Selecting the color combinations for your presentations should not be arbitrary or simply based on personal color preferences. As with all aspects of your presentation, you need to consider your message and the image you wish to project. Knowing the colors most color specialists consider "right" for presentations can be useful, as can color psychology in general. For instance, knowing that too much of a vivid yellow causes fatigue and even aggravation and that cool shades, such as blues and greens, have a calming effect could be important in supporting your messages. In addition, you should be sensitive to the cultural associations for some colors to ensure your colors do not deliver messages you do not intend.

The focus here is on selecting the colors that project best and promote legibility for the audience, and also on how you can draw the audience's eye to your most important message by effectively using color.

If you want more information on the design aspects, the psychology, and the cultural associations of colors, you should find the following sources useful:

- The Color Voodoo publications (most of them can be purchased through their Web site for under $30.00)
- www.presentersuniversity.com
- www.colormatters.com
- www.presentations.com
- www.3m.com
- www.lighthouse.org

The Lighthouse International site is particularly interesting since it reminds us that many people have impaired sight and have trouble seeing colors. While only a few people may be completely color-blind, many have trouble with distinguishing subtle shades of colors.

For everyone, the greater the contrast, the better when it comes to putting colors right next to each other in a presentation. Background and fonts that do not contrast sufficiently make the text difficult to read. Unless your company colors dictate differently, it is usually better to stay with the traditional primary or secondary colors or their combinations for business presentations and to avoid pastels.

The traditional color wheel (Exhibit 5.11), shows the primary and secondary colors that tend to work best in presentations. The color contrast chart shows how to

EXHIBIT 5.11
Basic Colors and Contrasts

Source: www.light-house.org/color contrast.html. Used with permission of the author, Aries Arditi, Ph.D., and Lighthouse International as the copyright holder.

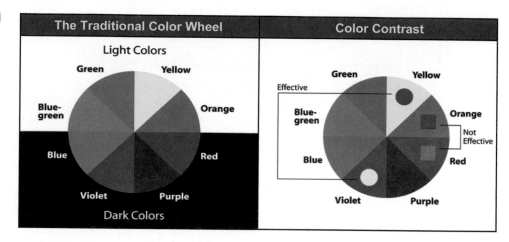

select opposites for strong contrast. It also demonstrates what happens when colors of the same hue are placed next to each other; the red square on the orange slice and orange square on the red slice do not allow enough contrast for easy legibility and the squares may not be visible to some people.

The secret of effective color choices is not so much the choice of one color but the choice of one in contrast to the others used with it: "Most people—or at least those of us without an art background—don't understand that the colors they choose are not as important as the relationships they create. Some colors work together, others fight against each other. Establishing sound relationship is key."[6] You want the colors you select for your presentation to work together, not against each other. In addition, you want the sharpest contrast, since the sharper the contrast the greater the legibility.

One principle of color relationships to keep in mind is that a lighter color appears to move outward and a darker color recedes; therefore, the lighter fonts show up better on dark background than a dark font on a white background. This is particularly true in a room somewhat darkened as is usual with PowerPoint presentations. Notice what happens in Exhibit 5.12 when the background colors are changed.

Clearly, the greater the contrast, the easier it is to see the font and, also, the sharper the letters appear. Similar color contrasts should guide you in selecting colors for shapes and objects. Look at the difference in the two slides in Exhibit 5.13 when the AutoShape colors are changed. Where is your eye drawn in the first versus the second?

The message you intend to emphasize should determine the colors you use. If your main message is as the title suggests in Exhibit 5.13—the "forces" affecting the industry—then making the force boxes yellow will draw the audience's eyes to them. If, however, you intend to emphasize the industry's profit splits, then the colors in the first version will work better since the yellow draws the eye and seems to project outward more. If the profit split is the main message, then the title for the first slide might be "Industry Forces Result in Dramatic Changes in Profit Splits."

EXHIBIT 5.12
Color Contrast of Fonts with Backgrounds

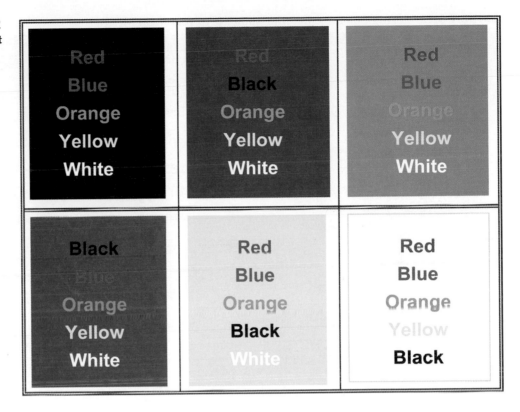

In summary, when using colors

1. Keep them simple and select colors that work well together.
2. Ensure the colors are easy to see when placed against each other.
3. Check text color, in particular, to see that it contrasts with background colors sufficiently to be clearly legible.
4. Make sure the colors support the image you want to project and the message you want to convey.

Also, light backgrounds in projected presentations create unnecessary glare that becomes uncomfortable for the viewers. Finally, you need to take into consideration the computer and the projection equipment that you will be using. If you are unfamiliar with the equipment and cannot test it ahead of time, your safest background will be black.

Selecting the Most Effective Fonts

With computer-projected presentations, recent studies have shown that a light font on a dark background (dark blue or black) is best; however, for overhead presentations, a dark font on a white background projects better in most settings. Some

EXHIBIT 5.13   Using Color to Direct the Audience to Your Main Message

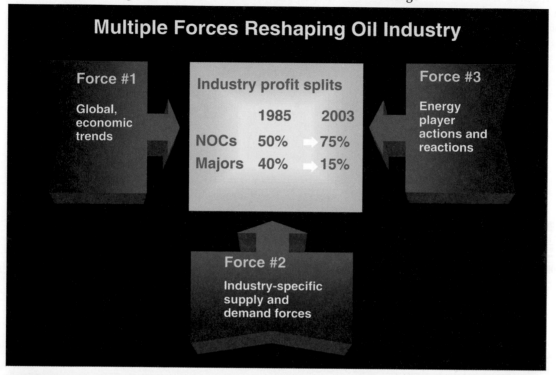

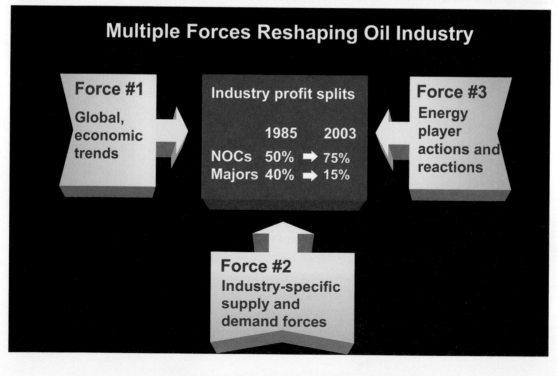

EXHIBIT 5.14   Examples of Poor Color and Font Selections

Black on white background does not show up well in computer-projected presentations and should be avoided

as should a serif font on any background.

If the font is too small, no one can read it.

ALL CAPS ARE HARD TO READ AND LOOK AS IF YOU ARE YELLING!

Initial Caps Are Distracting and Difficult to Read When Used for Text within Charts.

Underlining clips off the lower part of letters.

Red letters on blue backgrounds are fuzzy.

font colors are difficult to read on some backgrounds. For instance, red fonts on a blue background result in fuzzy images (see Exhibit 5.14).

Most presenters have been warned that the font needs to be large enough to be read from the back of the room in which you are presenting. Most of the time a font 20 points or larger will work for the text within the slides; however, when possible, you should check the room setup to be sure. Titles require a larger font, but you will probably find that the default for PowerPoint is larger than necessary and makes it difficult for you to have a title of any substance. You will find that 28-point size for the titles works well for most settings.

Recent studies in readability have found that in addition to the size of the font, the style matters as well. A sans serif font (such as Arial) is cleaner and easier to read when projected than a serif font (such as Times Roman) used for printed documents. You should thus choose a sans serif font for projected PowerPoint presentations (see Exhibit 5.14).

Capitalization is another element of font selection that you should handle carefully. You may be tempted to use all caps, thinking that this creates strong emphasis, but using all caps only makes the text difficult to read and gives the audience the sense that you are shouting at them. Using initial caps on all words within bulleted lists also decreases readability. Finally, never underline your text; it cuts off the bottoms of letters and makes the text more difficult to read. Use a larger font, bold, italics, or different colors for emphasis instead.

The bottom line is to make the font as easy to read and as comfortable for your audience as possible. The goal should be legibility, not simply aesthetics.

The following table is a summary of the guidelines for colors and fonts.

Guidelines for Using Colors and Fonts

1. Stay with the basic colors (primary or secondary).
2. Go for contrast in background and fonts and in AutoShapes or any objects or text placed next to each other.
3. Use a dark background (dark blue or black) for computer-projected presentations.
4. Use a white, cream, yellow, or light gold font on these dark backgrounds.
5. Use only a sans serif font, such as Arial, in computer- or overhead-projected presentations.
6. Make your font at least 20 points for text and 28 points for titles (depending on the size of the room).
7. Do not use the following:
   - All caps in titles or text.
   - Initial caps except in titles.
   - Underlining.
   - Red font on blue backgrounds.

MAKING THE MOST OF POWERPOINT AS A DESIGN AND PRESENTATION TOOL

The focus of this section is on using PowerPoint as a tool to communicate your content more effectively.[7] The major caveat in using PowerPoint, as with using any graphics in a presentation, is to recognize that the PowerPoint slides should enhance the presentation, not dominate it. No amount of flashy display can have the genuine impact of a meaningful, logical message delivered effectively.

Poorly designed slides, such as the one demonstrated in Exhibit 5.15, are responsible for much of the criticism and disdain for PowerPoint. This slide has too much "chart junk" or clutter (the zeros, unnecessary graphic elements, such as the background, and the 3-D effect). The 3-D effect and the legend make it difficult to read, the skyline in the background only detracts from the message, and the axes are unlabeled. As a result, the slide is more distracting than useful in conveying a message.

The slide is reproduced here as it appeared in a corporate presentation, with only the title changed to reinforce the message that just because PowerPoint provides all kinds of graphic augmentation for presentations, it does not mean that you should use them. Examples such as this one have led some organizations to ban the use of PowerPoint, which is unfortunate, for when used correctly, it can be a powerful and effective presentation tool. Its capabilities can help presenters in planning, preparing, and practicing their presentations, although its greatest strength is in the enhancements it provides to delivery.

EXHIBIT 5.15   An Example of a Poorly Designed PowerPoint Slide

It is not the aim of this section to teach you how to use PowerPoint as a computer software program, although it does include a few technical tips on using the program in case you are creating your own slides and want to know how best to obtain the results indicated in the examples. If you know how to use other Microsoft products, such as Word and Excel, you should be able to transfer those skills to PowerPoint. The primary focus is on effective slide design in PowerPoint with the goal of making your slides look better so that they communicate your content more effectively and give you a leadership edge.

The following discussions include guidelines on selecting and designing layouts and templates, inserting graphs, using animation, and delivering effectively using PowerPoint.

Deciding on Layouts and Templates

The most common format used in PowerPoint is the horizontal or landscape. To create slides for a PowerPoint presentation, you do not need to make any changes in page setup since PowerPoint defaults to the horizontal layout when you open the program. If you select new "blank presentation," you will see a white background with black font, which you could use to create a round-table, handout, or overhead presentation (see "Presentation Options" on the right side of the screen).

Technical Tips

- When opening PowerPoint, select the option <Open> or <New>. To design your own template, select <Blank presentation> or select a <Design template> that you want to modify and work in the master view.
- To insert additional slides, click on <Insert> and then <New Slide>. To have the text formatting and drawing tools visible, select them in your <View> and then <Toolbars> menus.
- For a text slide, be sure to select the title and text formatted slide so that the formatting you have set in your slide master will carry over to the slide.

If you plan to use your slides in a stand-up projected presentation and as a handout, you should create or apply a template with a dark background and light font; then, you can simply select "pure black and white" in the print options commands to print out a standard white background, dark font format (this will help avoid using up your ink cartridges).

Exhibit 5.16 shows the PowerPoint screen configured for easiest use by most people. This slide contains two text boxes because it is a title slide; the font size is larger than on regular text slides, and the text box is centered as traditional for the first slide of a presentation. The "Common Text Formatting" tools appear across the top of the screen. These include text typeface, which should always be a sans

EXHIBIT 5.16   The Opening Screen Shot in PowerPoint

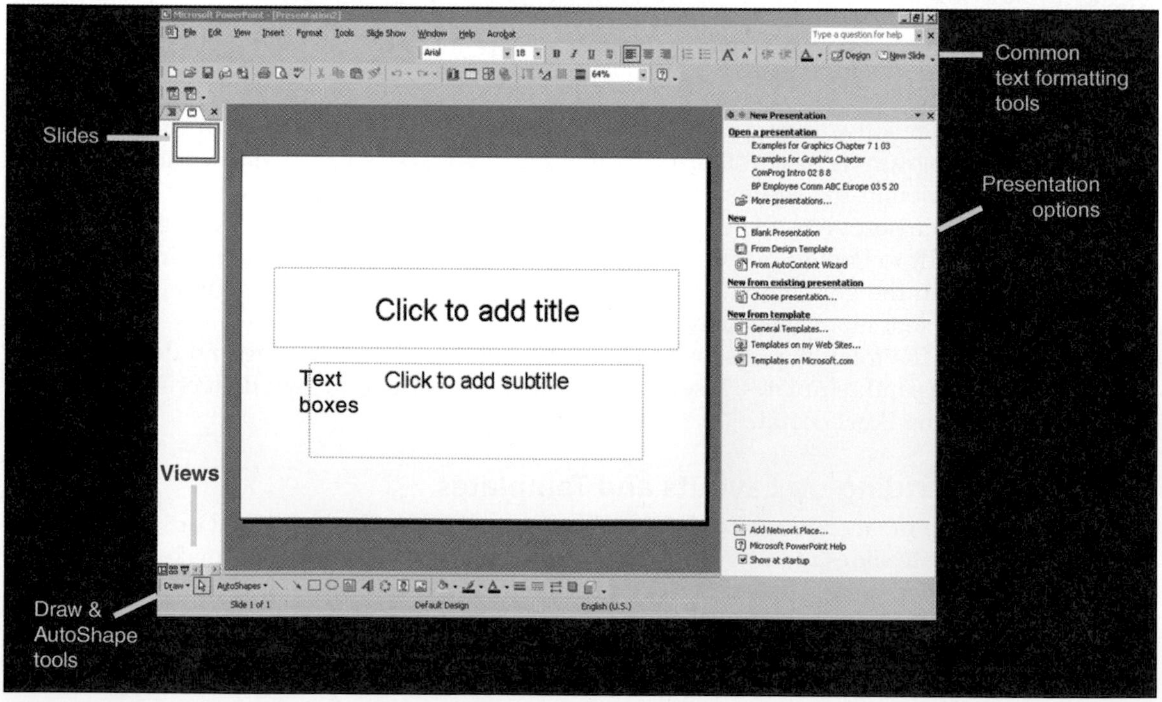

serif font such as Arial for PowerPoint presentations, and size, which should be no smaller than 20 points for most projected presentations (see font selection in the previous section). In addition, this line of icons shows selections, such as bold, italics, alignment, and color.

Using Templates

If you are creating a new presentation, you will need to select or design a template. Some of Microsoft XP's default templates conform to the graphic design and legibility guidelines contained in this chapter with little or no modification. The following are the most acceptable formats in XP:

- Artsy
- Ocean
- Compass
- Digital Dots
- Factory
- Fading Grid
- Fireworks

- Globe
- Lock and Key
- Mountain
- Mountain Top
- Soaring
- Stream

The dark background and the light font selection will work on most of these formats without being modified, although you may need to darken the backgrounds slightly on some of them to ensure enough contrast with your font and more reliable projection of the colors (see the color discussion in the previous section). You may also need to adjust the font size since it is often larger than it needs to be for most business presentation settings.

Designing Your Own Templates

Designing your own or modifying one of Microsoft's templates is a better approach than using one of Microsoft's standard templates. You want the template to reflect your company's image or your own personality and sense of style, or to reinforce or suggest your message.

Technical Tips

- To create an original background, select <Format>, then <Background>, and then <Fill Effects> and <Picture>. If you select <Apply to all>, it will become the background for all of your slides.
- If your background needs lightening, you might want to add a screen over it. You can do this by selecting the rectangle shape from the <AutoShapes>, filling it with a dark blue or other appropriate color, and selecting transparent so that your logo shows through. You may need to experiment with the level of transparency and the color to obtain the most effective appearance.
- Remember, to make changes to a template universal for the presentation, you should make them in the title and slide master views.
- Once you have created your individual template, you can save it as a template and reapply it to all future presentations by selecting <save as>.

EXHIBIT 5.17   Example of a Modified PowerPoint Template with Logo Embedded

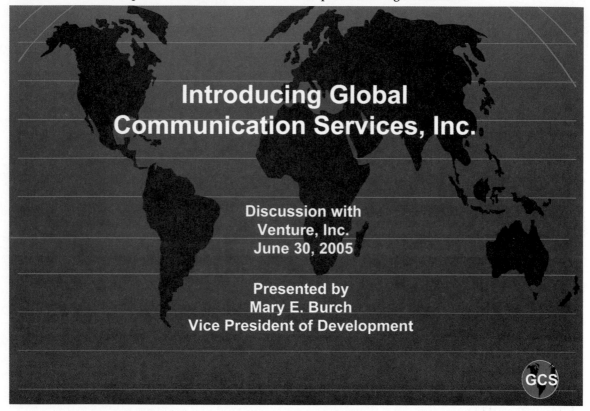

Also, creating your own template suggests you are willing to take the time to personalize the presentation and that you are not simply pulling something off the shelf that others could use. Creating your own template will mean that your presentation will stand out, as you probably would want. Again, you do not want the template format to detract from your presentation or to receive the audience's attention more than the message or the presenter. You should check your slides in slide view to ensure the background does not overwhelm the foreground (any text or graphics).

One way to personalize a template is to select a simple picture or your logo as the background. You do not want anything too complicated or showy since it could overshadow the content on the slides, as is the case in the cityscape background in Exhibit 5.15.

Exhibit 5.17 provides an example of an effective background using a modified Microsoft template with the company's logo inserted.

Creating Documents Using PowerPoint

PowerPoint, although primarily a presentation package, can be used to create documents that include graphics as well. The advantage of working in PowerPoint is that creating your graphics and then adding text is often easier and the saved

EXHIBIT 5.18 Example of a Report in PowerPoint—Portrait versus Notes View

Portrait View	Notes View
The most important question for measuring the success of the communication program is the one that asks the students if they feel their communication skills have improved because of the program. As the chart shows, the students have self-reported improvement every year since 2000. If the 2000 number were adjusted to allow for the lower scores in sections taught by first-time instructors, the score for 2000 would be 88%. Clearly, the students realize and acknowledge that their communication skills have improved as a result of the program.	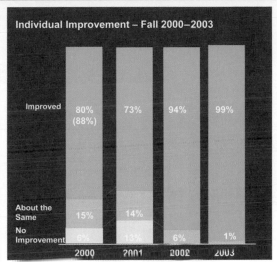

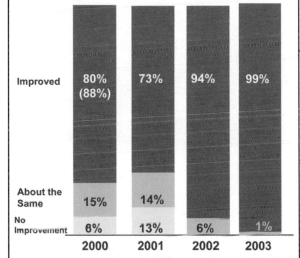

The most important question for measuring the success of the communication program is the one that asks the students if they feel their communication skills have improved because of the program. As the chart shows, the students have self-reported improvement every year since 2000. If the 2000 number were adjusted to allow for the lower scores in sections taught by first-time instructors, the score for 2000 would be 88%. Clearly, the students realize and acknowledge that their communication skills have improved as a result of the program.

document requires less memory than creating it in Word and importing graphic elements. Again, PowerPoint defaults to the horizontal or landscape format, but you can select portrait if you are creating a report or other document that you intend for your audience to read rather than see in a stand-up presentation. You can convert a presentation to the portrait layout after creating it in landscape, but you will probably need to make some adjustments to the graphics to make them fit effectively in the new layout. Therefore, it is better to select portrait before you start creating slides (open <Page Set-up> and select portrait) or plan to use the notes view as illustrated in Exhibit 5.18.

You might select the portrait layout if you have a number of graphs and want to ensure the explanations occur just above them. Exhibit 5.18 shows an example of a

EXHIBIT 5.19 Poorly Designed Graph Inserted into PowerPoint from Excel

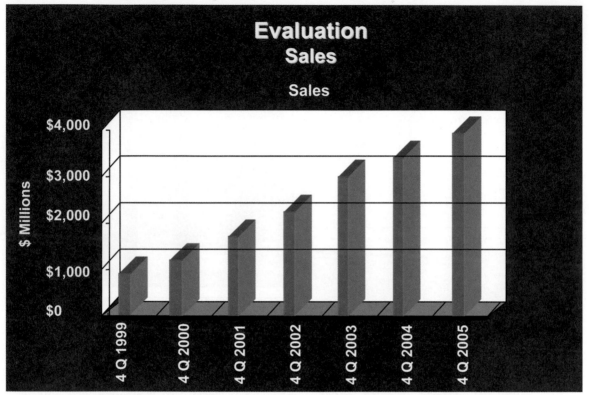

page from a vertical report created in PowerPoint. It also shows the notes view, which you can use as well to create a report. You would simply select the notes format when you print out the presentation for your audience.

Inserting Graphs and Other Objects

Many of the design faults that show up in PowerPoint presentations occur when people insert graphs or objects from other programs, Excel in particular. This section provides a few suggestions for avoiding and correcting the most common design problems. Exhibit 5.19 demonstrates a poorly designed graph for PowerPoint presentation purposes. Here are the problems:

- The chart has two titles, the one given in Excel and the one used in PowerPoint.
- Axis labels are not rotated to be read horizontally.
- Bars are too narrow; the space between should be smaller than the width of the bars.
- Use of 3-D makes reading the locations of the tops of the bars difficult.
- Chart junk clutters the exhibit: the zeros and the repetition of 4 Q with each year.
- The background of the graph is not consistent with the background of the presentation.

Some of these problems could be corrected in Excel before the graph is imported; however, it is often easier to correct them in PowerPoint (see the following Technical Tips box).

Technical Tips

- If you are creating a chart or bringing in a graph, select the title-only format for inserting new slides. You can then insert a table, graph, or clip art by selecting one of the icons from the "Common Insert Commands" located just above the text-formatting command line.
- You can also select the title with the type of graph or picture from the AutoLayout selections that come up when you hit <Insert>; however, you will probably need to adjust the location of the insert, and your graph will be linked to its source, for instance, your Excel spreadsheet.
- The following are some steps you can take to adjust an imported Excel graph:
  - Import or copy the graph into PowerPoint.
  - Stretch it as much as possible to fit your PowerPoint layout. Be sure you use the border marker in the corner so that you will be stretching both axes of the graph equally; otherwise, you will end up with a distorted graph. Also, get rid of the 3-D effect.
  - With the graph selected and highlighted, select the <Ungroup> command from the <Draw> pull-down menu to ungroup the graphics pieces in the graph. Ungrouping will cause you to have to de-link the graph from Excel; therefore, before you take this step, you should be sure you have completed your analysis and that your numbers are final. Microsoft will ask you if you are sure you want to ungroup the graph, and you must reply "yes." Now every number, line, symbol, and so forth, is separate, which means that you can easily move it, enlarge it, or alter it in some way, but it also means you can easily create chaos; therefore, as soon as you have adjusted any part of the graph and have it the way you want it in PowerPoint, you should <Regroup> it.
- Much of the work that needs to be done on a graph using the technique described here requires using the Drawing Tools. The "Common Drawing and AutoShapes Tools" are located at the bottom of the screen on the lower left side. The <Draw> menu contains commands you will frequently use when working with graphics and graphs in PowerPoint (Exhibit 5.16). The menus you open up when you click on <Draw> contain almost every command you need to adjust graphics pulled into PowerPoint.
- Just below <Group> you will see <Order>. <Order> allows you to select and place items in the foreground or background. For instance, if you create a box and you want it to have a color in it, you will need to select <Order>, <Send to Back> to push the colored box behind your text. Next, you see <Align or Distribute>, which will allow you to space your objects evenly. And finally, you see <Rotate>, which will allow you to turn your AutoShapes or any other drawing object or text at whatever angle you need.
- Once you have ungrouped the Excel graph, you will be able to rotate the axis labels to horizontal for easier reading, enlarge the font throughout, delete the gridlines and extra title, and delete legends and replace them if needed.

Your graphs should look as if they are part of the presentation, not pulled in at the last minute from Excel without concern for consistency in the formatting and clarity of the information being conveyed. Exhibit 5.20 shows the same graph reworked for projection in PowerPoint. It is now simple, clean, and easy to read.

Although you did end up with a graph that is more aesthetically pleasing, the main objective of these changes is legibility when the graph is projected. Taking

EXHIBIT 5.20
Corrected Bar
Graph
Imported
from Excel

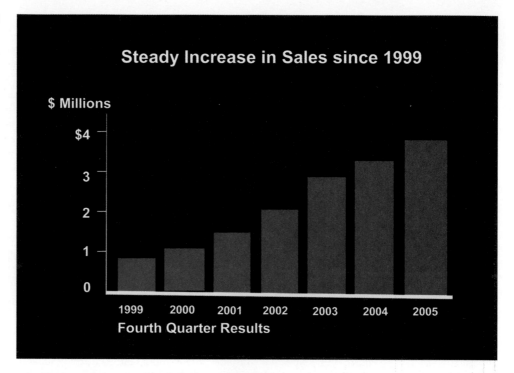

the extra time to make your imported graph easier to read and more attractive for a PowerPoint presentation is worth the effort; otherwise, your audience may think you are careless or not interested in their ability to read what you are presenting.

You can, of course, make the graph even more appealing by effective use of color and by following some of the design principles discussed previously, but the primary goal when adjusting any inserted graph or object should be to make it easier for the audience to get the message.

Using Animation

Animation is a great tool; however, it is easily overused and misused. The following guidelines will help you use animation effectively so that it adds to the impact of your presentation by supporting your main messages:

1. **Use animation only to control the delivery of the message or help the audience with the message.** Think carefully about how you can use animation to control the delivery of your content. For example, if you want your bullets to appear when you talk about each one instead of all at once, consider how long you will spend on each bullet. If you are going to discuss each item separately at some depth and length, then it would probably be worth the effort and slight distraction to have them appear one at a time; however, if you are going to talk about all of the bullets in more general terms, it would be better to have them all appear at the same time.

Although you should aim for one message on a slide, sometimes the overall message may have several layers or pieces to it. For example, if you have a complex message such as the one in the Exhibit 5.3, you might want to use animation. When presenting this slide, the presenter could use animation to control what the audience sees and when. You could bring in and discuss each arrow while building to the total picture. Seeing the whole slide with all of the pieces in place at one time could confuse your audience. They might not know where to look, so you would want to control their attention by bringing in the pieces as you talk about them.

Finally, make your animation keystroke driven rather than automatic so that you can control the building of the slide.

2. Do not overuse animation or add it just because you can. It will only distract the audience and even irritate them. Think about the spinning logo people sometimes place in a corner of their slides. Your eyes go to the logo or object no matter how hard you try to focus on the speaker or the other information on the slide.

3. If you decide to use animation to bring in text or AutoShapes, have them appear or come in from the most logical direction and the shortest distance. For example, in Exhibit 5.13, the arrow at the left should come in from the left, the bottom arrow from the bottom, and the right arrow from the right. While this seems intuitive, we have all sat through presentations with the objects flying in from all directions without rhyme or reason.

4. Avoid using several different animation techniques in one presentation. Decide on one or two main techniques and stay with them. Usually the more conservative the better, which means the "appear" choice is often the best one.

5. Make sure you test your animation by running your presentation in slide view from beginning to end. In fact, even if you are not using animation, you should always review your presentation in slide view since for reasons unknown, animation will sometimes appear that you did not intend (suggesting gremlins do exist). You can usually get rid of these gremlins by checking the Animation Schemes and turning off "Apply to all Slides" if it is selected.

As with all design guidelines discussed in this chapter, use animation only if it adds to or helps you in delivering your message.

The following five tips for better visuals presented by Jon Hanke, editor of *Presentations* magazine, typify much of the advice this chapter emphasizes:

1. **Remember that most eyes aren't perfect.** Because color-perception deficiencies are common, certain color combinations—including red/green, brown/green, blue/black, and blue/purple—should be avoided.
2. **Red should be handled with care.** Red is one of the most influential colors in your software palette—but it also carries negative cultural attachments, so use it carefully.
3. **Don't forget your basic black.** Often overlooked, black is a background color with useful psychological undertones; it connotes finality and also works well as a transitional color. Green is another background color with positive associations.
4. **Arrange colors from dark to light.** We perceive dark colors as being "heavier" than light ones, so graphic elements that are arranged from darkest to lightest are the easiest for the eyes to scan.
5. **Keep the eye moving.** Large, simple geometric shapes will be the first thing your audience focuses on; text will generally be the last. When designing visuals, keep innate scanning tendencies in mind.

Source: http://www.3m.com/meetingnetwork/presentations/pmag_better_visuals.html.

Hanke's fifth tip, to design your slide so that the audience's eyes keep moving, deserves some discussion. Although culture will determine how someone reads (right to left or left to right), most businesspeople are used to reading charts from left to right and top to bottom. You should think about how your graphics will direct the eye and where most of your audience will be inclined to look. Again, keep graphics simple, and design your slides so that the audience can scan them easily and naturally. Also, if you must create a design contrary to your audience's natural reading inclination, be prepared to guide them to the portion of the slide where you want their attention. This kind of guidance requires that you practice with your slides, making sure you can provide this assistance in reading easily and smoothly.

To summarize, when using graphics and PowerPoint, you want to follow these guidelines:

Top Ten Guidelines for Using Graphics and PowerPoint for a Leadership Edge

1. Decide on your message, determine what information or data best supports it, and then decide how best to show that data graphically.
2. Use graphics for the right reasons, such as to reinforce your message, to provide a road map of your presentation, and to support assertions.
3. Select the right kind of graph to illustrate your message.
4. Use integrity in selecting and designing all graphics, making sure any graphs do not distort the data.
5. Keep your graphic simple. The graphic should make your message easier to understand, not more difficult; however, make sure it is meaningful and actually says something.
6. Use a title that captures the "so what?" of your slide so that your audience sees immediately the message the graph is communicating.
7. Create your own PowerPoint template or modify the standard ones Microsoft provides so that the presentation reflects your personality or that of your company.
8. Make the font size and any graphic images large enough for the audience to see even from the back of the room.
9. Be careful with your color selections; go for contrast but be conservative.
10. Avoid overusing or misusing animation.

Finally, make the graphics and PowerPoint work for you, not against you. Use graphics as support of your message, and use PowerPoint as the tool it is intended to be. *You* should be the focus of the presentation. The slides are there to aid you, not replace you. Used correctly, graphics and PowerPoint will provide a leadership edge and help you project a positive ethos.

Exercise 5.1: Creating Graphs

1. Review the quantitative data that follows. You will see that you can make several conclusions based on this data. What do you see? Select *one type of comparison* (part to whole, time series, etc.) and roughly sketch out a slide to support the conclusion you have drawn from the comparison. (You do not need to use all of the data.) Write a title for the slide that captures the "so what?" of the graph.

Sales Data for Gizmo Company Products ($000)*			
	Product A	Product B	Product C	Total
January	85	26	7	118
February	94	30	8	132
March	103	35	8	146
April	113	40	7	160
May	122	45	13	180
June	130	30	10	170

*You may assume that the profit margins on each product are similar.

2. Use the same process to analyze this data and sketch out a slide. Remember to write a title that tells the audience what you want them to conclude from the data.

Quench Beverage Company—Cola Sales Data for the United States and Mexico ($MM)			
	2002	2003	2004	2005
U.S.	24.1	40.0	37.5	47.4
Mexico	39.9	34.8	23.8	19.9

Source: This exercise was developed by Beth O'Sullivan and Larry Hampton, Rice University. Used with permission.

Exercise 5.2: Selecting and Designing Graphics

For each of the following topics, decide on the best type of graph to support the message and then design the graphic. Do these very quickly, sketching what first comes to your mind. Do not worry about being artistic; instead, capture your own creative ideas.

1. Over the last five years, Company A has outperformed its competitor, Company B (increasing revenue, decreasing costs).
2. GMAT scores are not related to grades in MBA classes.
3. Widgets yield the majority of WidCo's profit.
4. The bonus percentage depends on employee title and rank.
5. Four forces are driving industry growth.
6. The project consists of three phases.

Exercise 5.3: Team Graphics and Oral Presentations

For this exercise, pretend you are in an investment group focused on stocks in the information technology sector and your group has been selected to deliver an updated presentation on the company/division discussed in one of the following *BusinessWeek* articles: "Chipping Away at Qualcomm's Chips" (June 16, 2003), "Pixar's Unsung Hero" (June 30, 2003), "Can HP's Printer Biz Keep Printing Money" (July 14, 2003), and "The Outcry over Terminator Genes" (July 28, 2003). Although these *BusinessWeek* articles work well for this exercise, almost any article that includes financial performance data will work as well.

Your audience will consist of potential investors in the company.

If you are not already working with a team, form a group of four to five people for this exercise. Each group will have 40 minutes to develop a 5-minute oral presentation that is heavily dependent on visual aids for communicating key ideas and maintaining interest. (Your team can choose who will present—not everyone needs to speak, although it is fine if you want everyone to deliver part of the presentation.)

Your presentation should convey the company's current situation and prospects. Your group may make an investment recommendation if you wish, but you are not required to do so. You do not need to use all the data in the article, and you may also add other information about the company (if it is from a reliable source!).

Each group member should offer suggestions about what key messages to include in your visuals. The team then needs to agree on the "storyboard," that is, the ideas to be conveyed and the content and sequence of graphics.

Use the paper and the markers provided or your computer to create the visual aids you will use for your presentation. Of course, in the real world, you would have more time to make your visuals look professional. For today, you should focus on your story, capturing key messages, expressing them graphically, and presenting them effectively (remember to include an effective opening, strong transitions, and an effective closing for your presentation). Your visuals may include quantitative charts, diagrams, qualitative drawings, and word slides (where needed). Be sure to do the following:

- Include a title chart with the names of the group members and the company.
- Write a title that tells the main message of the presentation.
- Create "so what?" titles for each visual.
- Limit your content or "body" visuals to a number you can comfortably present in 5 minutes

Source: This exercise was adapted from an exercise created by Beth O'Sullivan and Larry Hampton, Rice University. Used with permission.

Notes

1. Vogel, D., Dickson, G., & Lehman, J. A. (1986). *Persuasion and the Role of Visual Presentation Support.* Study sponsored by the University of Minnesota and 3M Corporation. The presentersuniversity.com site claims that "the human brain processes visuals 400,000 times faster than text [and] visual aids have been found to improve learning by up to 400 percent." *www.presentersuniversity.com/visuals.php.* They cite Knowledge Industry Publications, 1998, although the original reference could not be located and the numbers could not be verified.

2. Tufte, E. R. (2003). *The Cognitive Style of PowerPoint.* Cheshire, CT: Graphics Press.

3. For more on selecting and designing graphs, you might want to consult Gene Zelazny's *Say It with Charts.* New York: McGraw-Hill, 2001. Zelazny has spent years helping consultants turn complex data into understandable charts.

4. Tufte, E. R. (1983). *The Visual Display of Quantitative Information.* Cheshire, CT: Graphics Press, p. 53.

5. For examples of graphic distortion and how to avoid it and a discussion of visual ethics, see Tufte, E. R. (1983), & Kienzler, D. S. (1997). Visual ethics. *The Journal of Business Communication* 34, pp. 171–187.

6. Halverson, M. 3M Meeting Network—Choosing the Right Colors for Your Next Presentation," www.3m.com.

7. PowerPoint is the only presentation/graphics software discussed in this chapter because it has become the presentation standard, not to support or promote Microsoft and its products. All of the best practices presented would apply to any presentation or graphics software package.

Managerial Leadership Communication

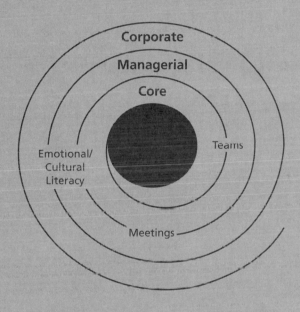

Corporate

Managerial

Core

Teams

Emotional/
Cultural
Literacy

Meetings

Chapter **Six**

Developing Emotional Intelligence and Cultural Literacy to Strengthen Leadership Communication

Emotional leadership is the spark that ignites a company's performance, creating a bonfire of success or a landscape of ashes.

Daniel Goleman, Richard Boyatzis, and Annit McKee (2001). "Primal Leadership: The Hidden Driver of Great Performance," *Harvard Business Review*

Our globalized, multicultural world requires leaders with a keen understanding of national cultures. By learning from other countries, culturally literate leaders build cultural bridges, enabling them to leverage culture as a tool for competitive advantage.

Robert Rosen (2000). *Global Literacies: Lesson on Business Leadership and National Cultures*. New York: Simon & Schuster

Chapter Objectives

In this chapter, you will learn to do the following:

- Appreciate the value of emotional intelligence.
- Take steps to increase your own self-awareness.
- Improve your nonverbal skills.
- Improve your listening skills.

- Mentor others and provide feedback.
- Realize the value of cultural literacy.
- Use a cultural framework to understand differences.

Leaders need strong interpersonal skills and an understanding of and appreciation for cultural diversity. Without these skills, leaders cannot communicate with and manage others effectively. Interpersonal skills have gained recent recognition among business leaders under the name of "emotional intelligence."[1] Emotional intelligence (EI) is the capacity to understand your own emotions and those of other people. This understanding provides a foundation for understanding and appreciating cultural differences, called cultural literacy here. It means being literate or knowledgeable about the fundamental differences across cultures.

Your emotional intelligence and cultural literacy affect the climate of the organizations you lead: "'Emotions are contagious. Research shows that they determine 50% to 70% of the workplace climate; that climate, in turn, determines 20% to 30% of a company's performance.' What's more, EI accounts for 85% of what distinguishes the stars in top leadership positions from low-level performers."[2] These numbers are too significant for a leader to ignore. The leader's emotional intelligence determines his or her success as well as the company's culture and performance, and understanding cultural differences begins with emotional intelligence.

For leadership communication, emotional intelligence and cultural literacy are as important as the strategy, writing, and speaking skills included in the core of the leadership communication spiral introduced in the first few chapters of this text. The need for keen emotional intelligence and cultural literacy becomes magnified when you interact with others in an organization, whether one-on-one, in groups, in meetings, or in teams; and it is this interaction that is the focus of the managerial ring of the leadership communication spiral.

Emotional intelligence and cultural literacy are necessary skills that allow you to interact with and lead others effectively, and the key to interacting with others and managing relationships successfully is communication: "The basis of any relationship is communication. Without communication—be it sign language, body language, e-mail, or face-to-face conversation—there is no connection and hence no relationship. The importance of effective communication skills to your Emotional Intelligence is crucial, and its value in the workplace is incalculable."[3]

While this entire book is dedicated to improving your leadership communication skills, this chapter is devoted specifically to understanding emotional intelligence and developing the ability to uncover what Weisinger calls the "emotional subtext," which means getting below the surface of the words, in many cases, to the meaning beneath. This ability is essential to emotional intelligence. The first sections of this chapter discuss the value of emotional intelligence and how to achieve it; the later sections on nonverbal communications, listening, people development, and cultural literacy will increase your ability to understand the emotional subtext.

APPRECIATING THE VALUE OF EMOTIONAL INTELLIGENCE

The company's culture reflects the emotional intelligence (or lack) of the company leaders, and the company leaders reveal that emotional intelligence through their communication ability and style. Think back to the example in Chapter 2 of the midwestern CEO who lambasted his managers in a memo because he thought their employees were not working long enough hours, citing the empty parking lot as one of his clues to the slacking workforce. What kind of personality does his e-mail reveal? What does it say about his attitude toward and relationship with his management team? What does it suggest about the company culture? The CEO's memo suggests emotional intelligence deficiencies since he shows little concern for the emotions of his audience and little control of his own. He appears very limited in his understanding of his audience and how best to motivate them.

The first version of the memo about the abuse of copy machines in Chapter 1 also exhibits limited emotional intelligence through its insensitivity to others and lack of awareness of how to motivate employees. The language in the first version, such as the use of passive voice ("It has recently been brought to my attention" and "Their behavior cannot and will not be tolerated"), and the threat ("Anyone in the future who is unable to control himself will have his employment terminated") suggest a culture that is authoritative and hierarchical, where management sits well above and separate from the employees. The language in the final version, however, suggests a company where the employees are part of a community with management: "We are revamping our policy. . . ."

Both of these examples show how the language that you use reveals the kind of leader that you are and the type of company that you run. Both are prime examples of how a deficiency of emotional intelligence can lead to communication mistakes, which in turn can lead to problems in the corporate culture and signal that cultural problems exist. All of the research into the importance of emotional intelligence demonstrates that possessing emotional intelligence is valuable to leaders personally and to the organizations they lead.

Understanding Emotional Intelligence

Reuven Bar-On, who developed the concept of emotional quotient in 1988, provides a technical definition of emotional intelligence. Emotional quotient (or intelligence) is emotional and social knowledge and the ability to

1. Be aware of, understand, and express yourself.
2. Be aware of, understand, and relate to others.
3. Deal with strong emotions and control your impulses.
4. Adapt to change and to solve problems of a personal or a social nature.[4]

This definition suggests that emotional intelligence begins with the ability to identify and manage emotions in ourselves and in others, but it extends also to the ability to translate these emotions into actions that show flexibility and personal and social problem-solving ability. It implies that the actions should have a positive impact on others. Exhibit 6.1 contains a diagram that breaks emotional intelligence

EXHIBIT 6.1 **Conceptualization of Emotional Intelligence**

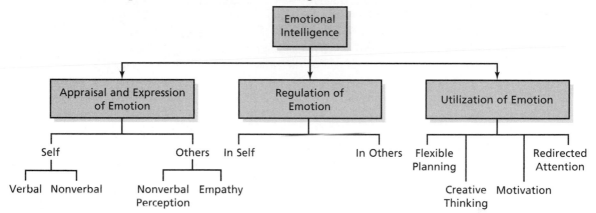

Source: Figure from Morand, D. A. (2001). The emotional intelligence of managers: Assessing the construct validity of a nonverbal measure of "people skills." *Journal of Business and Psychology* 16 (1), pp. 21–33. Figures based on Mayer, J., & Salovey, P. (1993). The intelligence of emotional intelligence. *Intelligence*, pp. 433–442.

down into components similar to those Reuven Bar-On cites. It illustrates the role of communication and the ways that emotional intelligence can be manifested.

The diagram contains three branches of emotional intelligence: (1) the appraisal and expression of emotions, (2) the regulation of emotions, and (3) the use of emotions. Another way to think about these three branches is as they might be expressed or revealed: through communication, by control, and by action. Leaders demonstrate their emotional intelligence by appraising situations and others and by expressing the appropriate emotions. In the first branch, the focus is on expressing yourself verbally and nonverbally, and on understanding others by reading their nonverbal cues and by empathizing with them. The middle branch focuses on the control of emotions in the self and in others. The far right branch deals with manifestation of emotional intelligence in actions, such as planning with flexibility, thinking creatively, motivating others, and redirecting attention or energy when appropriate.

Consider the midwestern CEO again; his emphasis is on the self, what he feels, and what is in it for him—all part of the left side of the diagram. His e-mail suggests little empathy and little regulation of his emotions. In the end, his e-mail fails to suggest flexible planning, creativity, redirection, or motivation of his employees toward the actions he desires. Effective leadership communication depends on being able to analyze an audience and develop a communication strategy for the context, which includes the left and middle branch of the emotional intelligence tree in Exhibit 6.1. The CEO has fallen short here, which carries over into the failure to craft and deliver the messages that will inspire his employees to act as he wants.

This example demonstrates how profoundly emotional intelligence influences your leadership communication ability, which in turn suggests your leadership style.

Connecting Emotional Intelligence to Leadership Styles

In *Primal Leadership*, Goleman, Boyatzis, and McKee argue that leadership styles fall into six broad categories: (1) visionary, (2) coaching, (3) affiliative, (4) democratic,

EXHIBIT 6.2
Leadership
Styles in a
Nutshell

Source: Adapted
and reprinted by
permission of
Harvard Business
School Press. From
*Primal Leadership:
Realizing the Power of
Emotional Intelligence*
by Goleman, D.,
Boyatzis, R., &
McKee, A. Boston,
MA 2002, p. 55.
Copyright © 2002 by
Daniel Goleman; all
rights reserved.

Style	How It Builds Resonance	Impact on Climate	When Appropriate
Visionary	Moves people toward shared dreams	Most strongly positive	When changes require a new vision, or when direction is needed
Coaching	Connects what a person wants with the organization's goals	Highly positive	To help an employee improve performance by building long-term capabilities
Affiliative	Creates harmony by connecting people to each other	Positive	To heal rifts in a team, motivate during stressful times, or strengthen connections
Democratic	Values people's input and gets commitment through participation	Positive	To build buy-in or consensus, or to get valuable input from employees
Pacesetting	Meets challenging and exciting goals	Because frequently executed poorly, often highly negative	To get high-quality results from a motivated and competent team
Commanding	Soothes fears by giving clear direction in an emergency	Because so often misused, highly negative	In a crisis, to kick-start a turnaround, or with problem employees

(5) pacesetting, and (6) commanding. These last two may have a negative impact on the organization (Exhibit 6.2).

Any one of these styles might be effective in the right situation, although the authors' research demonstrates that pacesetting and commanding rarely work, particularly in the long term.

The style of communication will differ from leader to leader and from organization to organization, and the leaders will reveal that style by how they choose to communicate with employees. Both the e-mail of the midwestern CEO and first version of the memo on the abuse of copiers suggest a commanding leadership style, for example, and it seems clear these styles would not be effective in motivating employees. On the other hand, visionary leaders would probably be very visible in the organization, speaking frequently in public internal forums, holding frequent meetings, and sending out statements that motivate and provide guidance to all of the employees. The coaching leaders would provide a strong, mentoring culture and probably place importance on training and development sessions and on management's responsibility for developing others. The affiliative leader would probably arrange forums for frequent interaction between management and employees and encourage management to walk the halls and be accessible, both one-on-one and in small groups. The democratic leader would probably hold frequent meetings as well, but he or she would also survey employees and establish methods to obtain employee input.

In the four positive styles, the leader's tone would be receptive and open, whereas in the pacesetting and commanding style, the tone would be closed and distancing. The pacesetting and commanding tone is suggested in the following: "It has been brought to my attention that some of you are abusing the copies" versus the tone of "We should work together to achieve a pay-as-you-go policy."

A leader might vary his or her leadership style when the situation warrants it, but the ability to select the most effective style for different situations requires the emotional intelligence to assess the situation correctly and assume the style appropriate for the context and audience. It means understanding that leaders reveal their emotional intelligence in their words and their actions.

Exhibit 6.3 contains the "major domains" of emotional intelligence with their associated personal and social competencies, further illustrating how emotional intelligence can be manifest in interactions with others and in attempts to communicate with and to lead them.

EXHIBIT 6.3
Emotional Intelligence Domains and Competencies

Source: Reprinted by permission of Harvard Business School Press. From *Primal Leadership: Realizing the Power of Emotional Intelligence* by Goleman, D., Boyatzis, R., & McKee, A. Boston, MA 2002, p. 39. Copyright © 2002 by Daniel Goleman; all rights reserved.

Personal Competence: These capabilities determine how we manage ourselves.

Self-Awareness
- Emotional self-awareness: Reading one's own emotions and recognizing their impact; using "gut sense" to guide decisions
- Accurate self-assessment: Knowing one's strengths and limits
- Self-confidence: A sound sense of one's self-worth and capabilities

Self-Management
- Emotional self-control: Keeping disruptive emotions and impulses under control
- Transparency: Displaying honesty and integrity; trustworthiness
- Adaptability: Flexibility in adapting to changing situations or overcoming obstacles
- Achievement: The drive to improve performance to meet inner standards of excellence
- Initiative: Readiness to act and seize opportunities
- Optimism: Seeing the upside in events

Social Competence: These capabilities determine how we manage relationships.

Social Awareness
- Empathy: Sensing others' emotions, understanding their perspective, and taking active interest in their concerns
- Organizational awareness: Reading the currents, decision networks, and politics at the organizational level
- Service: Recognizing and meeting follower, client, or customer needs

Relationship Management
- Inspirational leadership: Guiding and motivating with a compelling vision
- Influence: Wielding a range of tactics for persuasion
- Developing others: Bolstering others' abilities through feedback and guidance
- Change catalyst: Initiating, managing, and leading in a new direction
- Conflict management: Resolving disagreements
- Building bonds: Cultivating and maintaining a web of relationships
- Teamwork and collaboration: Cooperation and team building

According to Goleman, Boyatzis, and McKee, no leader possesses all of these competencies, but "highly effective leaders typically exhibit a critical mass of strength in a half dozen or so EI competencies."[5] Some competencies are certainly more important for effective leadership communication than others. These competencies are the focus of the remainder of this chapter, beginning with those included under self-awareness and self-management, moving through the relationship management competencies of developing others and managing conflict, and ending with increasing your social awareness by becoming more culturally literate.

INCREASING YOUR OWN SELF-AWARENESS

The first step toward emotional intelligence is self-awareness. Socrates said, "Know thyself," yet as most thoughtful people realize, knowing the self is not easy. In his book *Emotional Intelligence at Work,* Hendrie Weisinger calls self-awareness "the foundation on which all other emotional intelligence skills are built" and says that self-awareness is an ongoing process. He suggests that everyone exercise self-awareness at work by asking the following questions several times a day:

- What am I feeling right now?
- What do I want? How am I acting?
- What appraisals am I making?
- What do my senses tell me?[6]

The self-assessment at the end of this book's introduction contained a number of questions relating to emotional intelligence. If you have not completed it or skipped this portion, you might want to go back now and establish a baseline measure of your self-awareness and overall emotional intelligence.

Another way to become more self-aware is to take personality tests, such the Myers-Briggs Type Indicator (MBTI) discussed here. You may want to visit the Emotional Intelligence Consortium Web site (www.eiconsortium.org) since it lists and contains links to some self-assessment and 360-degree feedback tools. In fact, if you have never had the benefit of 360-degree feedback, or any feedback on your emotional intelligence, you will find such feedback often provides greater insight than personal assessments or personality tests. What is important to realize is that you can develop your emotional intelligence and by doing so improve your leadership communication ability, but you need to understand your strengths and weaknesses first.

Using Popular Psychological Profiles to Understand Yourself Better

Psychological testing can help you gain insight into your behavior and how you interact with others, and also how others interact with you. You can benefit from knowing yourself better and identifying characteristics that may hinder your ability to interact effectively with others. With this knowledge you can work toward modifying unproductive behaviors and perhaps, at a minimum, understand better why others respond to you as they do.

Numerous psychological profiling instruments exist for use by individuals and businesses. Three of the ones considered sound in their theory and applicability in a business environment are the FIRO-B, the Five Factors, and the Myers-Briggs Type Indicator (MBTI). Each can assist you in understanding yourself and others. Since the MBTI is the most widely used in business with over 2.5 million tests administered in organizations across the world,[7] the discussion here focuses on the MBTI to illustrate how you might use a personality test to understand yourself better and to manage others more effectively.

Using the MBTI

Katherine Briggs and Isabel Briggs Myers developed the MBTI using Carl Jung's concepts of personality types as the foundation for their personality assessments. Your individual personality type remains fairly consistent over time, although environmental influences can alter your responses slightly when you take the test. The MBTI consists of four dichotomies in 16 combinations. The dichotomies are as follows:

- Introvert (I) vs. Extravert (E)—indicates how you are energized.
- Sensing (S) vs. iNtuitive (N)—suggests how you interpret or understand the world.
- Thinking (T) vs. Feeling (F)—shows how you make decisions.
- Judging (J) vs. Perceiving (P)—suggests your approach to life and work.

A person's type is indicated by a combination of the letters according to his or her preferences in each of these dichotomies. Exhibit 6.4 lists the characteristics common to each of the individual letter designations.

An individual type could be an ESTJ, INFP, or any other of the 16 possible combinations. The combinations determine the personality type, not just one of the letter labels, although a letter may dominate.

The cartoon here illustrates how the types might differ even in something apparently as simple as telling time.

EXHIBIT 6.4
Descriptors
Commonly
Used for Type
Indicators

How Energized		How Interpret/Understand	
Extravert	**Introvert**	**Sensing**	**iNtuiting**
Outgoing	Introspective	The five senses	The sixth sense
External	Internal	What is real	What could be
Breadth	Depth	Present	Future
Interactions	Concentration	Utility	Novelty
External events	Internal reactions	Facts	Insights
Expressive	Reserved	Tangible	Theoretical
Gregarious	Reflective	Actual	Fantasy
Multiple relationships	Limited relationships	Practical	Ingenuity
Speak, then think	Think, then speak	Specific	General
Do-think-do	Think-to-do	Analyzes	Synthesizes
		Methodical	Random

How Make Decisions		How Live and Work	
Thinking	**Feeling**	**Judging**	**Perceiving**
Head	Heart	Control	Flow
Objective	Subjective	Run one's life	Let life happen
Reason	Mercy	Set goals	Adapts
Laws	Empathy	Decisive	Wait and see
Firm but fair	Compassionate	Resolved	Flexible
Just	Circumstances	Organized	Scattered
Clarity	Humane	Structured	Open
Critique	Harmony	Definite	Tentative
Detached	Appreciative	Scheduled	Spontaneous
Analytical	Involved	Product focus	Process focus

Starting with the man on the left and working across the characters, although we cannot identify all four letters of their types, we can infer that they most likely represent the following combinations within the types: SJ, NF, IN, EP. The SJ is very specific and decisive; the NF is general and focused on circumstances; the IN is concentrating and lost in internal thought; and the EP blurts out an answer without thinking and is not even sure what day it is. The cartoon demonstrates that even a small action can reveal something about the deeper personality of a person, although again, you should avoid jumping to conclusions and overgeneralizing about any type.

The Value of Knowing the MBTI

Knowing coworkers' types can help you as a leader understand how they are motivated and how better to manage them. For example, if you are having problems with a member of your group missing deadlines or being late for meetings, knowing that he or she is a "Perceiver" helps you to understand that their actions are not meant to be discourteous or disrespectful. You can then approach the behavior as a performance issue and provide feedback and perhaps coaching on the importance of better time management. That may not solve the problem completely, but if the employee performs well otherwise, you owe it to him or her and to your organization to recognize the inherent personality trait and respond appropriately to alter the undesirable behavior.

Awareness of personality types can be advantageous in team settings. If you are working with a group of individuals who are not collaborating and seem to enjoy working apart solving problems rather than as a team, you might infer that they are Introverts and pair them up for specific tasks. If you have the opposite situation, a team of Extraverts and one Introvert who rarely contributes to the discussions directly but whom you know to be able to contribute, you can pull the individual into the discussions directly with specific requests or questions.

Remember that no type profile or set of personality characteristics makes one person better than another. They just make them different in important ways. Also, no type is necessarily a better manager or leader, although studies have shown that certain types are better at some tasks than others. For example, those managers with "Feeling" as their decision-making preference are better at some components of emotional intelligence, such as experiencing empathy and recognizing nonverbal cues, particularly facial expressions.[8] That does not mean that leaders with a "Thinking" preference cannot or do not use feelings to make decisions; it only suggests that their first inclination is toward logic and that they may need to work a little harder at drawing out their emotional intelligence than the "feeling" person would.

Using a personality profile can help in developing your own self-awareness and understanding how best to interact with and manage others. As a result, it can contribute to personal development and to the dynamics of teams and even organizations. You need to keep in mind though that the profiles suggest how individuals are motivated and how they might approach certain situations; they do not predict behavior and certainly should not be used to create labels of individuals or even as ways to excuse a lack of performance of any type.

Finally, as an organizational leader, you need to understand the legal ramifications of such testing and the potential misuse of the information. You will thus want to check with your human resources or legal group if you are thinking of using the tests to help in team formation or dynamics, for instance, or to screen prospective employees, a widespread and growing use. A good source of information on the use of psychological tests in the workplace, including the legal issues, is Hoffman's *Psychological Testing at Work*.

Many assessments are available on the Web, although some require a fee and a psychologist to contact you with the results. You can take the MBTI for free online, and you receive your score and a report immediately. Over 30 personality tests as well as IQ tests are available at www.davideck.com. To appreciate the meaning of the results fully depends on understanding the tests and their intentions; therefore, if you plan to take any psychology test, you may want to consider talking the results over with someone licensed to give the test or, at a minimum, reading some of the many books available on them. For instance, on the MBTI, you might find Otto Kroeger's *Type Talk at Work* helpful. It is particularly useful in relating the test to the workplace and in explaining how different types handle different jobs and team situations.

Developing an Approach to Improving Emotional Intelligence

After the self-reflection and personality testing, can individuals really change their emotional intelligence? Goleman and others at the EI Consortium say "yes": "EI competencies are not innate talents, but learned abilities, each of which has a unique contribution to making leaders more resonant, and therefore more effective."[9] To do so requires that an individual be committed to change and willing to put in the effort. Goleman, Boyatzis, and McKee suggest the following steps "to rewire your brain for greater Emotional Intelligence":

Steps to Achieving Emotional Intelligence

1. **Who do you want to be?** Imagine yourself as a highly effective leader. What do you see?
2. **Who are you now?** To see your leadership style as others do, gather 360-degree feedback, especially from peers and subordinates. Identify your weaknesses *and* strengths.
3. **How do you get from here to there?** Devise a plan for closing the gap between who you are and who you want to be.
4. **How do you make change stick?** Repeatedly rehearse new behaviors—physically and mentally—until they are automatic.
5. **Who can help you?** Do not try to build your emotional skills alone—identify others who can help you navigate this difficult process.

Source: Reprinted from *Harvard Business Review.* From Primal leadership: The hidden driver of great performance. Goleman, D., Boyatzis, R., and McKee, A. December 2001. Copyright © 2001 by Harvard Business School Publishing Corporation; all rights reserved.

This approach calls on you, first, to assess your strengths and weaknesses; second, to obtain feedback from others on your strengths and weaknesses; third, to establish your goals; and finally, to map out a plan to achieve those goals. At the heart of changing is the self-awareness that you need to change. Once you have that awareness, a vision of your destination and a plan to get there, you can improve your emotional intelligence.

According to Goleman, "An emotionally intelligent leader can monitor his or her moods through self-awareness, change them for the better through self-management, understand their impact through empathy, and act in ways that boost others' moods through relationship management."[10] This section discussed developing self-awareness; the focus of the rest of this chapter is on the other side of emotional intelligence—relationship management through recognizing nonverbal communication, improving your listening skills, developing others more effectively, and appreciating cultural differences.

IMPROVING YOUR NONVERBAL SKILLS

The way you dress, walk and carry yourself, stand in relationship to others, use your hands, move your head, and change your facial expressions—all communicate to others. All of these are types of nonverbal communication or sending messages without using verbal language. As much as 65 to 93 percent of the meaning in communication is nonverbal.[11] Knowing something about nonverbal communication is clearly important for anyone wanting to improve his or her communication skills and is certainly important for any leader.

Nonverbal expressions are usually categorized into one of the following groups, some of which you may not have thought of as communication:

Categories of Nonverbal Communication

1. Appearance—looks, dress, grooming.
2. Paralanguage—vocal cues that accompany speech, such as volume, pitch, and rate.
3. Kinesics—body movements, such as gestures, posture, head movement.
4. Occulesics—eye movement, such as eye contact or looking away.
5. Proxemics—where you stand or sit in relationship to others.
6. Facial expressions—smiles, frowns, sneers.
7. Olfactics—smells.
8. Chronomics—the way time is used.

All of these affect how you are perceived and how you perceive others, yet studies have shown that people in general are not very good at interpreting nonverbal behavior accurately.[12] In fact, it is only in judging facial expressions that we tend to be correct. While the meaning of nonverbal communication involving body language differs substantially from culture to culture, researchers have identified six facial expressions that are consistently and universally interpreted across cultures: happiness, fear, sadness, surprise, anger, and disgust.[13] We often misinterpret other nonverbal communication, imposing our thoughts on others many times instead of accurately reading theirs. Beyond the common facial expressions, nonverbal signals are so dependent on culture and context that we need to take great care in interpreting them.

Developing a better understanding of nonverbal communication can help you in your communication to others and in your understanding of how your communications may be perceived by them. Nonverbal communication is too important for a leader to ignore; therefore, you may want to act on the following suggestions to improve your nonverbal communication skills:

1. **Learn as much as possible about any culture in which you will be interacting.** Much of the meaning of nonverbal communication depends on culture; therefore, you need to know something about the culture of individuals before you can fully understand their nonverbal behavior. Edward T. Hall, one of the first to research and write about culture and nonverbal communication, says that to understand people of a different culture, it is as important to know the nonverbal language (which he calls the "silent language") as it is to know the spoken language. He argues that most people, particularly North Americans, are not even aware of nonverbal language and its impact:

> Of equal importance is an introduction to the nonverbal language which exists in every country of the world and among the various groups within each country. Most Americans are only dimly aware of this silent language even though they use it every day. They are not conscious of the elaborate patterning of behaviors which prescribes our handling of time, our spatial relationships, our attitudes toward work, play, and learning. In addition to what we say with our verbal language, we are constantly communicating our real feelings in our silent language—the language of behavior. Sometimes this is correctly interpreted by other nationalities, but more often it is not.[14]

The discussion of cultural literacy later in this chapter will go further into some of the cultural differences, so for now, simply realize that nonverbal communication differs across cultures and misinterpreting it can result in serious miscommunication. Beyond the six universal facial expressions, few nonverbal signals carry the same meaning across all cultures. Therefore, anyone doing business with another culture must learn as much as possible about the role and use of nonverbal communication.

2. **Do not judge someone's actions out of context or leave the actions unexplored when important to you or the organization.** Remember that nonverbal behavior depends on context. What comes before and what will come after influence it. For instance, if someone walks past you in a corridor at work without speaking, you might assume that the person is irritated with you for some reason. You assign a meaning to the behavior that attributes an intention or motive to the other person. However, the action could have any number of explanations. Perhaps the person is simply absorbed in thought or perhaps not feeling well. If the individual is in the midst of writing a report and thinking about the analysis and perhaps an Introvert as well, then the person may simply be absorbed in thought. If someone on the team that is writing this report has shirked his or her responsibility, then the person could be irritated with that individual, not you. Taken out of context, which includes past actions not observable in the present moment and perhaps unknown to you, you cannot know for sure, so any interpretation on your part is a guess, and again, we have greater confidence in our ability to interpret nonverbal behavior than is warranted much of the time.

If it is important for you to know the motivation for the person's actions, you need to ask. Too often rumors and hard feelings grow in an office environment because people make assumptions based on nonverbal behavior.

3. **Develop your understanding or sensitivity to nonverbal cues.** Notice, for instance, when what someone says seems to differ from how they are saying it, often a very reliable nonverbal signal. If the words and the body movement seem in harmony, then the person is comfortable with what he or she is saying. If, however, the movements seem exaggerated or forced, then the person may be uncomfortable with the audience or with the subject. Pay attention to facial expressions, volume, pitch, and pace of the voice. To practice being more sensitive to nonverbal communication, you might want to engage a group in role-playing exercises, video them, and then discuss the nonverbal communication that occurs. Finally, if you want to review some of the most common explanations for nonverbal actions, you should look at the Center for Nonverbal Studies' Web site (www.members.aol.com/nonverbal2/diction1.htm). It contains a dictionary of 225 types of nonverbal behavior and is well researched and documented.

4. **Assess your own use of nonverbal communication.** The best way to see yourself as others see you is to videotape and watch yourself. To force you to focus on the nonverbal communication, watch the tape with the sound turned off. If you admire someone else's leadership image, then imitate the movements and

behaviors you observe. While you never want to be false and never can or should move too far away from your natural self, modeling the movements of others and practicing them until they are natural for you can be helpful in breaking habits that you want to change. You will find that confident speakers stand tall, establish eye contact, move with purpose, and use natural gestures to underscore or support their messages.

In addition to observing your body language, you should also listen to yourself giving a presentation, paying attention to your paralanguage (in this case, if on videotape, you would want to listen and not watch). Is your volume too loud or too soft? Do you talk too fast? Do you use fillers or allow meaningful pauses? Less skilled speakers often fill up any pauses with "uhs" or let each thought run right up into the next one. If you watch skilled speakers, you will see that they use silence effectively, allowing their audience to absorb their ideas and never rely on fillers of any kind.

You should also pay attention to how you dress and use the space around you. If you want to be accepted by your peers, you must dress the part. If you want others to see you as the one in charge, you must arrange your space to suggest your authority. Even where you sit at a table sends messages to others. How you arrange your office and your desk says something about you as a person. While all of these external symbols can mislead, they do communicate, and a manager must be sensitive to them.

Nonverbal communication is as meaningful as spoken words, even more meaningful in most situations. Leaders must pay attention to it in any communication situation and strive to be more observant of the nonverbal signals people send.

IMPROVING YOUR LISTENING SKILLS

Leaving listening out of any discussion of communication means leaving out at least 40 to 45 percent of the communication process.[15] Good listening skills are essential, and the lack of them hinders many people's careers. Most do not realize that good listening is hard work. According to Madelyn Burley-Allen in her book *Listening: The Forgotten Skill,* there are three levels of listening, with the highest level (Level 1) requiring more effort than people tend to expend:

Levels of Listening

Level 1—"Emphatic listening," where you refrain from judgment and listen with close attention, attempt understanding, and convey a sincere interest in the speaker's words.
Level 2—"Hearing words, but not really listening." Receivers pretend to hear and even respond; however, they do not understand the speaker's real intent because they are focusing on the words at a logical, nonfeeling level only.
Level 3—"Listening in spurts." Receivers tune in and out, hearing only part of what is said. They may even be pretending to listen when they are thinking about something else entirely.

While you should always aim toward maintaining your listening at Level 1, a number of barriers can interfere with listening, such as the following:

Common Barriers to Effective Listening

---

1. The speaker is talking about a subject of no interest to you or is boring. Although some blame for not listening falls on the listener, the sender carries responsibility as well.
2. You do not agree with the speaker; therefore, you do not listen to anything said or you think about counterarguments.
3. You may be more interested in what you have to say than in the other person. Extroverts easily fall prey to this communication breakdown.
4. You are distracted by other thoughts or by activities around you.
5. You have preconceptions about the subject or the speaker. Either you think you know what he or she is going to say before it is said, or you have already formed a judgment about the speaker or the content.
6. You respond emotionally to the words or ideas the person presents and, therefore, turn off your hearing to the rest.
7. You become so distracted by the person's delivery or something about his or her appearance that you shift your focus away from the words.
8. You only hear what you **want** to hear and fail to listen to anything else.

In addition to these barriers, we as so bombarded with noise every day that we become very good at filtering and hearing only what we want to hear. For example, think about how often you have the radio on in the car but do not hear a word the broadcaster is saying. Poor listening can easily become a habit, but it is one that managers must overcome to succeed as leaders in any organization. Obviously, some breakdowns in listening are more difficult to overcome than others, such as an uninteresting speaker; however, everyone can become a better listener in all situations with some effort. The following chart provides ten ways to improve your listening habits:

Ten Ways to Improve Listening Habits

---

1. Stop talking.
2. Stop thinking ahead to what you are going to say and turn off your own internal chatter.
3. Avoid multitasking (for example, talking on the phone while working at the computer or talking to someone in the room; attending to a lecturer while working at the computer).
4. Try to empathize with the speaker.
5. Don't interrupt, but ask questions if something is unclear.
6. Focus on the speaker closely, establishing eye contact if appropriate for the culture, but do not get in a "power stare."
7. Do not let delivery or appearance distract you.
8. Listen for ideas, not just for facts.
9. Listen with an open mind, not just for what you **want** to hear.
10. Pay attention to nonverbal cues and what is not said.

Again, good listening is not easy, but effective organizational leaders must be good listeners. Therefore, you should work on your listening skills just as you would any other communication skills. Practicing the following exercises may help sharpen your listening skills:

1. After a conversation with someone, or a lecture, or any event in which you were primarily a listener, try summarizing what the speaker said immediately, either on paper or in your mind.
2. In note-taking situations, look at the speakers and really listen to them; then record the main ideas, instead of trying to write down every word they say.
3. Practice paraphrasing others as they speak, but do not interrupt them.
4. Listen to a news story or something primarily factual and then try to summarize what you heard.

If you are not sure whether you are a good listener, you should take an inventory of your listening habits, either by making a list on your own, asking someone you trust to give you feedback, or taking a listening assessment. A little self-awareness will help you realize if improvement is needed and how much.

MENTORING OTHERS AND PROVIDING FEEDBACK

Developing others tests a leader's emotional intelligence. You need to be particularly sensitive to the feelings of others and able to establish ways to motivate and guide them that work with your personality and with theirs. You should recognize that employee development and management succession are two of your primary responsibilities as a leader, and you must want to foster the development of those around you and below you.[16] In addition to your own responsibilities in developing others, you are the model for the other managers in their roles as supervisors, mentors, and coaches.

Both mentoring (the longer-term coaching relationships) and coaching (the shorter-term, usually more specifically focused relationships) require a willingness to guide and help develop others as well as the ability to communicate effectively. One function that provides ample opportunity for you to use your emotional intelligence to develop others is by providing feedback. Providing constructive feedback is one of the leadership communication skills needed to guide others. After briefly discussing mentoring, this section will provide instruction on delivering and receiving feedback effectively.

Mentoring

All of the leadership communication skills discussed in this text so far—strategy, audience analysis, effective speaking and writing, and emotional intelligence—are required to be effective as a mentor. You should have a comprehensive strategy for providing mentoring throughout your organization and for you personally to mentor the managers working directly with you. You need to understand those you mentor in the way you would any audience and use all of the effective writing and speaking practices with them. Finally, emotional intelligence takes on even greater importance once you assume the role of mentor. You need to understand yourself and others, recognize the importance of nonverbal skills in communicating meaning, and be a skilled listener.

To build a successful mentoring program and establish successful mentoring relationships, you should establish roles and responsibilities for the mentor and the protégé. The Small Business Administration Web site provides a useful outline of the responsibilities for both.

Responsibilities of a Mentor

1. Provide guidance based on past business experiences.
2. Create a positive counseling relationship and climate of open communication.
3. Help protégé identify problems and solutions.
4. Lead protégé through problem-solving processes.
5. Offer constructive criticism in a supportive way.
6. Share stories, including mistakes.
7. Assign "homework" if applicable.
8. Refer protégé to other business associates.
9. Be honest about business expertise.
10. Solicit feedback from protégé.
11. Come prepared to each meeting to discuss issues.

Responsibilities of the Protégé

1. Shape the overall agenda for the relationship—know what you want!
2. Establish realistic and attainable expectations.
3. Be open in communicating with your mentor.
4. Establish priority issues for action or support.
5. Don't expect your mentor to be an expert in every facet of business.
6. Solicit feedback from your mentor.
7. Come prepared to each meeting to discuss issues.

Source: Information adapted from www.sba.gov/managing/leadership/mentor.html.

The mentor and the protégé must establish together an approach for working with each other and, if appropriate, set up a development plan with agreed upon objectives. They will also need to communicate regularly, but the protégé should be mindful of the mentor's time commitments and be realistic in his or her expectations. Mentors, on the other hand, owe it to protégés not to commit to more than they can deliver and to establish boundaries for the protégés.

Delivering Feedback

One of the most important abilities of a good mentor and coach is that of delivering feedback effectively. It is through feedback that people develop, particularly if the leader providing the feedback recognizes its potential value and uses it as a way to bring about the receivers' improvement. Feedback should include both praise and criticism. For feedback to be useful to the receivers, the feedback provider must be as specific as possible and use words that will motivate the receiver. For instance, to say, "Your presentation was not very effective" does not tell them much. They certainly would not walk away with anything specific that they could change. Instead, you might want to say, "Your presentation would have been easier for your audience to follow if you had stated your main message very clearly at the beginning, listing your main supporting topics, and then going through each of them in order."

The goal in feedback should be to connect with the receivers in such a way that they are receptive to what you have to say and leave with the specific information they need to perform differently in the future. Planning a feedback session requires the same effort in strategy development and audience analysis that you would apply for any communication situation. The following steps should work effectively when providing feedback in most business situations:

1. **Be well prepared for the feedback session.** Develop a strategy and analyze your audience. Then, have all of your facts and unbiased appraisal information at hand. Be aware of any cultural differences that may have influenced the person's performance or the way he or she may respond to your feedback. Also, think about all of the other communication strategy components: strategic objectives, medium, timing, messages.

2. **Create a receptive environment.** Depending on your primary objectives and the type of feedback you are providing, you may want to meet the receivers in their office or neutral locations. If your office seems most logical and you do not see any reasons for the receiver to be uncomfortable there, then at least come from behind your desk to welcome them into your office.

3. **Assume a comfortable demeanor.** Establish eye contact but not in a challenging way, smile, and exchange some small talk, if appropriate. Use the pronoun "I" instead of "you." For instance, instead of saying "You are not carrying your load on the team," say "I have noticed some distancing on your part from the team. Is there anything I should know? Or can I help you in some way?"

4. **Start by setting the context for the meeting.** If it is a yearly performance review, say so. If their performance has been below standard or their behavior has been disruptive, perhaps in a team situation, then start off briefly explaining the situation, focusing on the facts only.

5. **Move quickly into your main objectives, which should not be so numerous they overwhelm** (usually three to four at most). Have them organized so that you can move through them, pausing between each main point to allow the receiver to respond or ask questions.

Throughout, you should focus on behavior rather than the personality of the receiver, and you should be objective and specific. If the receiver is doing well, what can you say to reinforce success? If he or she is making mistakes, what specifically needs to be done differently? If your main focus is on a problem or issue, first try to bring out any positives in performance or actions, but do not make things up just to make the person feel better. If you can do so honestly, you should begin by focusing on what the receiver is doing well and mention any successes. Direct every criticism at an aspect of performance, behavior, or attitude that is correctable.

EXHIBIT 6.5

Source: Landsberg, M. (1997). *The Tao of Coaching*. Santa Monica, CA: Knowledge Exchange, 1997. Used with permission of Profile Books.

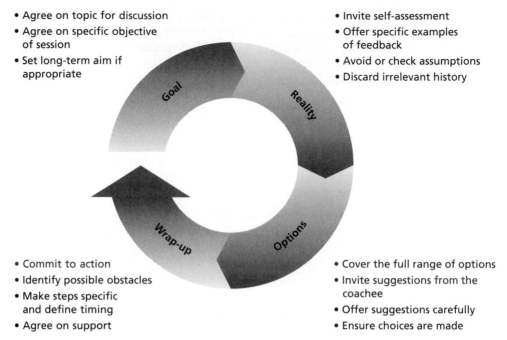

- Agree on topic for discussion
- Agree on specific objective of session
- Set long-term aim if appropriate

- Invite self-assessment
- Offer specific examples of feedback
- Avoid or check assumptions
- Discard irrelevant history

- Commit to action
- Identify possible obstacles
- Make steps specific and define timing
- Agree on support

- Cover the full range of options
- Invite suggestions from the coachee
- Offer suggestions carefully
- Ensure choices are made

6. **Ensure throughout that the receiver understands your points.** Do not take understanding for granted. Ask for questions or whether the receiver needs any clarification.

7. **Finally, close with next steps, being very specific about the actions you expect the receiver to undertake as a result of this feedback session and the timing for completing them.**

You may find it easier to remember the steps if you put them into the *GROW* model used by Max Landsberg in his book *The Tao of Coaching* (Exhibit 6.5).

Any good feedback session depends on listening and doing more asking than telling. You should always go into a session well prepared with specific facts and fair assessments. The goal should be to help the employee, to serve as a coach and mentor. If you display that attitude, the receiver will be much more receptive to your feedback.

Finally, a note on feedback from the other perspective. When others give you feedback, again listening is important. You do not want to be defensive. Listen attentively and show interest in what they are saying. If you feel they are being vague, ask for examples, but do not appear to be challenging them. There is a big difference in "I do not know what in the world you are talking about; do you have any examples of this?" versus "I am not sure I understand; could you give me an example?"

Theodore Roosevelt, the 26th President of the United States, said, "The most important single ingredient in the formula of success is knowing how to get along with people." Essentially, that is the thrust of emotional intelligence. People who relate well to others do better in the workplace and as leaders of organizations. They are able to motivate and inspire others to perform up to their potential, a skill every manager should possess. They are sensitive to the nonverbal communication around them. They are good listeners. They are sometimes called "people persons," which means they are interested in and care about other people, not just themselves.

To achieve emotional intelligence, you must have self-awareness and the ability to manage relationships or, in Goleman's words, personal competence and social competence. A good amount of social competence comes from understanding cultural differences and appreciating cultural diversity. The next section covers this hugely important part of emotional intelligence.

REALIZING THE VALUE OF CULTURAL LITERACY

We would hope the days of the "Ugly American" depicted in a book of that name published in 1958 are gone, although numerous Web sites suggest that is not the case, and examples abound of companies and businesspeople committing cultural gaffes and lacking sensitivity to cultural differences. For example, one global computer company, which planned to expand its business by partnering with companies in India, brought the future partners to a meeting at its headquarters, where cow hides were hanging in the elevators. How must the future partners have felt riding in an elevator surrounded by the skins of an animal that they hold sacred, with the slaughter of cows illegal in all but two states in India? Does that mean the company should change its decor for this one meeting? Perhaps not, but it should have a greater awareness of the cultural differences of countries with whom it plans to do business on any regular basis.

While bad examples are always easy to find since they are more visible to the public, examples are becoming more numerous of companies taking cultural literacy seriously and establishing comprehensive cultural diversity training. For example, Shell Oil Company has a diversity vision statement and conducts frequent diversity training sessions across all employee groups. Shell uses the "Iceberg of Differences" (Exhibit 6.6) to demonstrate how complex culture is and to illustrate how many cultural differences lie below the surface.

Gender, race, age, physical ability, nationality, religion, and language are the tip of the iceberg, and of course, an understanding of these differences improves a leader's ability to interact with internal and external audiences. An appreciation for all of the differences below the surface will increase a leader's emotional intelligence and greatly improve his or her ability to communicate effectively with today's typically diverse workforce.

Realizing the Importance of Cultural Literacy

Realizing the value of cultural differences is a key component of emotional intelligence. Only by understanding and appreciating cultural diversity can you know how best to communicate with all of the different audiences that form the complexion of most of the world's corporations today. More and more businesses are international, multinational, or global. Technology has enabled cross-global communication and made working across time zones, geographies, and nationalities a

EXHIBIT 6.6
The Iceberg of
Differences

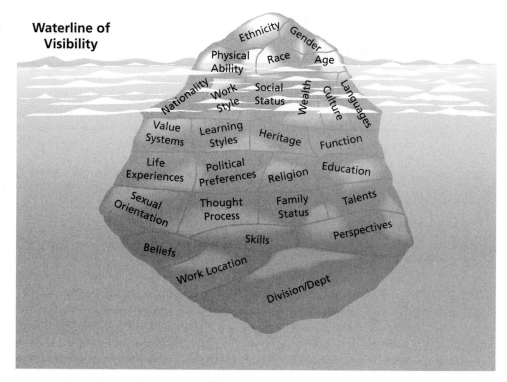

EXHIBIT 6.6
The Iceberg of
Differences

given for most managerial jobs. In addition, companies seek diversity in order to compete, and leaders need to be better educated about culture to take full advantage of the value diversity provides.

To be sure, academic learning about culture can provide only a basic level of cultural literacy: "Productive cross-cultural relationships require each individual to embark on a personal learning journey that initially can be even more frustrating than it is rewarding. Academic learning is useful, of course, but it is the direct knowledge accumulated in the day-to-day act of conducting business across cultures that is ultimately most meaningful. This is the kind of learning that allows people to understand not simply the surface signs of cultural differences . . . but, far more importantly, the invisible meanings beneath such differences. . . ."[17] Few would argue that to understand a culture fully, you must live it—breathing the air, speaking the language, existing as one with the people.

Finding standard, reliable frameworks to use in learning about cultural differences, as well as exposure to some guiding principles, will aid you in establishing a foundation on which to build a better understanding and appreciation of culture and its impact on the way we interact and communicate. This section provides those frameworks and principles and should help you approach diverse audiences with greater confidence and an appreciation for the differences. Understanding another culture requires setting aside a tendency to judge others and being open and flexible. In short, it demands that you draw on the best of your emotional intelligence.

EXHIBIT 6.7
The Layers of Culture

Source: Hofstede, G. (1997). *Cultures and Organizations: Software of the Mind.* New York: McGraw-Hill. Used with permission of the author.

1. A **national level** according to one's country (or countries for people who migrated during their lifetime)
2. A **regional and/or ethnic and/or religious and/or linguistic** affiliation level, as most nations are composed of culturally different regions and/or ethnic and/or religious and/or language groups
3. A **gender level,** according to whether a person was born as a girl or as a boy
4. A **generation level,** which separates grandparents from parents from children
5. A **social class level,** associated with educational opportunities and with a person's occupation or profession
6. For those who are employed, an **organizational or corporate level** according to the way employees have been socialized by their work organizations

Defining Culture

The term "culture" has numerous definitions, some rather narrow and others much broader. For instance, some think of culture as associated with levels of society or with nationality or geography. For anthropologists, culture is much broader: it is "the way of life of a people, or the sum of their learned behavior patterns, attitudes, and material things."[18] It is the way people make sense of and give meaning to their world. It is the frame of reference and the behavior patterns of groups of people. It includes social characteristics as well as physical characteristics, gender, age, profession, organizational function, and company structure and style. Culture is not personality. Culture is learned and shared equally by others of the same culture whereas personality is highly individual and influenced by our genes and our environment.

Geert Hofstede, a leading researcher on understanding cultural differences, provides a very useful way to look at the layers of the cultures to which we as people belong (Exhibit 6.7).

Countries, areas of a country, companies, and even functions within a company can have different cultures. Men and women exhibit cultural differences as well. Often these differences are thought of in a company context as diversity. Fortunately, most companies have come to realize the value of diversity and seek it; many are diverse naturally because they are truly global and contain different nationalities throughout the company.

USING CULTURAL FRAMEWORKS TO UNDERSTAND DIFFERENCES

The many books on international communication and on traveling in other countries, such as Roger Axtell's numerous "Do's and Taboos" of international business, provide guidelines on basic verbal and nonverbal communication in the major countries. They cover such topics as gestures to avoid, dining customs, gift giving, and even exchanging business cards. This section does not provide that kind of information. Instead, it provides frameworks and questions for you as a leader to use to analyze the diverse audiences to whom and with whom you will be communicating. The frameworks serve as tools to guide you to the areas of differences, and the examples provided illustrate some of those differences. The objective of this discussion is to move you closer to an acceptance level, where you are mindful and respectful of the many differences you will encounter in leading organizations today.[19]

A number of frameworks exist to help individuals define and organize the most important cultural differences. It is difficult to cover all of the most universal categories in which to place all the possible cultural differences, but cultural frameworks can be highly useful to bring insight into cultural differences and to help us approach culture systematically and nonjudgmentally.

One cultural framework that is particularly applicable to a business context was developed by Mary O'Hara-Devereaux and Robert Johansen for their book *Globalwork*. They argue that "while the learning process is endless, simple frameworks can help you develop a sense of competence. Understanding the various levels of diversity—physical, social, professional, functional, even spiritual— provides a good beginning. Learning to view each of these levels through the lens of language, context, time, power/equality, and information flow adds invaluable insights." One advantage of their framework is that it shows the interdependence of the variables, each crossing and interrelating with the other (Exhibit 6.8).

EXHIBIT 6.8
A Framework on Cultural Variables

Source: Adapted from O'Hara-Devereaux, M., & Johansen, R. (1994). *Globalwork: Bridging Distance, Culture, and Time.* San Francisco: Jossey-Bass Publishers. The information is used by permission of John Wiley & Sons, Inc.

The Five Cultural Variables in Holographic Relationship

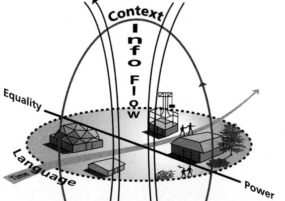

These variables are important to and applicable across all cultures. They are the variables anthropologists most often use when making distinctions about culture.[20] Understanding each of them will provide you with a platform on which to begin your audience analysis and determine your strategy for communicating and interacting effectively with people from other cultures.

Context

The first topic in almost any discussion of culture will be "context." Context was used in an earlier chapter as the term to denote what is going on around you that might affect the choices you make as part of a communication strategy. Its meaning here is slightly different since instead of focusing only on what is going on outside, it focuses also on what is going on inside people that affects the way they interact with others and understand communication events. In short, context is anything that surrounds or accompanies communication and gives meaning to it.[21] Context includes events, history, relationships, and status.

Cultures and professions can be arrayed on a spectrum ranging from low context to high context. Low-context cultures depend relatively little on existing relationships for meaning in communication and rely instead on explicit verbal messages. The United States and accounting and finance functions are low-context cultures. High-context cultures rely more extensively on relationships to understand meaning and place less importance on verbal messages. Japan and functions such as human resources and corporate communication are high-context cultures. Exhibit 6.9 shows the placement of cultures on the high/low-context spectrum.

EXHIBIT 6.9
Cultures as Usually Placed on the High to Low Context

Source: Cultures column from Copeland, L., & Griggs, L. (1986). *Going International: How to Make Friends and Deal Effectively in the Global Marketplace.* New York: Random House. Used with permission. Profession/function column, with additions in brackets, from O'Hara-Devereaux, M., & Johansen, R. (1994). The information is used by permission of John Wiley & Sons, Inc.

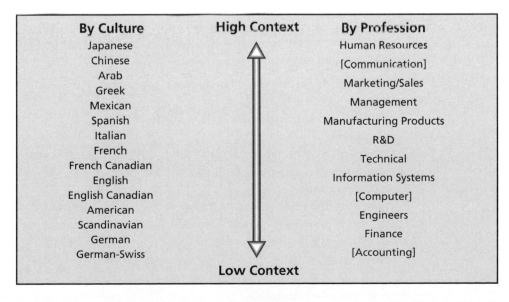

By Culture	High Context	By Profession
Japanese		Human Resources
Chinese		[Communication]
Arab		Marketing/Sales
Greek		Management
Mexican		Manufacturing Products
Spanish		R&D
Italian		Technical
French		Information Systems
French Canadian		[Computer]
English		Engineers
English Canadian		Finance
American		[Accounting]
Scandinavian		
German		
German-Swiss	Low Context	

One of the dangers of any discussion of cultural differences and classifications is stereotyping. It would be easy to overgeneralize about context differences. It may be typical for a person from the United States or for an accountant to rely less on context and more on the words that are exchanged, looking for actual facts and figures and not for the meaning between the words, the way the words are spoken, or the body language that might accompany the message. However, this stereotypical expectation will not be valid for everyone from the United States or for every accountant. The distinctions made in this discussion of context, as in the discussions of all the variables, describe characteristics that are typical of a group but will not necessarily be found in each member of the group. The goal is to make each of us more sensitive to the filters that are deeply embedded in our psyches that affect how we interpret the meaning intended by others in their communication with us.

Exhibit 6.10 illustrates some of the common differences between low-context and high-context culture that you might see in a business setting. As discussed earlier in this text, all communication exists in a context. Recognizing that the importance of context will differ from culture to culture is essential. For some cultures, context is more important than the words one individual might communicate to another. For others, getting to the point with words is all that matters.

Information Flow

The importance of context in a culture, high or low, influences how individuals approach exchanges of information and determines how messages flow between people and levels in organizations. It also controls who initiates communication and with whom, what kinds of messages are sent, what channels are preferred, and how formal or informal the exchange of information will be. U.S. businesspeople, for instance, are known for their directness and "bottom-line" mentality. They want the "so what?" right up front and do not want to read through a lengthy prologue to get to it. Information flow refers to "how" and "how fast" information is exchanged.

The following are some questions you should ask to understand better the cultural expectations of information flow:

1. How fast does a message travel from one part of the organization to another, from one person to another?
2. Does it and can it travel directly, or does it or must it go through levels or channels?
3. How much context is needed to ensure the information is understood?
4. How should information be linked and sequenced—or looped—to produce the intended results?
5. What are the most effective means of packaging information to produce the right responses?
6. Does the culture prefer words, graphics, or some combination?
7. How should the information be organized? Directly or indirectly?
8. Does the culture prefer written communication to oral?
9. Is the culture comfortable with informality in presentations or meetings?

EXHIBIT 6.10
Differences in Low- and High-Context Business Environments

Source: Table created with information adapted from O'Hara-Devereaux, M., & Johansen, R. (1994). The groupings and some examples supplement O'Hara-Devereaux and Johansen and draw on Hall & Hall (1989) and Samovar & Porter. The information is used by permission of John Wiley & Sons, Inc.

Areas	High Context	Low Context
Space	• Executive offices shared and open to all • May have several people in their office at one time, even with formal appointments • Stand close to each other in business conversations and may be offended if someone moves away	• Executive offices separated and access controlled • Expect to meet with one person alone and not have others lingering about during an appointment with someone • Set boundaries and will be uncomfortable if someone moves too close
Information	• Do not expect or want detailed information and feel irritated when pressed for it • Information shared with everyone • Comfortable in a sea of information	• Heavy reliance on detailed background information in written or verbal form • Information highly centralized and distribution controlled by a few people • Overload if information flows in a fast, disorganized manner
Relationships	• Relationships more important than objective data • Overlap between business and social relationships	• Objective (information based) rather than subjective (relationships based) • Business and social relationships compartmentalized
Status	• Authority and status more important than technical skills • Invitations to functions based on person's status rather than competence	• Competence given equal/more weight than position and status • Business meeting invitation based on competence
Meetings	• Meetings often announced on short notice; key people always accept	• Meetings with fixed agendas and plenty of advance notice
Decision Making	• Each new factor and item cautiously evaluated to be sure of implications	• Reluctance to act without a great deal of current information

Time

Henry David Thoreau, an American writer influenced by Eastern philosophical ideas and North American Indian culture, said, "Time is but a stream I go a-fishing in." This view of time is referred to in discussions of cultural frameworks as poly-chronic, that is, believing that time is a state of being consisting of many events occurring at once. Polychronic time is open-ended and flexible, and people are more important than promptness and schedules. The opposite cultural view of time is called monochronic.

People in monochronic cultures believe that time is linear, divisible, and consists of one event at a time. Time is a commodity and is meant to be measured and managed, conserved or wasted, spent wisely or foolishly. Events are scheduled sequentially, one at a time, and this schedule takes precedence over relationships and people. High-context cultures tend to be polychronic and low-context monochronic. For instance, North Americans see time as a scarce resource, and the expression "time is money" conveys the kind of value placed on time in U.S. business.

In addition to the polychronic/monochronic difference, cultures also differ in how they view the past, present, and future. Some see now as all there is and think it presumptuous to try to control or predict the future. Others value the past more. The typical North American is strongly oriented toward the future and devalues what is happening now as irrelevant. The following questions will help you understand differences in time orientation:

1. Does the culture emphasize promptness, or are people relaxed about starting times and even offended by those who arrive "right on time"?
2. Are they involved in several activities at a time, or do they do one thing at a time?
3. Do they take time commitments and deadlines seriously? How are appointments and schedules viewed?
4. How important is the way things were done in the past?
5. Are they more focused on the task or on people?
6. Do they expect privacy and respect private property?
7. What are their usual working hours?
8. When do they typically eat lunch and dinner?

Language

Language has been described as the "central influence on culture and one of the most highly charged symbols of a culture or a nation. . . . A language does not merely record and transmit perceptions and thoughts; it actually helps to shape both."[22] Although language usually presents the most obvious differences when people from different cultures come together, it is not just a matter of someone speaking Spanish and someone else speaking Mandarin. All cultural levels have language differences: industries, professions, functions, and even genders. As Deborah Tannen's research has found, men and women use language so differently at times that it is a wonder they ever connect. Language includes words, syntax, and vocabulary, as well as the various dialects and the jargon of disciplines.

Unfortunately, no easy way exists to solve the problems created by language differences. This is one place where the old adage "A little learning is a dangerous thing" bears out: "Without more than passing familiarity with the language of a culture, it is virtually impossible to scan the environment for business cues, negotiate, or evaluate performance."[23] Learning just a little bit of a language and trying to use it in a business context can cause serious problems, although most cultures would appreciate your interest and your attempt. In international business negotiations, you should always consider hiring your own interpreter even if you feel fairly comfortable with the language.

Power

Cultures differ tremendously in how they view power and equality. Some believe in strict hierarchies with clear distinctions between levels and formalized respect for people at the higher levels of an organization. Others see everyone as equal, and although a title may command some element of respect, it will not be as rigidly observed as in a hierarchical culture. Some cultures respect age; others do not. Some think education demands respect, while others see it as simply another item for a résumé. In other words, for some cultures, titles and position matter more than they do for other cultures.

Hofstede discusses the differences of power perception and practice in cultures as "power distance," which he defines as "the extent to which the less powerful members of institutions and organizations within a country expect and accept that power is distributed unequally."[24] He describes a major study measuring power distance from country to country in which the researchers found that some cultures view the possession of power by relatively few people and the resultant inequality as the norm. Such cultures have high power distance values. Other cultures see power as spread fairly evenly across all members and believe all people are equal, resulting in low distance values.

The survey results indicated "high power distance values for Latin countries (both Latin European, like France and Spain, and Latin American) and for Asian and African countries," and "lower power distance values" for the "U.S.A., Great Britain and its former Dominions, and for the remaining non-Latin part of Europe."[25] This difference in how power and equality are viewed leads to tremendous differences in how individuals approach reporting relationships within organizations, how they function on teams, and how they interact with one another on a daily basis. Exhibit 6.11 offers examples of some of the differences found in low power distance and high power distance workplaces.

The differences in how cultures view power affect leadership in particular. What might be considered leadership in one culture may be seen as tyranny in another. Managers who move outside of the culture they know must be particularly mindful of how the culture in which they have entered views power.

The following questions will help in determining and appreciating some of the differences in cultural perspectives on power and equality:

1. What is the attitude toward titles and positions?
2. Do individuals openly challenge authority?
3. Is the organization multilayered or flat?
4. How are decisions made (by one or many)?
5. Are subordinates consulted or told what to do?

EXHIBIT 6.11
Some Differences between High/Low Power Distance Workplaces

Source: Adapted from Hofstede, G. (1997). *Cultures and Organizations: Software of the Mind.* New York: McGraw-Hill. Used with permission of the author.

Low Power Distance	High Power Distance
• Inequalities among people minimized	• Inequalities expected and desired
• Interdependence between less and more powerful people	• Less powerful people dependent on the more powerful
• More educated hold less authoritarian values than less educated	• Both more and less educated show almost equally authoritarian values
• Hierarchy means inequality of roles, established for convenience	• Hierarchy reflects the existential inequality between higher and lower levels
• Decentralization is popular	• Centralization is popular
• Narrow salary range between top and bottom of organization	• Wide salary range between top and bottom of organization
• Subordinates expect to be consulted	• Subordinates expect to be told what to do
• Ideal boss is a resourceful democrat	• Ideal boss is a benevolent autocrat
• Privileges and status symbols are frowned upon	• Privileges and status symbols for managers are expected and popular

6. What is the attitude toward individualism?
7. How is status displayed?
8. What is the attitude toward women in business?
9. What is the attitude toward age?

A few differences in culture cut across context, information flow, time, language, and power. The following questions should help in diagnosing some of the general cultural differences not captured previously.[26]

General Beliefs and Attitudes

• What are the predominant religious influences?
• What are the holidays?

Agreements/Contracts

• What is the attitude toward agreements or contracts (firm or flexible and open)?
• How are negotiations conducted?
• How long might negotiations take?

Social Customs

• What are some customs related to lunch and dinner invitations?
• Should a guest bring a gift?
• What are appropriate greetings?
• What may be properly discussed?
• What gestures are to be avoided?
• What is the attitude toward talking about or showing feelings?

Finally, to conclude the discussion of culture, it may be helpful to dispel a few of the myths about working in other cultures:

1. **"We're Really All the Same."** As the discussion of cultural variables demonstrates, we are not all the same, and it can be dangerous to assume that we are.
2. **"I Just Need to Be Myself in Order to Really Connect."** While you never want to violate your own sense of identity and will even find it difficult if not impossible to do so, you do need to make an effort to understand cultural differences and may even need to go "outside of your own comfort zone in order to truly communicate your intent and keep your integrity intact."
3. **"I Have to Adopt the Practices of the Other Culture in Order to Succeed."** You should "adapt to" instead of trying to "adopt" the practices of another culture. Adopting can result in your being misunderstood and perhaps even considered disrespectful, as if you are mocking the culture. "You can and should adopt some practices of the other culture if they seem to be useful, desirable, and comfortable, or satisfying. The decision, however, should be based on thorough engagement with the culture, and with a good sense of your own cultural background and identity."
4. **"It's Really All about Personality."** While personality profiles, such as those discussed previously, are useful in helping to understand behavioral differences, drawing a direct correlation between a personality type and a culture can result in stereotypes that will limit your understanding of cultural differences. Also, "while the same range of personality types may exist within any given population, a culture's value orientations provide an overall framework for favoring one particular trait over another." Assuming that personality is the source of unfamiliar behaviors across cultures may cause a misreading of a cultural difference.

Source: Myths and directly quoted passages from Walker, D., Walker, T., & Schmitz, J. (2003). *Doing Business Internationally: A Guide to Cross-Cultural Success.* New York: McGraw-Hill. Used with permission of The McGraw-Hill Companies.

Even though you can only obtain a very basic level of cultural literacy from reading about the differences across cultures, having a framework for the cultural variables and using it to help you understand some of the differences provides a foundation on which to build the greater knowledge you will need if you do business with other cultures. At a minimum, the cultural frameworks, the examples of some of the differences, and the questions to help you probe differences should provide useful tools for your analysis of your audiences and for the development of your communication strategy. When you move outside of your own culture into another, you realize the value of learning as much as possible about the culture. If you plan to do business with another country for any length of time, you will ideally want to learn the language, while still realizing that if you are not fluent, you should use an interpreter before entering into business discussions or decisions.

This section provides a beginning and moves you toward a recognition of the importance and value of understanding and appreciating cultural differences, just as the entire chapter provides the information to start you on the road to greater emotional intelligence. Emotional intelligence and cultural literacy are essential in today's world and required for leadership communication. This chapter has provided an introduction to both. The next two chapters will build on this chapter by providing instruction on planning and conducting productive meetings and on building high-performing teams in a global environment. Your emotional intelligence and cultural understanding will affect your leadership in meetings and in teams, as it affects your leadership communication overall.

FURTHER READING

This chapter has referred to a number of excellent books on culture that would be worth reading in their entirety and would definitely help in further expanding an understanding of cultural differences.

Beamer, L., & Varner, I. (2001). *Intercultural Communication in the Global Workplace.* Boston: McGraw-Hill Irwin.

Bennett, M. J. (1993). Towards ethnorelativism: A developmental model of intercultural sensitivity. In M. Paige (Ed.), *Education for the Intercultural Experience.* Yarmouth, ME: Intercultural Press.

Hall, E. T. (1990). *Understanding Cultural Differences.* Yarmouth, ME: Intercultural Press.

Hall, E. T. (1989). *Beyond Culture.* New York: Anchor Books.

Hall, E. T. (1980). *The Silent Language.* Westport, CT: Greenwood Press.

Hofstede, G. (1997). *Cultures and Organizations: Software of the Mind.* New York: McGraw-Hill.

Lewis, R. (2000). *When Cultures Collide: Managing Successfully across Cultures.* London: Nicholas Brealey.

O'Hara-Devereaux, M., & Johansen, R. (1994). *Globalwork: Bridging Distance, Culture, and Time.* San Francisco: Jossey-Bass.

Rosen, R. (2000). *Global Literacies: Lessons on Business Leadership and National Cultures.* New York: Simon & Schuster.

Tannen, D. (1990). *You Just Don't Understand.* New York: Ballantine.

Walker, D., Walker, T., & Schmitz, J. (2003). *Doing Business Internationally: A Guide to Cross-Cultural Success.* New York: McGraw-Hill.

Exercise 6.1: Providing Feedback

The Case: Coaching Employees

You are the manager of a small group of people responsible for an introductory training program for new employees at your company. Your group consists of the following people:

- Rosanna, senior-level trainer with 12 years of experience, 10 at your company.
- Susan, senior-level trainer with 7 years of experience, 4 at your company.
- Hari, senior-level trainer with 15 years of experience, 2 at your company.
- Yang, administrative assistant, 7 years with your company.

Your group decides on the specific content of the training material based on the needs of the trainees, and then creates the materials (including lectures, handouts, and exercises), conducts the training sessions, and provides the feedback. Although the content for the training is fairly consistent from year to year, it does require some adjustments to match the number of attendees, the needs indicated in the assessments of the trainees before each session, and their course evaluations at the end of each session. The exercises in particular change frequently. Also, the instruction for each session depends on the previous session. The trainees receive feedback shortly after each session and must complete a lesson successfully before moving on to the next one. Thus, your group has two critical deadlines: one for preparing the materials and one for providing timely feedback.

Susan and Hari are both excellent trainers. In fact, their evaluations have been some of the highest of any trainers you have had working for you in the past, except for Rosanna, who has consistently received the highest rankings since you hired her 10 years ago. All of the trainers are very dedicated to the company and to their jobs. Lately, however, you have received negative comments about trainers' tardiness in returning feedback, particularly directed at Susan. Susan and Hari are what is called "Perceivers" in the Myers-Briggs Type Indicator terminology, which means they are easygoing, flexible, spontaneous, and open, all very positive qualities for trainers since it improves their ability to interact with the trainees and to be creative. However, it also means they are not very good at judging time, often wait until the last minute to get things done, and sometimes miss deadlines altogether.

Susan and Hari's frequent tardiness has caused extra work for Rosanna, who is always punctual and ends up having to complete some of Susan's and Hari's feedback forms and step in when they do not make their deadlines in creating materials. It also creates problems for Yang, since she has had to stay late and come in early several times to duplicate materials.

To ensure all feedback is delivered on time and that all materials are prepared ahead of time, you decide to try what you think of as "micromanaging," even though you do not like doing it. You meet with the group to establish (1) group deadlines for returning feedback and (2) specific responsibilities and deadlines for each lesson (divided up evenly among all of you). You want to make sure each of you has time to review the materials and make any adjustments before they go to the trainees, so you have specified that all materials be completed and sent to each of you at least a week before they need to be sent out for copying and distribution.

So far (you are just three months into the yearlong training program), Susan and Hari have frequently given handouts to Yang at the last minute and in some cases within as little as 10 minutes before a training session started, resulting in mistakes in the handouts and late starts for the sessions. They rarely make the one-week-ahead-of-time deadline to distribute their materials to the rest of the group, and they wait until the absolutely last minute to return their comments on the materials sent to them for review. Also, both have been late returning feedback to the attendees, and Hari has completely forgotten to prepare the materials for one of the training sessions, leaving you and Rosanna scrambling at the last minute to get them together. For the sake of your own stress level but, more important, to ensure the training program continues to receive positive reviews from senior management, you know you must talk to Susan and to Hari.

The Assignment

In breakout groups, answer the following questions:

- What are some of the issues you should resolve before talking to Susan and Hari?
- Should you meet only with both of them individually, with each member of the group individually, or with everyone at the same time?
- How should you conduct the session (consider using the GROW model)?
- How can you ensure the outcome will be what is best for you and for them?

After answering these questions, individuals may be asked to volunteer to demonstrate a feedback session based on the case.

Exercise 6.2: Improving Listening Habits

For this exercise, you will work with two other people. You will each assume one of three roles: speaker, listener, and observer. You will rotate the roles so that each person has an opportunity to participate in each one. The speaker should spend about two minutes telling the listener about an event or accomplishment that made him or her feel proud or happy while the third person observes. The listener should not interrupt at all in this one-way conversation. After the speaker is finished, the listener should tell the speaker what he or she heard—not only the facts but also some generalizations about the person made on the basis of the facts. The observer should then tell both what he or she heard and observed.

For example, if Galen tells Karim about a time he trained daily for three months to ride his bicycle in a charity marathon, Karim might tell him in return not only the facts he heard about Galen's training but also some assumptions about Galen: perhaps that he is motivated, dedicated to meeting his goals, and cares about the nonprofit organization for which he was raising funds.

Now, switch roles and repeat the exercise.

Source: Exercise created by Beth O'Sullivan and Deborah J. Barrett. Used with permission.

Exercise 6.3: Proactively Managing Diversity

Case: OmniBank's Diversity Efforts

You have recently been named the new president of OmniBank, a medium-size but rapidly growing suburban bank that meets the needs of individuals and small businesses. During the interview process you observed that, beyond the front office teller level, the more senior workforce at the bank is very homogeneous—mostly male and predominantly Caucasian. You have reviewed several marketing studies that profile your customer base and you realize that you not only have many customers of different ethnicities, but also have a large number of international customers.

As the new president, you decide it is important to launch a comprehensive effort to improve the diversity at the bank. You value diversity and believe that broadening your employee base as the bank grows will benefit everyone involved. Besides, it makes good business sense.

Your Assignment

You decide the company needs an improved hiring policy to jump-start its diversity efforts. In a group, list the steps you would take to establish such a policy and explain how you would ensure that it accomplishes your goal of greater diversity.

Exercise 6.4: Creating International Correspondence

The Case: PTI and Congoil

You are the vice president of operations for Production Tankers, Inc. (PTI), a U.S.-based oil services contractor that provides converted tankers to produce oil from offshore fields. PTI's converted tanker *Ocean Reliable* (*OR*) has been producing oil for Congoil P&P, a small but politically important division of a large West African national oil company, for the past seven years at a field called Naabila. Two years remain on the present contract. PTI hopes to renew the contract with Congoil for use of the vessel at another field when the present contract expires. You know in all honesty that other opportunities for the vessel are very limited. PTI's CEO has made the contract renewal a high priority for you and your group. Congoil pays PTI a fee of $43,000 per day for lease and operation of the *OR*, a rate that has allowed PTI to fully recover its initial investment in the vessel. Oil production has been running at around 7000 barrels per day, giving Congoil a revenue stream on the order of $140,000 per day at current prices.

Congoil owns Naabila field, is in charge of production operations, and bears all production costs. The large U.S. oil company Amproco serves as commercial and technical advisor to Congoil as part of the agreement granting it the rights to explore and produce other promising areas on the country's continental shelf. Amproco receives no payment for its advisory role and does not pay any share of the costs of operating Naabila field. Amproco is believed to have some influence with Congoil, although the nature of the relationship between the two companies remains rather obscure to outsiders.

Two years ago, as oil production at Naabila began to decline, Congoil asked PTI to install a small natural gas compression system aboard the *OR* so that they could implement gas lift operations, a technique used to help sustain production from aging fields. The need for gas lift had been anticipated, and PTI's contract with Congoil stipulated that if a gas lift compression system were ever installed, Congoil would reimburse PTI within 45 days for all documented costs. These costs came to $2.5 million and, under the terms of the contract, were invoiced to Congoil.

Gas lift operations began 18 months ago aboard the *OR*, but despite repeated requests from your operations manager and PTI's in-country business development manager, Congoil has not yet reimbursed PTI the $2.5 million. The difficulty seems to arise from Congoil's belief that some provisions of the contract are unfair and should be overlooked or set aside. Congoil's general manager, Syanga M'bweni Rugeiro, has maintained that installation of the gas lift compressor represents a capital improvement to the *OR*, and thus PTI should bear the cost. He and other Congoil officials have also objected to the fact that Congoil is contractually bound to pay PTI the $43,000 day-rate even if the vessel is not producing oil. They recall with considerable resentment an incident almost four years ago when needed repairs in conjunction with an extension of the original three-year contract required PTI to remove the *OR* from Naabila and take it to port for a 57-day period—during which they continued to pay the day-rate.

As vice president of operations, you have profit and loss responsibility for the *OR* and PTI's other production tankers. PTI's executives have made it clear to you that collecting the $2.5 million, preferably with annual interest of 8 percent, will have a material impact on the company's earnings for the current fiscal year, estimated by analysts to be in the range of $18.5 million on revenues of $390 million. Given the culture of PTI, you understand that securing payment from Congoil would be viewed very favorably and earn you additional status with your peers and superiors.

You decide to write a letter to Syanga Rugeiro requesting immediate payment of the $2.5 million. You have known Syanga for over seven years, and while you did not negotiate the original contract for the *OR*, you did negotiate the follow-on contract at the end of the first three years, when PTI agreed to reduce the original day-rate in exchange for the security afforded by a six-year extension. You feel that you know Syanga about as well as most Westerners get to know African officials, and you feel your relationship with him is sound. You know that he received his geology degree from the local university and later spent a year studying management at a British university. He speaks good English, and your business relations have been cordial. You have talked with him about his family and once even met his oldest son when Syanga brought him along on a business trip to Houston. He asked your assistance in getting the boy accepted into the engineering program at your undergraduate university, something you were happy to do.

Despite all these interactions with him, however, you have never felt that you understood Syanga very well. His Western education and business manner seem like a thin veneer over a much more substantial base of traditional African values and preferences. Your experience and some modest reading on the subject have indicated to you that the local West African culture is collectivist, high-context, high-power distance, polychronic, and risk and uncertainty avoiding. Decision making requires consultation among all affected parties, but nothing happens until the highest-ranking official involved signals his approval. You realize you have drawn most of these assumptions from your reading, but you feel you have also seen some of it in Syanga's actions. You feel you need to appeal directly to him to pay the $2.5 million owed to PTI.

You decide also to write a letter to Amproco's assistant country manager, Carl Mouton, asking for his help in getting Congoil to pay PTI the $2.5 million. You have met Carl on several occasions and have a number of common friends in the industry. Also, you have discussed the difficulties contractors can encounter doing business in West Africa. You believe that Carl might be able to influence Syanga to approve your request for payment.

The Assignment

In your role as PTI's vice president of operations, write two letters responding to the situation described in the case:

1. To Syanga Rugeiro requesting payment of the $2.5 million owed PTI, and
2. To Carl Mouton asking for his assistance in persuading Syanga to pay.

In addition, write a short (one page maximum) explanation of your communication strategy and how your knowledge of intercultural communication issues influenced the decisions you made in organizing the information in the letters, expressing your ideas, and developing an appropriate style and tone. In your explanation, please comment also on the choice of letters as the appropriate medium for your communication. If given the option, would you choose a different medium to communicate these messages? Please explain your response.

Syanga Rugeiro's address is 26-30 Avenida Presidente dos Santos, Dist. Norte 4, Kinuanda, Congola.

Source: This case and assignment were prepared by Charles R. McCabe. Copyright Charles R. McCabe, 2002. Used with permission.

Exercise 6.5: Preparing an International Briefing

For this assignment, you will work in groups to research, prepare, and deliver a 15-minute presentation with five minutes for questions and answers. The presentation will show how the culture of an individual nation or world region affects the local business environment and practices. As a starting point for your research and preparation, you should use the information in this chapter on cultural variables and determine the characteristics of your selected country against each variable. For example, is the country high or low context? How do they feel about power and equality? Your research should result in an international communication audit for the nation or region you select.

Although you will be presenting to your classmates, your team should develop its presentation with a specific business-related audience and purpose in mind; for instance, you might want to approach the presentation as a briefing for employees assigned to a newly acquired foreign subsidiary or a negotiating team about to embark on negotiations for an international merger. You should make your presentation appropriate in every respect to this specific audience. You may take a creative approach.

To promote breadth of learning and avoid repetition, each team is encouraged to select a different nation or region. You may choose from the nations and regions listed below.

Selected Nations and Regions

Any of the following Western European countries: Ireland, UK, France, Germany, Italy, Spain, Portugal, Scandinavia (as a region or individual countries)	Northern Africa or specific nations therein Northwestern South America (Colombia, Ecuador, Peru, Bolivia)
Argentina	Pakistan
Australia or New Zealand	Poland or Eastern Europe
Brazil	Russia
Central America	Southeast Asia or specific nations (Malaysia, Thailand, Vietnam)
Central Asia	Southeastern Europe, Greece or Turkey
Chile	Southern Africa or specific nations therein
China	Sub-Saharan Africa
India	The Middle East or specific nations therein
Indonesia	United States or Canada
Iran	Venezuela
Japan	West Africa or specific nations therein
Korea	
Mexico	

Exercise 6.6: Designing International Communication Programs

For this assignment, you are to work in teams to select a country in which a currently established company is not marketing its products. For example, you might look at Krispy Kreme and decide to market it in Germany. Each team is to research, prepare, and deliver a presentation of 20 to 25 minutes with five minutes for questions and answers, or 30 minutes total. The presentation will describe your marketing plan for the introduction of your company's product or service into a country outside of the United States. Your primary objective is to show that you understand enough about the country and its culture to argue that the country will be a successful target market for the product or service that you have selected. The presentation will address the business opportunity (the market), your product or service, the competitive landscape, your positioning, and your communication strategy (paying special attention to cultural differences).

The overall purpose of the presentation is to showcase to your CEO and senior executive team your team's approach to promoting and marketing your selected product or service. They will want to see your rationale and your preliminary plan for introducing and marketing the product or service.

You may select a company and country with the approval of your instructor. Your team must decide on (1) the company, (2) the product or service of that company, and (3) the country where the product/service will be introduced. You must be able to make a case for the introduction of your product or service; in other words, there must be a market for the product or service.

You might find the following site useful in determining your country and product: http://www.usatrade.gov/website/ccg.nsf/ccghomepage?openform. The U.S. Commercial Service is a service of the federal government whose mission is to help American businesses "compete and win in the global marketplace." Specifically, "The Commercial Service shall place primary emphasis on the promotion of exports of goods and services from the United States, particularly by small businesses and medium-sized businesses, and on the protection of United States business interests abroad." As part of that mission, the service provides market research for countries around the world.

Notes

1. The term "emotional intelligence" has been used by organizational psychologists for years, but it first became well known in business after the publication of Daniel Goleman's book by the same name.

2. Gary, L. (2002). Quoting Goleman in Becoming a resonant leader, *Harvard Management Update* 7 (7), pp. 4–6.

3. Weisinger, H. (1998). *Emotional Intelligence at Work.* San Francisco: Jossey-Bass.

4. Bar-On, R., & Parker, J. D. A. (Eds.). (2000). *Handbook of Emotional Intelligence.* San Francisco: Jossey-Bass.

5. Goleman, D., Boyatzis, R., & McKee, A. (2002). *Primal Leadership: Realizing the Power of Emotional Intelligence.* Boston: Harvard Business School Press.

6. Weisinger, H. (1998).

7. Hoffman, E. (2002). *Psychological Testing at Work.* New York: McGraw-Hill. For a discussion of the reliability of MBTI in studying manager personalities, see Gardner, W. L., & Martinko, M. J. (1996). Using the Myers-Briggs Type Indicator to study managers: A literature review and research agenda, *Journal of Management* 22 (1), pp. 45–83.

8. Morand, D. A. (Fall 2001). The emotional intelligence of managers: Assessing the construct validity of a nonverbal measure of "people skills." *Journal of Business and Psychology* 16, pp. 21–33; Gardner & Martinko (1996).

9. Goleman, D., Boyatzis, R., & McKee, A. (2002).

10. (2001). Primal leadership: The hidden driver of great performance. *Harvard Business Review.*

11. Albert Mehrabian found that 55 percent of our message is communicated through our body language and 38 percent through our voice, which means 93 percent of communication is nonverbal.

12. Goleman, D. (1991). Nonverbal cues are easy to misinterpret, *The New York Times,* p. C-1. Also, see Morgan, N. (August 2002). The truth behind the smile and other myths. Harvard Management Communication Letter.

13. Morand (2001).

14. Hall, E. T. (1959). *The Silent Language.* Westport, CT: Greenwood Press.

15. Nichols, R. G., & Stevens, L. (1957). *Are You Listening?* New York: McGraw-Hill.

16. Roche, G. R. (1979). Much ado about mentors. *Harvard Business Review,* January–February.

17. O'Hara-Devereaux, M., & Johansen, R. (1994). *Globalwork: Bridging Distance, Culture, and Time.* San Francisco: Jossey-Bass.

18. Hall, E. T. (1959).

19. The "acceptance" level of intercultural knowledge, as described by Milton Bennett (cited below), is the fourth stage of the Developmental Model for Intercultural Sensitivity. The stages are as follows: denial, defense, minimization, acceptance, adaptation, and integration.

20. For more on any of the variables, you would want to see any of the books by Edward T. Hall, a prolific researcher and writer on culture and the one to whom most recent writers on the subject refer. O'Hara-Devereaux and Johansen rely on Hall for some of their

examples. Also, if you desire a more complex, but also useful, framework, you should look at the one provided by Walker, Walker, and Schmitz in their book, *Doing Business Internationally.*

21. O'Hara-Devereaux and Johansen have pulled much of Edward T. Hall's distinctions on space under context, so this discussion will follow that combination as well.

22. Condon, J. C. (1975). *An Introduction to Intercultural Communication*, New York: Macmillan.

23. O'Hara-Devereaux and Johansen (1989).

24. Hofstede, G. (1997). *Culture and Organizations: Software of the Mind.* New York: McGraw-Hill, p. 28.

25. Hofstede, p. 26.

26. Driskill, L., Ferrill, J., Steffey, M. N. (1992). *Business and Managerial Communication: New Perspectives.* Fort Worth, TX: Dryden Press.

Chapter **Seven**

Leading Productive Management Meetings

There's nothing better than an in-person meeting. Nothing
yet has replicated that, as far as I know. For quick interaction,
e-mail and phone are great. But for really getting into something, a physical meeting is much better.

Jeff Bezos, Amazon.com's founder and CEO, *The Wall Street Journal*, February
4, 2000

Chapter Objectives

In this chapter, you will learn to do the following:

- Decide when a meeting is the best forum.
- Complete essential meeting planning.
- Conduct a productive meeting.
- Manage meeting problems and conflict.
- Ensure meetings lead to action.

A *Harvard Business Review* article several years ago reported that "11 million meetings . . . take place every day in the United States."[1] Today, that figure would probably be even higher with so many companies moving to team-based workplaces.
A survey conducted by UCLA and the University of Minnesota found that "executives on average spend 40%–50% of their working hours in meetings."[2] Another
survey cited in the same article indicated that "surveyed professionals agree that
as much as 50% of that meeting time is unproductive and that up to 25% of meeting time is spent discussing irrelevant issues."[3]

Given the dominance of meetings in business and how often people complain
about them, leaders need to be able to plan and conduct effective, productive
meetings. Doing so requires leadership communication skills and is important in
setting the precedent for the rest of the organization. As one specialist in meeting

management says, "Meetings matter because that's where an organization's culture perpetuates itself. . . . Meetings are how an organization says, 'you are a member.' So if every day we go to boring meetings full of boring people, then we can't help but think that it is a boring company. Bad meetings are a source of negative messages about our company and ourselves."[4]

To avoid creating a negative atmosphere around meetings in your company, you would want to avoid the seven deadly sins of meetings.

The Seven Deadly Sins of Meetings

1. People don't take meetings seriously.
2. Meetings are too long.
3. People wander off the topic.
4. Nothing happens once the meeting ends.
5. People don't tell the truth.
6. Meetings are always missing important information, so they postpone critical decisions.
7. Meetings never get better.

Source: The seven sins of deadly meetings. By Eric Matson and William R. Daniels. Reprinted from *Fast Company*, 1997, p. 27. Used with permission.

This chapter will help you avoid these seven deadly sins. You will learn to plan and conduct productive meetings by determining when a meeting is the best forum for achieving the required result; establishing objectives, outcomes, and agenda; performing essential planning; clarifying roles and establishing ground rules; using common problem-solving techniques; managing meeting problems; and ensuring follow-up occurs.

Meetings can be small or large, internal or external, frequent or infrequent. This chapter focuses primarily on small-group meetings intended to accomplish tasks or move actions forward inside an organization since these are the most prevalent type of business meetings.

DECIDING WHEN A MEETING IS THE BEST FORUM

Communication purpose and strategy should come first in planning meetings, as in all communication situations. You need to define a clear purpose and analyze your audience to determine whether a meeting is the best forum for what you want to accomplish. One of the frustrations with meetings is that they often seem unnecessary. Groups of all sorts can fall into a habit of meeting daily or weekly or monthly just because they have always done it that way. Beyond tradition or habit, they have no other reasons for meeting.

Even without what appears to be a specific business purpose, meeting periodically can be beneficial. For example, meetings can increase team, department, or company camaraderie. In company meetings, people see others they may not ordinarily see and feel connected to a larger group. Meetings with no specific business objective might have motivation, recreation, or networking as their purpose—all potentially important in certain organizational contexts. The frustration caused when attendees feel as if a meeting accomplishes nothing could perhaps be minimized by making it clear that the purpose for meeting is motivation, recreation, or networking. On the other hand, perhaps instead of a "meeting," what the group or company really needs is a social gathering or party.

In any case, you should be sure a meeting is the best forum for what you need to accomplish. No set rules apply to answer the question, "When is a meeting the best forum?" Referring to the three typical purposes for communication in business—that is, to inform, to persuade, or to instruct—will help you decide. For instance, if you decide your primary purpose is to inform, is a meeting required to convey the information or would an e-mail, memo, or maybe even a newsletter accomplish this goal more efficiently and effectively? If you decide your overall purpose is to instruct, is a meeting better for transferring the skills than an online instructional program?

You will also want to consider your audience. How do most of your employees like to receive information? Does your organization have an e-mail culture where people prefer to stay in their offices and communicate through e-mails, even to the person next door? Is your culture, on the other hand, one where people move up and down the halls and gather in the coffee room? Do you have mostly introverts, those who may prefer to work alone and may need meetings to pull them out of their offices, or extraverts, those who need other people to feel energized but can become distracted from tasks if meetings occur too frequently?

When you have something to communicate and are considering a meeting, you should first determine your overall purpose and consider the needs and preferences of your audience. With these issues settled, you can determine whether a meeting is the best forum for this communication. Use the following questions to direct you in deciding to meet or not:

- What is the purpose? What do I hope to accomplish?
- Will a meeting accomplish that purpose more efficiently? More effectively?
- Can I describe exactly the outcome I am seeking from the meeting?
- Is our group more productive when we meet?

COMPLETING THE ESSENTIAL PLANNING

Leaders often have assistants to handle the details associated with their meetings, but you will need to decide about the purpose, outcomes, agenda, setting, timing, and materials. To ensure your meetings are productive, you must conduct the necessary planning by answering the following questions:

- What is the purpose and expected outcome?
- What should be included on the agenda?
- Who should attend?
- What is the best setting?
- What is the best timing?
- What information will we need for the meeting?

EXHIBIT 7.1
Meeting
Purpose and
Expected
Outcomes

Objective	End Product
• Review past efforts at launching products in South America	• Brief description of each with highlights of what worked and what didn't
• Identify any problems or obstacles to product introduction	• List of potential problems or roadblocks in current proposed launch
• Determine possible approaches to overcoming problems	• Matching list of problem-resolving approaches for each roadblock

Clarifying Purpose and Expected Outcome

Meetings often have multiple objectives, but effective meetings, like good presentations and memos, usually have one main overall purpose. Your main purpose for meeting might be to inform, but you could also intend to persuade or even to instruct in the same meeting. The purpose of an informational meeting could be as significant as introducing a new vision or as mundane as providing a progress report intended to expedite a project. The purpose could be beyond the basic informing, persuading, or instructing. You could have as your purpose to solve a problem or make a decision. For example, a problem-solving meeting could have as its goal to determine alternatives for launching a new product in a new location; or for a decision-making meeting, the goal could be to walk out of the meeting having decided how the launch of a new product will occur.

The care you give to defining your purpose and objectives will determine the success of your meeting. As you begin to plan the meeting, write out your purpose and objectives very specifically; then, to start the meeting, tell the audience your intentions. You want everyone to know exactly why you are meeting and what you intend the meeting to accomplish.

In addition to the objectives, determine the outcome you seek from the meeting. It helps to make the outcome a tangible end product. For example, a meeting to discover and discuss the issues associated with introducing a new product for the first time in South America might have the objectives and end products presented in Exhibit 7.1.

If you have trouble defining an end product, your objective may not be clear enough or tangible enough to accomplish in a meeting. If they do not emerge from the meeting with end products, attendees may feel frustrated with not accomplishing anything. Although it takes some time and thought to list your objectives and end products for yourself as well as the attendees, doing so will ensure you avoid a meeting in which people feel they have wasted their time. It will move you toward conducting a productive meeting.

Determining Topics for the Agenda

The agenda should follow directly from the objectives and end products and should contain the information shown in Exhibit 7.2.

In determining the agenda topics and the meeting tasks, you will want to estimate the time it will take to cover each topic or, more important, to accomplish

EXHIBIT 7.2
Sample
Agenda

Date:	March 5, 2005	Location:	3rd floor conference room
Meeting called by: Beth Shapiro		**Attendees:**	See distribution list
Facilitator:	Alice Chang	**Please read:**	Memo from Beth on expectations, deadlines, etc.
Note taker:	Bill Smith	**Please bring:**	Memo, So. Am. Strategy Plan

Objectives
• Review past efforts at launching products in South America
• Identify problems or obstacles to product introduction
• Determine possible approaches to overcoming problems
• Assign tasks and establish deadlines

Agenda		
Time	**Topic**	**Responsibility**
8:30–8:40	• Introductions and review of agenda	Beth Shapiro
8:40–9:00	• Review of past launches in So. America (presentation)	Mario Cisneros
9:00–9:45	• Potential problems and solutions (brainstorming)	Alice Chang
9:45–10:00	• Assignment of action items	Beth Shapiro

Additional Information: This meeting will be the first of two. For this one, the goal is to surface all ideas, so each person should come prepared to contribute. At the end of the brainstorming session, we will decide as a group which solutions to pursue and the facilitator will assign tasks to the appropriate team members.

each objective; then, you should add at least five minutes to each topic to allow for transitions. You will want to make sure your timing is realistic for each topic and task. Try to anticipate where possible delays might occur and allow time to cover each topic and complete each task as planned.

Selecting Attendees

Selecting the right attendees is important to the success of a meeting. The attendees you invite should be the ones who can contribute to achieving your objectives. The selected attendees will usually include the decision maker(s), the budget holder (if different), those who must take action on the decisions, those with expert knowledge affecting the decisions, and representation from those affected by the decision. Sometimes it is obvious who should attend. For example, for a project team meeting, you would invite all team members. However, sometimes attendance is less clear-cut, and you must make decisions on the attendees. You can determine who should attend by asking the following questions:

• Who can supply information or input to the discussion or decision making?
• Who needs to accept the decisions so that implementation occurs?

- Who is necessary for you to reach a decision?
- Who needs to understand the information or actions to implement them?
- Who needs to feel part of the decision making?

Considering the Setting

You will want to consider the best setting for the kind of meeting you plan to lead. The setting considerations should include location, equipment, and layout of the room. If you have flexibility on the location, you should consider moving important meetings away from the office so that phones and messages do not distract attendees. For on-site meetings, you should establish ground rules that attempt to protect the meeting time as if it were off-site.

You will want to plan ahead so that these mechanics of meeting management do not interfere with the smooth progress of your agenda. For example, if you are planning an interactive meeting with discussion and an exchange of information, you will need flip charts and a room set up to allow people to see one another and to move around easily. If you are planning an information-sharing meeting with stand-up presentations and attendees sitting and listening, then you need to arrange for overheads or computer projections and ensure a setup that allows everyone to see the speaker and screen. Again, your assistants can manage these details, but you need to plan for them and arrange for the room layout to best serve your purpose.

Seating arrangements can be a critical part of room layout for some meetings. In a round-table meeting intended to provide an update on a team's progress, you might want to seat the team together on one side of the table with the audience on the other. However, if you anticipate some hostility or disagreement from the audience, you might intersperse team members with non–team members to suggest the entire group is part of the team or equal participants in the meeting. When arranging seating, you may occasionally need to think about cultural differences. In some cultures, the head of the organization always sits at the head of the table with others seated according to rank, and the head person may expect all attendees to remain standing until he or she has taken a seat.

If you are planning a virtual meeting (audio-conference, videoconference, or Web conference), with some or all other participants dispersed geographically, you will need to ensure someone has arranged for the phone conference call numbers, videoconferencing facilities, or net-meeting requirements. These arrangements need to be done far enough in advance to ensure connections are in place and all participants are informed of the arrangements and what they are expected to do to participate actively in the meeting.

Determining When to Meet

Setting a time for the meeting can be important. To accomplish your goals, you want people when they are at their best. Few leaders would call a team meeting on a Sunday morning after the Saturday night company Christmas party; however, many do hold weekly staff meetings first thing Monday morning when people's minds may be lingering on weekend activities. You should think about people's schedules and commitments as much as possible. If you are leading regular meetings, you may want to check with your attendees to get a sense of what works best for them. You should, of course, aim for the meeting time and day that will bring together the most productive group of people within the context of your company and the culture.

Meetings should be no longer than it takes to get through the agenda efficiently and productively. Most meeting planners say that 60 to 90 minutes is about as long as you can expect a group to remain attentive, so if you need longer, be sure to build in breaks and look for ways to vary the activities. Lengthy meetings will tax anyone's attention and patience; but if the purpose is significant, everyone is participating, and the meeting is progressing, most people are willing to endure the confinement for several hours.

Establishing Needed Meeting Information

You will want to anticipate and provide any information the group may need before or during the meeting to accomplish the meeting purpose. Too often attendees end up running down the hall to gather information after a meeting has started, which wastes time and suggests poor planning. If you have clearly defined your purpose and end products, you can review each one and think about what materials might be needed to facilitate the discussion and accomplish each objective. Ask yourself, What information will this group need to get from objectives to outcomes?

You will probably want to send the agenda out a few days ahead of the meeting so that others responsible for materials will come prepared. In addition, you will need to bring copies of the agenda with you since people often forget them.

Finally, if the meeting is a virtual forum, it is particularly important to plan ahead to ensure everyone is looking at the same information. If, for instance, you are meeting to discuss the latest numbers, you need to make sure the latest balance sheet has been sent and that any particular columns being discussed are highlighted.

CONDUCTING A PRODUCTIVE MEETING

If you have not done so beforehand, announce at the start of the meeting the decision-making approach that you plan to use, clarify leader and attendee roles and responsibilities, and establish meeting ground rules. In addition, the meeting will be more productive if your attendees know and use common problem-solving tools.

Deciding on the Decision-Making Approach

Your agenda will establish the order of the discussion, but how do you plan to make decisions? If attendees know the decision-making approach ahead of time, it will make the meeting run more efficiently. Company culture will often determine the decision-making approach as well as the format of the discussion. For instance, if the organization is very hierarchical and decisions come from the top, meeting attendees will expect to wait for you as the leader to make the decision. On the other hand, if the culture is open and employees are encouraged to challenge each other and even management, the attendees will expect to speak out and be involved in a process that builds to a consensus decision, which the leader then accepts.

To ensure a productive meeting, you will want to manage expectations by communicating to your attendees before or just after the meeting starts what the decision-making procedure will be. Will it be autocratic, with the leader making the decision on each item discussed before the group moves on to the next? Or will it be a democratic approach where the entire group votes on decisions or ideas? Or will the group use a consensus-driven approach to decision making? You as the leader will set the tone and establish the decision-making approach for the organization, which usually carries over into the meetings. Your approach may be so pervasive and well understood that you will not need to bring up the subject in a meeting; however, you may want to use different approaches for different types of meetings or problems, so you should make your approach clear for each meeting.

Clarifying Leader and Attendee Roles and Responsibilities

You should define the meeting roles and responsibilities before or after the meeting starts. Early definition of roles will help you avoid confusion. You might want to include the roles in the agenda as in Exhibit 7.2. The roles recommended for most meetings are as follows:

- Leader
- Facilitator
- Note taker
- Timekeeper

In a small, uncomplicated meeting, one person might play multiple roles, such as leader and facilitator or facilitator and timekeeper; however, it is usually better to separate the leader and facilitator roles, in particular. The leader can then focus on the content of the meeting while the facilitator looks after the process. In assigning roles, you need to be sensitive to diversity issues and people's strengths and weaknesses. You do not want to stereotype attendees into gender roles, for instance, always assigning the note taker role to a female. You also do not want to ask someone to facilitate a brainstorming session if that person tends to criticize every idea anyone else suggests. None of the roles should be minimized. All are important in helping a meeting progress smoothly toward its objectives.

Establishing Meeting Ground Rules

Ground rules should be established for every meeting, no matter how small or uncomplicated. Robert's *Rules of Order* served well in the past to provide strict rules for conducting a meeting. It still serves as the basis for ground rules in formal meetings today, particularly for community and civic organizations. Although the *Rules* may be considered too formal for contemporary business settings, leaders still need to establish either standing ground rules for all of their meetings or specific ground rules for each meeting. Quite often, companies need both. A company's standing ground rules may be based in its traditions or the company culture.

For instance, the company may have an intensive problem-solving culture in which all people are obligated to contribute in meetings, or it may have an avoidance culture that conditions people to shy away from any open conflict in meetings and avoid openly criticizing or questioning one another. Both could influence how the meeting is managed as well as the outcome.

Even the times that meetings start could reflect the culture, but you should never take for granted that everyone knows the traditions. For instance, every experienced person in a company would know that meetings always begin 10 to 15 minutes late, but those new to the company may see this as tardiness and be frustrated and even offended.

Ground Rules

- Meetings will start and end on time.

- Active participation by all is expected.

- No sidebars are allowed.

In most companies, the group will need to determine the ground rules at the beginning of each meeting. The facilitator should write them out so that everyone can see them. They should be actionable. They can be simple or elaborate. They should be specific to the company culture and the type of meeting.

The importance of ground rules cannot be overemphasized; however, they serve little purpose if not all attendees see them as an agreement, a contract that binds all present. If not enforced, the rules will appear to the attendees as an empty exercise with no value. If, however, ground rules are developed and enforced, the meeting will definitely be more productive.

For virtual meetings, a company will probably need to establish some special ground rules particular to the medium, such as the following:

Example Ground Rules for Virtual Meetings

- Introduce yourself when you join the meeting.
- State your name prior to your comments throughout the call.
- Avoid any side conversations since not all participants can hear them.
- Keep the speakerphone close to the person who is talking to avoid background noise.
- Avoid tapping pens or shuffling papers since these sounds may be exaggerated on the other end.

Using Common Problem-Solving Approaches

Your organization may already have preferred approaches to problem solving, which everyone knows and uses in meetings. If not, you may want to introduce some since most types of meetings will be much more efficient if attendees use common approaches to analysis and problem solving. If your organization does not have common analytical tools, you may want to select several from the ten listed here and teach your organization or group how to use them.

The value in using common analytical tools or problem-solving approaches is twofold: efficiency and creativity. The gain in efficiency is particularly evident when a group or a team is confronted with a complex or a politically sensitive problem. Having a common approach will allow all attendees to work on the problem in a similar way, which will save time and usually result in a better solution. Many of the approaches discussed here are designed specifically to open up the thinking of a group and thus increase creativity.

Shared knowledge of some approaches to analysis or problem solving allows you as the leader to say, "Let's use brainstorming or the six thinking hats to approach this problem." All attendees will then be able to jump right into the task.

Common analytical tools that work well in many different types of problem-solving meetings are as follows:

1. Brainstorming.
2. Ranking or rating.
3. Sorting by category (logical grouping).
4. Edward de Bono's *Six Thinking Hats.*
5. Opposition analysis.
6. Decision trees.
7. From/to analysis.
8. Force-field analysis
9. The matrix.
10. Frameworks.

1. Brainstorming

The goal of brainstorming is to generate an exhaustive list of ideas quickly. The characteristics of a brainstorming session are as follows:

- Each person is expected to contribute an idea.
- Ideas are not to be evaluated or judged in any way.
- Ideas must be recorded just as they are and be visible to all.
- Quantity is important, not quality.
- The facilitator's role is to keep the meeting moving and make sure all ideas are captured.
- The group stops when the ideas stop coming or when time runs out.

At the end of the brainstorming session, the group will emerge with a rather random, unorganized set of ideas. The next step will be to sort and organize, perhaps using one of the next two problem-solving approaches—ranking or sorting.

2. Ranking or Rating

Ranking or rating is performed with an existing set of ideas, perhaps generated from a brainstorming session. As the name implies, ranking involves selecting preferred ideas according to some clearly defined criteria. For instance, if you are looking for ideas about where to market a new product, you might generate 20 possibilities, then go back and select the top five based on your company's ability to implement them. Next, you might want to use a matrix similar to the one discussed here to evaluate the ideas according to value and difficulty, thus narrowing the list of five to the best one or two of the lot according to where they fall on the matrix. Again, the key to any useful ranking exercise is having group-determined criteria that will produce agreement on the best choices from the list.

3. Sorting by Category or Logical Groups

Sorting by category or logical groups requires a beginning list, although you might add items as they occur in the discussion as well. You also must have the categories of groups, which you should test to ensure they are logical. You can test the logic of your groups by asking the following questions: (1) are the groups mutually exclusive and (2) are they exhaustive? If the groups overlap at all, you need to reconsider them and come up with better categories. Once you have the categories, you can usually place the items in them fairly easily; coming up with the categories will often be more challenging than the actual sorting. The pyramid principle, introduced in Chapter 1, demonstrates how you might group ideas by categories in your key line of argument (Exhibit 1.10).

4. *Edward de Bono's* Six Thinking Hats

Edward de Bono designed his Six Thinking Hats approach to problem solving with the goal of encouraging open and complete thinking about a problem by separating ego (thinking your point of view is best to solve a problem) from performance (the actual solving of the problem). The Six Thinking Hats approach creates what de Bono calls "parallel thinking," which is thinking that involves looking at the problem in the same way. The example de Bono gives to illustrate parallel thinking is to imagine several people looking at a house from the same point of view, that is, all standing on the same side of the house. They would then more likely see the house in the same or very similar ways versus the differences that would occur if some people were looking at one side of the house and others another side. De Bono uses six distinct hats to represent six different ways of approaching a problem (Exhibit 7.3).

To use the approach in a meeting, the attendees would decide figuratively to wear the same hat for the discussion. For instance, they may decide they want to get all the facts out on the table, and thus assume the point of view of someone wearing the white hat; or they may feel they all need to think about the risks associated with an idea and all assume the point of view of someone wearing the black hat. Ideally, the group would spend time wearing all six hats to ensure they are looking at the problem from every point of view. Using the hats encourages people to move outside of their usual way of looking at a problem to see it from a fresh perspective. It also keeps the meeting focused on the problem and less on the participants' egos or desire to present their point of view. The result is that instead of a debate, the meeting attendees achieve parallel thinking, which de Bono says leads to more constructive problem solving.

EXHIBIT 7.3
Characteristics of de Bono's *Six Thinking Hats*

Source: From *Six Thinking Hats* by Edward de Bono. Copyright © 1985, 1999 by MICA Management Resources, Inc. By permission of Little, Brown and Company, (Inc.).

	Red	Emotions, intuition
	White	Facts, information
	Yellow	Benefits, positive values
	Black	Judgment, potential problems or risks, devil's advocate
	Green	Creativity, alternatives, ideas
	Blue	Cool, process control, organizing

5. Opposition Analysis

Opposition analysis requires the group to look at both sides of an issue. Some common techniques are to list the pros with matching cons, list advantages with matching disadvantages, or apply a test of meaning by using an is/is not approach. For instance, if a company is struggling with the wording of its vision statement, company leaders might assume not everyone defines the key words in the same way. They might then take each key word and decide if it means this, not this. For example, if the vision contained the words "world-class," that term could have different meanings to the various people involved in the discussion. If you wanted to establish a common meaning, you would ask people what "world-class" means to them and what it does not mean. Working through every key word in a vision using opposition analysis can be tedious, but it will elicit amazing differences in opinions, lead to greater clarity for all involved, and ensure the words selected provide the intended meaning.

6. Decision Trees

Decision trees, as discussed in Chapter 1, help break down a problem into its parts. They are particularly useful in finding a way forward through complex, many-faceted problems or issues. Decision trees take many shapes. To generate ideas in writing, for instance, you might state your recommendation or conclusion and then break out the major arguments and facts to support the conclusion. In analyzing a problem, you can use the decision tree to analyze areas of uncertainty or risk. For example, you might map out the decision to build a new coffee shop in a certain area of town using a decision tree to assess the risks as well as the opportunity.

7. From/to Analysis

From/to analysis is particularly useful in diagnosing change situations. It is similar to the force-field analysis discussed next, but it does not include the driving forces or restraining forces. The "from" describes the current situation, and the

EXHIBIT 7.4
From/to
Analysis
Using the 7S
Framework

Change situation: An IT group in a large medical facility needs to start providing broader MIS support for all of its internal clients.		
Selected 7S Categories	**From**	**To**
Strategy	Reactive, break-fix approach	Proactive, full-service consulting approach
Skills	Understanding of hardware and software	Understanding of consulting process and how to build client relationships
	Ability to diagnose and fix technical problems	Ability to anticipate and design processes and systems
Style	Reserved and behind the scenes Seen as followers	More outgoing and outspoken Seen as leaders
Structure	Hierarchical, clear reporting relationship and information sharing up and down only	Flatter, open, challenging, communicating up, down, and across

"to" matches changes that are needed to transform each of the "from's." The from/to analysis is particularly useful in communicating specific changes in activities or focus and works best if used with a framework designed for organizational diagnostics, such as the 7S framework. For instance, you might take the items from the 7S framework that are most important to change in an organization and develop a from/to for each one, as in Exhibit 7.4.

8. Force-Field Analysis

Kurt Lewin, a leading social psychologist, developed force-field analysis as a problem-solving tool to explore the problems and determine approaches to facilitate change in an organization. To use this analytical approach, you would take the following steps:

1. Carefully describe the current problem.
2. Describe the end state you desire.
3. Describe the driving forces included in the situation and pushing it in the direction it is currently heading.
4. Describe the restraining forces that are working against the driving forces and thus inhibiting the desired changes.

For instance, if you applied the force-field analysis to a problem of high turnover in your company, your analysis might be as illustrated in Exhibit 7.5.

By isolating the driving forces, you gain a better understanding of the problem, and then, by finding the restraining forces, you begin to see the reasons for the problems and perhaps ways to solve them. For instance, in the first bullet in Exhibit 7.5, internal competition is keeping the teams from functioning as teams and the current compensation or reward system is causing the competition. To expect people to

EXHIBIT 7.5 **Example of a Force-Field Analysis**

Current Situation

- Johnson, Inc.'s employee turnover rate is the highest in the industry
- Our reputation is that we "churn and burn"

Desired Future State

- Johnson, Inc.'s turnover rate one of lowest in industry
- Reputation for job satisfaction and enrichment

Driving Forces

- Competition within the teams
- Regional sales force confused over responsibilities
- Mentoring nonexistent
- Training inadequate

Restraining Forces

- Individual compensation structure rewards individual not team sales
- Regional structure allows overlap of some products
- Senior sales representatives in field; no time for new recruits
- Short time frame to make quotas

function as a team yet reward them as individuals is unrealistic. Therefore, to address the problem, the company would need to change its compensation system.

9. The Matrix

A matrix allows a group to evaluate or diagnose problems and the difficulties of making changes and can help a group decide on an approach. A decision-making matrix usually consists of four boxes with each axis assigned an evaluative label. Exhibit 7.6 demonstrates a matrix that a group might create to determine where to place its marketing efforts.

If you decide that a matrix will help your group in making a decision, you should first create the matrix by labeling the axes with the characteristics that are the most important in helping to reach a decision. In this case, the decision hinges on two key questions:

1. What is the value of reaching certain groups?
2. What is the difficulty?

Then, you can weigh the value against the difficulty and decide which is more important at this time. In the example above, the matrix has helped the group identify the key question: Should a marketing plan target customers first even though that will be more difficult, or should it go after an easier but lower value target?

10. Frameworks

As students of business know well, a framework exists for just about everything an organization might want to analyze. From McKinsey's 7S framework for organizational diagnostics to the Four "P's" of marketing, acronyms abound to diagnose or

EXHIBIT 7.6
Example of a
Matrix
Problem-
Solving
Approach

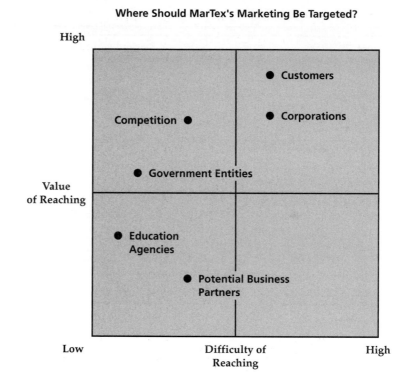

Where Should MarTex's Marketing Be Targeted?

analyze problems. Business frameworks may be original or already in use. Often the ones already in use work well initially but require modification to fit the specific situation and issues of a particular organization. If you use a framework, you will want to be careful not to force it. If you do, you risk invalidating the analysis.

Frameworks are useful and can be an excellent method for organizing analysis and problem solving. They serve as shorthand for discussion and can help simplify a complex idea and make it manageable. In addition, frameworks allow you to capture the elements of a complex problem visually. Further, they not only allow and encourage the logical organization of analysis, but also act as an effective communication device to illustrate the topics or questions being addressed.

MANAGING MEETING PROBLEMS AND CONFLICT

You will be able to stop or at least minimize most of the usual meeting problems by careful planning and by developing and enforcing ground rules; however, some issues may arise despite the best planning and meeting processes. All meeting leaders and facilitators must be prepared to handle problems in ways that will not interfere with the meeting objectives or those of the broader organization.

The primary responsibilities of a meeting leader are to plan the meeting, provide the content, anticipate problems, and ensure process facilitation. Fulfilling the last responsibility may call for the use of a skilled facilitator. A facilitator's primary responsibility is to ensure process problems do not interfere with the success of the meeting. Facilitators help to keep the meeting focused on the objectives and ensure redirection if it gets off track. Skilled facilitators should be prepared to (1) handle some of the most common meeting problems, (2) manage meeting conflict, and (3) deal with issues arising from cultural differences.

Handling Specific Meeting Problems

Exhibit 7.7 contains some of the most common meeting problems and methods to manage them. Careful planning and purposeful facilitation will solve most of these process problems; however, problems sometimes arise during meetings that are tied more directly to the personalities of the leader and the attendees than to corporate culture or the issues under discussion.

Two common problems in particular that can interfere with creativity are negative thinking and resistance to the ideas of others or changes of any kind. While a

EXHIBIT 7.7
Common
Meeting
Problems and
Approaches to
Managing
Them

Problem	Management Approach
1. **Confused Objectives and Expectations**	Create an agenda that includes objectives as well as end products Send agenda out ahead of time and review it at the beginning of the meeting
2. **Unclear Roles and Responsibilities**	Communicate roles and responsibilities with agenda or establish at the beginning of the meeting
3. **Confusion between Process and Content**	Separate the leader and the facilitator role Call time-outs for process checks as soon as confusion is expressed
4. **Drifting off Topic**	Stop and review meeting objectives. If digression continues, suggest • Discussion continue after meeting • Topic be placed on agenda for next meeting • Topic be tabled, stored for future (write topic down for all to see and make sure it is discussed at end of meeting if time allows or at an agreed future date)
5. **Data Confusion or Overload**	Control handouts to ensure all have the same version Create simplified data packs specific to meeting Exclude any data not directly relevant to objectives
6. **Repetition and Wheel Spinning**	Control the discussion by reminding attendees of objectives
7. **Time Violations**	Start on time. Allowing delays at the beginning of meetings cuts efficiency and sends the message that the leader is flexible on time Have a timekeeper If time limits are repeatedly violated, reevaluate agenda topics and time limits and build in cushion time

EXHIBIT 7.8
Negatives
Shut Down a
Discussion

devil's advocate can often stir up useful analysis, negativity—criticizing ideas without good reasons—is deadly in a brainstorming session, where it can destroy morale and shut down creative thinking completely. The leader or facilitator must address negativity immediately.

The best way to stop negativity is to establish a ground rule outlawing it. If no ground rules exist, then the facilitator will have to play a very direct role in confronting the person who is being negative. He or she may not even be aware of the negativity. If, however, the person persists, the leader of the group may need to call the person aside after the meeting, provide feedback on how counterproductive the negative comments are, and see if there may be something below the surface that is causing the negative responses. Exhibit 7.8 illustrates a few common negative comments. Imagine trying to have a constructive, creative discussion with such negative comments intruding into the meeting.

Resistance to the ideas of others is similar to negativism, but not as blatant. Instead of blurting out an obviously negative comment, the person may offer an opposing idea or present possible roadblocks. For some purposes, the leader might want to encourage the contrary ideas and even encourage someone to play devil's advocate to inspire better ideas as the group argues the pros and cons. If, however, the comments are disrupting rather than helping the discussion progress, the facilitator will need to step in and stop them. Exhibit 7.9 illustrates four techniques you might use to diffuse the situation so that the meeting can continue more productively.

EXHIBIT 7.9
Techniques to Manage Resistance

Technique	What You Might Say
Verify	"What I understand you to be saying is . . ."
Clarify	"I am not sure I understand your idea completely. Can you explain it in another way?"
Align	"Let's look at the problem from your point of view . . ."
Probe	"Tell me more about your concerns . . ."

Managing Meeting Conflict

When the common meeting problems turn into direct conflict, perhaps because of personality or factions within the group, facilitators may need to be more aggressive in their tactics. They must be prepared to manage the conflicts and the people involved before they interrupt meeting progress and in some cases even intrude into the overall working environment. Many approaches have been developed for managing conflict. One popular technique often used by negotiators calls on the individuals involved in the conflict to apply different levels of assertiveness and cooperation. They can approach the problem by competing, compromising, collaborating, avoiding, or accommodating. The matrix illustrates the trade-offs that occur when you select any one of these modes of conflict management (Exhibit 7.10).[5]

Any of the five modes may be used to allow the meeting to progress. However, collaborating is usually the best choice to manage meeting conflict because it calls on both sides to work together toward a common goal. Both sides can assert their points of view while still cooperating at a high level. Neither side feels as if it is losing anything; thus, both sides feel as though they have won, which results in a much more positive atmosphere for the meeting.

Although compromising allows the meeting to continue as well, it is usually not a choice to use frequently or for longer-term conflict. On the surface, a compromise

EXHIBIT 7.10
Conflict-Handling Modes

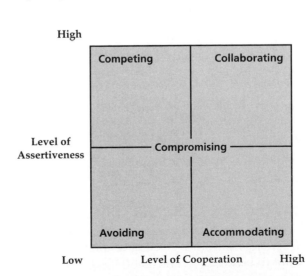

seems to be a win for both sides, but the ability of both sides to assert their opinions is only moderate and the level of cooperation is moderate as well. Therefore, neither side is likely to feel satisfied by the resolution; they will just accept it. If, however, a compromise is the only way to reach a resolution and will appease most of the group, it is better than the remaining three modes.

Competing, avoiding, and accommodating may be appropriate in certain situations, but they will usually only work as a short-term fix. In the competing mode one party wins, but the other loses. Thus, it frustrates the loser and even affects the others in the meeting as well since they may side with the loser or at least feel sympathy for his or her position.

Avoiding is not an optimal approach longer term since the problem is just buried and both sides feel frustrated. Neither side asserts the problems openly, and neither cooperates to achieve a solution. Avoiding the problem may work for a short time since it will allow the meeting to continue; but in a longer meeting, or in an organizational context, avoiding problems will usually result in an explosion or sabotage somewhere down the line.

Finally, in most organizational contexts, accommodating is not a good approach as a long-term solution since the level of assertiveness is so low that the conflicting parties may feel as if their opinions are not of value. This approach will allow a meeting to progress since the level of cooperation is high, which will mean the atmosphere of the meeting will not be negatively affected in the short term. Also, in some cultural contexts, cooperation and avoiding conflict may be preferred. Anyone who has to be accommodating too often, however, will become resentful and may eventually withdraw from the group.

Facilitators will find that they need to use all of these modes at one time or another to keep the meeting moving toward their goal; however, all but collaboration—and, if managed right, compromise—are short-term, quick fixes. If used over the long term, they can lead to dissension within an organization or with teams or any group holding a series of meetings.

If none of these modes seem the best for the situation, the facilitator may want to try one of the following methods of conflict management to calm the situation so that the meeting can continue:

1. Turn the question to the group.
2. Use the is/is not approach or a pro/con format.
3. Try listing points of agreement and disagreement.
4. Attempt to get at underlying assumptions.
5. Shift the discussion to the facts (put on the white hat).

Quite often, the white hat approach works well since it takes the emotions out of the moment and forces the group to be more objective and to look only at the facts.

Dealing with Cultural Differences

Chapter 6 contains a complete discussion of the importance of realizing cultural differences, but since meeting conflict may arise from cultural differences, you will want to be aware of some of the specific issues related to meetings. Recognizing

EXHIBIT 7.11
Cultural
Variables and
Meeting
Behavior

Cultural Variable	Some Examples of Differences in Meeting Expectations
Context	Individuals from a high-context society or functional area may expect meetings to include time for some casual conversation and relationship building.
Information Flow	People who expect information to come from one direction (top down, for example) may not feel comfortable contributing in a problem-solving or brainstorming session, for instance.
Time	Polychronic people may find agendas and a timekeeper artificial and uncomfortable. The time-is-money, schedule-driven mentality in the United States, for instance, would make them uncomfortable.
Language	People with a different cultural experience than that in the United States might find the bantering and joking exchange of United States attendees offensive, to the extent that they feel left out and isolated because of it.
Power	Societies in which position is equated with power may expect one leader, the person of highest position in the organizational hierarchy, to control a meeting and may be uncomfortable and even confused by the separation of the leader from the facilitator, for instance, or by a leader who takes a backseat for any reason.

some of these potential issues will help you manage many of them. Exhibit 7.11 presents the variables used in Chapter 6 and describes how differing culturally based expectations might disrupt a meeting.

These few examples illustrate only some of the obvious differences you might encounter when facilitating a meeting in today's global workplace. No one can know enough about every culture to prevent the occurrence of all the offending or marginalizing situations, but you can be aware of the differences and lead or facilitate the meeting in such a way that they do not cause anyone to feel uncomfortable. Of course, individuals acclimated to the culture of the company and the country in which the meetings are occurring will have adjusted and will conform, but new employees may not be used to the differences in customs and procedures. Again, you should analyze your audience (prospective meeting attendees) as you do your preplanning for the meeting. If you anticipate and plan adequately, you will mitigate or eliminate entirely most of the potential disruptions.

In addition to the differences arising from national, regional, and functional cultures, you will also encounter differences caused by personality. Recalling the MBTI discussed in Chapter 6, the Judging/Perceiving and Introvert/Extravert dichotomies will be the most obvious sources of problems in meetings. As you recall, the Judging personality is most comfortable with structure and schedules; Judgers like an agenda and will be uncomfortable if you do not provide and follow one. They also may take it personally if people are late for meetings, as many Perceivers are inclined to be. With Introverts, you will need to ensure they are given an opportunity, and in some cases even encouraged, to contribute, since Extraverts tend to dominate the discussion. Again, it is dangerous to generalize about personalities and how people will behave in a given situation, but being aware of some of the differences will help you lead and facilitate your meetings more effectively.

ENSURING MEETINGS LEAD TO ACTION

Recalling the seven deadly sins of meetings, number four was that nothing happens after the meeting ends. Unfortunately, inaction following a meeting is very common. A good meeting planner, however, can overcome this inertia by performing four steps:

1. **Assign specific tasks to specific people.** Giving the actions to a group is dangerous. The vagueness encourages moral equivocation, and inertia triumphs. When assigned a specific task, an individual is much more likely to deliver than a group will be. Accountability is increased when individuals are required to deliver.

2. **Review all actions and responsibilities at the end of the meeting.** Too often meetings just stop. Never let this happen. You should allow time for a review of actions and ensure the responsibilities are clear to all attending. Any next steps should be spelled out explicitly.

3. **Provide a meeting summary with assigned deliverables included.** If you have a note taker, that person should write up the minutes of the meeting, confirm with you on all action items and responsibilities, and send the minutes out to all attendees. The minutes do not need to include every word uttered at the meeting as they would in a traditional civic meeting run by Robert's *Rules,* for instance, but they should contain the main topics discussed and list every next step task, the person responsible, and the timing if appropriate.

4. **Follow up on action items in a reasonable time.** The leader should contact the responsible people shortly after the meeting to make sure they are clear about what they need to do and to see if they need help. This contact will serve as a gentle reminder and will be enough in most situations to ensure delivery. However, if someone habitually has trouble with deadlines, then the leader should contact that person again as the deadline approaches.

Although these steps may seem like micromanaging, if the meeting contained serious business objectives as it should have, then you are entitled to expect some action to come out of it. Otherwise, you risk sending a message that employees should not take meetings seriously, which will cause them to feel the meetings are busywork, the first deadly sin listed at the beginning of the chapter. Having your employees feel that meetings are a waste of time brings us back to where this chapter started, asking, "Is a meeting necessary?" If you decided that you needed a meeting to accomplish your purpose, you must ensure that it moves tasks forward and makes actions happen. The follow-up to all meetings is not micromanagement; it is simply good management and good leadership.

Exercise 7.1: Evaluating Experiences in Meeting Management

Think back to your most recent job and identify one small-group meeting that you attended. Jot down some key information about the meeting:

1. Who called the meeting?
2. What was it about?
3. Was there an agenda?
4. Was the purpose of the meeting accomplished?
5. After the meeting, were minutes distributed that outlined tasks and deadlines?
6. During the meeting, what role did you play all or most of the time (leader, scribe, facilitator, etc.)?
7. What could have been done to make the meeting more effective?

Now work with a partner to compare notes on the meetings you attended to identify similarities and differences in meeting organization and outcomes.

Source: Case and exercise developed by Beth O'Sullivan, Rice University.

Exercise 7.2: Planning a Meeting

Case: Wisconsin Frozen Delights

You have recently been named the new vice president for operations of Wisconsin Frozen Delights, a regional ice cream manufacturing firm located just outside of a large metropolitan area in Wisconsin. The following people report to you:

- Assistant vice president of operations.
- Administrative assistant to the vice president.
- Director of operations.
- Manager of manufacturing.
- Manager of purchasing.
- Manager of shipping.
- Manager of human resources.
- Regulatory compliance officer.

During your first tour of the facilities, you observed a number of safety hazards in the manufacturing areas and you also noticed that the factory and adjacent office areas do not have easy access for anyone with disabilities. You are concerned that the building is not in compliance with regulations under the Americans with Disabilities Act and that there are possible Occupational, Safety, and Health Administration (OSHA) violations.

The president has given you full authority to uncover safety concerns, determine areas in which employees have concerns about safety or disabled access, and fix the problems to make the company a safe and healthy place to work. You decide to call a meeting to set the tone for your new administration and to discuss the safety concerns.

The Assignment

Complete the following steps:

1. Decide whom to invite to the meeting.
2. Develop your objectives and end products.

3. Establish the agenda for the meeting.

4. Write a memo inviting your selected attendees to the meeting.

Source: Case and exercise developed by Deborah J. Barrett and Beth O'Sullivan, Rice University.

Exercise 7.3: Conducting a Problem-Solving Meeting

OmniBank's Diversity Efforts—Revisited

Look back at the OmniBank case in Chapter 6. You have decided to call a meeting to learn more about your current employee base and your recruiting efforts for new staff to investigate ways in which your bank can become more diverse. You want the meeting to be a problem-solving meeting that will help you get to know the employees and encourage them to contribute to the bank's new diversity approach. Select the problem-solving tool that you think would be most useful for your objectives and then write an explanation of how you plan to conduct the meeting to send to the attendees.

Notes

1. Jay, A. (1976). How to run a meeting. *Harvard Business Review,* March–April.

2. Introduction to Great Meetings, 3m.com/meetingnetwork/leadingroom/meeting-guide_make.html.

3. Introduction to Great Meetings.

4. Matson, E. (1997). Quoting William R. Daniels, American Consulting & Training in The seven sins of deadly meetings, *Fast Company's Handbook of the Business Revolution*, p. 27.

5. Borisoff, D., & Victor, D. (1999). *Conflict Management: A Communication Skills Approach* Boston, MA: Allyn and Bacon, discusses the use of the conflict-handling modes developed by K. W. Thomas and R. Kilmann.

Chapter **Eight**

Building and Leading High-Performing Teams

Teams are *not* the solution to everyone's current and future organizational needs. . . . Nonetheless, teams usually do outperform other groups and individuals. . . . And executives who really believe that behaviorally based characteristics like quality, innovation, cost effectiveness, and customer service will help build sustainable competitive advantage will give top priority to the development of team performance.

Jon Katzenbach and Doug Smith, *The Wisdom of Teams.* Boston: HBS Press (1993)

Chapter Objectives

In this chapter, you will learn to do the following:

- Build an effective team.
- Establish the necessary team work processes.
- Manage the people side of teams.
- Handle team issues and conflict.
- Help virtual teams succeed.

Since teams are now so prevalent in all organizations, business leaders need to know how to build and how to manage them to achieve high performance. Most businesspeople have experienced successful as well as unsuccessful teams. Unfortunately, unsuccessful team experiences may outnumber successful ones, a perception that has inspired the abundance of information on how to achieve successful teams. A Google search for the word "teams" yields over 10 million hits on every imaginable kind of team from kayak racing to continuous improvement.

Narrowing the search to include "business" with "teams" still yields over 3 million. A quick scan of the hits reveals that many are organizations, universities, and individuals offering training in how to develop a successful team. Obviously, many are seeking "the way" to build and maintain a high-performing team.

While no one way is likely to guarantee good results for all organizations, most of the skills you as a leader need to build and manage a high-performing team tie directly to your leadership communication ability. This chapter will guide you through the communication challenges involved in leading a team. You will learn how to build an effective team, establish necessary work processes, manage the people side of teams, and handle team conflict. In addition, you will receive some guidance on leading geographically dispersed teams (virtual teams), which are so prevalent in today's global workplace.

BUILDING AN EFFECTIVE TEAM

Building an effective team raises both organizational and individual leadership issues. In deciding to use teams across your company, you will want to look closely at the company culture and compensation structure to see if they both support teamwork. In the past decade, many companies have launched into the use of teams without establishing the organizational infrastructure for teams to succeed. If you are thinking of forming a team for specific tasks, you first need to determine that a team is the most effective and efficient approach to perform the task, solve the problem, generate the new ideas, or generally move your company forward in some way.

Deciding to Form Teams

Deciding to form a team is a process very similar to deciding to call a meeting. Both meetings and teams can alienate participants if they are not clearly the best approach. Before moving ahead to establish a team-based organization or to form teams individually, you would want to answer yes to the following questions:

1. Is a team the best approach to achieve the organizational objectives or a specific goal or targeted result?
2. Does the organization provide the necessary training in diversity, team dynamics, problem solving, and process management to ensure team members know how to manage team issues and processes?
3. Are the employees accustomed to creating and following team charters and ground rules, and do they know how to resolve team conflicts?
4. Does the current company technology effectively support team communication and collaboration? And do employees know how to use that technology (particularly critical for virtual teams)?
5. Are team performance measures built into the company compensation and performance systems?

Ideally, the answer to each of these questions would be yes; realistically, that may not be the case. Being able to answer yes to all of the questions will ensure a more productive environment for teams if your company intends to take full advantage of a team-based structure using teams throughout the organization. However, answering no to all but the first question does not mean that a team is doomed to fail. High-performing individuals working together in a team with a clear objective and the commitment to achieve it can be an effective team despite the environment. Having a supportive environment will simply make your role in leading and managing teams easier.

Forming Your Team

Once you have decided that a team is the best answer, you will need to look closely at how you will form that team. Companies often decide who should be on teams based on functional responsibilities, for instance. If you have the freedom to select the members, however, you will find Katzenbach and Smith's team basics framework useful in establishing the characteristics of a "real" team (Exhibit 8.1). In their team basics framework, the apex topics—performance results, personal growth, and collective work products—represent the outcome of the work of the team.

EXHIBIT 8.1
Katzenbach and Smith's Team Basics

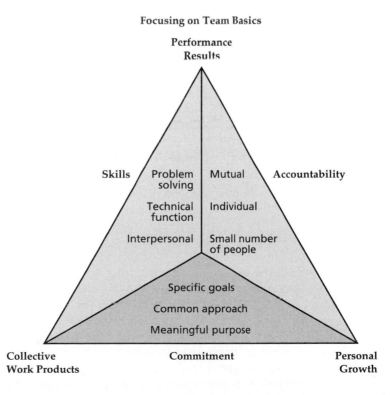

Focusing on Team Basics

Performance Results

Skills — Problem solving / Technical function / Interpersonal

Mutual / Individual / Small number of people — Accountability

Specific goals
Common approach
Meaningful purpose

Collective Work Products   Commitment   Personal Growth

The other items are the characteristics of what Katzenbach and Smith consider a "real" team:

- Complementary skills (problem solving, technical/functional, interpersonal).
- Accountability (mutual, individual, and small number of people).
- Commitment (specific goals, common approach, meaningful purpose).

Team members should have skills that complement rather than duplicate each other, although teams may develop some of the required skills after the team forms. All members need to recognize and accept mutual as well as individual accountability for the team's work products. The size of the team matters and affects accountability since a team that is too large will end up dividing into subteams and the work can become so diffused that accountability gets lost. Finally, the team must have specific goals, a purpose that is important to the organization, and a common approach to the work.

Having all of the team basics is more important to achieving high performance than team building exercises intended to mold a group of individuals into a cohesive, committed, mutually responsible unit: "By focusing on performance and team basics—as opposed to trying 'to become a team'—most small groups can deliver the performance results that require and produce team behavior."[1]

One of your first responsibilities as a team leader is bringing together the right people or, if you do not get to select the members, deciding how to work with the members you have to achieve the performance you desire. As the team leader, you will be the one to communicate to the members individually and collectively the reasons for their selection to the team, the team purpose and objectives, and your expectations of them as a team. The next section will help you communicate your expectations of the team as you work with them to establish the purpose, roles and responsibilities, ground rules, and communication protocol.

ESTABLISHING THE NECESSARY TEAM WORK PROCESSES

Once you have told the selected team members that they are on your team, you should schedule a launch or kick-off meeting. Teams tend to begin their work more effectively if you take the time to hold an official launch. Having a launch allows you to address many of the team work process steps discussed here. Although most teams will probably want to jump right into the work without spending the necessary time on process issues, leading them through development of the purpose, goals, and approach (the commitment side of the team basics framework) will help your team work more efficiently and effectively. The primary causes of conflict in a team are poorly defined goals and purposes and lack of clarity about the approach to the work and problem solving. Chapter 7 on meetings discussed the importance of using common problem-solving tools in meetings and provided some useful examples that work well with teams. In this section, you will learn how to address the issues of goals, purpose, and approach in your team launch by creating a team charter, action plan, and work plan.

Creating Your Team Charter

One of the first steps for your team will be to create a team charter or contract. A charter usually consists of the following:

1. Project purpose/goals.
2. Team member roles and responsibilities.
3. Ground rules.
4. Communication protocol.

Project Purpose and Goals

You may have already defined the team's specific purpose, but to make sure your team understands you and has internalized this purpose as a team, you should have them write down exactly what they see as their purpose for being a team. Is it a broad, organizational purpose, or is it narrow and specific to one division or one person? Simply expressing the purpose out loud is not enough. It must be written so that every member of the team can see it and agree to it.

The goals must support and clearly link to the purpose. They must be specific and measurable performance goals. For instance, the purpose of the team might be to establish a marketing strategy and promotional plan for MarTex, Inc. Then, the goals might be to (1) establish a profile of MarTex's current image, reputation, and market perception; (2) determine MarTex's value proposition, key messages, and target audiences; and (3) develop a marketing communication plan and materials to reach target audiences.

Team Member Roles and Responsibilities

Your team should define all roles and responsibilities for each team member at the first meeting. The roles to consider are similar to the roles in meetings: leader, facilitator, timekeeper, and note taker. The team should consider whether the roles will rotate or if the same person will perform the role throughout the project. In addition, the team needs to assign someone to be the meeting minder (coordinator) and/or work plan manager. This person is responsible for calling meetings or sending out reminders and making meeting arrangements. Depending on the size of the team and the project, the same person could also maintain the work plan, updating and making changes as needed and communicating them to the team.

Team Ground Rules

Teams need ground rules that the entire team participates in creating and agrees to follow. The rules should be determined at the first team meeting and become a permanent part of the team charter. The rules will probably resemble those the team would establish for meetings, but they will also be longer-term, governing the team's interactions between meetings as well. At a minimum, the team's ground rules should include topics, such as those listed in Exhibit 8.2. Some examples are included as well.

EXHIBIT 8.2
Ground Rule
Topics and
Examples for
Teams

Team Topics	Example Ground Rules
Leadership	One leader for the overall project, but lead persons assigned on the work plan will assume leadership for meetings on their topics.
Communication	The team will follow the communication protocol for all team communication.
Participation	We expect all members to participate equally and actively in all team activities and work.
Work Products	All members will contribute their share of the work, delivering end products complete and on time. The team will follow work plan action items and time line.
Conflict Management and Resolution	We encourage healthy debate about content within the meetings; however, the facilitator will directly address conflict that disrupts the team. Anyone who feels a conflict exists that is not being addressed has the responsibility to bring it to the facilitator or team for resolution.
Preparation	All members must be aware of agenda items for the day and have their portions of the work completed before the meeting starts.
Attendance	We require attendance at all team meetings. If an unexpected conflict arises, the member is responsible for sending in his or her work for the day and for notifying the team. A team member who misses more than three meetings risks being removed from the team.
Timing	We expect all team members to be on time for meetings. If teammates see they will be late, they must notify the team coordinator. Too many late appearances could result in being removed from the team.
Decision Making	The team will determine any decisions by consensus unless the team reaches an impasse, at which time the facilitator or leader can table the item for a future meeting, if appropriate, or call for a vote.
Laptops and Cell Phones	We will try to refrain from using our laptops and cell phones during team meetings. The exception is to retrieve information needed by the team during the meeting.

Ground rules should fit the culture of the organization and the personality of the team. Some teams like very strict rules with penalties while others prefer a more relaxed approach. You and the team will want to determine what approach is best for this team. Also, the team should build in periodic process checks to review the ground rules and be prepared to adjust the ground rules if they appear not to be working.

Communication Protocol

At their first meeting, you should tell the team how you plan to communicate with them on a regular basis and how you expect them to communicate with you. Also, the entire team should work out procedures for communicating with each other. Will they use e-mail or voice mail, for instance, or both, with each designated for a specific type of message? Is there a time of day or night that is off-limits for calling a team member or do some team members respond better and faster to e-mail than phone mail? You should consider the following questions in developing a team communication protocol:

1. What events or situations will trigger communication with each other?
2. When will we contact a member of the team versus the entire team? Do we copy the entire team on all e-mails? Are there some team members who prefer no calls at home or do not want to receive calls at a certain time?
3. Who will be our spokesperson for most team internal communication? For external communication (that is, with other groups within the company or even outside the company)?
4. What information needs to be communicated to the team? Should we provide regular updates on progress or limit communication to issues, requests, or announcements?
5. How should we communicate everyday messages, work plan items, end products, questions, emergencies, and the like? Which medium does our team prefer to use for everyday communication? Do some team members strongly prefer one medium to another?
6. To whom do we communicate problems, questions, concerns, and so on?

Exhibit 8.3 provides an example of a typical team charter for an internal team performing a marketing study for their company.

Using Action and Work Plans

For a team project of any complexity or length, an action plan of overall phases is useful and a specific work plan of all action items and end products with responsibilities and time lines is essential. Although any plan has to be updated frequently as the project unfolds, creating one at the beginning of the project is necessary for all team members to know exactly what needs to be done, by whom, and by when. It helps avoid duplication of effort, ensures all needed activities are included, and allocates adequate time for the planned actions.

Action plans allow the team to see the big picture of the project easily and help them organize the individual tasks into blocks of work that make it easier to manage the responsibilities and deliverables. The first step in creating the action plan is to establish the major phases of the project. A project of any complexity or length can usually be mapped into three to five phases. Any more than five phases makes the plan difficult to manage. The phases should correspond to the goals of your project. After you have determined the phases, you can then list the major activities

EXHIBIT 8.3 **Example of a Team Charter**

Team Charter for the MarTex Tiger Team (August 25, 2005)	
Purpose: To establish a marketing strategy and promotional plan for MarTex, Inc.	**Goals:** 1. Establish a profile of MarTex's current image, reputation, and market perception. 2. Determine MarTex's value proposition, key messages, and target audiences. 3. Develop a marketing communications plan and materials to reach target audiences.

Team Member Roles and Responsibilities

In addition to contributing to problem solving, analysis, research, and document content, members will have the following specific roles and responsibilities:

Amanda Shay	Team leader	Kick the team off and provide leadership overall. Create drafts of documents.
Miguel Serrato	Meeting facilitator, coordinator, timekeeper	Create agendas, manage the meetings, communicate meeting times and locations.
Tuyen Tran	Work plan master, costing expert	Create work plan, keep it up to date with changes, distribute to team.
Mary Prescott	Benchmarking/data gathering expert	Lead competitive image analysis.
Jane Sudduth	Branding/communication expert	Lead brand identity and message analysis.
Jodi Pliszka	Design specialist	Create sample promotional materials.

(continued)

within each one and the overall timing for the phase. You will see in Exhibit 8.5 following the action plan in Exhibit 8.4 that these activities become the action items in the work plan. The work plan becomes a more specific elaboration of the action plan.

The action plan phases should set up the main areas of work for the work plan. In fact, you might want to repeat the goals at the top of the plan as a reminder for the team.

Delivering the Results

A team's performance will depend on the team being able to deliver the results of its work. That usually means delivering a presentation, a report, or both. These tasks are often one of the major communication challenges that teams face.

EXHIBIT 8.3 (continued)

Team Charter for the MarTex Tiger Team	
Ground Rules:	**Communication Protocol:**
1. Meetings will start on time (penalties will be enforced for lateness).	***Who*** • Miguel will contact members for all meeting items.
2. Members must attend all meetings and be fully prepared to participate.	• Amanda will inform the team of any content issues or other issues from the company perspective. She is to be the only team contact with senior management.
3. We will stick to our agenda. Any important topics not on the agenda will be placed in the "parking lot"* for future discussion.	***What and to whom*** • All team-related information (meetings, work plan, questions, etc.) will be sent to all team members.
4. No sidebars are allowed.	• Correspondence on subteam work will go to members involved only.
5. No negatives are permitted at any time.	
6. Work plan responsibilities must be fulfilled and on time.	***How*** • We will meet daily for the first week. Then, we will meet as needed. Any team member may call a meeting if needed, but he or she must coordinate through Miguel.
7. Consensus approach will be used for decision making, although the leader has right to call for a vote if necessary.	• We will communicate primarily through e-mail unless urgent; then, we will use phone mail.
8. Any conflict will be handled immediately, first by the facilitator and then by the whole team if necessary.	• Documents will be sent through e-mail and will always contain the initials of the last person working on them and the date and time.
	• Home phone calls are limited to extremely important team business, such as a last-minute emergency that will cause missing a meeting.

*"Parking lot" is the team's name for items that are important but not for discussion at that meeting or time.

Chapter 2 provided guidance on avoiding problems when creating team documents and outlined the single-scribe and the multiple-scribe approaches. The purpose here is simply to emphasize the importance of including the steps required to create your documents or presentation in your team work plan.

You will want to include all tasks to create and complete your document or presentation in the action steps of your work plan. Teams typically underestimate the time it will take to create and complete a document or presentation as a team. They make this mistake because they do not push far enough into the details of document or presentation creation and completion. On the work plan, for instance, a team may be tempted simply to write "Create report" as their action step, which

EXHIBIT 8.4
Example of a
Team Action
Plan

MarTex Tiger Team Action Plan

Phases	Current image, brand identity	Value proposition, key messages	Marketing plan and materials
Actions	• Determine approach to perception analysis • Assess current marketing and promotional efforts	• Conduct surveys and interviews • Identify gaps in perception and materials • Identify audiences • Determine value proposition and messages	• Develop marketing plan • Create preliminary marketing materials • Pilot test plan and materials
Timing	Sept 1–Sept 15	Sept 15–Sept 30	Sept 30–Oct 27

EXHIBIT 8.5 Example of a Team Work Plan

Phase 1 Goal: Establish a Profile of MarTex's Current Image, Reputation, and Market Perception

Action Items	Responsibility	End Products	Deadline
Determine approach to perception analysis			
• Create framework and approach	Miguel & Amanda	Framework	9/2
• Establish benchmarking criteria	Mary & Jane	Benchmarking criteria	9/5
• Determine how best to obtain client and marketplace perceptions	Miguel & Amanda	Perception plan	9/8
• Create data instruments (survey interview guides)	Mary & Tuyen	Survey and interview guide and schedule	9/9
• Test survey and interview guides	Mary & Tuyen	Revised version	9/12
• Determine who among competitors to include	Miguel	List of target competitors	9/12
• Determine who among clients to include	Amanda	List of target clients	9/12
Assess current marketing and promotional efforts			
• Research competitors' current promotional efforts	Tuyen & Jodi	Portfolio of material	9/14
• Analyze their marketing approaches	Tuyen & Jodi	Summary of approaches	9/14
• Obtain and evaluate their marketing materials compared to ours	Tuyen & Jodi	Comparative matrix	9/16

does not begin to capture the many steps involved. Instead, the work plan should contain steps, such as the following:

Typical Steps in Creating and Completing Documents or Presentations

1. Develop communication strategy.
2. Decide on medium (round-table or stand-up presentation, formal written document).
3. Determine format and layout. If creating a presentation, this would include selecting your PowerPoint template.
4. Develop outline, storyboard, or ghost pack.
5. Divide up slides or sections.
6. Create first draft.
7. Pull the sections together into one document.
8. Test for coherence and reorganize if necessary.
9. Rewrite sections and complete any editing.
10. Read the entire document or presentation as a team.
11. Perform final proofreading.
12. Practice if a presentation, allowing time for revisions if needed; print and bind copy if a document.

Listing all the steps will ensure the team allows enough time for the creation and completion of their document or presentation. You want to plan for this work just as you do for the research and analysis. Otherwise, you risk not allowing enough time, and the resulting rush may prevent you from delivering the high-quality end product that is characteristic of a high-performing team.

Learning from the Team Experience

Team members want to learn from the experiences of being on the team, which calls for reflecting on the team work processes. Teams working together over an extended period of time should build in periodic process checks. Doing so allows them to determine which processes are working well and which may need to be changed. They should revisit their roles and responsibilities, ground rules, and communication protocol. At the end of this chapter, you will find a sample form to assess team process performance. In addition to periodic reviews during the work, the team should schedule time as a team to debrief on the experience at the end of the project. Each team member can then learn from the experience, and the team leader will be able to capture the lessons learned from the team's experience for the benefit of future teams in the organization.

The team leader will also want to provide feedback on the performance of individual members and ask for feedback on his or her performance as a team leader (see sample evaluation form in exercises at the end of this chapter). The feedback may cover people issues as well as work process activities, although many of the people issues will be avoided if the team leader ensures the team attends to the work process activities.

The following list of steps for avoiding team trouble summarizes the process steps previously discussed.

Keeping Your Teams Out of Trouble

---

1. Have an official team launch including an introduction to the team and a creation of a team charter.
2. Obtain any needed training in team management, such as facilitations skills, meeting management, problem solving, and conflict resolution.
3. Develop and post team ground rules and expectations for team behavior.
4. Educate team members about what to expect in team development, such as the traditional stages of forming, storming, norming, and performing.
5. Anticipate the roadblocks to team performance early and deal with them.
6. Provide regular opportunities for feedback among team members and make sure it is done properly.
7. Provide feedback to the team leader on what is working and what isn't.
8. Build in team process checks to monitor the effectiveness of the team.

Source: Adapted from Bens, I. (1999). Keeping your teams out of trouble. *Journal of Quality and Participation* 22 (4), pp. 45–47.

MANAGING THE PEOPLE SIDE OF TEAMS

Teams bring together the best talent available to solve a problem; however, sometimes these talented people clash. The previous section covers the more mechanical side of managing team processes, but the success or failure of a team often depends on the softer issues associated with the people and how well they work together. Just as emotional intelligence is important for individuals, it is also important for groups. One way to improve the team's emotional intelligence or ability to work together smoothly is for the team to take time to know something about each other's current situation, work experiences, expectations, personality, and cultural differences. This knowledge may not result in team bonding or friendships, which are more the by-product of teams than the goal, but since these softer issues influence how the person behaves as a team member, the knowledge can help the team avoid conflict and help you as the leader anticipate any problems or performance roadblocks.

Although team members will get to know each other through day-to-day interactions while working together, the team members can shorten the learning curve by discussing the following information at the first team meeting:

1. Position and responsibilities
2. Team experiences
3. Expectations
4. Personality
5. Cultural differences

Position and Responsibilities

What are the person's responsibilities outside of the team? If in a company setting, what is the position (not just title) of the individual within the company? What does the person do for the company? What are his or her day-to-day responsibilities and workload? As was discussed in Chapter 6, high- and low-context preferences affect various functional groups within organizations as well as cultures, and these differences will influence the person's expectations of team dynamics.

Also, unless the individual is relieved of all other responsibilities to work on the team, responsibilities outside of the team will influence the time and commitment available for the team, which could leave other team members resentful, particularly if they are unaware of the extent of the individual's outside commitments. While work outside the team is never an excuse for an individual not to carry his or her share of the team work, the team benefits by knowing about the outside demands both for the sake of understanding, and also for helping the team to assign team responsibilities. This knowledge is particularly useful, for instance, when managing someone who tends to overcommit.

Team Experiences

How often have the members worked on a team and on how many teams? If they are new to the team experience, they will need more education in team dynamics, work approaches, and expectations. What kinds of experiences have they had—positive and negative? The team could perhaps learn from discussing both what worked well and what did not work so well on other teams. A decidedly negative team experience could affect a member's attitude toward teams in general; getting that out in the open can help mitigate negative attitudes.

Expectations

What do the members expect from the team and team experience? Do their goals align with the team goals? Are their goals focused more on the project or the process? Are they on the team only to advance their careers? For example, a team member who sees working on the team primarily as a way to garner management attention may pursue individual goals rather than working for team goals. He or she may dominate presentations to management or violate team communication protocol by communicating with management without the team present. The rest of the team will then become frustrated and even angry with this attention-seeking team member.

Another example, frequently encountered in a business school setting, occurs when a team is divided between members who want to learn and get the most out of a project or team experience and those who simply want to receive the reward, in this case a good grade. When a team divided like this makes work assignments, instead of giving those who do not know a subject the opportunity to learn it, they assign the substantive work expediently to the person most familiar with the subject to improve their odds of getting the better grade. The people who are there to learn then become frustrated because they feel their learning experiences are limited.

When team members have different expectations and goals, they may work at cross-purposes. This again underscores the importance of establishing goals at the beginning and making sure each member accepts them.

Personality

Chapter 6 discussed the MBTI as a way to help understand individual personalities and how they affect the way people work. Team performance can benefit if the members understand how each other's personalities may affect work behavior and group interactions. For instance, if a Perceiver is frequently late (and while a type characteristic is not an excuse), the other team members will at least know not to take it personally. Knowing the characteristics of different personality types on your teams can contribute to your ability to lead and manage them as well as help you function constructively as a team member. It will help you understand others and how they take in information and approach problem solving. For example, if you know that a member is an Introvert and he or she withdraws from the conversation, you will realize that the person is probably not angry or upset, but simply thinking, and you as leader may want to draw him or her out.

Cultural Differences

Team members' understanding of cultural differences can affect a team's ability to function. Some examples of particular team issues that may arise from diversity are aligned with the cultural variables presented in Chapter 6 and discussed in Exhibit 8.6.

EXHIBIT 8.6 Cultural Variables and Examples of Potential Team Issues

Cultural Variable	Some Examples of Differences in Team Expectations
Context	• Individuals from a high-context society or functional area may expect teams to socialize some to allow time to build relationships. These individuals could be offended if the social time included discussion of work issues. • Some high-context people may be so dependent on nonverbal cues that they find working electronically limiting. A high-context person may feel that e-mails fail to capture the meaning of the message and need more direct interaction with others on the team.
Information Flow	• Businesspeople from different cultures expect information to flow in a certain way. Some, for instance, may not understand when the team's communication protocol has established only one person as the main contact with senior management; they may see that as face time for them with people of power and resent the team setting limits on their interactions. Others may not be comfortable with including all team members on e-mails when they want to communicate with the team leader. • Some cultures see information as something that is freely shared, and others as a source of power they need to protect. Failure to share information openly on a team can result in hard feelings and a lack of trust, which can completely undermine the team's working relationship and the quality of their work.
Time	• A polychronic person may find action plans and work plans too linear and may not appreciate the importance of attempting to manage time so intensely. • Some people may be very relaxed about meeting times and even deadlines for deliverables, which can cause conflict and place teams in a bind. • Team members may not share the same single-task focus, causing the single-task person to fear that the multitasking individual is not committed to the task or is not well organized.
Language	• Persons from a different cultural experience than that in the United States, for instance, might find joking exchanges offensive; they may see it as a way to keep them from bonding with the team. • Some may have problems with the amount of jargon that tends to emerge in a team environment as well.
Power	• Persons from cultures in which power and position are equated may not recognize the team leader as a person of power if the leader is of the same rank in the company and may resent that person's attempts to lead the team in any meaningful way, for instance, in resolving conflict or determining the best solution when the team is divided. • Some may have trouble seeing team members as equal partners in the project.

Discussing these topics will serve as the first steps toward building the team's emotional intelligence. In research on the importance of developing group emotional intelligence, Druskat and Wolff found that "to be most effective, the team needs to create emotionally intelligent norms—the attitudes and behaviors that eventually become habits—that support behaviors for building trust, group identity, and group efficacy. The outcome is complete engagement in tasks."[2] Openly discussing some or all of the five topics presented in this section—position and responsibilities, team experiences, expectations, personality, and cultural differences—will shorten the time the team needs to develop trust and a group identity.

It seems obvious that the more team members know about each other, the better; however, too often, teams fail to take enough time up front to understand each other as people. Discussing these topics at the team launch and working to develop the team's combined emotional intelligence will help the team avoid some of the conflicts that typically arise.

HANDLING TEAM ISSUES AND CONFLICT

Despite all of the best planning and time spent getting to know each other, teams will likely experience conflict. Some of it will be useful and some not, but the odds are that it will occur. As Katzenbach writes, an effective team is "about hard work, conflict, integration, and collective results."[3] Working on a team is not easy, but the benefits can be very rewarding for the team members, and the results can be much better for the company. Obtaining the best results can depend on the team's ability to manage conflict. Just as individuals and teams must be able to disagree in meetings, teams need to know how to manage conflict in their overall team activities.

Types of Team Conflict

Internal team conflict will usually be one of four types:

1. Analytical (team's constructive disagreement over a project issue or problem).
2. Task (goal, work process, deliverables).
3. Interpersonal (personality, diversity, communication styles).
4. Roles (leadership, responsibilities, power struggles).

Analytical

Analytical conflict emerges when team members disagree about substantive project issues, approaches to problem solving, or proposed answers to major questions. This type of conflict is usually constructive for the team since it leads to better answers and greater creativity. It should be encouraged and recognized for the value it brings. Deriving value from analytical conflict, however, requires that the team separate personality from issues, which is not always easy. The individuals involved must not take disagreements personally. They must see someone's questioning not as a personal attack but as a way to explore and understand all sides of an issue. Putting on the "black hats" (from de Bono's Six Thinking Hats discussed in Chapter 7) can help team members think critically while removing any associations with personal issues.

Further, a team that wants to be as creative as possible and explore issues rigorously should have a ground rule encouraging members to disagree. For this ground rule to succeed, team members must view analytical conflict as constructive. If it takes on a destructive tone, there is usually a problem below the surface that the team needs to confront.

Task

The second form of team conflict concerns tasks or, quite frequently, a team member's not attending to a task. For example, a team member may not deliver the work product completed or may miss a deadline for an action item. All team members could be at fault if they have not been clear and specific about the expectations for the work product (thus the value of the end product column in the work plan). However, the individual team member may be at fault if his or her commitment level is not high enough to ensure the task is done well and delivered on time. Having a ground rule that sets this expectation establishes the responsibility for every team member to deliver work products complete and on time. If they do not, this kind of conflict can destroy a team.

Interpersonal

Interpersonal conflict can be very disruptive to a team as well. Differences in personality types or cultural backgrounds often cause this kind of conflict. Conflict can also emerge from differences in core values and even ethics. Personality conflict can arise over differences in attitudes. For instance, if one team member has a playful, jocular attitude toward life, and another takes everything very seriously, the joker could offend the more serious teammate. Personality conflict can also arise over goals and expectations. For example, one team member may see the work the team is doing as a valuable learning experience and enjoy the team problem solving and give-and-take; another may see the team's work as a means to an external end, perhaps a way to gain a promotion or recognition, and thus focus only on the end product, demanding team perfection. Unfortunately, ground rules may not be enough to resolve these kinds of conflicts; the team will thus need to apply some of the approaches to handling team conflict discussed later in this chapter.

Roles

Teams can usually minimize conflict over roles by taking time at the beginning to establish the roles and responsibilities of each member. Role conflicts can still occur if the team gets off course, or individuals start intruding into one another's task area. Conflicts can also occur if individuals have different expectations of the leader's role. One member may see the leader as primarily a facilitator who keeps things moving along smoothly, while another may see the leader as the one to take charge and tell others what to do. Again, clarity about roles and clear ground rules defining team interaction should help manage these kinds of problems.

Whatever the source of the conflict, if it is disruptive, the team needs to address it or risk failing to accomplish planned objectives—and certainly jeopardize obtaining results of the highest quality. The conflict will become distracting and prevent the team from being productive and turning out quality work. The methods and techniques presented in the next section will help teams manage team conflict.

Approaches to Handling Team Conflict

Most teams will use one of the following three approaches to managing conflict:

1. One on one: Individuals involved work it out between themselves.
2. Facilitation: Individuals involved work with a facilitator (mediator).
3. Team: Individuals involved discuss it with the entire team.

One on One

Quite often, a team will decide that the first step in the team's conflict resolution procedure will be to have the two individuals work out the issues alone. However, this may not be the best approach. The approach should be based on the type of conflict and the personalities of the individuals. For example, if the conflict is a personality conflict and both individuals are Introverts, leaving them alone to solve the problem will probably not yield much progress. Even with an Introvert and an Extravert, the one-on-one approach may not work in a personality conflict. On the other hand, if the problem relates to a task and one member thinks another is not carrying his or her load, the two might be able to discuss it and come to some understanding.

If the individuals decide to resolve the issue themselves, they should follow common ground rules for conflict resolution. They may want to use the following guidelines to manage the discussion:

1. Each person should start in a white hat mode, stating the facts as he or she sees them.
2. Both should listen carefully to the other and not interrupt. Setting a time limit for each person may help manage the exchange of information and avoid the more aggressive person dominating too much.
3. Then, both should explain how they see the issue in relationship to the team and how it may disrupt team functioning.
4. Next, the individuals should suggest approaches or ideas to resolve the issues.
5. Finally, they should agree on an approach, write it out, and sign it.

Exhibit 8.7, developed by Deborah Borisoff and David A. Victor, presents a more detailed way of approaching one-on-one conflict management discussions.

You could use these steps in most conflict resolution situations, but you will find that they will work particularly well for teams. A memory device to help remember the steps is to think of them as the *Five "A's"* and make them action steps.

Chevron Chart of Five "A's"

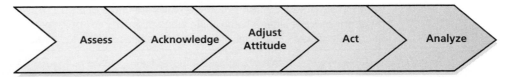

Assess | Acknowledge | Adjust Attitude | Act | Analyze

EXHIBIT 8.7
Steps to
Integrative
Conflict
Management

Source: From
Borisoff, D., & Victor,
D. *Conflict Manage-
ment: A Communica-
tion Skills Approach.*
Published by Allyn
and Bacon, Boston,
MA. Copyright 1997
by Pearson Educa-
tion. Adapted by
permission of the
publisher.

Steps	Description
Assessment	• Allow yourself time to calm down and to evaluate the situation • Gather appropriate information or documentation • Assess your compromise points • Assess what the other party wants • Make a preliminary determination of the appropriate conflict-handling behavior for the situation, relationship, environment
Acknowledgment	• Listen to the other party's concerns • Try to understand his or her viewpoint
Attitude	• Avoid stereotyping and making predeterminations • Try to remain objective • Remain as flexible and open as possible
Action	• Observe how the other party communicates verbally and nonverbally • Watch your use of language and nonverbal communication • Stick to the issues; don't go off on tangents • Don't make promises you can't keep • Don't present issues in a win-lose context • Don't sidestep the issues • Be sincere and trustworthy • Try to remain open-minded and flexible • Use the appropriate conflict-handling behavior and be able to revise your behavior according to how the transaction progresses • Listen, repeat, clarify information
Analysis	• Make sure all parties' concerns are articulated and considered • Summarize and clarify decisions • Review procedure for implementing any changes

Facilitation

Having a third person work with the clashing individuals apart from the team is often the best option. If the team decides to use this approach, the facilitator should be skilled in managing conflict. Research indicates that a facilitator can encourage constructive debate and achieve resolution by following the steps below:

Steps to Facilitate Team Conflict

1. Identify and examine the differences to gain understanding of all perspectives.
2. Establish a rule that all involved must listen politely and not interrupt.
3. Have the individuals in conflict paraphrase each other's concerns.
4. Openly address the concerns and translate what they are saying if necessary.
5. If translation is necessary, confirm your understanding of their message.
6. Invite constructive feedback as soon as issues are in the open.
7. Be assertive as a facilitator, intervening when misinterpretation or personal attacks interfere.
8. Bring the discussion to closure, stating what has been agreed and what the next steps will be.

Source: Adapted from Bens, I. (2000). "Facilitating Conflict." *Facilitating with Ease!* San Francisco, CA: Jossey-Bass. Used with permission.

Team

When a team decides all members should meet to solve the problem, they should have a very specific approach in mind and should select one person to facilitate the discussion. They should also take care not to appear to be "ganging up" on one person. If the problem involves one person not performing his or her share of the work, the team might want to select one member to meet with the slacker first, and only then meet with the slacker as a team. For the team meeting, the team should appoint a spokesperson to present the team's views rather than having everyone confront the individual. They should even use caution in how they sit around the table to avoid all sitting on one side with the offending party on the other as if in an inquisition.

If the problem is broader and involves several team members or the team as a whole, the team should manage the discussion by following the steps below:

1. List the concerns, using facts not feelings (white hat again), trying to capture any differences in perspective.
2. Describe how the conflict is at odds with or interferes with the team's purpose or objectives.
3. Reach agreement on what the main issue is as a team, ensuring all team members have a chance to be heard and all related issues are on the table.
4. Keep the discussion focused on the facts of the main issue and avoid any personal attacks or side issues.
5. Determine if the issue(s) can be resolved by a better understanding of or better implementation of the team's ground rules.
6. Then, write out what the team agrees to do and adjust the ground rules to cover the issue if appropriate. Make sure all actions and responsibilities are clear to everyone on the team.
7. Establish a fallback plan should the conflict continue.

In all team conflict situations, you should make sure your team avoids the following mistakes to help keep the conflict from escalating:

Conflict Resolution Mistakes That May Cause Conflict to Escalate

1. Avoid forcing team members to choose among given options or limited alternatives.
2. Avoid becoming too dependent on having others resolve team problems because dealing with conflict may be difficult or awkward.
3. Avoid the temptation to ignore conflicts altogether.
4. Prevent individual team members from giving into the group, who later act as though they are victims of group pressure.
5. Prevent team members from talking about team issues outside of the team setting.

Source: Adapted from Fisher, K., Rayner, S., & Belgaard, W. (1995). *Tips for Teams: A Ready Reference for Solving Common Team Problems*. New York: McGraw-Hill, Inc. Used by permission of The McGraw-Hill Companies, Inc.

Finally, teams can prevent most, if not all, team conflict by clarifying and agreeing on their project purpose and goals, defining team member roles and responsibilities, establishing and following team and meeting ground rules, developing a communication protocol, and devoting time to improving their group emotional intelligence.

HELPING VIRTUAL TEAMS SUCCEED

More and more companies are using virtual teams to connect their personnel in offices around the globe. In fact, research has shown that today "most teamwork is virtual" with it being rare "to find all team members located in one place" in organizations.[4] As one recent book on virtual teams reported, "The boundary-crossing, virtual team is the new way to work."[5] After September 11, 2001, with the increase in the worldwide threat of terrorism, many companies have cut back on business travel and started focusing even more on the use of remote technologies and virtual teams. It is thus important for all business leaders to know how to help virtual teams succeed. Although virtual teams are common, many companies do not know how to ensure that they function as effectively as a co-located team would. Virtual teams require special effort, and it should not be taken for granted that people who are effective in traditional teams will also work well in a virtual team setting. There are marked differences.

Defining Virtual Teams

Virtual teams are teams whose members are geographically dispersed and rely primarily on technology (telephone, computer, video, or some combination) for communication and to accomplish their work as a team. The geographical separation can range from global dispersion to simply being in different locations within a single company facility. Exhibit 8.8 illustrates one way to think about the difference between traditional and virtual teams: a traditional team might be working around a computer; the virtual team is *in* the computer or other technology.

Identifying Advantages and Challenges of Virtual Teams

Virtual teams provide several advantages for companies today: lowering travel and facility costs, reducing project schedules, allowing the leveraging of expertise and vertical integration, improving efficiency, and positioning to compete globally.[6]

EXHIBIT 8.8
Virtual Team vs. Co-located Team

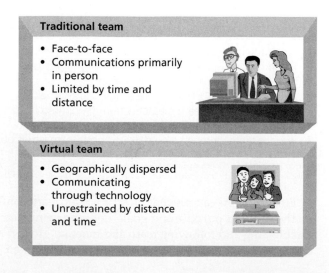

Traditional team

- Face-to-face
- Communications primarily in person
- Limited by time and distance

Virtual team

- Geographically dispersed
- Communicating through technology
- Unrestrained by distance and time

Some have even argued that virtual team structures may lead to greater team creativity "as a result of more openness, flexibility, diversity, and added access to information."[7]

On the other hand, virtual teams also provide challenges, particularly in communications:

- Much of the context of communication, so important in high-context societies, is lost, particularly if teams rely on voice or text technology only. Even members from low-context societies will find virtual communication more of a challenge since they cannot see nonverbal cues, which represent as much as 80 to 93 percent of the meaning people receive in face-to-face communication.
- Cultural differences can become amplified, and personality conflicts more pronounced. Virtual teams must work harder to build relationships and get to know each other as people.
- It is difficult to share and discuss complex information (diagrams, balance sheets, etc.). Projection technology with videoconferencing is improving but still not perfect, and for networked meetings and conference calls, teams often encounter problems with different document versions and with materials not being formatted for easy and quick focus on the right information.
- Connection and trust are difficult to build in a virtual environment, and the lack of trust may put a virtual team on a "collision course."[8]

Addressing the Challenges of Virtual Teams

Since training can address some of the challenges of virtual teams, companies need to be prepared to provide additional resources and training for the people working on virtual teams. They must be trained in how best to use the technology on which their communication will depend. They will need additional diversity training since "culture is pervasive and even more transparent in virtual working than in face-to-face collaboration."[9]

A virtual team needs to have even more structure than a traditional team and must spend even more time on basic good team practices, such as having a clear purpose and objectives, establishing ground rules, creating work plans, and developing team communication protocols. Virtual team members will need to spend planning time talking through the pros and cons of the meeting options as well as the communication media as part of their team communication protocol (Exhibit 8.9). What are the advantages yet challenges of meeting in different places and at different times by using e-mail, voice mail, fax, or computer conferencing with delayed response? Of meeting at different times and in the same places using shared electronic work space? Of meeting at the same time and in different places with conference calls, videoconferencing, or computer conferencing? And how often should they meet face-to-face? They need to determine which option works best for their personalities, cultural differences, the type of team tasks, and the team timing.

By establishing a virtual team room, that is, a shared electronic work space, team members can start to create a team identity and perhaps begin to develop the

EXHIBIT 8.9
Virtual Team
Meeting
Options

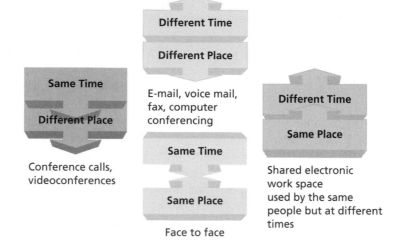

connection that is needed to succeed as a team. The team room provides a way to meet and a routine for all to share in developing ideas and documents (the "same place/different time" way of working). The team will need to implement procedures for the use of the space and for informing colleagues about progress.

Studies have shown that many virtual teams fail because of people problems.[10] As previously mentioned, trust is vital to the success of a virtual team. Unfortunately, trust is not something training can address. It is up to the team members to build it with each other. Jill Nemiro's research on the importance of trust in virtual teams shows that it is difficult to establish and takes time to develop: "Trust developed from a sense of accountability, from seeing that others followed through on what they said they would do. Trust was also based on a belief in the expertise of others, and on positive, ongoing experience with one another."[11] Just as with a co-located team, virtual team members must be committed to the team and the team's work. They must deliver what they promise, on time, and according to the team's expectations. With a virtual team, a high level of commitment is even more critical than with a traditional team.

In summary, according to an article in *The McKinsey Quarterly*, a virtual team needs the following to be successful: (1) shared beliefs, (2) a "storehouse of credibility and trust," and (3) a shared work space.[12] The shared beliefs come from the team discussing fundamental questions about how they plan to approach the problems, examining areas of potential conflict, and taking time to resolve any differences. To build a storehouse of credibility and trust, each team member needs to "pay careful attention to the way others perceive them." In addition, they need to "deliver on their promises, and do so on time; consider other people's schedules; deal straightforwardly with colleagues; and respond promptly to e-mails and voicemails."[13] Creating a shared work space means that they need to establish a virtual team room through the technology available to them. It should allow them to communicate easily and to share in developing ideas and documents.

A virtual team needs to do all that a co-located team does and more to succeed. They must devote time to the team process and people side of teams. They must communicate frequently and have frequent electronic meetings. Ideally, they should meet in person at least once, if not more. Meeting in person at the launch can speed up the needed trust building. In their in-person meeting, the virtual team should exchange information on position and responsibilities, team experiences, expectations, personality and learning styles, and cultural differences. If an in-person meeting is not feasible, then they will need to devote technology-mediated time to these topics.

Virtual teams are praised, but they are also condemned. On one side, they are hailed: "The new workplace . . . will be a virtual workplace, where productivity, flexibility, and collaboration will reach unprecedented new levels."[14] Others lament the loss of the "human moment" and see decreased performance, confused collaboration, increased anxiety, and diminished creativity when people work virtually.[15] Virtual teams, however, are here to stay, and their presence will probably increase. They make sense for most businesses today. They can provide benefits for both the company and the employees. For them to succeed, however, companies need to be able to answer the five questions with which this chapter started, placing an even greater emphasis on the middle three:

1. Does the organization provide the necessary training in diversity, team dynamics, problem solving, and process management to ensure team members know how to manage team issues and processes?
2. Are the employees accustomed to creating and following team charters and ground rules, and do they know how to resolve team conflicts?
3. Does the current company technology effectively support team communication and collaboration? And do our people know how to use that technology?

If the answer is yes, then the company has taken some of the basic organizational steps to help virtual teams succeed. That leaves it to the members of the team to do their part. If they follow the instruction provided in this chapter for all teams—combining complementary skills, establishing shared work processes and approaches, devoting some time and attention to the people side of their teams, and constructively managing team conflict—the odds of having a high-performing team are increased tremendously.

To conclude this chapter, it may be helpful to review the activity phases of any team: getting started, doing the work, and delivering the results. The activities within each phase can be thought of as the communication challenges that leaders must meet to support the team. Exhibit 8.10 (contributed by John Kimball Kehoe) provides a summary of the challenges discussed in this chapter:

This chapter has discussed the best approach to ensuring all team activities run smoothly so that the team achieves its objectives. It has provided team leaders and team facilitators tools to help them build and manage a team. No doubt, leading a team and working on a team present some challenges, but with the right approach, a team can work through the challenges, achieve high performance, and, in the end, "outperform other groups and individuals."

EXHIBIT 8.10
Summary of Team Work Phases and Challenges

Work Phases	Leadership Communication Challenges
Getting Started	• Selecting team members and communicating to them individually and collectively the reasons for their selection • Establishing the team charter and confirming the understanding/ acceptance of it by all team members • Making sure that roles and expectations of team members are clear and accepted • Setting ground rules for the way the team will work • Creating a team communication protocol
Doing the Work	• Guiding or facilitating team meetings • Giving feedback (positive and negative) as work is done • Coordinating the work done by team members; making sure everyone is kept informed • Dealing with and resolving conflicts • Keeping people outside the team informed of what the team is doing when appropriate
Delivering the Results	• Preparing the presentation or report of the team's work • Delivering the presentation or report • Debriefing the experience of the team (what went well and what did not) • Closing out the team, if appropriate

FURTHER READING

Katzenbach, J. R. (1998). *Teams at the Top: Unleashing the Potential of Both Teams and Individual Leaders.* Boston: Harvard Business School Press.

Katzenbach, J. R., & Smith, D. K. (1993). *Wisdom of Teams: Creating the High-Performance Organization.* Boston: Harvard Business School Press.

Katzenbach, J. R. (1998). *The Work of Teams.* Boston: Harvard Business School Press.

Exercise 8.1: Assessing Team Performance and Developing an Improvement Approach

Part 1—Team Assessment

Using the form provided on page 259, assess the team work processes of a team that you have worked with for a while. Your answers are intended to help your team reflect on its performance to date so that it can make any improvements that may be needed. After completing the assessment individually, you should compare your answers with other team members and discuss any differences in scores.

Scale:	Needs Improvement	Average	Excellent
	1	2 3 4	5

1	2	3	4	5	How effective is your team in using tools (agendas, team objectives, action plans, or work plans)?
1	2	3	4	5	How productive are your team meetings?
1	2	3	4	5	How orderly and systematic is the team in its overall approach to team projects?
1	2	3	4	5	How conducive is the team atmosphere to effective communication?
1	2	3	4	5	How effective are your team processes?

1. Has your team established ground rules?   Yes   No

2. Do all members of the team have an equal opportunity   Yes   No
   to participate?

3. Have all members of the team shared equally in team   Yes   No
   responsibilities and workload?

4. Do all members function as team players (as opposed   Yes   No
   to putting themselves before the team)?

Part 2—Team Performance Improvement Plan

1. Complete the following table as a way of assessing your current use of team process tools. Make each item as specific and actionable as possible.

Team Tools	Actions We Have Taken	Actions We Plan to Take
Team Objectives		
Team Ground Rules		
Meeting Agendas		
Action Plans		
Work Plans		

2. Complete the following table as a way of determining what you want to continue or change about your current team processes.

Team Activities	What Has Worked	What Needs to Be Improved
Meeting Productivity		
Project Management		
Communications		
Division of Labor		
Team Learning		

3. Working with your team, list the overall actions your team plans to take to ensure your team continues to perform well.

Exercise 8.2: Assessing Team Members and Providing Feedback

Using a team you have worked with for some time, apply the scale below to evaluate each team member *including yourself* according to the attributes listed. Write the number in the space provided, total the column, average the contribution of this member, and place comments on strengths and weaknesses against the attributes. You will need to complete a separate form for each team member and for yourself.

Scale:	Needs Improvement		Average		Excellent
	1	2	3	4	5

Evaluator: Date:		Name of Team Member Being Assessed:	
Attribute	**Number**	**Comments:**	
1. Positive attitude toward team's work			
2. Completed equitable amount of work			
3. Participated actively in all meetings			
4. Cooperative (easy to work with)			
5. Team player (worked with team, not alone)			
6. Made meaningful contributions to team discussions, process, and products			
7. Good listener, responsive to ideas of others			
8. Good problem-solving ability			
9. Good at synthesizing team ideas			
10. Dependable (team could count on him or her)			
Total contribution of this team member (total of column divided by 10)			

After completing the forms, meet with your team and review the assessments, using the following approach:

Approach to Providing Constructive Team Member Feedback

The goal of this exercise is to provide constructive feedback to your team members to help them be better at working in a team environment. You want to be honest and specific but, most of all, constructive in everything you say. Note: You may want to review the information on giving and receiving feedback in Chapter 6 before completing this portion of the exercise.

1. Using the evaluation form that you have completed for each individual in your group, select one or two areas of strength and improvement for each person in your group. You should also have a specific example for both.
2. Ask for a volunteer in your group to be the first recipient of the feedback.
3. Then, move from person to person in the group, presenting the strength and then the improvement area for the first recipient. The person receiving the feedback should listen only and not respond unless he or she needs to ask a clarification question. After receiving the feedback, the recipient should simply say "Thank you."
4. After everyone has delivered the feedback to the first person, move to the next person to that person's left until all people in the group have received feedback.

For this exercise to be open and honest and to ensure the information leads to the team improving its approach to working together, it is better that the individual team assessment and information provided in the team's discussion remain confidential to the team; therefore, you should not discuss it with anyone outside of your team.

Exercise 8.3: Managing Team Conflict

Consider each of the following five scenarios and decide what may be causing the team's problem (task, interpersonal, or roles) and what steps the team could take to resolve the issues. Consider which of the suggested team conflict resolution approaches would work best (one on one, facilitation, or team) and work out how you would structure the discussion. You may want to go back to Exhibit 7.10 on conflict-handling modes and consider one of the approaches discussed there.

Work independently for about ten minutes, then share your ideas with a breakout group, rotating leadership of the discussion after each scenario. You should assume that all of the teams in these scenarios are working on a project that will last several months, so they must resolve any issues they have—merely appeasing one or more members would not be a viable long-term solution.

1. Team One often spends much time discussing alternatives and ideas for their various projects and cases in their MBA program. One of the members often interrupts and is disrespectful of others' ideas. She says, "I don't know why we have to spend so much time discussing alternatives when the answer is already so obvious!"

   What is going on here and how can the team change the disruptive behavior of their member?

2. Team Two often meets over lunch since their class schedule this semester is so full. Two international members of the five-person team have started bringing food to the meetings, which are held in the university's small "breakout" rooms. One member really objects because he dislikes the strong smell of garlic and curry in the small room. He calls the other American team members to complain, saying, "We've got to do something—I can't stand the smell anymore!"

   What is the source of the conflict and what should the team do?

3. Team Three has met to bring together sections of a final report for their marketing class. The team leader is expecting everyone to arrive with complete text sections that they can easily integrate, but one member comes in with only an outline, another comes in with a bulleted list of text items, and another arrives without any of his sections written.

   Why is the team in this predicament and how can they prevent this type of misunderstanding from occurring in the future?

4. Team Four has a strong team charter and every member participates. On a major semester project, the team decided to divide up the work and check in with each other every few days. One member, Gary, is not sure he understands his part of the work. He does his best to complete his section, but he has also been working part-time on the side and turns his work in to the group the night before it is due. The rest of the team members review his work and decide it is unacceptable; they spend all night reworking his section prior to handing it in. As the next project starts, the team is concerned that Gary's work will continue to be late and of substandard quality.

   What may have led the team to this conflict and how should the team approach Gary to resolve it?

5. Team Five meets on a regular basis every Wednesday at 7:30 a.m. before classes begin. Ellen was on time for the first few meetings, but lately she has been arriving late, often bringing donuts for the other members; she doesn't seem concerned about being late, and she does get right down to business, but one of the other members is really becoming upset about this, saying, "I have to get up at 6:00 to be here on time, but I can make it, why can't she?"

   How should the team handle this issue?

Source: Scenarios developed by Beth O'Sullivan, Rice University. Used with permission.

Exercise 8.4: Launching a Virtual Team

The Case: Zarate Tech Goes Virtual

Zarate Tech has a sales group of 120 located in Chicago, Atlanta, Los Angeles, London, and Sydney. The sales group generates and qualifies leads, meets with existing and potential customers, negotiates deals, and offers technology solutions, focusing primarily on customer relationship management (CRM). The sales force conveys requirements to Zarate's offices in Chicago and London, matching staff capacity with the quantities and types of products needed. The sales group also performs customer service functions, including tracking and confirming delivery and quality of products and solutions. Overall, the sales group moves $2.1 billion of products and consulting services each year.

Traditionally, the company's philosophy was that the sales staff must remain small and in close contact; therefore, they meet in person frequently in either London or Chicago. They see their manufacturing facilities as marketing tools to demonstrate the company's commitment to quality, on-time delivery, and products customized to meet specifications. Despite its focus on providing the latest in CRM technology for its customers, the COO, Jan Ciampi, who oversees Zarate's accounting, finance, and information system, feels the company is behind in its use of technology to manage its sales, sales group interactions, and team communication and problem solving. While Zarate has e-mail, an intranet, and a state-of-the-art internal accounting and telecommunications system, the company rarely uses its technology for team interactions and communication. Although all salespeople have laptops to use on the road, they use them primarily for generating reports and handling e-mail.

You have recently been hired as the new vice president of worldwide sales to help modernize the work processes of the sales group. Senior management is particularly interested in your improving how the company communicates across distances, shares and captures company information, and makes use of computer technology for client and team meetings. They feel the sales group spends too much time and money flying to meetings and even commuting to work. They know some direct contact with customers is important as well as internal meetings of the sales team, which usually consists of a sales rep, account manager, technical engineer, logistics coordinator, and IT technician; however, they wonder if some of these meetings could be handled virtually. They are also considering using a remote sales force structure with the salespeople working from their homes instead of coming into the office, which they think would allow them to cut office overhead.

Last week at the company's annual budget planning meeting in Chicago, Ciampi announced the formation of a team to investigate how best to move the sales group toward using virtual team technology and how to encourage them to use the intranet, video technology, and computer network systems to connect, manage accounts, and work and meet directly online. You will be heading up the team. Your charge is to determine what it will take to ensure the sales group accepts the new way of working and knows how to work effectively as a virtual team.

Once you have decided who to include from your sales group and also from the training, development, and communication departments, you need to draft a memo announcing the project to the team and scheduling the team launch. One of your immediate challenges is that your team will be scattered across all of the offices with many of them on the road constantly. So, you yourself must confront the challenges of working virtually. In fact, you realize that this team could end up serving as a model for how to work effectively as a virtual team, but you also realize that motivating the sales group to change from their current ways of working and providing the training they need to work effectively using virtual technology will be a challenge.

The Assignment

Draft the memo to your team establishing the project objectives and inviting them to the team launch, which you have decided to hold in person in the Chicago office. Then, establish an agenda for the meeting and your approach to working as a team. Next, outline what you see as the challenges to this project and some of the best practices in working virtually that you think will help your team get off to a good start.

Notes

1. Katzenbach, J. R., & Smith, D. K. (1993). *Wisdom of Teams: Creating the High-Performance Organization.* Boston: Harvard Business School Press.
2. Druskat, V. U., & Wolff, S. B. (2001). Building the emotional intelligence of groups. *Harvard Business Review* 79 (3), pp. 80–91.
3. Katzenbach, J. R. (1998). *The Work of Teams.* Boston: Harvard Business Press.
4. Duarte, D. L., & Snyder, N. T. (2001). *Mastering Virtual Teams.* San Francisco: Jossey-Bass, p. xi.
5. Lipnack, J., & Stamps, J. (2000). *Virtual Teams.* New York: Wiley, p. 6.
6. Duarte & Snyder, p. 4.
7. Nemiro, J. E. (2001). Connection in creative virtual teams. *The Journal of Behavior and Applied Management* 2, No. 2 (Winter–Spring), also available online at www:jbam.org/articlesarticle2_8.htm.

8. George, J. M. (1996). Virtual best practice: How to successfully introduce virtual team-working. *Teams Magazine* (November), pp. 38–45.

9. Simons, G. Meeting the Intercultural Challenges of Virtual Work. From http://www.diversophy.com/news_info/downloads.htm.

10. Lipnack & Stamps (2000).

11. www.jbam.org/articles/ article2_8. htm.

12. Benson-Armer, R., & Hsieh, T. (1997). Teamwork across time and space. *The McKinsey Quarterly*, pp. 19–27.

13. Benson-Armer & Hsieh (1997), p. 25.

14. Townsend, A. M., DeMarie, S. M., & Hendrickson, A. R. (1998). Virtual teams: Technology and the workplace of the future. *Academy of Management Executive*, p. 17.

15. Hallawell, E. M. (1998). The human moment at work. *Harvard Business Review*, January–February, pp. 1–8.

Corporate Leadership Communication

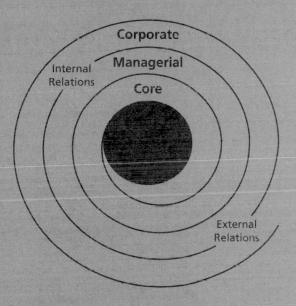

Chapter **Nine**

Establishing Leadership through Strategic Internal Communication

Personal leadership is about communication, openness, and a willingness to speak often and honestly, and with respect for the intelligence of the reader or listener. Leaders don't hide behind corporate double-speak. They don't leave to others the delivery of bad news. They treat every employee as someone who deserves to understand what's going on in the enterprise.

Louis V. Gerstner, Jr., *Who Says Elephants Can't Dance?* New York: Harper Collins (2002)

Communication is always critical but never more so than when you're trying to get others to see and do things differently. . . . If leaders want to change the thinking and actions of others, they must be transparent about their own. If people within the organization don't understand the new thinking or don't agree with it, they will not change their beliefs or make decisions that are aligned with what's desired.

Jeanie Daniel Duck, *The Change Monster: The Human Forces That Fuel or Foil Corporate Transformation and Change.* New York: Crown (2001)

Chapter Objectives

In this chapter, you will learn to do the following:

- Recognize the strategic role of employee communication.
- Assess internal communication effectiveness.
- Establish effective internal communication.
- Use missions and visions to strengthen internal communication.
- Design and implement effective change communication.

One of the major responsibilities of an organizational leader is communication with employees. Fraser Seitel, former senior vice president of public affairs for Chase Manhattan Bank, argues that it is the most important responsibility: "Employee communications is the most important part of a CEO's many responsibilities. . . . If employees believe in the CEO—trust him [her] and respect him [her]—then they become agents to convince other publics of the goodness of the programs and the company."[1] By communicating effectively with employees, however, CEOs are not simply creating ambassadors of goodwill for their companies; they are providing direction, establishing a positive and productive working environment, and influencing their bottom lines.

Effective internal communication provides organizational direction and employee motivation. Based on their research into 530 companies, Ragan Communications found that "CEOs are not just communicating because they want to be thought of as nice people. They have discovered that effective internal communications will help them achieve their vision for the company and will motivate employees to do their best work."[2]

Organizational direction comes from leaders having created and effectively communicated a clear and meaningful vision. Developing and communicating a vision is one of the most important and visible communication tasks of senior management.

Employees are motivated when, through words and actions, the leaders carefully translate the vision and strategic goals into terms that are meaningful to all employees. To do so requires analyzing audiences, targeting messages, and creating communication strategy. Motivating employees also requires listening to them and using emotional intelligence to connect with them. Leaders who appreciate the importance of connecting with all employees through communication and through their actions see results: "An attractive communication climate can contribute significantly to the long-term success of a company. Managers should therefore pay serious attention to the internal communication climate by providing each employee the adequate information and the opportunities to speak out, get involved, be listened to, and actively participant."[3]

Direction setting and the creation of a motivated, productive workforce alone are reasons enough to pursue effective internal communication. Effective employee communication clearly results in higher organizational performance and increased productivity.[4] In addition, effective internal communication has a measurable financial impact. As one recent study of the ROI of 267 major corporations found, internal communication significantly influences financial performance: "Companies with the highest levels of effective communication experienced a 26 percent total return to shareholders from 1998 to 2002, compared to a −15 percent experienced by firms that communicate least effectively."[5]

From daily informational exchanges and interactions with employees to creating and communicating visions, strategic objectives, or other direction-setting messages, to helping employees understand and support major changes, internal communication requires leaders to use all of their best leadership communication skills. Thus, all of what you have learned about leadership communication in this text so far is applicable to your being an effective communicator with your employees—in particular, that you project a positive ethos, create meaningful, purposeful messages, analyze audiences and target your messages, develop communication strategy, and lead through emotional intelligence.

This chapter focuses on establishing leadership through strategic communication with employees. It describes the role of strategic employee communication and how to ensure your employees are equipped to make the greatest possible contribution to the success of your organization. It also discusses how to develop and use vision and mission statements to lead the organization and provides an approach to effective change communication, an essential type of communication in today's rapidly changing workplace.

RECOGNIZING THE STRATEGIC ROLE OF EMPLOYEE COMMUNICATION

For employee communication to play a strategic role in an organization, the leader must realize its importance in accomplishing the company's strategic objectives and performance goals and integrate it into the company's overall strategy and business processes. You want to ensure all internal communication aligns with and reinforces the company's strategic objectives, from the mission and vision to the guiding principles to the operational, performance, and financial goals. The company's strategic messages feed into any communication strategy that you would create within an organization.

For example, suppose one of a company's strategic objectives is to eliminate the current functional silo approach to decision making and bring the leaders of different business units together to make decisions jointly for the good of the company instead of just their individual units. The communication objectives would be (1) to ensure all business units receive the same corporate message that joint decision making is now a priority and (2) to establish forums (meetings if appropriate) for the joint decision making to occur. Your first responsibility will be communicating your message clearly; your second will be persuading the managers to act on it and seeing that they do.

Ensuring that employee communication connects to the strategic objectives requires integrating the internal communication into the company's basic operational processes. If, for example, a company undertakes a yearly business planning process, it will want to integrate communication into the business plan by building in specific communication objectives and milestones. Communication needs to be a topic on the agenda of meetings and a subject of management discussions of strategic objectives and planning; otherwise, it will be neglected and seen as unimportant.

Your communication to employees needs to support the strategy and the performance goals, and all communication with them needs to position them to help you achieve those goals. Therefore, you should think about how best to accomplish the following basic employee communication objectives:

1. Educate employees in the company vision and strategic goals.
2. Motivate employee support for the company's strategy.
3. Encourage higher performance and discretionary effort.
4. Limit misunderstandings and rumors that may damage productivity.
5. Align employees behind the company's performance objectives and position them to help achieve them.

To accomplish these goals, your messages need to be clear, consistent, and targeted. Effective employee communication is both the product—the messages that the organization wants to transfer—and the process—the conduit for transferring the messages. You will need to pay attention to both, and developing a communication strategy for your internal audiences will help you do so.

ASSESSING EMPLOYEE COMMUNICATION EFFECTIVENESS

If you are a new leader in an organization or otherwise not sure about the effectiveness of the internal communication, before developing an internal communication strategy, you may want to use the scorecard in Exhibit 9.1 to uncover how your organization stands in relation to the best practices for internal communication. The scorecard uses the components presented in the model here and establishes a range of performance. The "x's" will be mostly on the left side for a company with an effective employee communication program in place. If, however, the "x's" fall more on the right side of the scale, the company may want to look at improving those components where they fall short.

To obtain a comprehensive appraisal of the current internal communication practices, you would probably want to ask a representative sample of your management team and employees at different levels to complete the scorecard as well. Where a company is on the scale beside each component indicates how much time and effort you will need to devote should it be necessary to improve the current employee communication practices. For example, if the current media now in use are not reaching employees, you will want to find more effective ones immediately. No matter how clear, consistent, and targeted the messages, if they are not reaching the intended audiences, they are useless. If you find key managers are uninvolved and unsupportive of communication efforts, you may need to coach and encourage them to accept responsibility and accountability for the success or failure of employee communication. Once you have pinpointed areas for

EXHIBIT 9.1
Scorecard of
Current
Employee
Communi-
cation

Source: Barrett, D. J. (2002). Change communication: Using strategic employee communication to facilitate major change. *Corporate Communication: An International Journal* 7 (4), pp. 219–231. Used with permission of Emerald Press.

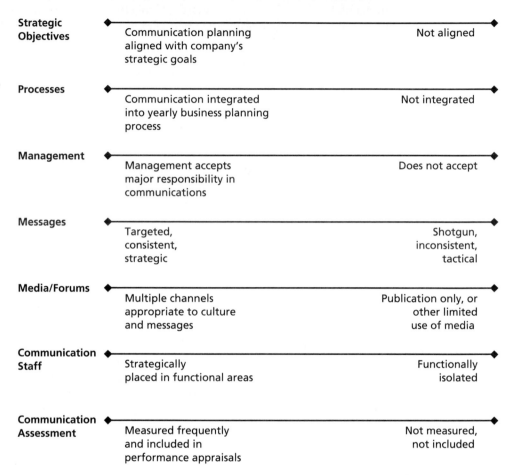

Where are the company's employee communication practices at present?
Place an "x" on the scale below to indicate your preliminary assessment:

Strategic Objectives
Communication planning aligned with company's strategic goals — Not aligned

Processes
Communication integrated into yearly business planning process — Not integrated

Management
Management accepts major responsibility in communications — Does not accept

Messages
Targeted, consistent, strategic — Shotgun, inconsistent, tactical

Media/Forums
Multiple channels appropriate to culture and messages — Publication only, or other limited use of media

Communication Staff
Strategically placed in functional areas — Functionally isolated

Communication Assessment
Measured frequently and included in performance appraisals — Not measured, not included

improvement, you should take steps to close the gaps and work toward establishing the effective internal communication approach described in this chapter. Otherwise, your internal communication will not be as effective as it needs to be to support your company's strategy.

ESTABLISHING EFFECTIVE INTERNAL COMMUNICATIONS

Although creating the internal messages that are to be sent to your employees is your primary leadership responsibility, you also need to pay attention to the other main components of any good communication strategy in your effort to ensure your internal communication supports and assists in accomplishing your company strategy. The strategic employee communication model in Exhibit 9.2 is

EXHIBIT 9.2
Strategic Employee Communication Model

Source: This model and the research into the best practices on which it is based appear in Barrett, D. J. (2002). Change communication: Using strategic employee communication to facilitate major change. *Corporate Communication: An International Journal 7* (4), pp. 219–231. Used with permission of Emerald Press.

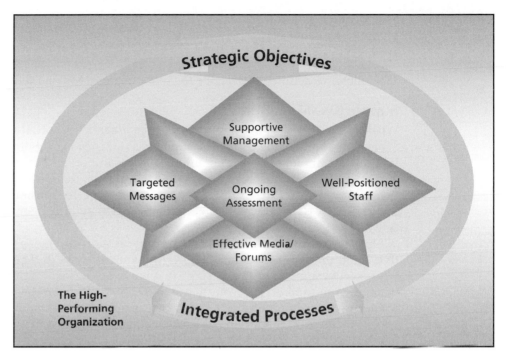

designed to help you. It builds on the communication strategy framework introduced in Chapter 1 to show how you might want to think about developing your strategy for internal communication.

First, it shows the linking of the company's strategy and strategic messages and suggests the business process integration as a band that ties all of the pieces of an internal communication strategy together. Then, it brings in the components of any communication strategy, such as messages and media, and introduces other employee communication components, such as supportive management and well-positioned staff, which best practice research indicates are necessary to have effective employee communication.[6]

To ensure your internal communication is comprehensive, you will want to use an analytical approach to developing a communication strategy as has been suggested throughout this text for any of your important communication. The model serves as a framework for creating your internal communication strategy. In addition, the definitions of each of the components provide benchmarks for you to measure your program against the best practice ideal to work toward achieving.

At its core, the model shows that effective internal communication consists of the following:

1. Supportive management
2. Targeted messages

3. Effective media/forum
4. Well-positioned staff
5. Ongoing assessment

The following definitions describe the best practice approach to each component:

Supportive Management

What does it mean to have supportive management? In short, it means that managers should model the communication behavior they expect of their employees. If you want employees to see communication as important in your company, you and all other managers need to demonstrate it. Such demonstrations may mean that managers are directly involved in and assume responsibility for relaying important messages to their direct reports, but they also openly communicate upward and across their peer groups.

Showing management support for communication also means including effective communication on managers' performance reviews and recognizing those who excel in some way. The message that you want to send to the organization is that communication is everyone's responsibility and is not to be limited to the activities of the communication staff. Since employees are much more likely to behave as they see their managers behave than to follow written principles, you and other managers need to demonstrate support for and belief in the value of communication.

For example, if you want to promote an open, free exchange of ideas, you need to encourage and establish media and forums for communication to flow up, down, and across the organization. The leaders need to accept good and bad news without penalizing the messenger. In fact, the fear of speaking out can lead to ethical quandaries in some organizations where an employee witnesses something that is questionable but is afraid to bring the news to management. In addition, it can lower employee productivity because they have no outlet or recognition for improvement ideas. You and the other leaders in the organization set the tone for an open or closed culture. Without management's positive examples to establish a high priority for open and honest communication, the channels of communication will not flow freely and the rest of the organization will not see communication as important.

Targeted Messages

As has been emphasized throughout this text, effective communication depends on making all messages specific to the audience receiving them. Therefore, you need to analyze your many internal audiences and work with other managers to establish groups by function and level and then develop messages each group will understand. While the core messages communicated within the company must be consistent across the company and in all external messages, you may need to present messages to specific groups with a slightly different emphasis and maybe even slightly different language. That does not imply that the meaning changes, only the words that are used. The targeted messages need to be relevant and meaningful for each targeted employee group yet consistent with the company's overall strategy and messages, such as those found in the mission, vision, and guiding principles.

For example, each business unit or division may need to create a version of important messages for its employees or convert the overall message from the corporate center into digestible and actionable messages the employees can understand and act upon. They may even have their own vision statement specific to their goals in support of the company's vision. This kind of specific message tailoring usually requires the help of individuals closest to the employee groups, so after establishing the overall major messages for the organization, you may want to enlist help in the wording of the messages that follow to each group.

Effective Media and Forums

While most organizations have traditional media and forums for conveying information, companies should not take for granted that all employees receive the information through the company's preferred channels. Companies may need to communicate internal messages through several different media to reach all employees. You need to look critically at the media, decide when different situations require different media, and survey employees to determine if they are receiving the intended messages through the selected media.

For example, many companies produce expensive and elaborate employee newsletters and magazines periodically, yet if they were to survey employees on how many read them, they might find that employees do not see much value in them and that they would prefer receiving something less elaborate and more frequent, such as e-mails or recorded voice messages. Gordon Bethune, the CEO of Continental Airlines, was known for leaving global messages for all employees every Friday in voice mail. These informal, frequent messages were much more effective in reaching the Continental employees than more formal publications or meetings.

If you find that your employees prefer direct, face-to-face communication over indirect, print, or electronic media, you will need to develop systems and procedures to allow for frequent exchanges among employees at all levels. For example, UPS would hold what they called "three-minute" meetings every morning at all regional locations to deliver important information for the day and to solicit feedback. This way they encouraged frequent two-way dialogue and made sure they reached all employees with key messages, even those employees not connected to voice mail and e-mail.

Of course, if you decide you want to encourage face-to-face communications, you may need to consider providing training in diversity, interpersonal communication, and meeting management to assist those managers doing most of the communicating in addressing the real needs and interests of their employees effectively (see Chapters 6 and 7).

Well-Positioned Staff

As an organizational leader, if you are serious about ensuring that communication is integrated into the company operations and strategy and positioned to help you deliver strategic messages, you will want to consider the placement of your professional communication staff. Research indicates that the communication staff must be positioned close to the most important business issues and decisions and involved in the strategic and business planning processes for internal communication to be fully effective. They need to have a "seat at the table." For most organizations, that means the highest-ranking communication person must be at the same level as company presidents and vice presidents. To understand the company's strategy and to participate in the decision making, the senior communication officer must be directly connected to the highest levels of the organization.

If your organization is large enough to have several full-time communication professionals and wants to encourage communication up, down, and across the organization, you should locate them at all levels of the organization. Having communication staff close to different functions or within each business unit signals the importance of communication and provides local expertise when you need to tailor your messages to these different groups. When isolated and seen only as producers of publications, the communication professionals will not be positioned to help the other managers deliver and measure the impact of either routine or major change messages.

Ongoing Assessment

For internal communication to be effective, you need to demonstrate clearly that you consider good communication to be valuable and important. As is well known, what matters in an organization is what is measured. Therefore, you will want to include communication ability and performance in the assessment of the employees. Your organization should evaluate communication effectiveness as part of each employee's individual performance appraisal and give appropriate recognition for excellence.

Employee evaluation forms should include questions on how well employees are communicating to others in their department as well as to people outside of their groups. Are they open and sharing information frequently enough? Do they encourage others to communicate with them? How do they respond to bad news, for instance? Such openness has been found to be one of the major deterrents to unethical practices. It is not as easy to hide questionable activities if all employees feel as though they are being held accountable for communicating everything that is going on within the company openly and honestly.

In addition, you should ensure that your organization assesses companywide communication effectiveness formally and frequently against clearly defined goals. Assessment procedures should include ascertaining whether important messages are reaching all employees and how well these messages are understood. In response to the assessments, you should establish ways to ensure that improvement occurs when you uncover breakdowns in communication.

The quickest way to obtain a picture of the "what" and the "how" of internal communication is to send out very short surveys to a stratified sample of the organization. Depending on which channels work best for the organization and the different groups in the company, these surveys can be sent out electronically through e-mail or on the company intranet or distributed as hard copy. Web-based survey companies, such as SurveyMonkey, make it very easy to send out surveys electronically and also make it easy to synthesize the results quickly. Phone surveys work as well, again depending on the culture and the company's preferred way of communicating.

Using the model or a similar analytical framework to develop your internal communication strategy and aiming toward reaching some of the best practices discussed in this section will help you achieve improved internal communication. It is up to you and the other leaders of the organization to make communicating with employees a priority and to set the tone for how the organization views employee communication. Failing to approach internal communication strategically and realize its importance will hinder any organization from achieving its performance goals and limit any leader's ability to accomplish his or her goals.

USING MISSIONS AND VISIONS TO STRENGTHEN INTERNAL COMMUNICATION

The strategic employee communication model provides an analytically rigorous approach to internal communication that works particularly well with the process side of communication, such as media selection, supportive management, and ongoing assessment; however, leaders need to spend most of their time on the content side. You must ensure that the strategic objectives and the messages are clear, unambiguous, meaningful, and understandable for internal communication to be effective.

Missions, visions, values, and guiding principles make up one category of major strategic messages that most organizations convey to their employees. Your ability to establish and communicate the mission and the vision effectively strengthens your position in leading the organization. Leadership communication must include how best to create and deliver these core messages to ensure they are strong and meaningful and not simply feeble slogans good only for adorning coffee cups. You want the vision and mission in particular to guide employees' efforts toward achieving your company's strategic goals.

This section answers the following questions:

1. Why are missions and visions important?
2. What are missions and visions?
3. When are they most effective?
4. How do you build them?

Understanding the Importance of Missions and Visions

In their book *Built to Last,* James Collins and Jerry Porras argued that visions play an essential role in a company's performance, but to do so, they must be clear, relevant, and directed toward delivering a genuinely useful service or product. They found that the companies they labeled "visionary" achieve the highest profitability: a single dollar invested in general market stocks in 1926 would have grown to $415 by 1990. That same dollar, invested in a "visionary company" with a clear, functioning vision and mission statement, would have reaped $6,356.[7]

Effective mission and vision statements are important to a company for the following reasons:

1. Inspire individual action, determine behavior, and fuel motivation.
2. Establish a firm foundation of goals, standards, and objectives to guide corporate planners and managers.

3. Satisfy both the company's need for efficiency and the employees' need for group identity.
4. Provide direction, which is particularly important in times of change, to keep everyone moving toward the same goals.

An organization's success can be facilitated by its having a clearly stated, credible, intelligible, actionable, and meaningful vision and mission statement. While organizational leaders usually develop and communicate the mission and the vision, all employees need to understand and accept them.

Defining Missions and Visions

The words "mission" and "vision" are quite often used interchangeably; however, they should not be, and doing so can result in confusion. Since definitions differ slightly from company to company, as the leader, you may first want to establish your definition. The following discussion provides definitions and examples of both words.

Missions

A mission is a statement of the reason a company exists that is intended primarily for internal use. It should ensure that employees understand the company's purpose by defining a company's basic business (i.e., types of products or services provided or markets served). It should establish a single, noble purpose and an enduring reality.

The following table contains a few mission statements to demonstrate this definition:

Company	Mission
Ford	"We are a global family with a proud heritage, passionately committed to providing personal mobility for people around the world. We anticipate consumer needs and deliver outstanding products and services that improve people's lives."(http://homepages.wmich.edu/~s9obrie1/bus%20270%20pro%203.htm)
Sun Microsystems	"Solve complex network computing problems for governments, enterprises, and service providers." (http://www.sun.com/aboutsun/coinfo/mission.html)
Jones Graduate School of Management	"The Jones School is dedicated to quality education, personal attention, outstanding research, and integration with the greater community." (www.jonesgsm.rice.edu)
Goodwill Industries of the Lowcountry (SC)	"Goodwill Industries of the Lowcountry is a community resource dedicated to helping individuals with disabling and disadvantaging conditions achieve their fullest potential by offering choices and opportunities that determine how and where individuals live and work. These choices and opportunities are provided through employment, rehabilitation, and residential services." (www.beaufortonline.com)

Visions

A vision statement establishes the company's aspirations. It describes an inspiring new reality, achievable in a well-understood and reasonable time frame. Companies often use visions for internal and external audiences, although their greatest purpose is usually to guide internal actions. They should reflect the company leaders' willingness to project into the future. A vision usually starts with the words "to become" or "to create."

The following table contains a few vision statements to demonstrate this definition:

Company	Vision
Ford	"Our vision is to become the world's leading Consumer Company for automotive products and services."
Sun Microsystems	"Everyone and everything connected to the network."
Jones Graduate School of Management	"To be a premier business school with international recognition and stature of the highest order. It will prepare future business leaders to make substantial contributions to the well-being of society."
Goodwill Industries of the Lowcountry (SC)	"We pledge to be a not-for-profit leader in the provision of services, which promote the individual's fullest potential, to include employability, integration and inclusion in the community where the individual lives and works. We serve people with physical, mental, emotional, economic and social obstacles."

One way to differentiate a mission statement from a vision statement is to think of the mission as the "here and now" and to think of the vision as the future. What is most important, however, is that a company have a clear definition of its reason for being (mission) and of where it wants to go (vision); whether one is called a mission and the other a vision matters less than that both exist and the organization knows what they are and which is which.

Ensuring the Mission and Vision Are Effective

To be useful in guiding employees, both the mission and the vision need to be perfectly clear in their meaning and specific to the company. You can apply the following tests to determine how meaningful and specific they are.

To test a mission, the leaders should look for the following characteristics:

- Inspirational and suggestive of excellence.
- Clear, making sense in the marketplace.
- Stable but flexible enough to last with only incremental changes.
- Beacons and controls when all else is up for grabs.
- Aimed at empowering employees first, customers second.[8]

To test the vision, the organizational leaders should ask if it does the following:

- Suggests goals and provides a direction.
- Inspires and prepares for the future but honors the past.
- Applies specifically to the company, providing details that are actionable.

Of course, a vision statement and a mission statement interact, which means that a vision may give rise to a new mission, and a redefined mission may require a changed vision for implementation.

Building an Effective Mission and Vision

In his essay "The Vision Thing," Todd Jick explains three approaches to building a vision:

- CEO/leader developed.
- Leader–senior team visioning.
- Bottom-up visioning.[9]

Depending on the company culture, any of the three could work effectively. If, for example, a company is larger or fairly hierarchical, management would probably want to use the CEO/leader approach. If, on the other hand, the company is very much a team-based organization or structured more in a matrix, it might want to use the leader–senior team visioning approach. Finally, if the company is a relatively small, flat organization, management might ask a team of employees to develop the vision. For example, a team of 60 employee volunteers developed the Whole Foods Market's "Declaration of Interdependence," which contains their motto, "Whole Foods, Whole People, Whole Planet," and their guiding principles.[10]

For most companies, some combination of the three approaches seems to work most effectively. This combination approach consists of first having the company's leaders and senior leadership team create initial vision and mission statements and, then, having employees at different levels participate in refining them. A mission and vision that emerge at the end of a more interactive process will more likely resonate meaning for employees at all levels of the organization. The danger of developing a mission and vision in isolation at the top of the organization is that lower-level employees may not understand the leaders' intentions and will not feel any ownership of the statement.

You might take the following steps in a leader-led, interactive, employee-involved approach to building a mission and a vision:

1. Create Initial Draft

Bring the "right" employees, usually a cross section of organizational leaders, together to create the initial draft of the mission and vision.

To arrive at the mission, the leadership team should work through the following questions:

- What do we do?
- What are our core products, concepts, or services?
- What are our collateral products and services?

- Why is what we do important?
- What if our company no longer existed?
- What is our value proposition?

To arrive at the vision, the team should work through the following:

- What does it take for us to succeed in today's marketplace?
- What will it take in the future?
- What are our current strengths and weaknesses?
- What are our major opportunities and threats?
- How might we increase the value we bring to our stakeholders?
- What do we want to become?
- How do we want competitors and the world to see us?

2. Clarify the Meaning

After the group has answered these questions and completed the first draft, they should look at it critically, word by word. One approach is to take each word and ask what it means. For example, the company vision might read as follows:

> To be the market leader in providing high-performing, cost-effective computer products and services to enable systemwide success for all of our customers.

Then, the exercise to determine the real meaning behind most of the rather abstract words in the vision might look as follows.

Word or Phrase	Means	Does Not Mean
Market Leader	Recognized by peers for innovation	A certain market share percentage
High-Performing	Fast, high-quality, free from defects, low maintenance, compatible with industry standards	The fastest with complete compatibility with all other hardware
Cost-Effective	Competitive	Lowest cost
Computer Products and Services	Central computing, client server, hardware with service and support for all our manufactured products	Peripheral computer equipment such as printers, scanners, external drives, and so forth, with service and support for other companies' products
Systemwide Success	Success for critical enterprisewide hardware	Success for interfaces and compatibility with all other manufactured products

3. Tell the World in 25 Words or Less What You Are and What You Want to Become

The mission and the vision need to be more than slogans; at the same time, they need to be concise enough that people can remember them. Again, however, they

EXHIBIT 9.3
Relationship of Mission to Vision to Strategic Objectives

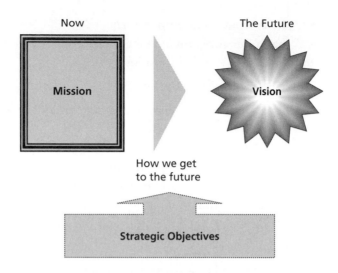

must be meaningful; while some companies have created visions that captured a lot of meaning in just a few words, it is very difficult to do so.

4. Develop the Strategic Objectives to Make the Vision Specific and Actionable

The strategic objectives should be specific actions designed to help (1) accomplish the vision and (2) bring a sustainable competitive advantage. They are usually measurable targets, divided into quantitative goals (such as financial, market share, or productivity) and qualitative goals (such as personnel development, reputation). Exhibit 9.3 illustrates how the mission, vision, and strategic objectives relate to each other.

Exhibits 9.4 and 9.5 illustrate how the strategic objectives should support the vision. Strategic objectives help to make a vision more meaningful and actionable. Notice in Exhibit 9.4 that the supporting relationship between the strategic objectives and the vision is indicated by the use of the word "by."

EXHIBIT 9.4
Example Vision with Strategic Objectives

Vision: To be the market leader in providing high-performing, cost-effective computer products and services to enable systemwide success for all of our customers by

- Creating seamless integration of all system critical components.
- Providing products of a superior value at prices at or below all major competitors.
- Supplying management of all products and support for all systems.
- Establishing partnerships to ensure customers have integrated, highly reliable systemwide solutions.

5. Hold Cascading Meetings with Employees to Test the Mission and the Vision

Cascading meetings offer a way to involve as many employees as possible in testing the mission and vision. These meetings or workshops usually start with the upper levels of the organization broken into functions or divisions and then give way to cross-level, functional, or divisional meetings. The first level of these workshops will usually focus on creating and refining the vision and making sure the group involved agrees with the specific language and the meaning of that language to them.

The next round will usually involve a "working draft" of the vision so that the attendees will feel comfortable suggesting changes. After this round, the leaders may want to regroup and consider which changes to accept and then produce a draft of the vision that incorporates the suggested changes from the other employee groups.

The final round of vision workshops will include a cross section of the next levels, functions, or divisions of the organization. If the organization is large, it will not be practical to involve all employees, so managers should select a representative group from the levels, functions, or divisions. At this point, the vision should be considered "final" and ready to roll out across the entire organization.

The major reason to approach the development of the vision in face-to-face workshops of this sort is to begin to build support for the vision. Involving the employees in this way makes them feel part of the process. In addition, it can break down some of the barriers to change and allow management to obtain important input from the organization in shaping a vision that is meaningful at all levels.

With most companies, once a few levels or groups of the organization have been involved and a good cross section of employees have had a chance to react to the mission and vision, management can feel fairly comfortable that the mission and the vision statements are acceptable and ready for the outside world to see. Exhibit 9.5 shows an example of a vision, mission, and the strategic objectives for a major international chemical company.

Although following the steps outlined in the vision development process here takes time, the process will ensure the creation of a mission and a vision that will guide the actions of the organization. Employees need to know why the company exists and where it plans to go in order to ensure that their actions support the mission and contribute to accomplishing the vision.

Going through some sort of visioning discussion and particularly following a cascading workshop approach can strengthen internal communication by bringing forward agreements and disagreements even among senior management so that the company can create a common, shared view of its focus and direction. In fact, in some cases, the process of creating the vision may do more to bring the company together by clarifying its direction than the end products that come out of the process—the mission and vision statements.

EXHIBIT 9.5
Example
Vision with
Mission and
Strategic
Objectives

MISSION

A customer-driven organization, providing industrial chemical products and creative solutions in select markets around the world.

VISION

Major Chemical's Inc.'s vision is to become the preferred partner in providing industrial chemical products and creative solutions for our customers by—

STRATEGIC OBJECTIVES

- Conducting business based on a foundation of environmental responsibility.
- Running all operations efficiency but safely.
- Generating profitable growth of 15 percent over the next five years.
- Improving the satisfaction of our customers, employees, and shareholders.
- Conducting every aspect of our business guided by our values.
- Developing internal measures of how we are operating and how well we "walk the talk" for our customers and employees.

DESIGNING AND IMPLEMENTING EFFECTIVE CHANGE COMMUNICATION

Organizational change is inevitable yet rarely easy. Many change efforts fail to deliver the value the company seeks. For instance, mergers are one of the most frequent causes of major organizational change, but only a few yield the anticipated or hoped for results. A *Harvard Business Review* article reports that companies spent $3.3 trillion in 1999 on mergers and acquisitions, yet "less than half ever reached their strategic and financial goals."[11] The reason for this failure will usually rest on the softer side of the merger, the side of culture, process, and people.

The greatest difficulty leaders face in bringing about change involves the people. To achieve successful change, leaders must confront the challenges of reaching the employees through effective leadership communication before, during, and after any major, companywide change programs. Without effective employee communication and a rigorous approach to the leadership communication, a change program has little chance to succeed.

In "Leading Change: Why Transformation Efforts Fail," Kotter lists "undercommunication" as one of the major reasons change efforts do not succeed. As he says, "Transformation is impossible unless hundreds or thousands of people are willing to help, often to the point of making short-term sacrifices. Employees will not make sacrifices, even if they are unhappy with the status quo, unless they believe that useful change is possible. Without credible communication, and a lot of it, the hearts and minds of the troops are never captured."[12]

The organization's leaders bear the primary responsibility for successfully communicating the rationale for the changes, the implementation plans, and the impact on the company as a whole and on the individual employees. The leaders will need to decide how much communication will be enough and to establish how to manage the change communication effectively. The following discussion will take you through a leadership approach to change communication that begins with determining the scope of the communication program. Next, you will learn a best practice approach to structuring a change communication program that includes establishing a change communication leadership team and leading the organization through interactive change meetings.

Determining the Scope of the Change Communication Program

The magnitude of the proposed organizational changes and the effectiveness of the company's current internal communication practices will determine the scope of the change communication program. To help you determine how comprehensive the communication program needs to be and where you should start, you should first assess how effective your company's current internal communication practices are and decide if they are strong enough to support major change.

You may want to use the scorecard presented in Exhibit 9.1 or a similar instrument as a way to start your assessment. If you find the current approach to internal communication lacking, you will probably need to include improvement approaches in the change communication plan. For example, if you find that the media the company is currently using are not effectively reaching all employees, how will you reach them with major change messages? If you find your management team currently does not see communication as one of its primary responsibilities, how can you depend on them to communicate the change messages effectively?

Thus, before jumping into a major change program, you will need to take stock of your current internal communication practices and make improvements if necessary. Otherwise, the internal communication will not be able to facilitate the changes by ensuring all employees understand and accept them.

Next, you should ask the following questions to help you determine how widely felt the effects of the change will be:

1. Is the proposed change a major transformation for the company or does it only consist of incremental adjustments?
2. Is the change companywide or business unit specific?
3. How many employees are involved and affected?

If the changes are major and essential to company performance, you will want to develop a complete change communication plan as part of your change program. Exhibit 9.6 demonstrates three possible levels of communication effort, depending on the extent of the change proposed.

For a simple change in policy, for example, you could probably succeed by using level 1: "basic" communication. You will still want to target your messages, but you will send them out to the organization and probably not assess or follow up on their delivery. For a more complex change, such as the introduction of new performance measures and reward systems across all groups, you might choose the "strategic" level, using several media to ensure all employees receive the information on the changes and holding meetings to ensure managers, in particular, understand when and how to use the measures. You

EXHIBIT 9.6
Levels of
Change
Communica-
tion Effort

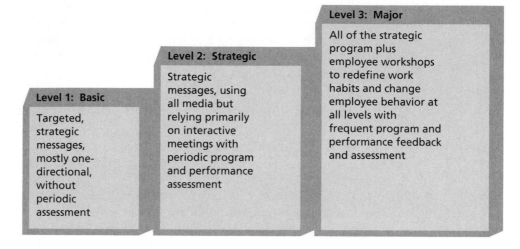

Level 1: Basic

Targeted, strategic messages, mostly one-directional, without periodic assessment

Level 2: Strategic

Strategic messages, using all media but relying primarily on interactive meetings with periodic program and performance assessment

Level 3: Major

All of the strategic program plus employee workshops to redefine work habits and change employee behavior at all levels with frequent program and performance feedback and assessment

would probably follow up with an assessment at some point to make sure all employees understand the proposed changes and their impact on them. For a major change, such as merging two companies, moving the company in a new direction, or developing new products or services, you would probably want to select level 3: "major" and develop a complete change communication program using the following approach.

Structuring a Communication Program for Major Change

Exhibit 9.7 provides an example of a three-phased change communication plan for major change. Each of the three phases specifies actions the leaders would want to take to develop and implement the change communication strategy. Even though a broad organizationwide change program would not flow linearly or as neatly as depicted in Exhibit 9.7, you should still create a simple overview map of how you expect the change communication plan to progress. Creating such a plan will be useful for thinking through program staging issues and ensuring consideration of all important actions and their timing.

As you know from the discussion in Chapter 8 on team action and work plans, action plans require frequent updating to remain accurate in guiding activities. They evolve as the project unfolds; therefore, you will need to build in periodic feedback loops to capture information coming in that affects the plan once the change program is under way. Also, you know that in addition to this high-level action plan, you will need a very detailed work plan to specify all actions, responsibilities, and deadlines.

Phase 1: Design Change Communication Strategy and Plan

The first phase of strategy development is critical to the success of any change communication program. You should use your best leadership skills to guide the organization away from initiating changes immediately without first determining

EXHIBIT 9.7
Three-Phased
Change
Communica-
tion Action
Plan

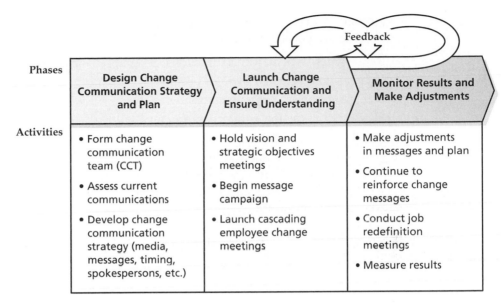

Phases	Design Change Communication Strategy and Plan	Launch Change Communication and Ensure Understanding	Monitor Results and Make Adjustments
Activities	• Form change communication team (CCT) • Assess current communications • Develop change communication strategy (media, messages, timing, spokespersons, etc.)	• Hold vision and strategic objectives meetings • Begin message campaign • Launch cascading employee change meetings	• Make adjustments in messages and plan • Continue to reinforce change messages • Conduct job redefinition meetings • Measure results

Feedback

what specific actions are needed and how best to communicate them. You should think carefully about the specific changes the employees will need to understand and make in their day-to-day jobs to accomplish the major companywide change objectives. The from/to problem-solving tool introduced in Chapter 7 will be useful in analyzing and capturing the specific changes at all levels and of all types (see the example in Exhibit 7.4).

You need to develop a communication strategy that includes audiences, media, messages, spokespersons, and timing, at a minimum. Also, you may need to assess the current employee communication situation to determine if you have the media/forum currently in place to ensure that change messages will reach the intended targets. You must know where the communication breakdowns are and how best to reach the organization with the key change messages.

Before assessing the current communication practices or developing the strategy, you may want to put together a team to help you since major change requires a lot of leadership's time and attention. A change communication team (CCT) can assist you in analyzing the needs and implementing the change communication program. A full-scale change communication program requires resources dedicated to communications. Depending on your organization and the type of changes, you will probably want the team to consist of a multilevel, cross-functional group of employees and managers representative of the organization. Having diverse, frontline, operational employees on the team provides definite benefits if you are expecting widespread change affecting all employees. It can often mean the difference between the employees accepting the changes or rejecting them as another management fad of the day. Such a team will often become part of the mechanism to ensure the changes remain after the "official" team no longer exists.

Although your CCT membership needs to reflect the culture and structure of your company, you should select employees with the following basic characteristics:

- Representative of all levels, functions, geographic locations (if relevant).
- Respected and trusted by their peers.
- Open and honest communicators.
- Skilled at interacting with others and facilitating discussions.

You will also want to ensure that you select employees who can break away from their regular duties to dedicate the time needed. The employees on the team need to be fully dedicated since they will need to work rapidly to make any needed improvements in employee communication, develop the strategy, and launch into aggressive communication with the entire organization.

Having a team dedicated to communication will make the change program run much more smoothly. In addition to helping develop the strategy, they can serve as change ambassadors who can reach deep into the organization to ensure widespread understanding of the change messages.

After you have established the core CCT and the team has completed the preliminary analysis and strategy development, you may want to break the team into subteams to focus on different aspects of the change communication strategy. Exhibit 9.8 provides an example of how a CCT might fit into the organization and how the subteams might be organized. In this example, some of the subteams correspond to the components of the strategic employee model, but others are outgrowths of the preliminary assessment and the specific areas determined to be priorities for change communication in this company. The subteams will probably work independently, but to be most effective, they need to interact frequently to avoid duplication of effort and ensure no issues remain unresolved.

A strong CCT serves as the linchpin of the development and implementation of the change communication strategy and plan. The team can provide information

EXHIBIT 9.8
Sample
Change
Communica-
tion Team
Structure

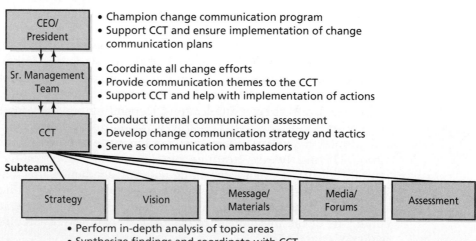

from management to the organization, help translate messages to employees at all levels, and bring credibility to the change communication effort. One additional result of a CCT is that having a cross-functional, multilevel team will help the organization see communication as a responsibility of all employees.

Phase 2: Launch Change Communication and Ensure Employee Understanding

The first step in launching the change communication plan is to start communicating the change messages, getting them out to the organization through the media determined in your analysis. If a company already has an acceptable vision, you may want to measure the organization's understanding of it and reinforce it before launching into delivery of the change messages. Often, however, the vision no longer works for a company undergoing major changes, and you will need to create a new vision with strategic objectives to support it. Since you need to move fast, the most efficient approach may be for the company's leaders to convene and develop a new initial vision that captures the company's new direction, but to be most effective, you would want to build the development of the vision into the change process and use the leader-driven, employee-involvement approach described previously in this chapter. Allowing employee involvement in the creation of the vision during major change will increase their understanding and acceptance of the new direction and what the changes mean to them.

Once the vision is in place and you have launched your communication campaign, you will want to start bringing the organization into the change more directly and specifically. To do so means you and other managers and perhaps members of the CCT will need to meet personally with all employees. These should be interactive meetings in which you communicate the case for change and major change messages. The format should allow for and encourage employee questions and reactions to the proposed changes. Your goal in these meetings is to ensure employees really understand the change messages and know what they mean to them personally and how they are to perform their jobs. All employees need to feel a part of a change process, and the more they can contribute to the change discussions, the more they will start to internalize the proposed changes.

Phase 3: Monitor Results and Make Adjustments

As soon as you feel you have reached the entire organization with the change messages and after you have held meetings with the employees to communicate with them directly, you should plan to stop and assess the employee understanding. It is a good idea to survey a cross section of the employees and conduct a few carefully planned focus groups. Once you have the results, you will know if you need to make any changes in the messages or media and if you need to conduct additional meetings. You may find that you need to conduct some job redefinition sessions that will allow employees to discuss how their specific job activities will need to change within the altered organization.

It helps employees to understand the changes if they can see the key objectives as they are now and as they will be in the new organization once the change

EXHIBIT 9.9
**Example of a
From/To Table
for Strategic
Objectives**

Strategic Objectives	From	To
Providing computer products at superior value	Hardware, software, and solutions for all computers	Hardware and solutions for servers and complex enterprise systems only
	Value to us, but high cost to customer	Low cost, high value to customer
Creating integration	Fragmented products and services in isolated pockets	Connected components within the enterprise system

program is completed. Again, a from/to analysis is useful in determining the changes and explaining them to employees. For example, a computer company might have the from/to for its strategic objectives as illustrated in Exhibit 9.9.

Once the employees can see the changes at a higher level, you would probably want to have supervisors meet with them to develop the specific changes in each job function. Again, the from/to works well. The employees would look critically at what their job entails now and what it will involve as a result of the change. For some employees, the change may be small, which will be reassuring to them. For those who have to make major changes in the way they work, these sessions should help make those changes more tangible to them, which again could be reassuring since any ambiguity around the changes would be removed.

Throughout the change process, you should involve as many managers as possible in the change meetings and job redefinition sessions. Not only will their involvement show their support for the change program, but it also allows them to see employees at work in the organization in ways that differ from day-to-day operations. Often hidden talent emerges in interactive employee meetings. Managers may want to elevate some of the high performers to different positions in the organization during or after the change program. Also, your CCT may want to recruit some of the employees who stand out to serve as additional ambassadors and even facilitators for future change meetings.

Just as you want to communicate aggressively at the beginning of the change program to help employees understand the new direction and the meaning of the changes, you will want to communicate successes along the way and ensure the organization hears how well the change program is progressing. Finally, at what you see as the end of the change program, you will need to measure the results.

Underlying any successful change communication program are the continual signals along the way that change is happening and that the change is making a positive difference in the way the company operates. The program will not be judged a success unless it makes a meaningful difference not only for the employees but also for the company overall. Communication is the key to ensuring that the organization sees and understands the differences being brought about by the changes. Without a well-planned and executed change communication strategy, no change program can succeed.

In conclusion, from the day-to-day exchanges to the major efforts associated with change, internal communication is important to the success of any organization. The strategy for internal communication consists of the basic components of any effective business communication strategy, such as audience analysis, targeted messages, and appropriate media, but it is also much more than processes and products. Internal communication holds an organization together. Good internal communication provides the direction needed to reach strategic and financial goals and encourage productivity. It enables the smooth operation of the organization when interwoven seamlessly into all other processes of the organization. You will need all of your leadership communication skills to inspire employees to support you in achieving the organization's strategic and financial goals, and it is through skilled, strategic internal communication that you will accomplish leadership.

Exercise 9.1: Merging Benefits

The Case: Huge Co. Revisited

Huge Co. (you may want to review the facts in the Huge Co. case in Chapter 2) has now developed the new benefits program for the software managers based on the consulting company's report, which incorporated an assessment of best practices in the industry and consultation with benefits managers at both companies. The new program has the following features:

- Life insurance options will be unchanged for employees from both premerger companies. Huge Co. will pay for a base level of insurance (two times salary) and the employee can elect to pay for additional coverage.
- A flexible spending account is a new key feature, under which employees can set aside pretax dollars for medical spending or dependent care. This will be a new feature for the CC employees.
- A vendor who is new to both companies will provide medical insurance, but the new company offers a broader choice of physicians than either plan previously, and employees will retain several choices about the type of plan they enroll in. Employees who actively participate in exercise classes and other health maintenance activities will receive additional credit toward health care deductibles.
- Dental/orthodontic insurance is optional and, if elected, is paid for by the employee.
- Vision will not be offered, but would be covered under the flexible spending account.
- The company will match 401K contributions up to 12 percent of salary, and stock options will be offered to high-performing software engineers.

The change team (CT) has managed the major integration of the two companies, and they have asked for your input on a task that has a smaller scope but is essential to the continued success of the company: advising the software engineers of both companies about their new plan. As Mariel Salinas, the former benefits manager at Computer Co, your new position will encompass all the benefits for the two merged companies.

Mariel believes the new plan is consistent with the mission and vision of the merged companies and that it really is the "best of both worlds" in merging the plans from the two companies. The new flexible spending account will be attractive to the software engineers. Most of the other key features of the plans remain fairly similar with only a few key changes.

The Assignment

You, as Mariel, have been asked by the CT to develop a communication program to roll out the new benefits to the approximately 5500 software engineers across the company, which still has offices in four different countries. You are expecting delivery of the booklets with all the key details of the plan within two weeks. In the meantime, you must consider the other steps you will need to take to convey this information, the media you will use, the sequence of events, and the content of the communications about the new plan. Develop the communication program to submit to the CT. Remember that a key reason for the merger was adding the software engineers from Computer Co to the Huge Co. team; they need to understand the new plan and also to feel that they are valued members of the new team.

Exercise 9.2: Communicating Bad News to Internal Audiences

The Case: The HADWIT International Services Company

In 1993, you decided to open a small oil field services company based in Houston, Texas. Two friends from graduate school agreed to join you as investors, and you agreed to manage the business. Your company, Have Data Will Travel International Services Company (HADWIT), provides geological/geophysical consulting and computerized interpretation of the 3-D seismic data collected by surveyors working from boats offshore in the Gulf of Mexico, the North Sea, and the Pacific Rim. HADWIT data is critical to the exploration and production (E&P) companies because it forms the basis for decisions on where to invest in oil and gas exploration and development. Many of your clients are major oil companies—such as Shell, Exxon/Mobil, and BP/Amoco—as well as a number of independents operating all over the world.

HADWIT's Initial Success

You began operations with ten employees and trained them well. You are now up to 58 professionals with very specialized backgrounds in geology or geophysics and E&P data analysis. You wanted to develop a company known for high-quality services, and you wanted a stable, loyal workforce to represent you to the client. Your partners agreed with this philosophy, and you provided above-average salaries, paid vacations, health insurance, and annual bonuses.

As the company expanded, you placed employees overseas in offices in Singapore and Aberdeen, Scotland, to meet clients' on-site needs. Things were going well: employees were happy, and the investors were satisfied with their return on investment. You credit some of the success to your fairly flat, team-based organization (see Exhibit 9.10).

You have been operating on a substantial profit margin. Until recently, you had been billing out your professionals at two times their gross salary, but the market will now

EXHIBIT 9.10
The HADWIT Team

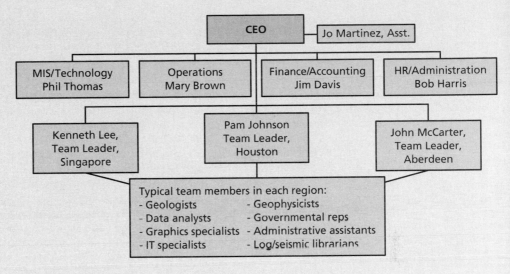

support only 1.5 times gross salary, which leaves you with no capacity for underutilization of people or resources. You have, however, been very generous in the past with bonuses for completing projects ahead of schedule and just for doing good work. In addition, your benefits package is beyond industry standards with you picking up 80 percent of the premiums.

Market Changes Creating Need for Cost Cutting

In 1998–1999, however, the oil industry went into a major downturn, with oil prices falling and corporate mergers tightening the market for everyone. Even though prices rebounded some in 2000, your customers' E&P budgets were still strictly constrained; the ensuing decline in HADWIT projects led you to cut costs by dismissing four employees who were not performing up to par, cutting back on company perks, such as cars and expense accounts, and reducing travel budgets. Now, after September 11, 2001, the collapse of former corporate giants, and a sluggish economy, the demand for your services has fallen more; thus, HADWIT has experienced a serious loss of revenue coupled with increased costs.

So far, the numbers this year are not looking good. In fact, you estimate that profit will be down by around 25 percent this quarter and possibly even 50 percent by the first quarter of 2003. Your partners are losing patience with the last few months of negative cash flow. Although they understand that HADWIT is a market-driven business and you cannot increase demand for your services, they think that your costs are still too high, and they want you to consider laying off a significant portion of your workforce.

CEO Contemplating Cost-Cutting Measures

To date, you have run a first-class operation and have spared no costs when it comes to providing what your employees need, especially when they are overseas and out of the office working in your clients' facilities. In fact, compared to your competitors' costs, your research shows that your overhead for each employee averages about 15 percent more per year. In addition, you have just purchased the latest computer hardware and software, which allows you to (1) work more efficiently, (2) provide data services others cannot, and (3) connect virtually across the globe. While you know you can cut some of your overhead, you fear that doing so will result in unhappy employees and dissatisfied customers and will not be enough to turn the company around.

This brings you to the possibility of closing offices and laying off employees. Most of the employees have been with the company for several years and all are doing excellent work. In addition, many of your clients depend on having the pick of your staff on-site anytime they want them; up to now, this "on demand" team formation has never been a problem since you have had the staff to cover client preferences. Your company is built on the principle that HADWIT should provide clients what they want, when they want it, and where they want it. Thus, you expect that letting staff go will cause some clients to be very uneasy about doing business with your company, particularly since most of your employees have direct relationships with your major clients.

Your clients like having people on the ground in Singapore or Aberdeen. Although they can adjust, it will take away from their flexibility and sense of having a "local" service provider. Even though you may be able to convince the customers that this is a short-term move that will not affect the quality or speed of your services, some of them will not take the news well. You fear that you even run the risk of losing them, which you certainly cannot afford, given the current negative cash flow. You hope that you can convince your clients that since you have all the equipment you need to service any company anywhere in the world from your offices in Houston, they need not worry. Also, since most of the consultants work on-site, you can still send your people to work with clients in the North Sea, or in any other location, as long as the client picks up per diem (daily) expenses.

Partners Demanding Drastic Measures

You have seen the oil industry recover from cycles like this one before, so you hope that if you can hold out a while longer, things will turn around; however, you meet with your partners, and they want action now. After some heated discussion, you agree to start reducing your costs by 25 percent immediately, which you know will mean you are going to have to let some portion of your workforce go after all.

Your first step following the meeting with the partners is to look for additional ways to cut costs without downsizing staff. You decide to decrease the company's contribution to health and dental insurance, cancel all bonuses, and eliminate paid vacations. You consider even asking all employees to accept a 10 percent salary cut for next year. Also, you decide that you will have to close your offices in Aberdeen and Singapore, even though you know your clients will not be happy about it. That means you will have to let four administrative support staff people go, two in Aberdeen and two in Singapore, and will need to relocate all of the technical staff to Houston, where you will centralize all operations. After your initial analysis, however, you see no way to reach the targeted numbers without a substantial reduction in staff. You are extremely concerned about the effect these cuts will have on your company and your people.

You decide to hold a meeting with the management team, which includes all of your direct reports (team leaders in each location, who will be protective of their staff in each country and want to keep their locations open). In the meeting, you want to work through all possible ways to reduce costs and look at which staff you can cut. You realize, also, that given the seriousness of the messages you will be sending internally and externally, you need to devote some of your own time to consider your most important audiences and the messages to send to them.

The Assignment

First, develop a communication strategy for all of your internal audiences. Second, write a memo to the management team delivering the news about the need to cut costs and downsize the workforce and inviting them to the meeting. This memo is an opportunity for you to lay out any issues to be considered and any concerns that you have about the situation as well as tell them what you expect them to do in general and in preparation for the meeting. Think carefully about this audience. While you will want to provide the truth about what is to happen, you also need to try to allay their concerns as much as possible. These are the leaders in your organization and some of your best people, and you certainly do not want to lose any of them at this crucial time in the company's history. Thus, you need to consider the tone you use and the information these managers will want to have and need to hear. Third, develop an agenda for the meeting establishing objectives, end products, and content.

Source: Case and assignment developed by Deborah J. Barrett and Beth O'Sullivan. Copyright 1999. Substantially revised 2002. Used with permission.

Exercise 9.3: Developing a Change Communication Strategy

The Case: Rescuing Fly High

The management of Fly High knew they needed to turn the company around immediately. They were constantly rated low in customer satisfaction polls, they were the worst in handling baggage (more lost and more damaged than any of their major competitors), the complaints from passengers had grown by 25 percent, and the employee morale was at it lowest level ever. Fly High was losing money and on the verge of having to lay off hundreds of its 50,000 employees.

The board was placing the company's future in the hands of a new CEO and the management team she was bringing with her. The board had essentially cleaned house, but then it was not the first time new management had been brought in to try to turn things around. Fly High had gone through constant change in leadership at the top as well as frequent downsizing and reorganizations, but they had not been able to turn the company around.

The company needed to make drastic changes and fast, and they needed to make them across the entire company, from baggage handlers to pilots. From the reservation desk to the hangers to the corporate offices and the rest of the employees scattered across the globe, no one talked to anyone else and no one worked together. In fact, the different locations seemed knowingly or unknowingly to work against each other and against the goals of the total company. Some of the middle- and lower-level management adopted an extreme command and control and silo thinking approach to managing, while others used a team-based, participative, cross-functional culture. Employees had reached a point of complacency and cynicism. They lacked a performance ethic and felt management was not open to their ideas about the company. Cutting across all of the levels in the organization was a lack of trust for Fly High management and now a lot of skepticism that this new management team would make a difference.

Fly High needed a major change program across the entire company involving all levels of the organization; however, the internal communication was so poor that they did not know where to begin. Communication across the organization or up or down the organizational chain of command was almost nonexistent. A recent HR survey had revealed specific problems in internal communications: key messages across the company had changed so often that employees were confused and unclear as to the company's vision, many employees felt afraid to express their ideas or concerns, and management appeared isolated and nonreceptive to the employees at lower levels of the organization. It was clear that the company seriously needed to improve internal communications before any change program could have impact.

The Assignment

As part of this new management team, you are charged with addressing the communication challenges and establishing the change communication program. Outline the steps you would take and develop an action plan for improving communication that will feed directly into the larger change program that Fly High needs to undertake.

Notes

1. *Ragan Survey of CEO Communications* (2001). A Ragan Research Report, supported by the International Association of Business Communication, p. 6.

2. *Ragan Survey of CEO Communication* (2002), p. 7.

3. Smidts, A. Pruyn, A. T. H., & van Riel, C. B. M. (2001). The impact of employee communication and perceived external prestige on organization identification. *Academy of Management Journal* 49, p. 1059.

4. Clampitt, P. G., & Downs, C. W. (1993). Employee perceptions of the relationship between communication and productivity: A field study. *Journal of Business Communication* 30, pp. 5–28. Downs, C. W., Clampitt, P. G., & Pfeiffer, A. L. (1988). Communication and organization outcomes. In G. M. Goldhaber & G. A. Barnett (Eds.). *Handbook of Organizational Communication*, Norwood, NJ: Ablex, pp. 171–212. Frank, A., & Browness, J. (1989). *Organizational Communication and Behavior: Communicating to Improve Performance*. Orlando, FL: Holt, Rinehart & Winston. Jablin, F. M. (1979). Superior-subordinate communication: The state of the art. *Psychological Bulletin* 86, pp. 1201–1222.

5. *Connecting Organization Communication to Financial Performance: 2003/2004 Communication ROI Study (2004)*. Watson Wyatt Worldwide.

6. The components in this model emerged from the best practices in employee communication found in interviews conducted with and research conducted on several Fortune 500 companies. While no company exemplified all of the best practice components exactly as presented in the definitions, they each serve as the ideal components of effective employee communication. The model was created by Deborah J. Barrett based on this research. The model and some of the research have been presented by Deborah J. Barrett at Association for Business Communication and International Association for Business Communication conferences. They are published in her article, Change communication: Using strategic employee communication to facilitate major change, *Corporate Communication: An International Journal* 7, pp. 219–231, which appeared in 2002. It is used with permission of Emerald Press.

7. Collins, J., and Porras, J. I. (1994). *Built to Last*. New York: Harper.

8. Peters, T. J. (1988). *Thriving on Chaos: Handbook for a Management Revolution*. New York: Alfred A. Knopf, pp. 399–408. Peters uses these characteristics in a discussion of effective visions, but many of them apply more to missions as defined in this chapter.

9. Jick, T. D. (1989). The vision thing. Harvard Business School Case, pp. 1–7.

10. www.wholefoodsmarket.com.

11. Ashkenas, R. N., & Francis, S. C. (2000). Integration managers: Special leaders for special times. *Harvard Business Review*, November–December, pp. 108–116.

12. Kotter, J. P. (1995). Leading change: Why transformation efforts fail. *Harvard Business Review on Change*. Boston, MA: Harvard Business School Press.

Chapter **Ten**

Leading through Effective External Relations

> A CEO is ultimately responsible for the growth of a company as evidenced by its financial performance, its capacity for self-renewal, and its character. The only way you can measure character is by reputation.
>
> Roberto Goizueta, CEO, Coca-Cola, quoted in *Fortune*, March 6, 1995

> To become well regarded, companies must deserve it. They must develop coherent images and a consistency of posture internally and externally. Identity and self presentation beget reputation.
>
> Charles J. Fombrun, *Reputation: Realizing Value from the Corporate Image*. Boston: Harvard Business School Press (1996)

Chapter Objectives

In this chapter, you will learn to do the following:

- Develop an external relations strategy.
- Build and maintain a positive corporate image.
- Work with the news media.
- Handle crisis communications.

A positive public image or reputation affects a company's ability to achieve all other measures of success. Reputation Institute says that the companies with the best corporate reputations outperform all others in terms of market share and share value.[1] For example, the top five companies in its list of 20 of the best in corporate reputation in the United States—Johnson & Johnson, Coca-Cola, Intel, Ben & Jerry's, and Wal-Mart—combine good reputations with strong financial performance. Hill & Knowlton, one of the leading public relations firms, found in its study of corporate reputation that 94 percent of the CEOs surveyed consider corporate reputation to be "very important" to achieving their "strategic business objectives."[2]

Negative public sentiment hurts internal and external reputation, resulting in lost morale among employees and a loss in market share for the company. Managing the public's perception of a company is one of the primary jobs of company leadership, and the leader's personal image affects the company image. Hill & Knowlton's *Corporate Reputation Watch* reports that 84 percent of the CEOs responding to the survey believe that the CEO's reputation "extremely influences" the corporate reputation, and 77 percent report that CEOs are primarily responsible for managing their company's corporate reputation.[3]

Just as the leaders determine the personality of the company on the inside, they also shape the outside image as well. A company has an ethos just as an individual does. The goal of organizational leaders is to ensure that the company's ethos is positive—that all external audiences consider the company honorable, trustworthy, and ethical. Managing external relations effectively is essential to achieving that goal and essential to leadership communication in any organization.

Any communication activity that touches a company's outside constituencies—such as advertising, sales promotions, direct marketing, or public relations—falls into the category of external relations. All of these are important and influence how the public perceives a company. Also, these activities must all be coordinated as part of an overall external relations campaign so that all messages are consistent and delivered effectively. However, the focus of this chapter is primarily on the activities usually considered public relations, including press and media management, philanthropic activities, community involvement, investor relations, and external publications (for example, annual reports and company magazines). Companies must manage all aspects of external relations very carefully. They all affect the company's public ethos. In most organizations, the leadership communication skill of the managers has the greatest impact on that external ethos through their involvement in public relations.

This chapter provides guidelines to help manage external relations in day-to-day encounters and in crisis situations so that the company projects a positive image. You will learn how to apply the communication strategy model introduced in Chapter 1 to external relations, how to shape a positive image, how to deal with the media, and, finally, how to manage crisis communications.

DEVELOPING AN EXTERNAL RELATIONS STRATEGY

Effective external relations require a sound communication strategy. As you have done with other communication situations, you can use the communication strategy framework, Exhibit 10.1, to guide you in addressing the entire range of external

EXHIBIT 10.1
Communica-
tion Strategy
Framework

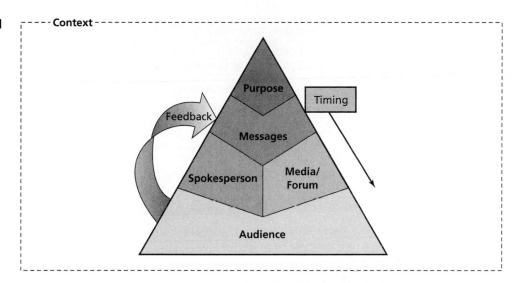

audiences. With the framework in mind, you can take the following steps to create a strategy for external audiences:

1. Clarify your purpose and strategic objectives.
2. Identify your major audiences or stakeholders.
3. Create, refine, and test your major messages.
4. Select, limit, and coach your spokesperson(s).
5. Establish the most effective media or forum.
6. Determine the best timing.
7. Monitor the results.

Clarifying Your Purpose and Strategic Objectives

A company must have a strategy for all of its external relations activities: managing the press and media, coordinating philanthropic activities and community involvement, establishing relationships with the financial analysts or investor groups, and creating and distributing all publications that touch stakeholders. A central and consistent purpose radiating from the very top of the organization should govern all external communication activities. As discussed in Chapter 6, the CEO and his or her direct reports determine the personality of a company, and as discussed in this chapter, that personality influences the corporate reputation, the ethos of the company. Given these lines of influence, it is clearly the responsibility of the CEO and his or her staff to establish a strategy for external relations.

Ideally, a company's internal ethos and external image will be consistent with a few central themes permeating all day-to-day activities as well as any crisis situations that may arise. The major corporate themes usually embody the vision, mission, and strategic objectives, as discussed in Chapter 9. The logos, slogans, letterhead, business cards, and any promotional materials, often called collaterals,

EXHIBIT 10.2
Mission Statement for the Houston Grand Opera

Source: www. houstongrandopera. org.

The mission of **Houston Grand Opera** is to bring larger and more diverse audiences together for exciting opera in a financially responsible way.

Supporting Principles of **Houston Grand Opera** will

- Be defined by the **excellence** of its work.
- Provide a **memorable** experience.
- Be artistically and administratively **imaginative, balanced,** and **responsible.**
- Make an **impact** locally, regionally, nationally, and internationally.
- Communicate a **welcoming** atmosphere, be accessible to all, and create an atmosphere of inclusiveness.
- Hold **discovery** as a valuable goal in itself.

reinforce these themes. Although the logos and slogans cannot capture all of the company's themes, they should reflect the major ones and certainly suggest the personality of the organization. Leaders will want to approach the development of all promotional materials strategically and analytically to ensure support for as well as consistency with the corporation's strategic purpose and objectives.

For example, a few years ago, the Houston Grand Opera (HGO), one of the premier opera companies in the world, decided to change its promotional materials. It started by putting together a team to study the company's current and future strategy. The HGO team determined that the messages it wanted to send to the public were that HGO is "fun, for everyone, and innovative." The team surveyed subscribers and nonsubscribers to obtain the public's perception of the opera company. After a few months synthesizing the results and discussing them internally, HGO emerged with a new mission for the company (Exhibit 10.2).

After developing and testing the mission, HGO launched another team to establish its new logo and look. At first, they met some resistance to changing the logo since HGO had used the current logo for years, and the traditional operagoers loved the look and feel of it (Exhibit 10.3). It had dignity and suggested something solid and long-standing. However, HGO's general director and several of the

EXHIBIT 10.3
Example of Logo Change to Emphasize New Message

Logos used with permission of David Gockley, director of the Houston Grand Opera.

| Previous Logo | New Logo |

community leaders who supported the opera felt that the logo needed to be changed to reflect more directly HGO's innovative leadership in the opera world. After several months of surveys and focus groups, the team recommended the new logo (Exhibit 10.3).

The new logo suggested a company that was both traditional and innovative and captured the message of HGO being expansive yet inclusive. Through the new logo and the promotional activity that accompanied it, HGO was able to reinforce its messages to its public: HGO is innovative, fun, and for everyone. Soon afterward, the connection of the mission and the logo to the strategy of the company became obvious to the public when HGO unveiled a season with a perfect balance of traditional and innovative operas.

A company's messages to the public are intertwined with everything that touches that public; to avoid confusion and unwanted associations, the messages communicated in all external materials should be clear and consistent. With this foundation in place, the company can then create specific messages for specific events as needed, from announcing new products to handling crisis communication situations. All organizations must have central, overarching messages or themes that they intend to deliver to the mass of individuals called their "stakeholders."

Identifying Major External Stakeholders

A company's external stakeholders consist of any persons, groups, or organizations outside of the company that may be affected by the company's activities or influenced by its messages and image. The stakeholders are all audiences for the company's messages. Depending on the company and industry, a list of stakeholders could include many or all of the following:

1. Media
2. Community
3. Customers
4. Investors
5. Analysts
6. Board
7. Partners
8. Distributors
9. Suppliers or vendors
10. Trade associations
11. Unions
12. Interest groups
13. Retirees
14. Competitors
15. Government agencies
16. The public at large

The list should include anyone even remotely touched by the company's products or services.

Once the company has identified its stakeholders, it needs to establish priorities for reaching each one with its general message as well as specific messages tailored to individual groups. Again, the messages must be consistent, although they may differ slightly in their wording to ensure the audiences receiving them understand them. While companies need to be careful not to exclude any audience or minimize its importance, priorities are necessary to an organized approach. Companies do need to determine how important as well as how difficult it is to reach each stakeholder.

EXHIBIT 10.4
Example
Matrix
Analyzing
Stakeholders

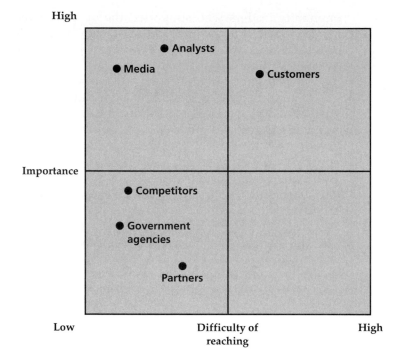

Asking the following questions will help in prioritizing the external stake-holders:

1. Who shapes or influences business or community opinions?
2. Who are the high-profile leaders in the community?
3. Who is well respected? Who is feared?
4. Who has high levels of responsibility within the community?
5. Who do others regard as important or powerful in the area?
6. Who is actively involved in the community?
7. Who is in a demographic group affected by the company?
8. Who has a financial or emotional stake in the company?
9. Who has the most to gain or lose because of what happens to the company?
10. Who has a clear role in regulations or policies affecting the company?
11. Who can undermine the company's external relations campaign?

Exhibit 10.4 illustrates how you might use a matrix to determine the importance as well as the ease of reaching the different stakeholder groups.

Creating Your Major Messages

Messages aimed at external audiences are far more vulnerable to interference, interruptions, and barriers than messages to internal audiences. Many external audiences will be only weakly motivated to attend to your messages, and they will often be ignorant of much of the knowledge you can assume for your internal audiences. For example, while you may be able to assume that an internal audience will know the jargon of your industry, you cannot assume that outsiders will. Thus, using industry jargon can become a barrier to communication. In addition, you would hope for the best intentions from internal audiences; however, for external audiences, assuming the best can be dangerous.

You should be able to prevent the interruptions and overcome the barriers to reach your external audiences successfully if you ensure all of your external messages conform to the following criteria:

- Honest
- Clear
- Consistent
- Meaningful

Honest

Not all audiences can see through false or deceptive messages, but a company can do more harm to its reputation by getting caught lying than by telling an unpleasant truth. Honesty should be one of the underlying values and guiding principles of your company's communication activities for external audiences as it is with internal audiences.

Clear

Assuming your messages are clear is often not enough when dealing with external audiences. Just as you must scrutinize important internal messages, you should also test messages for external audiences to ensure they will understand them as intended. Companies often use focus groups for this purpose.

Consistent

Consistency is essential in the messages a company delivers to its public. Internal and external messages must be consistent. Also, messages delivered to different audiences must be consistent. Consistency does not mean messages cannot be tailored to the different stakeholders. The wording must be targeted to the specific audience, and it may differ slightly or the emphasis may shift to accommodate the varying needs and interests of different stakeholders, but the core message must remain the same.

Meaningful

Finally, the messages must be meaningful. Too often companies water down their external messages so much that they no longer communicate any substance. This weakening of the message is particularly a problem in a crisis, but occurs at other times as well. In some cases, the company may not have taken the necessary time to determine what it is that it wants to communicate. In other cases, companies are intentionally equivocating or making the message ambiguous to avoid sending a negative message, to sidestep possible legal problems, or to obfuscate the facts.

EXHIBIT 10.5
Example of
Ambiguity in
a Press
Release

FDA Statement

Media Inquiries: 301-
827-6242
Consumer Inquiries:
888-INFO-FDA

FOR IMMEDIATE RELEASE
Statement
October 13, 2003

FDA Statement on Foodborne Illness Risk Assessment

The U.S. Food and Drug Administration (FDA) today issued the following
statement:

The headline of a story on the risk of illness from food, "Food Attack Likely,
FDA Says" that ran under "Washington in Brief" in the October 11th
Washington Post mischaracterizes the FDA report.

FDA prepared this qualitative risk assessment to accompany two new final
rules, published October 10th, to improve food safety and security. It
discusses both unintentional and intentional contamination of the food
supply, because the goals of food safety and security are closely linked.

In drafting the risk assessment FDA relied heavily on the regular occurrence
of foodborne illness outbreaks from accidental contamination in reaching
the "high likelihood" prediction. The FDA report did not say there is a high
likelihood of a terrorist attack in the next year. It did say there is a high
likelihood of a significant foodborne illness outbreak in the next year (as
there is every year) and that one possibility is that the outbreak would come
from a terrorist attack. The actual "likelihood" of a significant terrorist
attack on the food supply in the next year is difficult to quantify precisely.

Finally, the report is not "declassified" as the article asserts. FDA compiled
the report, which was never classified, from the open literature.

A press release sent by the U.S. Food and Drug Administration (FDA), printed
in its entirety in Exhibit 10.5, makes ambiguous statements while discussing
problems caused by ambiguity in previous releases of information to the public.
What the FDA's 12-page report contains is as follows:

> "The agency has considered, for the purposes of risk characterization, the known
> exposure to food that has been inadvertently contaminated and the past incidents of
> deliberate contamination, as well as the evidence that terrorists have targeted our
> food supply. In light of this information and the uncertainties attendant to character-
> izing the risk of an act of food terrorism, FDA has concluded that there is a high
> likelihood, over the course of a year, that a significant number of people will be
> affected by an act of food terrorism or by an incident of unintentional food
> contamination that results in serious foodborne illness."[4]

EXHIBIT 10.6
The Press's
Coverage of
the FDA Story

Food Attack Likely, FDA Says

WASHINGTON IN BRIEF
Saturday, October 11, 2003;
Page A13
Washington Post

There is a "high likelihood" within the coming year of a deliberate attack or accidental outbreak in the U.S. food supply that sickens a large number of people, the Food and Drug Administration said yesterday.

Although no specific threats were identified, the FDA said it came to the conclusion because of recent food-borne outbreaks and recent reports that al Qaeda was plotting to poison the food supply.

"FDA has concluded that there is a high likelihood, over the course of a year, that a significant number of people will be affected by an act of food terrorism or by an incident of unintentional food contamination that results in serious food-borne illness," the agency said in a declassified report.

The food supply was especially vulnerable because of the broad range of biological and chemical agents that can be used, the FDA said.

The agency said salmonella, E. coli 0157:H7 and ricin pose a significant threat because of their easy dissemination in food. Anthrax and botulism were considered the most deadly.

What appeared in the newspaper is illustrated in Exhibit 10.6. When an organization sends unclear messages, the organization risks misinterpretation by the media and by the public. If, in addition, the organization has obscured the information, intentionally or unintentionally, by embedding the "sound bites" (concise messages designed to capture the "so what?" in broadcast journalism) in long releases or complex reports, as in the example here, the organization risks distorted messages being conveyed to the public.

Messages that an organization sends to the broadcast media for transmission to the public need to be very brief so that they conform to the length of the typical sound bite. The essential information—the who, what, when, where, why, and how—must be covered in 10 to 20 seconds. Certainly, such conciseness can result in loss of substantive meaning; therefore, to counter media dilution, companies should create the sound bites themselves. In addition to the sound bite version, however, companies should have at their fingertips the details behind the "so what?" message.

Messages need to be concise and simple, but they also need to contain enough real information to be meaningful to any audience. The habit of using business jargon may interfere with clear communication, as discussed in Chapter 3. Other messaging faults can lead to consequences that are more serious. Business pronouncements that contain doublespeak (the use of ambiguous and often mean-ingless language) or fluff not only will frustrate your public and leave your com-pany open to misquoting and misunderstanding, but also may cause your stakeholders to feel as though they are being deceived, which can destroy a com-pany's ethos. For example, look at the following company announcement of pend-ing layoffs:

> "As a result of our recently completed cost rationalization study, Proteus, Inc., will be performing some staff reduction activities in order to rightsize the organization and eliminate redundancies in the human resources area. We expect these workforce adjustments to start right away with some repositioning of staff and with termination services provided for all those employees who may be displaced."

No doubt the company is going to be firing employees, but by choosing to at-tempt to obscure the bad news, the company risks creating a strongly negative im-pression with their stakeholders.

In summary, when developing external messages, company leaders need to spend the time to ensure all messages are honest, clear, consistent, and meaning-ful. The time spent in the beginning will be fully justified if it avoids confusion or negative communication to any stakeholder. In the end, it is the company's repu-tation that will suffer, and trying to correct misconceptions or a negative image is much more difficult than spending the time up front to communicate with all stakeholders effectively.

Selecting and Coaching the Spokesperson(s)

Selecting the right spokesperson to deliver external messages can be almost as criti-cal as the messages themselves. Three major rules apply to selecting spokespersons:

1. They must be at the right level for the problem.
2. They must project a positive ethos.
3. They should have received media training.

The rank of the spokesperson sends a message in itself. For instance, if the per-son is too high-ranking for the message being delivered, it could suggest that the issue being discussed is more important than it is. If the person is too low-ranking, it could signal that the company does not view the issue as important enough to warrant the CEO's time. An example from a fairly recent crisis com-munication situation concerns the Ford and Firestone/Bridgestone controversy, involving rollover accidents in Ford Explorers. Some people were very critical of

Firestone/Bridgestone's choosing a vice president to address the public instead of the CEO, as Ford did. Although Firestone/Bridgestone may have had very good reasons for its decision, the public felt that the company did not view the accidents and resulting deaths as important enough to justify the CEO's time.

Next, the spokesperson must project a positive ethos. His or her credibility must be above reproach; otherwise, no message he or she delivers will be received as intended. Ethos relates to both how the person appears to the public and how close he or she is to the situation. For example, in a crisis situation involving a pipeline explosion, an engineer on-site would have more firsthand knowledge and could answer the media's questions more specifically on the causes and what happened mechanically; medical personnel would have better answers on the injuries; and depending on how serious the explosion is, the highest level executive may be needed to suggest the company's concern for the injured. Deciding on the spokesperson is not easy and can require as much deliberation as is required for creating the messages.

Thinking back to the sources of ethos discussed in the introduction, it is best to select the spokesperson based on the following three of French and Raven's sources of power:

1. Legitimate—position or title.
2. Referent—charisma.
3. Expert—knowledge.

Even if the spokespersons possess all of the sources of ethos, however, they should still receive media training before facing the press. Many companies provide formal media training for any employees who might have to face the media at any time. That training will usually include the who, what, when, and where of dealing with the media as well as coaching on projecting a positive image (see "Working with the Media" later in this chapter).

Establishing the Most Effective Media or Forum

Deciding on the most effective media or forum to ensure reaching the identified stakeholders is yet another critical component of external relations. A company will often use several different media to reach external audiences, depending on the importance and magnitude of the communication event. For example, when the SEC was investigating Putnam Investments, Putnam used every available medium to reach its stakeholders. They sent letters to investors and e-mails to internal audiences; they crafted a carefully written press release for the news media and conducted a press conference with them; they posted releases, letters, and a video clip of two senior-level executives explaining the investigation on their Web site; and they published a "tombstone" (advertising statement).

Exhibit 10.7 describes each of the most frequently used external media and the limitations on using each one effectively.

Determining the Best Timing

Depending on the context, the timing of an external message can be critical. As discussed in Chapter 1, you must ask yourself what is going on around your communication event that will influence how your audience receives your message.

EXHIBIT 10.7
Characteristics and Limitations of External Media or Forums

Media/Forum	Characteristics	Limitations
Press Conferences	Meeting to which media are invited. Company spokespersons present prepared statements and usually take questions as well. May or may not be broadcast.	Most influential media may not come. Require careful planning and practice for the participants, not only in delivering the statements but in anticipating the questions.
Press Releases	Short, usually no more than one page definitive statement intended to be quoted by the media. Start with the most important information and end with the least (releases are cut from the bottom); also contain contact information. Intended for wide media distribution quickly.	If sent as a blast fax and not followed up with personal contact, a press release has a hit-or-miss effect; therefore, it may not reach the intended audience and may attract no media interest or coverage.
Fact Sheets or Backgrounders	Compilation of relevant information for the press or for analysts. Usually contain information similar to a press release but presented in bullet form with highlights emphasized.	Must be carefully crafted to ensure the major messages are captured and enough supporting information is supplied to appear substantive. Too short to provide much more than the sound bites.
Press or Media Kits	Usually contain the following: • Press release • Fact sheet of company history • Relevant biographies and pictures • Contact information • Video clips	Limited in space or press tolerance, so information must be carefully organized for selective reading.
Hotlines	Easily established numbers for stakeholders to call with specific questions or comments.	Require coaching of respondents to ensure consistency of responses. Need constant oversight.
Web Sites	May be a specially designed Web site for a particular event or an addition to the company's current Web site. Convenient method for reaching a broad audience. Allow for rapid dissemination of information that can be persuasively crafted.	Creation should be by a Web site design expert. To be effective, it should meet the necessary criteria of an effective site: easy to navigate and informative, with contact information.
Tombstones or Advertising Statements	Notices published in newspapers intended to reach the public with a specific message from the company.	Expensive. May be dismissed by the public as simply advertising.
Analyst's Briefings	Usually a presentation in person or as a phone or videoconference. Include a short prepared statement on financial performance with backup financial information.	Require time to prepare materials and answers to anticipated questions and reliable financial analysis.

EXHIBIT 10.7   (continued)

Media/Forum	Characteristics	Limitations
Town Hall Meetings	Local gatherings of selected stakeholders. Usually include prepared statements but allow for informal but controlled interaction between company representatives and stakeholders.	Need to be facilitated skillfully or can turn into gripe sessions if the message being communicated is bad news.
Editorials	Allow company to voice an opinion on newsworthy topics.	May not be widely read.

For example, announcing a major layoff at the same time as your company is promoting and advertising its expensive sponsorship of a major sporting event will cause many employees to be even more resentful than they might have been if the announcement had been better timed. Google's announcement of its new e-mail product on April 1 was certainly questionable timing since it left many thinking it was an April Fool's joke.

Also, the sequencing of the messages around a communication event should be taken into consideration. For instance, if you are involved in a merger communication event, you will need to consider the timing of every announcement down to the minute for both internal and all external stakeholders. Ideally, you would want your internal audiences to receive the announcement first, but often the best timing for a merger announcement is not the best time to reach employees, for instance, early enough on Monday to influence the stock price. Depending on the company's public profile, how and when the public hears or sees the announcement will affect how they respond to it, just as when the announcement hits the market will impact investors' responses around the globe. Legal and regulatory requirements could also affect the timing of any announcements related to a merger.

Monitoring the Results

Finally, measuring the impact of your messages on your major constituencies is important, but it is also can be difficult, expensive, and time-consuming. Larger, well-known companies will find their reputations monitored for them in yearly surveys, such as *Fortune*'s "Most Admired List," Harris Interactive's "Reputation Quotient," or The Customer Respect Group's online reports.

Two of the most common methods used to obtain feedback from external stakeholders are focus groups and surveys (phone, Web, or mail). Holding effective focus groups and conducting useful surveys, however, require very careful planning and a clear and specific purpose. In-house employees must be proficient at survey methods and analysis to obtain reliable results. If they are not, a company should hire one of the many PR, external relations, or HR consulting firms that offer these services, since the established firms have efficient and effective approaches to conducting focus groups and surveys and to analyzing the results.

In addition to periodic focus groups and surveys, companies should establish a procedure for frequently monitoring their Web presence by checking online news and chat rooms and, depending on their product or service, consumer activist sites. Even entering its company name into a common search engine will yield some indication of the conversation about the company on the Web. They may also want to subscribe to a clipping service, which will collect any media hits whether broadcast, newsprint, or Web.

However companies decide to measure the results of their public relations activities and their reputation, they need to make sure they target all constituencies. They must have a strategy for routine as well as periodic comprehensive assessments of their public perception. The key is being proactive, anticipating responses, and planning ahead for what, when, and how monitoring will occur.

BUILDING AND MAINTAINING A POSITIVE CORPORATE IMAGE

Warren Buffet is quoted as saying, "If you lose dollars for the firm, I will be understanding. If you lose reputation for the firm, I will be ruthless." Reputation affects the bottom line, and even the strongest companies will have difficulty surviving damage to their reputations. Organizational leaders must give high priority to establishing and maintaining a positive corporate image.

All companies can learn something about effective management of external relations by looking at others that are considered good at it. In *The State of Corporate Communications,* written by Hill & Knowlton and based on research conducted by Yankelovich Partners, the corporate communication chiefs identified the companies listed in Exhibit 10.8 as good at managing the different types of external relations.

EXHIBIT 10.8
Which Companies Are Considered Good at External Relations

Source: *Corporate Reputation Watch* (October 1997). *The State of Corporate Communications,* written by Hill & Knowlton and based on research conducted by Yankelovich Partners. Use with permission of Hill & Knowlton.

Type	Company
Media Relations	1. Microsoft
	2. Coca-Cola
	IBM
	GE
	Disney
Corporate Public Relations	1. Coca-Cola
	2. Microsoft
	3. GE
Corporate Identity	1. Coca-Cola
	2. IBM
	Nike
Government Relations	1. Boeing
	2. GE
	Phillip Morris
	AT&T
Investor Relations	1. Microsoft
	Intel
	2. GE
	Coca-Cola

EXHIBIT 10.9
Most and Least Respectful Web Sites—Companies and Scores

Source: *2004 Online Customer Respect Study of the Country's Largest 100 Companies.* Online reference: www.Customer-Respect.com. Used with permission. The average score was 6.2.

Most Respectful (Top 12)	Least Respectful (Bottom 12)
Microsoft (8.7)	UnitedHealth (4.5)
Hewlett-Packard (8.6)	PepsiCo (4.4)
IBM (8.5)	Northrop Grumman (4.2)
Bank of America (8.2)	Morgan Stanley (4.1)
Medco Health Solutions (8.1)	Prudential Financial (3.9)
Intel (7.9)	Boeing (3.9)
Albertson's (7.8)	Lockheed Martin (3.7)
Kmart (7.8)	Sysco (3.7)
Walgreen (7.8)	Pfizer (3.6)
UPS (7.7)	Weyerhaeuser (3.5)
AT&T (7.6)	Johnson Controls (3.2)
Wachovia (7.6)	Supervalu (2.7)

If this survey were conducted today, the Internet would have an effect on how the companies ranked. A Customer Respect Group's *2004 Online Customer Respect Study of the Top 100 U.S. Companies* looked at how well companies manage their Internet customer relations. They established what matters to Internet customers and found the following criteria at the top: simplicity, privacy, responsiveness, transparency, and attitude. Interestingly, responsiveness is very low for some of the world's most respected companies despite the risk of losing customers. Customer Respect Group found 70 percent of the consumers surveyed move their business to a competitor if they do not receive a timely response in their 2002 study. Exhibit 10.9 shows the most respectful and least respectful Web sites out of the 100 largest U.S. companies.

CustomerRespect.com found that 37 percent of the companies did not respond at all to customer inquiries, while 41 percent responded in 48 hours, 12 percent in 72 hours, and 10 percent in more than 72 hours. Importantly, Customer Respect Group found a correlation between those companies with a low "Customer Respect Index" and a publicized lack of respect for shareholders and employees.[5] They argue that "respect for the customer, respect for investors, respect for employees, are all borne out of self-respect and moral fiber." In other words, the lack of respect a company shows for its customers may suggest a lack of respect for its investors and its employees and a fundamentally flawed ethical core. Whether the logic follows exactly may be questionable, but the study shows that customer respect does affect image and potential profitability.

Everything a company does influences public opinion and reputation; therefore, every company should look carefully at building a positive reputation. In *Reputation: Realizing Value from the Corporate Image,* Charles Fombrun identifies six ways companies can build and maintain a positive corporate image:

1. Design campaigns to promote the company as a whole.
2. Carry out ambitious programs to champion product quality and customer service.
3. Maintain systems to screen employee activities for reputation side effects.

4. Demonstrate sensitivity to the environment.
5. Hire internal communication staff and retain public relations firms.
6. Demonstrate "corporate citizenship."[6]

This list reveals the importance of being proactive and comprehensive in fostering corporate reputation. The company needs to be perceived as one unit with one unified message, no matter how many individual business units may exist or how globally diverse it may be. It needs to place a high priority on customer service and ensure all employees realize their importance as representatives of the company. Shaping a positive corporate image involves every employee and the total commitment of senior management. It also involves taking advantage of the resources available to help, from internal communication professionals to public relations firms. In fact, for a large, global company in particular, the assistance of a strong public relations firm is invaluable. These firms have the contacts in local communities and the news media and can often do more to build a reputation than a public advertising campaign.

Building and maintaining a positive corporate image require having an external relations strategy that is vigilant, vigorous, and comprehensive. It involves developing a strategy for managing the press and media, making meaningful and sincere philanthropic contributions, being actively involved in the community, obeying all of the legal and regulatory requirements of investor relations, and ensuring all external communication vehicles carry honest, clear, consistent, and meaningful messages to all stakeholders. One mistake in any of these areas can cause repercussions from which a company may never recover.

WORKING WITH THE NEWS MEDIA

The mistakes or missteps that tarnish a company's reputation are most often uncovered and publicized by the news media. To increase chances for favorable treatment, it is important for a company to establish a positive relationship with the media and for every senior manager to know how to work effectively with them. Hill & Knowlton's 2002 Corporate Reputation Watch survey reported that CEOs see media criticism as "the greatest threat to corporate reputation." Any leader of an organization should know why the media are important, when to talk to them, and how to manage encounters with them.

Understanding the Media's Role and Importance

Print, broadcast, and Internet media are the primary channels for much that is communicated in our society. While some coverage is given to business in almost all traditional media, certain newspapers and TV news networks and programs provide more coverage of corporations than others. A recent study by Media Tenor found that *The Wall Street Journal, The Washington Post,* and *USA Today* publish most extensively on corporate management, with *The Wall Street Journal,* not surprisingly, providing three times the coverage of the other two.[7] Unfortunately, as the Media Tenor study also found, the media are much more likely to pick up a negative story than a positive one. As is well known, the bigger the story, the more media attention it attracts, and since the media are businesses, they seek the news that will sell.

Since all major newspapers and most TV networks provide coverage of major corporations and are definitely interested in sensational news from smaller companies, every company needs to recognize the importance of the media and take the time to meet the local media representatives and learn a little about their needs and interests. In addition, companies need to understand the value of positive public relations and realize that establishing a relationship with the media, either directly or through a public relations firm, can open the door to a tremendous amount of "free" publicity. Of course, "free" is relative since companies have to pay for public relations resources and services; however, if handled effectively, a good public relations campaign will usually reach more people more economically than an advertising campaign. A public relations campaign can also achieve more positive results since most people are more skeptical of advertising than they are of what they think of as "news."

Deciding When to Talk to the Media

Interactions with the media can allow a company to reach a large and globally dispersed audience, present their point of view proactively, and establish a positive public ethos. However, a company must be cautious and think through the answers to these key questions before deciding to talk to the media:

1. What will the company gain by talking to the media and what might it lose?
2. Why would the media be interested in your company or your story?
3. Could your story potentially fall within the context of a negative story about another company or topic?
4. Who is the reporter? Is he or she reputable and known for covering "real" news or for doing features or lighter reporting?
5. Do you have all of the facts that a reporter might seek on the story?
6. Will you be able to come across as knowledgeable and credible?
7. Will the coverage result in additional positive interest in your company?
8. What are the ways an interview could turn negative?

Preparing for and Delivering a Media Interview

Any leader or high-level manager should receive training and, ideally, specific coaching in preparation for an encounter with the media. The training should include the following at a minimum: preparation for the interview, performance during the interview, and steps to take afterward.

1. Preparation

Preparation is key to an effective interview. You should never go into an interview without it. You must not only have the content well under control but also know how to dress and how to appear credible to the reporter. You should develop your strategy with a public relations expert. That strategy should include the description and understanding of the context, target audiences, strategic objectives, and major messages. You should work with the content and know it well enough that you need only minimal notes. Ideally, in the live interview, you should be able to speak without notes. You should know something about the reporter's background and mode of operation in interviews, and you should establish ground rules with him or her before the interview starts. Finally, you should practice in a setting similar to the one in which the interview will be conducted.

2. Performance during the Interview

If you are being interviewed over the phone, you want to be very well prepared and have your notes handy, although you do not want to sound as though you are reading. You want to keep all of your answers simple, thinking in terms of sound bites. If you respond with long sentences or complicated prose, the writer will do the cutting to get the sound bite, taking control of the message out of your hands and greatly increasing the odds of your being misquoted. If you give clear and concise responses, the reporter will be more likely to use your words, which will make it more likely that what you say is exactly what is published or broadcast. Also, you should be very careful to stay focused on your message and not let the reporter take you away from it.

If the meeting with the media is a press conference, you will have a prepared statement to deliver, but after that, you must be ready to answer any questions that may arise. You should have full command of information and subjects closely related to the main messages of your statement. You may bring notes with you, but again, make sure they are sound bites and that you know them well. If you have to read responses, you will not look confident, so your notes should be very brief and have only facts or any numbers you might need. You want to dress appropriately and look pulled together. Most of all, you want to be yourself and maintain your composure no matter what questions are thrown at you.

Exhibit 10.10 provides ten rules for dealing with the media that apply for any media encounter, but particularly when meeting with them in person.

As a final note for any encounter with the media, remember that nothing is "off the record"; never be misled into believing that it is. Always be very careful what you say and do in the presence of the media, and always tell the truth.

EXHIBIT 10.10

Ten Rules of Effective Communication with the Media

Source: Adapted from Burger, C. How to meet the press. From *Harvard Business Review*, July–August 1975. Copyright © 1975 by Harvard Business School Publishing Corporation; all rights reserved.

1. Talk from the viewpoint of the public's interest, not the company's.
2. Speak in personal terms whenever possible.
3. If you do not want some statement quoted, do not make it. There is no such thing as "off the record."
4. State the most important fact at the beginning.
5. Do not argue with the reporter or lose your cool.
6. If a question contains offensive language or simply words you do not like, do not repeat them, even to deny them.
7. If the reporter asks a direct question, he [or she] is entitled to an equally direct answer.
8. If you do not know the answer to a question, simply say, "I don't know, but I'll find out for you."
9. Tell the truth, even if it hurts.
10. Do not exaggerate the facts.

3. Steps to Take after the Interview

After the interview, reporters may or may not let you see how they are going to report your statements. Most often, however, they will not. If the story has a longer lead time and is more a public interest piece than hard news, they may allow you to see it. You should certainly review it if possible. If they do not offer, then ask. If the story is breaking with a short lead time, you will have to trust that they quote you exactly, emphasizing again the importance of being very careful about what you say and providing the sound bites for them. Whether you have a chance to review the story as written or not, you should still follow up by thanking them and, if appropriate, complimenting them on how well they conducted the interview or the importance of the topic. Building strong relationships with the media is important and will serve you particularly well should you ever face a crisis communication situation.

HANDLING CRISIS COMMUNICATIONS

At one time or another, most companies will face a crisis. A situation requiring crisis communication involves "a specific, unexpected and non-routine event or series of events that create high levels of uncertainty and threaten or are perceived to threaten an organization's high priority goals."[8] If the company has established and maintained a positive relationship with the media and their stakeholders, the job of managing the crisis will be somewhat easier.[9] In fact, "an important part of crisis planning . . . entails identifying stakeholders prior to a crisis and cultivating positive relationships with these groups. . . . The organization's leadership plays a fundamental role in establishing value positions with key stakeholders before a crisis as well as after the event."[10]

Although establishing positive relationships with external audiences prior to a crisis will help in all but the most extreme situations, no amount of goodwill can guarantee the positive coverage that is necessary to avoid permanent damage to a company's reputation. History is full of examples of companies handling a crisis well and not so well. Johnson & Johnson's effective handling of the Tylenol tampering incident is legendary, while Exxon's bungling of the Valdez oil spill is infamous. More recently, the world witnessed how companies and a city responded to one of the worst crises of modern time, the destruction of the World Trade Center buildings in New York City. No one was untouched by the disaster, and examples of effective and ineffective communication efforts during the crisis abound, from the companies located in or near the World Trade Center to organizations scattered across the world, which had to decide how to reach their employees with the news and how to answer their questions about performing their daily duties.

The following guidelines will help companies respond appropriately in most crisis situations.

1. **Develop a general crisis communication plan and communicate it.** No organizations should take for granted they have no risk of encountering a crisis. Nothing will replace preparation and a knowledgeable, informed workforce to implement it.

2. **Once the crisis occurs, respond quickly.** Implement your plan immediately. The first few hours are critical. While you need time to gather the facts, you must do so quickly so that you are the first to the media with the information they need to write a story.

3. **Make sure you have the right people ready to respond and that they all respond with the same message.** Corporate crises of any significance require the CEO's response. In fact, one of the criticisms of Exxon's handling of the Valdez disaster was that the CEO sent two lower-level executives to Alaska. Other executives should also be trained to respond appropriately to the media in a crisis situation and should be prepared to accept the responsibility for implementing the communication plan. The people preparation includes at least minimal training for all employees who might come in contact with the media, even if that training consists simply of telling them where to refer questions. The designated spokespersons should be accessible and visible and should deliver a consistent message.

4. **Put yourself in the shoes of your audience.** What do they want and need to know? What will be their major concerns? You want to focus on the facts but ensure that you touch the feelings of the people on both sides of the crisis. Craft messages that are honest and compassionate.

5. **Do not overlook the value of the Web.** Use of the Web during a crisis is essential today. Reporters as well as the public and even employees often go to a company's Web site for information during a crisis; therefore, every company should include use of the Web in any crisis communication plan. You can use the Web as a virtual crisis communication center for internal and external audiences.

6. **Revisit your crisis communication plan frequently.** Since situations and people in companies change constantly, you must build in periodic reviews and revisions of your plan. Any major changes to the plan need to be communicated to the employees responsible for implementation. One way to make the plan easier to update is to keep it on the company's intranet.

7. **Build in a way to monitor the coverage.** You may want to use a clipping service to collect media hits. Also, again, the Web can be a tremendous resource for measuring the response of the public to your messages.

8. **Perform a postcrisis evaluation.** Management should look critically at what worked and did not work and collect the lessons learned for the future. In addition, the company needs to develop a strategy for moving forward and quickly communicate it once the crisis is under control.

Just as managing the crisis and most of the communication that surrounds it falls to the company leaders, often the CEO, establishing the direction out of the crisis is the CEO's responsibility as well. As Lou Gerstner, CEO of IBM from 1993 to 2002, writes in his book *Who Says Elephants Can't Dance?:* "So there must be a crisis, and it is the job of the CEO to define and communicate that crisis, its magnitude, its severity, and its impact. Just as important, the CEO must also be able to communicate how to end the crisis—the new strategy, the new company model, the new culture."

All companies, no matter the size, must have a crisis communication plan. Nothing will replace being prepared. When a crisis happens, it is too late to develop a communication strategy and select target audiences, create appropriate message content, and choose spokespersons. Everyone must be ready to move quickly or the company risks its reputation, and lost reputation results in lost morale for employees and a loss in market share for the company.

To conclude, managing external relations effectively is essential for organizational leaders; however, external relations do not exist in isolation. Companies must link all communication activities to ensure that what the outside world sees and hears reflects what the inside world lives. As one CEO said when interviewed in a survey of 2000 top private and public sector organizations conducted by Aon Consulting, "The fundamental truth, which you only discover when you have gone through the fires of hell, is that your reputation will always mirror the absolute reality of who you are. . . . Anyone who thinks that they can change their reputation without changing the company is mistaken."[11] Today, more than ever before, the public expects companies to demonstrate social responsibility and to behave ethically in all that they do internally and externally.[12]

All leaders of organizations must realize that their companies' reputations depend on their internal ethos and the perceptions of their many external stakeholders. They cannot ignore the importance of establishing and maintaining a positive reputation or the necessity of effectively managing external relations to obtain and keep it.

Exercise 10.1: Communication with Customers after a Crisis

The Case: Spree Cruise Lines Revisited

(Begin by reviewing the facts in the Spree Cruise Lines case from Chapter 1.)

Within several days after the cruise returned to New Orleans, Tara had been able to learn more about what happened on the ship. Approximately 350 passengers made their own arrangements to fly home and disembarked from the ship in Cozumel, but the remainder stayed on board. The cruise line offered them a shipboard voucher of $100 per person, but there were still some extremely unhappy customers.

Marcie Smith, the senior vice president of sales and marketing, has asked Tara to draft a letter for her signature to be sent to all customers who were aboard that cruise, whether they disembarked or stayed aboard. Since research shows that many cruisers are repeat customers, upper management approved an offer of a 50 percent discount on another 3- to 5-day cruise so that these passengers might give Spree Cruise Lines a second chance. The cruise line set up a special booking phone number to accommodate the return guests, 1-800-724-4000; the offer stipulated that new reservations must be made within the coming year to qualify for the discount.

The Assignment

Draft the letter to go out to all of the customers who were on the cruise, offering them the discount and explaining the terms of the offer.

Exercise 10.2: Writing a Press Release

The Case: Spree Cruise Lines Revisited, Again

Teams of mechanics greeted the *Sensation* upon its arrival back in New Orleans. They were able to repair the ship sufficiently so that the propulsion system would hold up for the next few cruises, which were already fully booked. As the vessel departed for its next trip, teams of city engineers carried out tests to determine whether the vibrations reported from the last trip were indeed linked to the vessel's departure from port. They concluded that the vibrations were indeed caused by the vessel: they had nothing to do with the malfunctioning propulsion system that hampered the last cruise, but the vibrations did seem to relate to the frequency set up when the engines were run at a particular power level. The vessel's captain could easily be directed to reduce power during departures and entries into port.

Even though the vibration and frequency problems could easily be solved, Spree's vice president of operations decided to accelerate the timetable for the dry dock, which had initially been planned to occur in several months. The vessel would go into dry dock for a multi-million-dollar makeover, including a new purser's lobby, new restaurant decor, upgraded passenger rooms, and a complete engine system refurbishment. The dry dock would require about two months, during which time one of Spree's other ships, the *Plenitude*, would serve the New Orleans market.

The Assignment

Draft a press release announcing the dry dock plans for the *Sensation*. Include any other information that you feel should be addressed and be prepared to discuss your reasoning for including specific pieces of information. As you know from the chapter, any messages to external audiences must be clear and unambiguous. So be very careful with the language you use. Also, press releases serve two primary purposes: They inform the public and they create an image. Your press release should conform to the following guidelines:

1. Answer the journalist's questions of who, what, where, when, and why.
2. Place your most important information in the first sentence or two.
3. Since news editors cut press releases from the bottom up, you need to make sure all of the most important information comes as early in the release as possible, leaving the "nice-to-knows" to the end.
4. Place contact information (name and phone number) at the top.
5. Try to limit the release to one page, but if it runs over, type "more" in the center of the first page.
6. Leave adequate margins and double-space.
7. Use concise sentences (think in terms of sound bites) and proofread carefully.
8. At the end of the release, use -30- to indicate it is the end.

Exercise 10.3: Developing External Communication Strategy

The Case: HADWIT, Revisited

Review the HADWIT case in Chapter 9, paying particular attention to the information on HADWIT's relationship with its clients.

The Assignment

Develop a complete communication strategy including all of the external audiences you need to consider. After developing the strategy, write a letter to your clients explaining the changes you will be making at the company.

Notes

1. The best corporate reputations, *The Wall Street Journal* (1999).
2. *Corporate Reputation Watch,* Hill & Knowlton (2001).
3. Ibid.
4. *Risk Assessment for Food Terrorism and Other Safety Concerns,* http://www.cfsan.fda.gov/~dms/rabtact.html#i), October 7, 2003.
5. *Online Customer Respect: Study of Fortune 100 Companies* (2002), p. 7.
6. Fombrun, C. J. (1996). *Reputation: Realizing Value from the Corporate.* Boston, MA: Harvard Business School Press.
7. Media Tenor International, March 2003.
8. Seeger, M. W., Sellnow, T. L., & Ulmer, R. R. (1998). Communication, organization, and crisis. In M. E. Roloff (Ed.), *Communication Yearbook,* Vol. 21, pp. 231–275. Thousand Oaks, CA: Sage.
9. Ulmer, R. R. (2001). Effective crisis management through established stakeholder relationships. *Management Communication Quarterly* 14 (4), pp. 590–615.
10. Ulmer (2001), p. 594.
11. Steve Marshall (2003), CEO of Railtrack, quoted in *Corporate Reputation: Not Worth Risking,* p. 3.
12. Kitchen, P. J., & Laurence, A. (2003). Corporate reputation: An eight country analysis. *Corporate Reputation Review* 6 (2), pp. 103–117.

Appendix **A**

Transition Words

THOSE FOR TIME

a few minutes later
after
afterward
as
at last
at length
at present
at this instant
at this point
before
before this
finally
from this time on
from time to time
immediately
in the first place
in the meantime
instantly
later
later in the day
meanwhile
next

not long after
not long afterward
now
occasionally
once
presently
quickly
shortly
since
since then
some time ago
sometimes
straightway
suddenly
then
until
when
whenever
whereupon
without delay
yesterday

THOSE OF PLACE

above
around

at the right
at this place

before

below

beyond

farther

from

here

here and there

hereabouts

in front of

in the distance

in the foreground

in the middle

near

nearer

on this side

opposite

over

somewhat nearer

there

where

wherever

THOSE OF CONTRAST AND COMPARISON

as

as if

as paradoxical as this may seem

as though

but

by

either

else

equally important

however

in comparison to

in comparison with

in contrast to

in spite of

just as surely

much more interesting

neither

nevertheless

no

nor

notwithstanding

of even greater appeal

on the contrary

on the other hand

otherwise

quite as evident

rather

similarly

still

though

unless

whereas

with

yet

THOSE OF REASON AND RESULT

admittedly

as a result

because

consequently

for example

for this purpose

for this reason

granted that

hence

if unless

in case that

in order that

in particular
in this way
in as much as
inevitably
naturally
notwithstanding
obviously
on that account

since
so that
therefore
though it is true
thus
under these conditions
with a view to

THOSE OF ORDER

as mentioned above
as mentioned previously
first, second, last, etc.
in conclusion
in the first place, etc.

in the last place
so far
the aforementioned
to conclude

THOSE OF ADDITION

accordingly
additionally
also
and
another
as a matter of fact
besides
besides all this
finally
for example
for instance
furthermore

in addition to
in fact
in other words
in short
indeed
likewise
moreover
namely
neither/nor; either/or
similarly
such as
too

THOSE OF RESULT, CONCLUSION

all things considered
as a result
as we have seen
as we now see
clearly then
consequently
due to the fact that

for these reasons
hence
so
then
therefore
thus
ultimately

THOSE OF EMPHASIS

after all	obviously
apparently	of course
assuredly	remember that
certainly	the fact remains
granted	to be sure
it is true that	to return to
keeping in mind	true
no doubt	undoubtedly
nobody denies	unquestionably

THOSE OF SUMMARY

all in all	in summary
altogether	in the final analysis
finally	to summarize

Appendix **B**

Successful Case Analysis and Discussion

The ability to read and learn from cases is an important skill for any business leader. Cases provide examples of good and bad business decisions along with enough of the story for you to learn from the challenges and approaches in them. They also provide an opportunity to test your business judgment and decision-making ability in the context of real business problems.

As is typical of problems within an organization, a case rarely provides facts and information you would like to have before making a decision. Therefore, you must be able to think critically and uncover the assumptions underlying the case information.

You must also learn to be comfortable with ambiguity in the information as well as in the "answers." In fact, one of the most valuable lessons to learn from case analysis and discussion is that there is no one "right" answer. A good case is open to many interpretations and the case problems to many possible resolutions.

Since case analysis and discussion are standard approaches to learning in the business school classroom, this appendix is intended to help you approach both with some of the traditional techniques needed to succeed in the case classroom and to obtain the most out of the case experience. The discussion here contains hints on how to do the following:

- Perform a successful case analysis.
- Contribute to a case discussion.
- Organize a case analysis report.
- Stay within the ethical boundaries of case discussions.
- Get the most out of the learning experience that case discussions provide.

PERFORMING A SUCCESSFUL CASE ANALYSIS

To prepare for a case discussion, you should approach the case analysis as follows:

1. Skim the case quickly.
2. Write out what you see as the central problem(s) in the case.

3. Read the case through more carefully, highlighting key issues and facts to support the central problem.
4. List the possible solutions to the case problem.
5. Select a solution and develop your defense.
6. Outline how you would implement the solution.

When reading the case, you should focus on exploring the problems and pulling out the issues and the facts instead of focusing on specific courses of action. You might find it helpful to think about approaching a case as you would the analysis of a short story. Try looking for the conflicts and sources of tension, outline the plot of the story, and examine the motives of the characters involved.

CONTRIBUTING TO THE CASE DISCUSSION

In the case classroom, you will want to sit where you are visible, if possible, which usually means sitting in the middle of the room at the case discussion leader's eye level. You want to avoid the far right or left unless you are unprepared and want to lower the risk of the discussion leader calling on you, although you should not show up to any case discussion unprepared. Doing so wastes your time, your colleagues' time, and the discussion leader's time.

To benefit from the case experience, you must be prepared to contribute positively to the discussion whether in the classroom or with your team. You should not assume a combative pose, although you can and should challenge ideas. Instead of attacking people, challenge the ideas and look for ways to work toward building on their point of view or ideas. What most discussion leaders want to see is an active exchange among class members, not simply a routine Q&A between the discussion leader and the class.

Most case discussions will begin with the discussion leader asking for someone to summarize the case. This type of contribution provides a chance for you to speak up early in the discussion, before the rapid exchange that soon erupts once the discussion gets started. If you are new to the case discussion or perhaps hesitant to jump in, you may want to take advantage of this opening opportunity to speak. The following are usually considered legitimate contributions to a case discussion:

1. Summary of case.
2. Your solution.
3. An alternate solution to one suggested by a classmate.
4. An explanation of any underlying assumptions in the case.
5. Transition to another area of the case.
6. Connections to other cases read for this class.
7. Clarification of relevant financial or quantitative information.
8. Application of an analytical approach.
9. Synthesis of key learnings from the case.

10. A summary of the discussion.
11. Suggested next steps.

Overall, you want to avoid broad generalizations or superficial statements.

ORGANIZING A CASE ANALYSIS OR REPORT

If you are not given a suggested organizational structure for writing your case analysis, you will probably want to use one of the following popular structures:

1. Inductive or indirect.

   - Strategic issues and problems.
   - Analysis of problems.
   - Recommendations.

2. Deductive or direct.

   - Recommendation or solution.
   - Support for solution or evidence for recommendation.
   - Brief discussion of alternative solutions.

3. Issues and results (executive).

   - Crucial strategic issues.
   - Assumptions about issues.
   - Recommend strategies.
   - Justification for recommendation.
   - Plan of action.
   - Expected results.

4. Elimination of alternatives.

   - Discussion of at least three alternative solutions.
   - Summary of why only one is the best.
   - Reinforcement of that one.

5. Pros and cons.

   - Introduction of two best solutions.
   - Advantages and disadvantages of each.
   - Conclusion, recommending the preferred alternative.

6. Thesis-antithesis-synthesis.

   - Solution.
   - Counters or objections to that solution.
   - Combination with solution emphasized.

What is most important in writing your analysis is that you organize it logically and make it easy for the reader to find your analysis of the problems and clear explanation of any solutions.

STAYING WITHIN THE ETHICAL BOUNDARIES OF CASE ANALYSIS

Staying within the case ethical boundaries means you do not do the following:

1. Pass along case notes or old case reports to students who have not yet taken the course.
2. Discuss the case with someone who has not yet had the case in class.
3. Attempt to find out "what happened in the case" (as if what the company did was the correct answer, or that someone else's "right" answer is right for you).
4. Contact a case company without permission to gather more information about the case situation.
5. Identify the real company in a disguised case.
6. Take advantage of group members by letting them do the bulk of the work instead of reading and analyzing the case yourself.

GETTING THE MOST OUT OF THE CASE EXPERIENCE

As with most learning experiences, you get out of the case method, what you put into it. To get the most out of the case experience, you should do the following:

1. Prepare for the discussion by skimming, reading, thinking about the case.
2. Emphasize the student-to-student learning over the teacher-to-student learning.
3. Listen carefully to colleagues and synthesize their ideas and yours to develop your own critical analytical abilities.
4. Develop your own personal system of case analysis.
5. Remember, case analysis is designed to sharpen your analytical skills.

Usage Self-Assessment

Instructions: Each of the following sentences requires adding or changing punctuation (or a word or two) or correcting usage errors. *You should keep your changes to a minimum. Do just what is necessary to correct any errors. Avoid completely rewriting sentences.* Sentences may contain more than one error.

You should allow approximately 30 minutes to complete the assessment and should not go beyond a maximum of 45 minutes.

After completing the assessment, compare your responses to the answer key that follows.

1. A group of our top executives, account directors and myself met to discuss the need for change across the company.

2. Everyone must complete their monthly report before they can leave for the holidays.

3. Balancing the books, and completing performance appraisals is the worst aspect of the job.

4. My boss thinks its selfish not to share all of my ideas with John, I think its prudent.

5. By having a clear vision and strategic direction, our clients will be better served in the future.

6. In John Smiths new book Watching Giants Fall, the best chapter is "Saving the Corporation".

7. Since Finance has lead the list in placement opportunities in the past, many M.B.A.'s still select it as their concentration.

8. This approach will create shareholder value, and increase the markets confidence in our companies continued success.

9. Mary worked on the report to long, now its past the deadline set by the home office.

10. The team members cannot expect to do good if they never practice their speech, therefore, I do not understand why they think to constantly complain will get them anywhere.

11. ABC Corporation decided to redesign their website so it appeals to a wider customer audience.

12. Having been employed by Johnson, Inc., for 8 years, his dismissal with only one day notice caught Bill completely off guard.

13. Scheduling all full time employees and to actually expect to need part-time people as well is to optimistic in my opinion; we never have received that many orders in the Summer, but their has been more activity this quarter then ever before.

14. Three major newspapers, The New York Times, The London Herald, USA Today and The Washington Post, carried full-page ads for the new e-commerce cite. It must have cost the company a small fortune which is such a waste since no Web savvy person pays attention to this anymore.

15. The board of directors ran out of time before our Department could deliver the quarterly report, therefore, we will have to come back tomorrow at 10:00 am.

16. Ms. Zavier claims to have been VP for Operations at Jones and Porter, Inc., from May, 1994 to June, 1998, but between you and I, she does not seem to know that much about Operations management.

17. The team knew there was a problem when Mary exclaimed, "You going out of town last weekend caused us to miss the deadline"!

ANSWER KEY

Instructions: After completing the usage self-assessment, compare your responses to this answer key. The corrections are in **bold** to make them more visible for you. The number in parentheses at the end of each sentence is the number of corrections *required* in the sentence. Other answers besides those provided here are possible.

1. A group of our top executives, account directors, and ~~myself~~ **me** met to discuss the need for change across the company. **(2) The way to test this one is to say, "A group of us met." You would not say, "A group of we met"; thus, you need to use a pronoun in the objective case (in this case, "me").**

2. Everyone must complete ~~their~~ **his or her** monthly report before ~~they~~ **he or she** can leave for the holidays. (2)
   Or: **All employees must complete their monthly report before they can leave for the holidays.**

3. Balancing the books~~,~~ and completing performance appraisals ~~is~~ **are** the worst aspect**s** of the job. (3)

4. My boss thinks **it's** selfish not to share all of my ideas with John~~,~~**;** I think **it's** prudent. (3)

5. By having a clear vision and strategic direction, ~~our clients will be better served in the future~~ **we will serve our clients better in the future.** (1)

6. In John Smith's new book, *Watching Giants Fall,* the best chapter is "Saving the Corporation~~".~~**."** (4)

U.S. business communication standards call for periods and commas to be placed inside quotation marks. Many other country standards do the opposite. Follow the standards of the corporate headquarters.

7. Since ~~F~~**finance** has ~~lead~~ **led** the list in placement opportunities in the past, many M.B.A.'s [apostrophe is optional] still select it as their concentration. (2)

8. This approach will create shareholder value~~,~~ and increase the market**'s** confidence in our compan~~iesy~~**y's** continued success. (3)

9. Mary worked on the report **too** long~~,~~**;** now**,** **it's** past the deadline set by the home office. (4)

10. The team members cannot expect to do ~~good~~ **well** if they never practice their speech~~,~~**;** therefore, I do not understand why they think to ~~constantly~~ complain **constantly** [or complaining constantly] will get them anywhere. (3)

11. ABC Corporation decided to redesign ~~their~~ **its Web site** so **that** it appeals to a wider customer audience. (3)

Selection of "its" or "their" is country specific.

12. Having been employed by Johnson, Inc., for ~~8~~ **eight** years, **Bill was caught completely off guard by** his dismissal with only **one day's** notice ~~caught Bill completely off guard~~. (3)

13. Scheduling all full-time employees and ~~to~~ actually **expecting** to need part-time people as well ~~is~~ **are too** optimistic in my opinion; we never have received that many orders in the ~~S~~summer, but ~~their~~ **there** has been more activity this quarter ~~then~~ **than** ever before. (6)

14. ~~Three~~ **Four** major newspapers, *The New York Times, The London Herald, USA Today*, and *The Washington Post*, carried full-page ads for the new e-commerce ~~cite~~ **site. The ads** must have cost the company a small fortune, which is such a waste since no Web-savvy person pays attention to this **form of advertising** anymore. (7)

15. The board of directors [if you capitalized it, count it as one error] ran out of time before our ~~D~~department could deliver the quarterly report~~,~~; therefore, we will have to come back tomorrow at 10:00 a.m. (3)

16. Ms. Zavier claims to have been VP [if you wrote it out, that is okay] for Operations at Jones and Porter, Inc., from May~~,~~ 1994 to June~~,~~ 1998, but between you and ~~I~~ **me,** she does not seem to know that much about ~~O~~operations management. (3)

17. The team knew there was a problem when Mary exclaimed, "Your going out of town last weekend caused us to miss the deadline~~"!~~!" (2)

Scale:

    0–10 = In good shape
  11–18 = Need some review
  19–25 = Need more review
  26–52 = Need lots of review

Appendix **D**

The Business of Grammar

Each specialization has a jargon. To know how to talk about style and usage at an advanced level, you need to know the jargon of grammarians. Also, the more you know about the foundation of a language, its grammar, the more confident you will be in using it.

Grammar, just as any subject, needs to be reviewed periodically. What follows is a brief review of traditional English grammar designed to give you the basics of the business of grammar so that you can be proficient in the business of leadership communication.

PARTS OF SPEECH

Following Priscian's Latin grammar in the 6th century A.D., the first grammarians broke the English language down into eight parts of speech: *nouns, pronouns, verbs, adverbs, adjectives, prepositions, conjunctions,* and *interjections.* The use of Latin grammar causes problems when we try to apply the different labels of the parts of speech because the classification definitions are not consistent:

1. Three parts of speech are defined by meaning—*noun, verb,* and *interjection.*
2. Four by function—*adjective, adverb, conjunction,* and *pronoun.*
3. One by function and form—*preposition.*

When you start paying attention to how words work in sentences, you quickly realize that you can determine the part of speech by the position of the word in the sentence. For example, if you were asked what part of speech the nonsense words "rehpog" and "gud" are in the following sentence, you would recognize "rehpog" as a noun and "gud" as a verb because of their positions and the context provided by the other words: The *rehpog gud* a deep tunnel in the woods.

What follows is a brief explanation of the eight parts of speech.

1. **Nouns.** Nouns name persons, places, things, and abstractions. Properties of nouns are more appropriate for Latin, but in case you hear the terms for the properties, the following definitions should help you:
   a. **Number**—singular (one) or plural (many). Plurals are indicated by *-s* or *-es,* which will be pronounced: *s, z, ez,* or, *iz.*

    b. **Case**—in Latin, there were five cases. Cases did in Latin what word order does in English.

- Nominative or subjective—subject (*David* gave the report to Mary.)
- Accusative—direct object (David gave *the report* to Mary.)
- Dative—indirect object (David gave *Mary* the report.)
- Genitive—possession -'s (*David's* report is complete.)
- Ablative—preposition (from, with, in, etc.)

2. **Verbs.** Verbs show action or states of being. There are two kinds of verbs:

    a. Active verbs express action.

        (1) **Transitive** active verbs require objects.

           Example: The CEO *gave her* the report.

                    V   I.O.   D.O.

        (2) **Intransitive** active verbs are complete without objects.

           Example: He *ran*.

    b. Linking verbs express a state of being. They may be followed by predicate adjectives or predicate nominatives.

        (1) Predicate adjective

           Example: She is brilliant.

        (2) Predicate nominative

           Example: She is the boss.

Either active or linking verbs may appear with auxiliary (or helping) verbs, such as *can, could, may, might, must, shall, should, will,* or *would*.

    Five terms apply to verbs:

    a. **Person**—*who* is performing the action or doing something.

First:	person speaking (I, me)
Second:	person spoken to (you)
Third:	person spoken about (he, she, they)

    b. **Number**—*how many* are performing the action or doing something.

Singular	Plural
I am	We are
You are	You are
S/he is	They are

    c. **Tense**—*when* the action is performed.

Present:	I am; action taking place now
Past:	I was; action that has taken place
Future:	I will be; action that will take place
Perfect:	I was to be; action that took place at one time in the past; indicated in English by a verb phrase: will go, was going, had gone, etc.

d. **Mood**—the *attitude of the speaker* or way in which the speaker thinks about the action.

    Subjunctive: conditional, contingent, possible, contrary to fact; if he were (thought mood)

    Imperative: command, request, prayer (will mood)

    Indicative: statements and questions (fact mood)

e. **Voice**—indicated by the *relationship* between the verb and the subject.

    Active: The subject performs the action.

        Example: *He* hit the target.

    Passive: The subject is what is acted upon.

        Example: *The target* was hit by him.

Another way to think about the passive voice is to focus on the *actor* in the sentence instead of the subject. Ask yourself who is performing the action and where he or she is positioned in the sentence. The actor is *before* the verb in the active voice and *after* the verb in the passive voice.

Quite often, the passive voice will be constructed as it is in this sentence without identifying the actor.

    Examples: The target was hit. (By whom?)

    The report will be written. (By whom?)

Verbals make up a subgroup of verbs. Verbals are formed from verbs, but they function as nouns, adjectives, and adverbs. The three types of verbals are the following:

a. **Gerund**—an *-ing* form of a verb that functions as a noun.

    Examples: *Finishing* the report was all that occupied Pierce's mind. Mary hoped the team's *completing* the report ahead of schedule would impress her boss. (Note the possessive before the gerund.)

b. **Participle**—a verb form ending in *-ing* if present tense and *-ed*, *-en*, or *-d* if past that functions as an adjective.

    Examples: A *malfunctioning* computer is worse than no computer.

    A *completed* report is a relief.

c. **Infinitive**—the root form of the verb preceded by *to* that may be used as a noun, adjective, or adverb.

    Examples: *To finish* the report was all that occupied Pierce's mind. (noun)

    He has a report *to finish*. (adjective modifying report)

    He has gone *to finish* the report. (adverb modifying gone)

3. **Pronouns**. Pronouns take the place of nouns. A pronoun must refer to a specific noun, called its antecedent or referent, in the same or a previous sentence. An English pronoun must agree with its antecedent in person and number. Pronouns have the following gender properties: masculine (he), feminine (she), neutral (it).

We have six types of pronouns in the English language:

a. **Personal** pronouns—refer to a specific person or thing mentioned previously.

First:	I, me, my, mine, we, us, our, ours
Second:	you, your, yours
Third:	he, she, it, him, her, his, hers, its, they, them, their, theirs

b. **Relative** pronouns—can function as connecting words and reference words. As connecting words, they are used to relate subordinate clauses to main clauses. As reference words, they refer to and stand for their antecedents, making the repetition of the antecedent unnecessary.

Simple relative pronouns:	who, which, that
Compound relative pronouns:	whoever, whomever, whichever, whatever, whatsoever

c. **Demonstrative** pronouns—pointing words used to indicate which one or ones: this, that, these, those.

d. **Reflexive** pronouns—used to indicate that the action is reflected or comes back to the subject: myself, herself, themselves, ourselves, etc.

e. **Indefinite** pronouns—pronouns that do not refer to any particular person or thing. The most common ones are the following:

> any, anybody, anyone
> everyone, everybody, everything
> some, someone, somebody, something
> one, none, nobody
> other, another, all, many, each, both, either

Be very careful with agreement in number—singular or plural—when using indefinite pronouns. They are the ones that often cause mistakes in pronoun antecedent agreement.

Remember to say *Everybody must file his or her report.* Employ the following verb test: Would you say, "*Everybody is*" or "*Everybody are*"? Since the verb would be *is*, you know that the indefinite pronoun is singular and requires a singular pronoun for reference.

All of the indefinite pronouns in the *any* and *everyone* groups are *singular*. *Some* and *none* may be singular or plural depending on the meaning in the sentence.

Example: *Some* of the employees *were* upset over the decision.

But—

Some of the confetti *was* left on the floor.

A related pronoun reference, which often causes problems in business communication, is the reference to a collective noun, such as *board, committee, corporation, department,* or *company.* In the United States, collective nouns are usually thought of as singular and take singular verbs and pronouns. For example, in the United States, a company is treated as singular and would be referred to by "it," as in the following example: "Brown & Partners, LLP, is considered successful in its market area." In other countries, such as Great Britain and Australia, a company is treated as plural, which would mean that the previous sentence would read: "Brown & Partners, LLP, are considered successful in their market area." As with other differences across countries, you should usually follow the conventions of the country in which the company has its headquarters.

    f. **Interrogative** pronouns—used in questions: *who, whose, whom, what, which*. A pronoun must agree in person (1st, 2nd, or 3rd) and number (singular or plural) with its antecedent noun. Remember that *who* stands for people. *Which* stands for things and objects and denotes properties.

        Also, with pronouns, watch the cases. Is the pronoun performing the action or receiving it? Use *I, who, he, she* in the subjective case (action performers) and *me, whom, him, her* in the objective cases (action receivers).

Say: Divide the money between him and me.

Not: Divide the money between he and I.

You need to take care to use the correct case since the incorrect pronoun is used often in casual conversation and, unfortunately, on the radio and television as well. Trust your knowledge of the use of the pronoun: Ask, is it functioning as an actor or as a receiver? Do not be misled by common misuse. Also, since the use of pronouns is a foundation for our grammar, no amount of misuse will make it correct.

4. **Adjectives.** Adjectives modify (describe or point out) nouns and pronouns by telling color, kind, size, amount, or other qualities.

5. **Adverbs.** Adverbs modify verbs, adjectives and other adverbs, telling when, where, how, or to what extent.

    Modifiers in English do not have to agree with the nouns or words that they modify, but we do use endings to indicate degrees of comparison.

    a. **Positive (no comparison):** good, bad, large, useful

    b. **Comparative (comparison between two):** better, worse, larger, more useful

    c. **Superlative (comparison among three or more):** best, worst, largest, most useful

Most modifiers add *-er* and *-est* endings, a few use *more* or *most,* and some, such as good and bad, have special forms. With one-syllable words, you will usually add *-er* and *-est,* but there are some exceptions, so be careful. With many *two-syllable* words and practically all words with *three or more syllables,* you should use *more* and *most.* Some modifiers, such as *unique* and *ubiquitous,* are absolute in their meaning and cannot be used as comparatives or superlatives. The phrases "more unique" and "most unique" are illogical and should not be used.

Remember to place modifiers close to the word(s) being modified so that the sentence is clear and not ambiguous. Watch for *dangling modifiers* in particular.

Example: Balancing the books, the accounts had to be recalculated.

        (*Accounts* cannot perform the task of balancing, thus the dangling modifier.)

6. **Prepositions.** Prepositions show relationships between other words.

   One way to recognize the largest group of prepositions, those indicating position or direction, is to think of anything that you can do to a log: across, around, at, beside, beyond, in, over, out, through, to, and under.

   Another commonly used group shows relationships of words or phrases to other words in a sentence: as, of, except, for, besides, etc.

7. **Conjunctions.** Conjunctions join other words or connect two or more grammatical units.

   The three types of conjunctions in English are as follows:

   a. **Coordinating conjunctions:** and, or, for, but, yet, nor, so

   b. **Subordinating conjunctions:** after, as, although, as if, because, before, even though, if, till, until, when, since, unless, whenever, where, whereas, while

   c. **Conjunctive adverbs:** however, therefore, nevertheless, thus, then

   A reminder about punctuating conjunctions: **Coordinating** conjunctions require a comma before them if they join two independent clauses (see examples that follow).

   > Example: Zhang finished writing the report last night, and she plans to give the rest of the group copies today.

   However, coordinating conjunctions should not have a comma if they separate an independent and dependent clause:

   > Example: Zhang finished writing the report last night and plans to give the rest of the group copies tomorrow.

   Subordinating conjunctions make the sentence following them dependent, so they only need a comma before them if the following clause is nonessential to the meaning of the sentence:

   Essential (no comma needed):   Lee left the company because he found another job.

   Nonessential (comma needed):   We need to finish the analysis by tomorrow afternoon, because Ms. Johnson needs to take it with her to the board meeting tomorrow.

   Conjunctive adverbs require a semicolon before them and a comma after them when they join two independent clauses. They require a comma only if they start a sentence, and they need commas around them if they serve as interrupters.

   > Examples: The analysts are reporting on the company's performance in the morning; *however,* the word on the street is that the news will not be good.
   >
   > The analysts are reporting on the company's performance in the morning. *However,* the word on the street is that the news will not be good.
   >
   > The analysts are reporting on the company's performance in the morning; the word on the street, however, is that the news will not be good.

8. **Interjections.** Interjections express emotions: Ouch!, Ah!, etc.

SENTENCE STRUCTURE

The parts of speech are combined to form the following larger structures:

1. **Phrases** are groups of two or more words, which act as a single element in a sentence but do not have a *subject* (what is talked about) and *predicate* (what is said about the subject).

2. **Clauses** are groups of words with subjects and predicates. Clauses are main (independent) if they can stand alone and still make sense and subordinate (dependent) if they depend on a main clause to make sense:

   a. **Independent clause**

      Example: The employees were pleased with the extra holiday this year.

   b. **Independent clause followed by a dependent clause**

      Example: The employees were pleased with the extra holiday until they were told that they would have to make it up next year.

   c. **Dependent clause followed by an independent clause**

      Example: Because the employees were pleased with the extra holiday, management decided to make it permanent.

   If a clause is introduced by a *subordinating conjunction* (after, although, as, as if, because, before, if, since, because, or whereas), it is a *dependent clause*. A dependent clause cannot stand alone, so when you have used a subordinating conjunction, always make sure that your clause is attached to an independent clause.

3. A **sentence** is an independent clause that contains both a subject (could be implied and not stated) and verb. Sentences are traditionally said to convey a complete thought; that is, they make a meaningful statement.

   The three types of sentence structures are as follows:

   a. A **simple** sentence consists of one independent clause by itself.

      Example: We are going to work now.

   b. A **compound** sentence consists of two or more independent clauses, joined by a coordinating conjunction (and, or, but, for, so, yet) or a semicolon.

      Examples: We are going to work now, and we would like you to join us. We are going to work now; we would like you to join us.

      Remember to use strong punctuation to separate two independent clauses. A comma alone is too weak and would create a comma splice. No punctuation between two independent clauses creates a run-on sentence.

      Comma splice: We are going to work now, we would like you to join us.

      Run-on: We are going to work now we would like you to join us.

   c. A **complex** sentence consists of at least one independent clause and one or more dependent clauses.

      Example: *Although* you would like to extend the lunch hour to two hours, we are going to work now and want you to join us.

   In a complex sentence, the dependent clause is usually set off by a comma if it begins the sentence as in the previous example.

If the dependent clause comes after the independent clause, as previously mentioned, the punctuation depends on the conjunction and if the following clause is essential or nonessential.

Examples: We are going to lunch now and want you to join us, *although* you would like to extend the lunch hour to two hours.

We are going to lunch now and want you to join us before it is too late.

The four kinds of sentences are as follows:

1. **Declarative**—usual straightforward statement that may be active or passive.

   Example: We are going to work now.

2. **Imperative**—begins with *you* (stated or implied) and issues a command or request.

   Example: Go to work now.

3. **Interrogative**—begins with a finite verb or a question word and ends with a question mark.

   Examples: Get to work now?

   Who did you say was going to the meeting?

4. **Exclamatory**—ends with an exclamation mark.

   Example: We are going to work *now!*

A FINAL NOTE ON THE STUDY OF GRAMMAR

English grammar and the rules that govern its use need to be reviewed just as any other subject needs to be from time to time. People tend to forget what they do not use regularly. Also, usage rules do change because the way that we use our language influences the way we expect it to be used, and there are some differences among academic, journalistic, and business writing. Journalism, in particular, has influenced usage since we hear and see the reporters and newscasters daily. A knowledge of grammar helps you to recognize the differences between everyday, casual usage and the more traditional, correct usage, and it develops your recognition for what can be changed and what cannot. As you realize now after reviewing traditional grammar, usage may vary, but the basic structure of a language—the grammar—remains constant.

Certainly, you can use the language without understanding its foundation or workings, just as most people use the computer without knowing what makes it run or drive a car without knowing how the engine works; however, by knowing how something works and the terminology for its parts, you have a greater sense of freedom and control. How often have you said or heard someone else say upon reading a sentence with a mistake in it, "I don't know exactly what's wrong, but it just doesn't sound right"? Now, perhaps, you will not only recognize that it is wrong but also know why and what options you have to correct it.

Index